PLAGIARIZING THE VICTORIAN NOVEL

How can we tell plagiarism from an allusion? How does imitation differ from parody? Where is the line between copyright infringement and homage? Questions of intellectual property have been vexed long before our own age of online piracy. In Victorian Britain, enterprising authors tested the limits of literary ownership by generating plagiaristic publications based on leading writers of the day. Adam Abraham illuminates these issues by examining imitations of three novelists: Charles Dickens, Edward Bulwer Lytton, and George Eliot. Readers of *Oliver Twist* may be surprised to learn about *Oliver Twiss*, a penny serial that usurped Dickens's characters. Such imitative publications capture the essence of their sources; the caricature, although crude, is necessarily clear. By reading works that emulate three nineteenth-century writers, this innovative study enlarges our sense of what literary knowledge looks like: to know a particular author means to know the sometimes bad imitations that the author inspired.

ADAM ABRAHAM is a Postdoctoral Fellow at Virginia Commonwealth University. He is the author of *When Magoo Flew: The Rise and Fall of Animation Studio UPA* (2012) as well as articles on Victorian literature and culture.

CAMBRIDGE STUDIES IN NINETEENTH-CENTURY
LITERATURE AND CULTURE

General editor
Gillian Beer, *University of Cambridge*

Nineteenth-century British literature and culture have been rich fields for
interdisciplinary studies. Since the turn of the twentieth century, scholars and
critics have tracked the intersections and tensions between Victorian literature and
the visual arts, politics, social organization, economic life, technical innovations,
scientific thought – in short, culture in its broadest sense. In recent years,
theoretical challenges and historiographical shifts have unsettled the
assumptions of previous scholarly synthesis and called into question the terms of
older debates. Whereas the tendency in much past literary critical interpretation
was to use the metaphor of culture as 'background', feminist, Foucauldian, and
other analyses have employed more dynamic models that raise questions of power
and of circulation. Such developments have reanimated the field. This series aims
to accommodate and promote the most interesting work being undertaken on the
frontiers of the field of nineteenth-century literary studies: work which intersects
fruitfully with other fields of study such as history, or literary theory, or the history
of science. Comparative as well as interdisciplinary approaches are welcomed.

A complete list of titles published will be found at the end of the book.

PLAGIARIZING
THE VICTORIAN NOVEL

Imitation, Parody, Aftertext

ADAM ABRAHAM

Virginia Commonwealth University

CAMBRIDGE
UNIVERSITY PRESS

CAMBRIDGE
UNIVERSITY PRESS

University Printing House, Cambridge CB2 8BS, United Kingdom

One Liberty Plaza, 20th Floor, New York, NY 10006, USA

477 Williamstown Road, Port Melbourne, VIC 3207, Australia

314-321, 3rd Floor, Plot 3, Splendor Forum, Jasola District Centre, New Delhi - 110025, India

79 Anson Road, #06-04/06, Singapore 079906

Cambridge University Press is part of the University of Cambridge.

It furthers the University's mission by disseminating knowledge in the pursuit of education, learning and research at the highest international levels of excellence.

www.cambridge.org
Information on this title: www.cambridge.org/9781108493079
DOI: 10.1017/9781108675406

First published 2019

A catalogue record for this publication is available from the British Library

ISBN 978-1-108-49307-9 Hardback
ISBN 978-1-108-71724-3 Paperback

Contents

Illustrations

Acknowledgments

I began research for this project under two brilliant supervisors: John Bowen and Robert Douglas-Fairhurst. Both proved to be insightful, demanding, and kind. To John I owe the original impetus for the book, and he reminded me to write it when I thought that I would write something else instead. To Robert I am indebted for his encouragement, generosity of spirit, and attentive reading of every word, with a scholar's acumen and an editor's care.

The earliest stirrings of this book began at Columbia University. I am grateful to Alan Stewart for his good advice. Nicholas Dames read a prototype for one section of the book, although neither of us knew it at the time. James Eli Adams has become a true mentor at Columbia and beyond, and he has offered useful critiques of this book at various stages. At the University of York, I was guided by Trev Broughton and Matthew Campbell. For literary tourism and extracurriculars: Megan Bryan, Margarita Maira Serrano, Sam Smart, Michael Smith, Ronald Trogdon, Imke van Heerden, and Rosanna Wood. And for hosting me when I was homeless, I want to thank Nick and Catherine Wolterman.

At Oxford, I enjoyed productive conversations with Mishtooni Bose, Helen Small, and Daniel Tyler. For companionship, support, and general cheer, I thank Cara Bartels-Bland, Sarah Green, Emily Jennings, Ulrike Künzel, Maximilia Lane, Becky Lu, Richard Porteous, Franz Rembart, Alice Schneider, Diba Shokri, Erfan Soliman, Kirsty Souter, Carissa Véliz, and my fellow occupants in the unnamed flat: Amin Ebrahimi and Naomi Funabashi. The experience would have been far poorer if I did not belong to a cohort of two, so I am grateful to Ushashi Dasgupta for countless conversations on Dickens and more. Matthew Bevis, Valentine Cunningham, and Sally Shuttleworth proved to be careful interlocutors to this work; they were keen to challenge me on many a fine point. Seamus Perry and Paul Schlicke dutifully read every word, and I was pleased by their thoughtful responses.

It is perhaps a truism that one should never meet one's heroes, lest they disappoint. But Victorianists are so kind that I suspect the truism does not obtain. Through circuitous circumstances, I got to meet four senior scholars who profoundly influenced the pages that follow. Louis James published his seminal book on working-class fiction in 1963; in Canterbury, he was willing to meet me for tea. I met Michael Slater at an academic conference, in Dublin; at the conference dinner he recounted his fascinating life story. Further, this book exists, in part, because of John Sutherland. His *Victorian Novelists and Publishers*, which I found in a second-hand bookshop, changed my life. In London, I was able to tell him so. Finally, back in the United States, at a party, I met one of the deans of Dickens studies, Robert L. Patten. He proved to be interested in my work, and he helped to advance the project at a critical moment.

I presented early incarnations of some material at the Dickens Universe, in Santa Cruz, California. I am grateful to the organizers of the Nineteenth-Century Seminar: Lorraine Janzen Kooistra, Tricia Lootens, Jennifer McDonell, and Sharon Aronofsky Weltman. I also want to mention my fellow participants, including Alexander Bove, Maia McAleavey, Daniel Pollack-Pelzner, and Joanna Robinson. Carra Glatt told me to make up my own word (I suppose I did). For an invitation to subsequent Dickens Universes, I am happy to thank John O. Jordan, John Bowen, James Buzard, James Eli Adams, Jonathan Grossman, Helena Michie, and Ryan Fong.

Virginia Commonwealth University has been a warm and welcoming place for a postdoctoral fellowship. I am truly grateful to David E. Latané for making it possible. There are many colleagues to thank as well. Nicholas Frankel has read my pages and proposals when he probably should have been doing something else. I have enjoyed conversations with Sachi Shimomura and Dale Smith, and I owe a lot to their institutional memories. I am grateful to Katherine Saunders Nash, who has shared her thoughts on research and teaching, and to Rivka Swenson, who invited me to speak at the English Faculty Forum. For conversations and guidance, I want to thank Winnie Chan, Richard Fine, Catherine E. Ingrassia, Shermaine M. Jones, Mary Caton Lingold, and Ivy Roberts. And I was pleased to join VCU alongside Mimi Winick as fellow Victorianist and postdoc.

This book is an archival study, and it would not exist without the collections found in libraries and archives in both the United Kingdom and the United States and the dedicated professionalism of those who work there. To list them here does not discharge my debt, but it's a start: the

Bodleian Library, Oxford; Christ Church, Oxford; St. Catharine's College, Cambridge; the British Library; the Fales Library and Special Collections, New York University; the New York Public Library; the Widener and the Houghton Libraries, Harvard University; and the Beinecke Rare Book and Manuscript Library, Yale University.

An early iteration of some of Chapter 1 appeared in *Dickens Quarterly* 32, no. 1 (March 2015), and sections of the Prologue, Chapter 1, and Chapter 2 were printed as an article in *SEL Studies in English Literature 1500–1900* 57, no. 4 (Autumn 2017). I acknowledge the respective editors, David Paroissien and Logan Browning, for showing interest in my work, and I express gratitude to the publishers for permission to reprint.

At Cambridge University Press, this book began life under the auspices of one editor, Linda Bree, and it came to fruition under another, Bethany Thomas, who championed the manuscript when it was something of an orphan. I am grateful to both and to Carrie Parkinson, for guiding me through the process. I also want to thank the series editor, Gillian Beer, for approving the project. Rose Bell provided careful copy-editing, and Anna-Claire McGrath created the index. The two anonymous readers for the press offered potent suggestions; the chapters that follow are better because of their efforts.

Ambika Tewari has endured this book with curiosity and good cheer, and she has tolerated a long-distance relationship longer than most mortals could. I thank my sisters, Shara and Nina, and their respective families, for showing a continual interest in my curious undertakings. Last, I dedicate this book to my parents, Ronald and Marcia Abraham, who have supported me through a wandering life with more love than anyone can deserve.

Prologue

The first book tyrannizes over the second.

                        – Ralph Waldo Emerson

Unoriginality is nothing new. Walter Jackson Bate quotes a scribe from 2000 B.C. who feared that everything had already been said before.[1] Marilyn Randall suggests the complexity that is involved when one ventures into the regions of originality and unoriginality: "The history of 'plagiarism' is tentacular, involving not only concepts of copyright and intellectual property, but also questions of authorship, authority, originality, and imitation."[2] Indeed, intellectual property has been vexed long before our own age of YouTube parodies and online piracy. In Victorian Britain, enterprising authors tested the limits of literary ownership by generating plagiaristic publications based on the leading writers of the day. Confronting the mass of nineteenth-century imitations, one encounters anonymous and pseudonymous texts; part-issue and penny publications; works that are incomplete, infrequently or never reprinted, rarely read, woebegone, lost. What is more, there is a degree of instability at work in such paraliterary offerings. In 1741, Solomon Lowe wrote to Samuel Richardson to commiserate about the opportunists who capitalized on the success of Richardson's novel *Pamela*; Lowe referred to "the Labours of the press in Piracies, in Criticisms, in Cavils, in Panegyrics, in Supplements, in Imitations, in Transformations, in Translations, &c."[3] A similar diversity is on display in a twentieth-century *Dickensian* article, which claims that Charles Dickens "suffered at the hands of literary hacks of the period, who, having no imagination or ability of their own, adapted, continued, plagiarized or stole the fruit of his brain."[4] That this anonymous author resorts to four verbs – *adapted, continued, plagiarized, stole* – suggests some indecision about what is going on.

    By uncovering ephemeral, scurrilous texts – in many cases ignored or undertheorized for the past century and a half – this book charts their interactions with their sources. These texts form something of a countercanon or a subgenre, a neglected counterpart to the "Victorian Novel" as taught in universities and construed by literary criticism.[5] Margaret Cohen refers to the "great unread," and John Sutherland, among others, demonstrates how our canon of frequently read and reprinted novels is only a small fraction of the century's fictional output.[6] This book focuses attention on works that are drawn to three centripetal figures – whether for inspiration or exploitation, whether to emulate or to castigate – in order to deepen and complicate our understanding of nineteenth-century authorship. The book argues that imitative works illuminate their sources and the literary culture that produced them. Surprisingly, these imitative works usurp authorial identity and control, thus compelling the three test cases – Charles Dickens, Edward Bulwer Lytton, and George Eliot – to pivot away from the imitators, to undercut or outperform them, and to change narrative modes and publication formats in order to distinguish him- or herself from the epigones. There is, I will show, something of a continuity or a continuum between the source texts and their successors. In what appear to be instances of reverse chronology, imitative works that come *after* a literary source in fact change that source – or at least our understanding of it. Through an archival study of print material found in libraries in the United Kingdom and the United States, I recover plagiaristic texts that altered literary history and that demonstrate a more dynamic relationship between what is original and what is unoriginal.

The range of terms that could be used to describe this corpus, with varying degrees of accuracy, is vast indeed: *imitation, adaptation, appropriation, transformation, repetition, re-mediation; satire, parody, pastiche, travesty, burlesque, lampoon, caricature, spoof, forgery, counterfeit, hoax; intertext, metatext, hypertext; sequel, prequel, continuation, fanfiction, remake, revival, reboot; paraphrase, summary, condensation, digest, précis; allusion, quotation, reference, parallel, homage; copy, piracy, palinode, plagiarism, palimpsest.*[7] While the present study will not investigate every one of these historically complex terms, it is worth noting that formal and generic shifts are at work when one surveys what Gérard Genette calls "literature in the second degree."[8]

Originality has its adherents. Johann Joachim Winckelmann states, "Of scholars and artists, general history immortalizes only inventors, not copyists, only originals, not collectors."[9] By 1840, Thomas Carlyle's lecture "The Hero as Man of Letters" could praise the "original man" who is not a "borrowing or begging man."[10] Isaac D'Israeli, however, sounds a little less certain: "It is generally supposed that where there is no QUOTATION, there will be found most originality."[11] He settles for a syllogism: if this, then that. Paul K. Saint-Amour suggests that originality (so-called) may be little more than the result of an "originality effect": "the great individuals loom large because others are blotted out, forgotten."[12] For Robert Macfarlane, "Originality and plagiarism are in many ways the invisible men of literary history."[13]

That history can be traced to the Greeks. Plato was skeptical of the arts: poets, in his estimation, rank somewhere below gymnasts and prophets.[14] In the Platonic theory of Forms, our world of phenomena is the reflective shadow of inaccessible ideas; therefore, human works of representational art are merely copies of the copy. Aristotle, on the other hand, is the great theorist of *mimesis*: "it is an instinct of human beings, from childhood, to engage in mimesis" because "everyone enjoys mimetic objects."[15] Nick Groom notes that "mimesis is commonly translated as 'imitation,'" but Richard McKeon finds that "the term is vague, inadequate, primitive."[16] Groom adds that mimesis further suggests "portrayal, representation, reproduction, copying, aping."[17] Despite its liabilities, the term *imitation* has been used in English to suggest the practice recommended by classical rhetoricians for orators and writers.[18]

In the neoclassical period, "capturing the spirit of the original author" was the admirable goal of any imitation – hence the many poetic reworkings of Horace.[19] Through imitation, a writer finds him- or herself. "Your own Wit will be improved," claimed Henry Felton, in 1709.[20] According to Samuel Johnson's *Rambler*: "When the original is well chosen and judiciously copied, the imitator often arrives at excellence, which he could never have attained without direction."[21] In 1832, *Fraser's Magazine for Town and Country* suggested that a writer "must accumulate a stock of ideas by extensive reading, and improve his style by the sedulous study of the best models."[22] "Stock" is a suggestive word, since it implies a storehouse, a financial instrument, and a cooking process in which matter is simmered and reduced to its essence. Robert Browning, in 1842, could still subscribe to the ancient ideal: "Genius almost inevitably begins to develop itself by imitation."[23] In a more mundane frame of mind, James Brander Matthews reminds us that "[t]he man who plants cabbages imitates too."[24]

According to various literary-historical accounts, the so-called Romantic movement in Great Britain deviated from this imitative tradition. Zachary Leader refers to "spontaneity, originality, genius," and Linda Hutcheon cites a similar trio, "genius, originality, and individuality"; K. K. Ruthven asserts that under such conditions, "the text is an autonomous object produced by an individual genius."[25] Opposed to this Romantic figure is the "the scribbler, the journalist or literary drudge."[26] Robert Macfarlane, drawing on the work of George Steiner, distinguishes *creatio* ("creation as generation") from *inventio* ("creation as rearrangement"), with the autonomous Romantic author striving for the former.[27] Macfarlane writes, "1840 can usefully be considered as the high-water mark of originality as *creatio* in Britain."[28] Yet from 1839 to 1840, as John Sutherland indicates, fifteen imitations of *The Pickwick Papers* (1836–37) were on sale.[29] At a moment when *creatio* seemed ascendant, *inventio* was not far behind. Tilar J. Mazzeo further complicates the story: Romantic writers "did not, in fact, insist on the impossible goal of ex nihilo creation that has often been attributed to them." Rather, "Romantics were centrally concerned with narrative mastery, domination, and control over borrowed materials."[30] Samuel Taylor Coleridge, famously, was accused by Thomas De Quincey of "unacknowledged obligations" and "barefaced plagiarism," particularly of German sources that Coleridge translated but failed to assimilate. The irony, in De Quincey's retelling, is that the poet did not *need* to steal; yet "[w]ith the riches of El Dorado lying about him, he would condescend to filch a handful of gold from any man whose purse he fancied."[31]

For Alexandre Dumas, "the man of true genius never steals, *he conquers*."[32] Dumas knew of what he spoke. He employed a number of writers to work as his subalterns, in various forms of collaboration. August Maquet, it has been asserted, is the actual author of *The Three Musketeers* (1844) and *Twenty Years After* (1845), but only the name "Alexandre Dumas" appeared on the title pages of these products of corporate authorship.[33] By 1896, the *Scottish Review* could proclaim, "There are no greater borrowers than those whom we regard as the classics of literature."[34] H. M. Paull takes the argument a step further: "The history of plagiarism is indeed the history of literature.[35] Such a statement can be corroborated by canonical writers who, at different times, have been accused of pilfering from others: Chaucer, Montaigne, Marlowe, Shakespeare, Jonson, Webster, Milton, Molière, Voltaire, Sterne, Scott, Coleridge, Tennyson, Dickens, George Eliot – a veritable Norton anthology of literature.

If *plagiarism* can refer to the efforts of a brilliant author as well as the careless essay of a hasty undergraduate, then perhaps the term is too vague to be of any service. Thomas McFarland, in *Originality and Imagination*, defines *plagiarism* as "the appropriating, in the name of an individual's needs, of the insignia of another individuality, and it is therefore censured in a way that imitation and influence are not."[36] The "therefore" is not quite earned here: why "censured"? Why is allusion noble and plagiarism a fault – the "Original Sin of literature," for Stephen Orgel, or rather "the unoriginal sin," according to Robert Macfarlane?[37] A more cogent exposition can be found in Peter Shaw's article on "Plagiary." He defines *plagiarism* as "the art of using the work of another *with the intent to deceive*."[38] Shaw also finds in plagiarism a "hysterical revolt against the tyranny of originality" and compares the plagiarist to the kleptomaniac; as in De Quincey's account of Coleridge, "what is stolen may not be needed."[39] In the nineteenth century, Ralph Waldo Emerson made the point that "it is as difficult to appropriate the thoughts of others, as it is to invent."[40] Some plagiarists work quite hard at it; they bury clues, cover their tracks, paraphrase, update metaphors. Yet all this effort, for Shaw, demonstrates "the desire to be caught," a need for "self-exposure."[41] If one does not want to be caught, surely the safest course is abstinence. Martin Amis, whose 1973 novel *The Rachel Papers* was plagiarized, believes that "there must be something of the death wish in it."[42] Indeed, plagiarism is a form of self-abnegation, an unwriting of the self, an erasure.

For Hillel Schwartz, plagiarism is a "cultural addiction" and "a defiance of capitalism."[43] Yet plagiarism predates capitalism in its modern, industrialized forms. The English word derives from the Latin *plagiarius*: a kidnapper, someone who abducts children or slaves. "[K]idnappers in Cicero's time were called plagiarii," explains one nineteenth-century journalist.[44] The root, *plaga*, can refer to a net, which could be used to capture people, but it can also refer to a stripe or a lash, as in the punishment inflicted.[45] The metaphoric use of *plagiarius* is attributed to the Roman writer Martial. A number of his epigrams refer to literary thievery, sometimes practiced by Fidentinus: "Rumor has it, Fidentinus, that you recite my little books in public just like your own. If you want the poems called mine, I'll send you them for nothing. If you want them called yours, buy out my ownership."[46] Martial here asserts the monetary value of his literary productions; poetry is a commodity that can be bought and sold. In Epigram 52, the word *plagiaro* is used, in reference to the "kidnapper" of Martial's "little books."[47]

These epigrams were translated into English verse, in 1577, by Timothe Kendall. Soon after, forms of the word *plagiarism* appeared in English. At the end of the sixteenth century, Joseph Hall referred to "a Plagiarie sonnet-wright."[48] The more familiar *plagiarism* and *plagiarist* can be traced to 1621 and 1674, respectively, according to the *OED*. But through the seventeenth century, the word *plagiaries* could still refer to those who steal physical books. In *A Dictionary of the French and English Tongues*, Randle Cotgrave translates the French word *plagiarie* as "a booke-stealer, or booke-theefe" but also as "one that fathers other mens workes upon himselfe."[49] By 1775, *plagiary* approached our modern understanding, as in John Ash's definition: "one that clandestinely borrows the thoughts or expressions of another."[50]

In the eighteenth and nineteenth centuries, a species of "source hunter" or "plagiarism hunter" arose: journalists who performed pre-electronic-era searches to discover borrowings and concordances.[51] Tennyson referred to "editors of booklets, bookworms, index hunters, or men of great memories and no imagination."[52] Such hunters were "eagle-eyed" or "argus-eyed"; Harold Bloom calls them "those carrion-eaters of scholarship, the source hunters."[53] The *Spectator*, in an article entitled "The Cry of Plagiarism," explains their motivation and method: "There are some genial critics who seem to make it their business to catch the literary man tripping, entrap him into telling an apparent lie, and then confront him with parallel columns."[54] Besides the ironic note of "genial," this passage casts the plagiarism hunter as the aggressor, looking to "catch" or "entrap" a victim. Sir Walter Scott, one such victim, railed against the practice: "It is a favorite theme of laborious dulness to trace out such coincidences; because they appear to reduce genius of the higher order to the usual standard of humanity, and, of course, to bring the author nearer a level with his critics."[55]

Other writers shared this skepticism about plagiarism hunting and the usefulness of promoting "originality" as a literary virtue. In the words of Emerson, "There never was an original writer. Each is a link in an endless chain."[56] He developed these ideas further in an 1876 essay, "Quotation and Originality," which argues that "there is no pure originality. All minds quote. Old and new make the warp and woof of every moment. There is no thread that is not a twist of these two strands."[57] Paul K. Saint-Amour uses the term "apologists" to describe those who want to minimize the category of plagiarism or absolve individual cases.[58]

For many, the charge of plagiarism could be forgiven if the alleged plagiarist improved upon the source. An anonymous article, "Recent Poetic Plagiarisms and Imitations," published in the *London Magazine* in the early nineteenth century, articulates this point.[59] "Few readers care how a man's ideas are come by, so they be forcibly and fervently brought out" (601). Originality is not prized here, rather the strength of an argument. One important innovation in this article is the suggestion that "[n]ew thoughts and new modes of expression are literary property" (597). This marks a transition from an eighteenth-century view that a writer owns only the words on the page to a later view that "modes of expression" – "tone, style, and voice," according to Mazzeo – are the rightful property of any author.[60] Now a plagiarist could borrow the *style* of another. Yet the *London Magazine* separates "culpable plagiarism" (that is, "without improvement") from a more productive kind (597). The article develops an optimistic narrative of art as progressive, accumulative; the plagiarist-poet "should regenerate the thoughts of his inferiors, giving them the cast of his own mind" (598). Such benign plagiarism rescues "[i]solated ideas, originating with men of scanty imagination," which otherwise would have been lost (598). The poet-plagiarist thus provides a service to humankind, as long as he or she fully assimilates the source in question.[61]

Plagiarism in Anglo-American culture is not, strictly speaking, a crime. For Alexander Lindey, "Plagiarism and infringement are not the same thing, though they overlap."[62] Saint-Amour calls plagiarism "an ethical rather than a legal transgression," and Peter Shaw finds it to be "a breach of professional ethics."[63] In the Romantic period, plagiarism was more of an aesthetic category: to plagiarize is to write badly, to fail to exert Percy Bysshe Shelley's "power of assimilating" over found materials.[64] Yet the development of copyright law in eighteenth- and nineteenth-century Britain necessarily informs any study of Victorian literary reproduction.

***

How dare you thus unlawfully invade
Our Properties, and trespass on our Trade.

– Edward Ward

Although authorship and plagiarism have origins in the ancient world, copyright is "a specifically modern institution."[65] Mark Rose, in *Authors and Owners: The Invention of Copyright*, argues that this institution was born at a particular historical moment in "printing technology, market-place economics, and the classical liberal culture of possessive individual-ism." For Rose, "Copyright is founded on the concept of the unique individual who creates something and is entitled to reap a profit from those labors."[66] The philosophical foundation lies in John Locke: a man owns himself and therefore owns his own labor.[67] The legal development of copyright also led to a changed understanding of works of art them-selves. "No longer simply a mirror held up to nature, a work was also the objectification of a writer's self," Rose explains. He makes the canny point that the novel and the biography, two forms that specialize in clarifications of the self, grew in prominence after the advent of copyright.[68] As the law developed in Great Britain, a key distinction was made between idea and expression. "Dressed in language, the writer's ideas became a property that could be conveyed from owner to owner in perpetuity according to the same principles as a house or a field."[69]

The older, medieval view of literary property was that whoever owned a manuscript could do what he or she liked with it. If a bookseller purchased a manuscript from an author, then that bookseller could print it, burn it, cut it into pieces, rewrite it, or sell it to a competitor. Buying a manuscript was no different from buying linen or cloth. For Rose, "True copyright is concerned with the rights in texts as distinct from the rights in material objects."[70] John Sutherland finds this notion rooted in a Platonic view that a work of art transcends any particular manifestation.[71] In the eighteenth century, Johann Gottlieb Fichte separated "physical [*körperlich*] and ideal [*geistig*] aspects of a book."[72] William Enfield, in a 1774 pamphlet, drew on William Blackstone in order to divide the "corporeal" from the "incorporeal": "corporeal" are things of the senses, and "incorporeal" are, according to Blackstone, "creatures of the mind."[73] For Enfield, both types can be deemed property and thus protected by law.[74]

One thing that you cannot copyright, it seems, is style. Although D'Israeli maintained that "an author can have nothing truly his own but his Style" and the *London Magazine* article found that "modes of expression" (597) belong to an author, copyright law does not cover style per se.[75] Trevor Ross explains that "copyright protects the expression of a style in a work, but not the style itself to the degree that it can be abstracted from expression."[76] Style, which a reader may perceive and appreciate, is not protected by law: only the particular manifestation of that style in a text. Ross points out the irony that "copyright is grounded on a notion of individuation yet is indifferent to individual achievements in style."[77] This issue will return in the chapters that follow. Charles Dickens and Edward Bulwer (later Lytton) could, to some extent, protect particular novels under the auspices of copyright, but the Dickensian or Bulwerian style so important to the success of those works was fair game for the aspiring imitator. This exception for style, as delineated by Ross, runs counter to the history of copyright – a domain that has grown temporally, spatially, and conceptually over the years.

Copyright in England was born in a 1710 Act of Parliament, although Adrian Johns notes that the word *copyright* was "nowhere used in the original law."[78] In previous centuries, forms of proto-copyright existed through royal patent and the Stationers' Company of London (chartered under Queen Mary, 1557). These two modes of protecting authors and booksellers often fell into conflict.[79] After the Regulation of Printing Act lapsed in 1694, a fifteen-year period followed in which piracy ran rampant; no authority was in place to stop it. Evoking the image of the *plagiarius*, Daniel Defoe, in a 1710 periodical, complains about literary kidnapping: "these Children of our Heads are seiz'd, captivated, spirited away, and carry'd into Captivity." In the same work, he also endorses "a Law to prevent Barbarity and Pyracy."[80] Such a law received royal assent from Queen Anne and was enacted on 10 April 1710.[81] Under the terms of the law, older works were protected for twenty-one years; new works, for fourteen years, after which rights reverted to the author, if living, for another fourteen years.[82]

Through the nineteenth century, Parliament occasionally expanded the term of copyright but did little to expand or clarify the breadth of its coverage. In 1814, the term was extended to twenty-eight years or the life of the author – whichever was longer. This decision "put the author at the very centre" of what had previously been a law to protect the interests of booksellers.[83] Such an adjustment also meant that copyright in a work necessarily died with its biological author – an innovation that living writers with children found unsettling and unfair. Thomas Noon Talfourd, lawyer, playwright, Member of Parliament, and friend to many writers, introduced a number of bills from 1837 to 1841 to extend copyright's length once again. Although he lost his seat, in 1841, a new law was enacted, on 1 July 1842: now the copyright term was forty-two years or the life of the author plus an additional seven years – whichever was longer.

John Feather points out that the 1842 law "was ambiguous about abridgements, anthologies, magazine and newspaper articles, translations, dramatizations and many other matters."[84] Because early copyright law rarely addressed such paraliterary works, decision-making rested in a series of legal cases. As early as 1704, Defoe warned that a book, perhaps costing one pound, could be undercut by cheap condensations, "perswading People that the Substance of the Book is contain'd in the Summary of 4*s.* price."[85] Yet eighteenth-century authorities "gave wide latitude to derivative works, including abridgments, sequels, and translations."[86] In *Gyles v. Wilcox*, a legal case from 1740, the Lord Chancellor decided that an abridgement "may with great propriety be called a new book" because of "the invention, learning, and judgment" required.[87] *Dodsley v. Kinnersley*, a 1761 case, deemed that an abridgement of Johnson's 1759 novel *Rasselas* was "not a piracy."[88] In the 1774 case *Anonymous v. Newbery*, the Lord Chancellor determined that a particular abridgement was "not an act of plagiarism" but rather "an allowable and meritorious work."[89] By the nineteenth century, according to Augustine Birrell, many believed that "a good, honest abridgement was a new book and in no sense a piracy."[90] Robert L. Patten sums up the matter thus: "in Britain both the law and the courts had allowed parodies, sequels, adaptations, abridgements, and some kinds of imitation to be protected by copyright."[91] The interplay between original works and their derivatives will be examined in the chapters that follow. Yet this Victorian phenomenon was not unprecedented.

***

> . . . books always speak of other books, and every story tells a story that has already been told.
>
> – Umberto Eco

During the eighteenth century, *Robinson Crusoe* (1719), *Gulliver's Travels* (1726), *Pamela* (1740), and *Tristram Shandy* (1759–67) were subject to a variety of "autographic" and "allographic" successors.[92] These terms, employed by Nelson Goodman in *Languages of Art*, were redefined by Gérard Genette to refer to works that are produced by their originating artists (autographic) or by others (allographic).[93] In the case of *Robinson Crusoe*, Daniel Defoe published an autographic sequel, *The Farther Adventures of Robinson Crusoe; Being the Second and Last Part of His Life, and of the Strange and Surprizing Accounts of His Travels round the Three Parts of the Globe* (1719). For the allographic, the numbers are legion. J. K. Welcher counts 277 eighteenth-century imitations, and variants continued to appear well into the nineteenth century, including *The Catholic Crusoe* (1862), the hopeful *Le dernier Crusoe* (1860), and *Der schweizerische Robinson, Oder der Schiffbrüchige Schweize-Prediger und Seine Familie* (1812, later filmed, by Walt Disney, as *The Swiss Family Robinson*).[94] For David A. Brewer, *Gulliver's Travels* is similarly "an inexhaustible public resource."[95] Welcher counts some four hundred variants by approximately two hundred different writers. Gulliver himself appears as the "author" of many such offerings, even when the texts have little to do with Jonathan Swift's book.[96]

In a study of Samuel Richardson's *Pamela*, Thomas Keymer and Peter Sabor create a vivid picture of an eighteenth-century novel's complex afterlife. "Richardson's novel is valuably illuminated by the appropriations and transformations, the resistant readings and creative misreadings, that followed its publication."[97] Within a year of *Pamela*'s appearance, in November 1740, publishers offered *Pamela Censured, Anti-Pamela, The*

True Anti-Pamela, and *Shamela*. In Keymer and Sabor's account, *Pamela's Conduct in High Life* and its ilk compelled Richardson to prepare an autographic sequel, which he published in December 1741 (dated 1742). Indeed, it became clear that "he alone no longer controlled, and could not close down, the fictional world he had opened."[98] Earlier, in May 1741, Richardson wrote an advertisement, "*To the PUBLICK*," disavowing *Pamela's Conduct* and promising his "OWN CONTINUATION ... with all convenient speed."[99] As Richardson wrote privately, "I saw all my Characters were likely to be debased, & my whole Purpose inverted."[100]

Walter Scott, who served as a professional model for many Victorian writers, saw his own fiction reproduced, parodied, and staged throughout the nineteenth century. Ann Rigney refers to a "Waverley phenomenon," comprised of derivative texts that evince "a desire to prolong and intensify the memory of stories that had given pleasure."[101] Rigney argues that "[t]he usual way of judging the cultural impact of writers is by counting the number of new editions and sales figures. An alternative is to examine the intensity with which the work is replicated in other cultural expressions."[102] In fact, the Waverley phenomenon expanded beyond print culture to include Scott-inspired place names throughout the English-speaking world, such as Waverley Place, in New York City. The dramatists were often the first to appropriate Scott's narratives. After *Guy Mannering* appeared at Covent Garden, in 1816, "virtually all of the novels of the Great Unknown were immediately staged within months of their publication."[103]

Among prose imitations, *Walladmor, Frei nach dem Englischen des Walter Scott* was published in Germany, in 1823, with two further volumes in 1824. Supposedly translated from a novel by Scott, *Walladmor* was in fact written by the pseudonymous Willibald Alexis. He claimed that if he were ever imprisoned, "he would write a novel in the style of Scott."[104] This little jest contains the suggestion that an author's style can be seen as a form of escape, an intellectual flight from the bounds of confinement; on the other hand, this statement also implies that to write like Scott is itself a form of imprisonment. Seamus Perry argues this point regarding G. K. Chesterton, whose parody of Robert Browning makes the poet seem trapped by his own style: "a sort of prison from which he could not escape."[105] With some inexactitude, L. H. C. Thomas calls *Walladmor* a "parody" but also a "forgery" of "Scott's technique as a novelist"; an alleged translation that is also forgery (or parody) indicates some of the formal confusion that confounds such works.[106] *Walladmor* was itself translated into English, by Thomas De Quincey, in 1825.

For Rigney, *Ivanhoe* is "the Scott novel that has generated the greatest number of versions of itself on page, stage, and screen."[107] H. Philip Bolton identifies *Ivanhoe; or, The Jew's Daughter* (aka *Ivanhoe; or, The Jew of York*) as the earliest dramatization; it opened at the Surrey Theatre, on 20 January 1820, soon after the book's publication.[108] Condensations of this three-volume novel, in the form of chapbooks, also appeared, including *Ivanhoe; or The Knight Templar, and the Jew's Daughter* (1821). Bolton estimates that forty-two such "penny dreadful" publications derived from this one title.[109]

To catch a glimpse of this Waverley phenomenon, consider two nineteenth-century prose iterations of *Ivanhoe: Richard of England* and *Rebecca and Rowena*. *Richard of England; or, The Lion King*, a curious reworking of *Ivanhoe* elements, was published anonymously and is attributed to Thomas Archer. The central love triangle is retained; King Richard and the crusades grow in prominence; and the story of Rebecca and the Templar is diminished. Archer changes the names of Scott's fictional characters: Ivanhoe is now Eustace de Vere; Cedric becomes Oswald; Rowena, Alena; and Rebecca takes her mother's name, Rachael (sometimes Rachel). While ostensibly a new narrative (hence the title), *Richard of England* frequently descends to verbatim plagiarism. A description of Rowena is applied to Alena, and Archer borrows liberally from Scott's tournament: "Five knights, chosen by lot, now advanced slowly into the area; a single champion riding in front, and the other four following in pairs."[110] Yet Archer deletes the mention of Scott's credited source (the Wardour manuscript) as well as the narrator's sudden glance at a future perspective: "Their escutcheons have long mouldered from the walls of their castles."[111] By cutting analeptic and proleptic references, Archer flattens the historical dimensions of *Ivanhoe*; *Richard of England* retains the surface pleasures of Scott's narrative but not its depth. In other places, the plagiaristic novel simplifies the language of its predecessor ("the fearing discomfiture and disgrace" becomes "fear of being conquered"), and archaisms are modernized ("script" becomes "stripped").[112] Although much of *Ivanhoe* takes place in the north, *Richard of England* relocates scenes to southern England and London in particular – to move closer, perhaps, to the urban readers who were its likely audience. "The scenes of the past," Rachael explains, "are about to be reacted here."[113]

Rebecca and Rowena: A Romance upon Romance (1850) also extends Walter Scott's novel, but the function is now parodic. Written by William Makepeace Thackeray and attributed to his pseudonym Michael Angelo Titmarsh, *Rebecca and Rowena* is an example of Rigney's "desire to prolong" a narrative. What is more, Thackeray's work stands as a correction to its forerunner: "Ivanhoe's history *must* have a continuation."[114] Like many readers before or since, Thackeray believed that Ivanhoe belongs with Rebecca, the daughter of Isaac of York. Rowena, "that vapid, flaxen-headed creature," is "unworthy of Ivanhoe."[115] In the process of continuing and correcting Scott's novel, Thackeray transforms its characters into Thackerayan characters: melancholic, hypocritical, despairing, shallow. Ivanhoe himself, like many characters in *Vanity Fair* (1847–48), gets what he wants and regrets it. Further, it is appropriate that in this imitative work King Richard is recast as a plagiarist; he claims to have written the music and lyrics to a song, but "he had stolen every idea."[116] While Thackeray was willing to steal ideas from Walter Scott, he resists describing a scene of hunger because such was already achieved by Dante: "my efforts may be considered as mere imitations."[117]

Beyond this attention to *Ivanhoe*, Scott's mode of historical writing was replicated in the early Victorian period by successors such as William Harrison Ainsworth, whose historical novels include *The Tower of London* (1840) and *Old St. Paul's: A Tale of the Plague and the Fire* (1841). G. P. R. James, one of the most plodding of Scott's epigones, was, for the *Edinburgh Review*, a clear disciple: "his whole tastes and modes of thinking have grown into a singular harmony with those of the great original from which he drew."[118] Even as late as 1880, in French-speaking Canada, the phenomenon could still be felt. *Le manoir mystérieux*, by Frédéric Houde, plagiarized Walter Scott's 1821 novel *Kenilworth*.[119]

Indeed, the urge to imitate did not end with the death of Scott, in 1832. In the pages that follow, I analyze plagiarisms, parodies, and imitations of the Victorian novel – the successors to the successors to Defoe, Swift, Richardson, and Scott. One feature that imitated Victorian novels share with their eighteenth-century forebears is that many are what Terry Castle calls "charismatic texts": "those with an unusually powerful effect on a large reading public."[120] The charismatic text "creates in readers a desire for 'more of the same'"; further, there is a "deep unconscious nostalgia for a past reading pleasure."[121] Despite this continuity, one could cite many ways in which the conditions of printing and bookselling changed by the mid-nineteenth century from the days of Pope and Johnson: steam printing, machine-made paper, rail travel, increased literacy, the growth of periodicals, the expansion of circulating libraries, and the reduction of taxes on knowledge.[122] For Brewer, the quintessential eighteenth-century literary derivative employs "character migration" – fictional characters stray from their textual origins. As he states, "[T]he characters in broadly successful texts were treated as if they were both fundamentally incomplete and the common property of all."[123] This process certainly continued: for example, Samuel Pickwick, of *The Pickwick Papers*, strayed into all manner of literary, subliterary, and non-literary variants. Victorian imitation also drew attention to the figure of the author and evinced an effort to embody or impersonate the successful novelists of the day.

***

Piracy, Plagiarism and Confusion.

– Daniel Defoe

One problem with Victorian imitation is what to call it. Earlier, I offered a long list of potential candidates, and I have already discussed *imitation* and *plagiarism*. It lies beyond the scope of this book to delineate every terminological possibility, but in this section, I will investigate three terms that could be used to describe the efforts of spurious Victorians: *adaptation, sequel*, and *parody*. The last, because of its historical complexity, requires a lengthier treatment.

In some ways, *adaptation* may be a more appropriate term than *plagiarism* for some of the imitative works examined in the chapters that follow. Linda Hutcheon, in *A Theory of Adaptation*, refers to "deliberate, announced, and extended revisitations of prior works."[124] These terms accurately describe Thomas Peckett Prest's many revisions of Dickens's early narratives; Prest's efforts were "deliberate" in that they were no accident, "announced" in so far as each title is a clear corruption of an earlier one, and "extended" in that each publication extends the limits of a Dickens text. Sarah Cardwell further compares literary or "cultural adaptation" to "biological (genetic) adaptation." In the former, as in the latter, there is a process of species survival: some genetic elements in a source text are passed on to subsequent generations.[125] Whereas the biological form of adaptation supposes improvement over time, Hutcheon mentions the reverse assumption in the case of literary adaptations: "an adaptation is likely to be greeted as minor and subsidiary and certainly never as good as the 'original.'" Yet adaptations offer "the comfort of ritual combined with the piquancy of surprise" – a formula that could also serve for sequels.[126]

Autographic and allographic sequels, as I explained, flourished in eighteenth-century Britain, and this book will consider a number of nineteenth-century examples. Sequels, of course, are more familiar to twenty-first-century audiences than antique forms such as *palinode*, and Marjorie Garber points out that the most familiar sequel is the New Testament, which turns the Hebrew Bible into a "prequel" and thus an "Old" Testament.[127] Garber refers to a "sequel-effect," by which the ontology of a text is changed by the appearance of a successor; the earlier text is now designated "the original."[128] Terry Castle memorably states that "sequels are always disappointing" because readers "persist in demanding the impossible: that the sequel be different, but also *exactly the same*"; yet sequels inevitably create difference.[129] Genette, ever methodical, divides what he calls "continuations" into four categories: "*proleptic*" (our sense of the sequel), "*analeptic*" (a prequel), "*elleptic*" (that which fills a narrative gap), and "*paraleptic*" (a new narrative that runs concurrently, like a subplot).[130] On the other hand, D. A. Miller offers some skepticism about the possibility of sequels and prequels. That which is outside a novel is non-narratable, such as the "quiescence" before the beginning and after the end.[131] Further, that which is non-narratable does not generate stories and therefore cannot be the source of sequels and prequels (by the same logic, closure is also impossible, because narrative is the thing that narrates and cannot be expected to stop).[132] Thackeray, in *Rebecca and Rowena*, responds to the condition that Miller describes: "the books we delight in have very unsatisfactory conclusions, and end quite prematurely with page 320 of the third volume."[133] Obviously, this was a publishing convention: there was no artistic reason for novels to appear in three (rather than four or seven) octavo volumes of roughly three hundred pages each.[134] Anticipating Garber's sequel-effect, Thackeray refers to *Ivanhoe* as "the former part of this history."[135] The efforts of allographic sequels, such as *Rebecca and Rowena*, is to push beyond the temporal and generic limitations of any "original" text.

Rebecca and Rowena is also a work of parody. Regarding this word and its near synonyms, the experts agree: "Dictionary definitions do not help"; "[t]he dictionaries are not helpful" and "not very helpful here."[136] What are parody, burlesque, travesty, burlesque travesty? It depends on whom you ask and when you ask. M. H. Abrams, in *A Glossary of Literary Terms*, uses *burlesque* as the keyword. *Burlesque* probably comes from the Italian word *burla* ("a joke or a trick") and was ascendant in the seventeenth and eighteenth centuries.[137] Burlesque "does not require a specific literary model," which draws it away from parody.[138] George Kitchin blurs the distinction between burlesque and parody, although he agrees that burlesque can target either literary or extra-literary subjects, such as "Balliol week-end parties."[139] To add to

the complexity, Abrams separates high and low burlesque, and John
D. Jump further divides the field into four categories: "Travesty,"
"Hudibrastic," "Parody," and "Mock-Poem" or "Mock-epic."[140]
Travesty, in turn, comes from *travestire*, "to disguise" or "to change
clothing."[141] Travesty debases, brings high matters low; it is thus the
reverse of mock-heroic, which elevates the mundane. To add to the
chaos, Genette prefers the eighteenth-century French word *pastiche*,
from the Italian *pasticcio* ("paste" or "mixture"); Margaret A. Rose
explains that pastiche is "used as a synonym for parody ... especially
in French literature."[142] Fredric Jameson further defines *pastiche* as
"blank parody, parody that has lost its sense of humor," and David
Bromwich explains that "parody and pastiche are hard to tell apart"
because "parody and writing are hard to tell apart."[143]

To escape the verbal quagmire, it makes sense to return to origins.
Parody, like *plagiarism*, is rooted in the ancient world and thus predates
the various coinages of *burlesque*, *travesty*, and *pastiche*, all of which
responded to contemporary (often fleeting) artistic forms. In part because
of its antiquity, *parody* is used as the central term by two important
theorists, Linda Hutcheon and Margaret A. Rose. Moreover, parody,
both the word and practice, was ascendant in the nineteenth century. An
1819 article in *Blackwood's Edinburgh Magazine* refers to "this age of
parody."[144]

The first parodist, according to Aristotle, was Hegemon of Thasos.[145]
None of his work has survived. The English word *parody* comes from *ode* (a
song or a chant) and the prefix *para*, which can mean "alongside" but also
"against" – consider a paralegal or a paradox. A *parode* is a song "sung in
imitation of others," and *parodia* suggests "singing beside," which could
mean "off key" or "in another voice."[146] Hutcheon insists that *parodia* does
not imply ridicule; it is "repetition with difference."[147] For Seamus Perry,
parody is a "counter-song."[148] In the ancient world there was a *Deiliad*, "an
Iliad of cowardice," according to Genette; and the parodic work
Batrachomyomachia, which concerns a mock-Homeric battle between
frogs and mice, is extant.[149]

One traditional view is that parody is bad, aesthetically and morally.
William Hone stood trial in December 1817 when he parodied Christianity
in a number of publications (he was acquitted).[150] Later in the century,
Matthew Arnold called parody "a vile art," and George Eliot denounced it
as a "moral imbecility" and a "befooling drug."[151] In the preface to *Hamlet
Travestie* (1810), John Poole states, "The objection most commonly urged
against burlesques and parodies in general, is, that they tend to bring into

ridicule and contempt those authors against whose works they are directed."[152]

More often, nineteenth-century critics lauded the virtues of parody. Francis Jeffrey, writing anonymously in the *Edinburgh Review*, offers a definition:

> to be able to borrow the diction and manner of a celebrated writer to express sentiments like his own – to write as he would have written on the subject proposed to his imitation – to think his thoughts in short, as well as to use his words – and to make the revival of his style appear a natural consequence of the strong conception of his peculiar ideas.[153]

The final clause is striking: the notion of a "natural consequence" in which style flows from idea. It is noteworthy that Jeffrey suggests that parody focuses on the "celebrated" rather than the obscure writer; to borrow from the unknown and unrecognized may well constitute plagiarism. However, ambiguities develop in this passage, especially Jeffrey's use of "his." With "the subject proposed to his imitation," does "his" refer to the writer who is being imitated or the one creating the imitation? Similarly, consider "the strong conception of his peculiar ideas." Whose ideas? The parodist or parodee? Further, "to think his thoughts in short" might mean to think his thoughts as result or consequence, but the phrase could also mean to think his thoughts, only now shortened or truncated. Nonetheless, Jeffrey is enthusiastic about parody: "it commonly has the advantage of letting us more completely into the secret of the original author."[154] This espousal of parody continued as the century progressed. The *Athenaeum*, in 1871, still conflated *parody, burlesque,* and *caricature* but conceded that parodic modes increase, rather than decrease, the stature of their targets: "A man who finds himself the subject of a caricature may thank his stars that he is thought worth the caricaturing."[155] By 1885, the *Saturday Review* could enthuse, "[T]o parody a writer is really to pay a compliment to his popularity."[156] More recently, Bromwich has summarized this optimistic view: "*That it can be parodied*, most readers would admit, is one good test of an individual style."[157] Somewhat tautologically, then, a writer is parodied because he or she is worth the parodying.

From the early nineteenth century to the early twentieth century, collections of parodies generally meant collections of poems. *Rejected Addresses; or, The New Theatrum Poetarum* (1812) is comprised of supposed compositions from Wordsworth, Coleridge, Lord Byron, Walter Scott, Robert Southey, and others (only three of the entries are prose); *The Poetic Mirror; or, The Living Bards of Britain* (1816) presents a familiar list of

Byron, Scott, Wordsworth, and James Hogg (himself the presumed author). In the 1880s, Walter Hamilton compiled six large volumes of parodies; only one-third of the last volume covers prose. By 1912, Arthur Quiller-Couch could write in another anthology, "The material, then, on which Parody works is Poetry."[158] There are good reasons for an identification between poetry and parody. Lyric poems tend to be short and so lend themselves to both parodic treatment and to anthologizing. Further, nineteenth-century poetry offers two features ready made for parody: namely, the built-in repetitions of meter and rhyme. Many parodies recreate the rhyme scheme of a target poem; some even rhyme *with* the original poem – a form of silent or supplementary rhyme.

Parodists of prose fiction, on the other hand, often have longer sources to emulate, and these sources generally lack the obvious, systemic structuring of conventional verse. That said, masters of prose parody have produced worthy collections, such as Thackeray's *Punch's Prize Novelists* (1847), F. Bret Harte's *Condensed Novels and Other Papers* (1867), and Max Beerbohm's *A Christmas Garland* (1912). Furthermore, Simon Dentith makes the case that nineteenth-century novelists such as Jane Austen, Thackeray, and Eliot use parody "as a kind of guarantee of their own realist credentials."[159] This tradition recalls Cervantes and Henry Fielding: the novel employs parody to correct and move beyond its predecessors. Dickens, too, deploys parody in his fiction. To cite one of many examples, Kate, in *Nicholas Nickleby* (1838–39), reads aloud from a three-volume novel entitled *The Lady Flabella*, a wicked parody of the silver-fork or fashionable school of fiction.[160]

However, this study is not an account of parodic, imitative, or plagiaristic works produced *by* canonical writers but rather versions *of* the canonical produced by others. Unfortunately, there is no satisfactory English word that encompasses all of the examples in the chapters that follow. Carrie Sickmann Han suggests "continual reading" for the efforts of those who write successors to Victorian novels, and David S. Roh offers the phrase "disruptive textuality."[161] It is striking that these recent coinages, helpful as they both are, move in opposite directions: continuity versus discontinuity. Because of the terminological difficulties, I will employ *aftertext* as an umbrella term. Genette in fact refers to "after-texts" to describe "revisions and corrections made to an already published text."[162] I will broaden the scope of *aftertext* because it is concise and multivalent. Victorian aftertexts were published after – that is to say, chronologically – and many are "after" the manner, sense, style, or creative ambitions of some earlier text or writer. In some cases, aftertexts are also "after" their sources in a more aggressive way, as in the threatening phrase "I'm coming after you." Aftertexts come after, in more than one sense, as they simulate and interrogate their predecessors.

***

Je prends mon bien où je le trouve.

– Molière

This book offers a new kind of reception history. Along with sales figures and reviews in periodicals, literary imitations tell us a great deal about how a novel was received by its initial audiences. Robert Darnton, writing on book history, finds that "[r]eading remains the most difficult stage to study in the circuit that books follow."[163] Readers, with few exceptions, leave no traces; Michel de Certeau says that "[r]eading takes no measures against the erosion of time . . . it does not keep what it acquires."[164] Imitative authors, perhaps unwittingly, perform a useful literary–historical function. Because such authors capture – or attempt to capture – the essence of their sources, each imitation necessarily records at least one reader's response. Francis Jeffrey, in the aforementioned review, argues that "the copy presents no traits but such as are characteristic."[165] Although Jeffrey was reviewing a work of parody, his use of the word "copy" suggests that various forms of imitative writing could perform such a function.

Aftertexts, as described in the pages that follow, enlarge our sense of what literary knowledge looks like: to know a particular author means to know the (sometimes bad) publications that the author inspired. This argument draws on the teachings of textual criticism and the distinction made between the *work* and the *text*. G. Thomas Tanselle argues that "the work can only be reconstituted through the application of critical judgment to each element of every surviving text"; the work, then, transcends its manifestations in individual, printed texts, "subjected to the hazards of the physical."[166] In a better-known formulation, Roland Barthes agrees with the distinction but inverts the definitions: "the work is a fragment of substance, occupying a part of the space of books (in a library for example)," whereas "the Text is a methodological field."[167] Following the Anglo-American tradition of Tanselle and Jerome J. McGann, I want to refer to the *work* as the totality of a literary existence. Further, I propose that the work (so defined) should include aftertextual productions: plagiarisms, parodies, sequels, and so on. A conventional view would find that such excrescences are peripheral to the study of literature and the arts; Peter Lamarque, for instance, argues that parody and forgery "are not part of,

and do not contribute to, the oeuvre and its achievement."[168] His reason is
that parody is humorous and forgery dishonest. The following chapters
will undermine this stance and broaden our sense of the literary work
(Lamarque's "oeuvre"). Arguments in favor of the validity of aftertexts as
a source of literary knowledge depend on the notion of dichotomy: that
which is not-x helps us to see with greater clarity that which is x. As Joseph
Loewenstein remarks, "Transgression is one of the historian's most useful
data."[169] Alexander Welsh makes a similar case for pathology as an epistemological practice: to examine that which is ill or aberrant (i.e. literary
plagiarism) increases our understanding of the healthy subject.[170] Such
dichotomizing stands at the root of the European literary tradition; ancient
librarians separated genuine from spurious texts for each author and
termed them "*gnesioi*" and "*nothoi*."[171] One cannot produce a canon unless
there is something that is not in it.

In the nineteenth century, aftertexts proved to be more than an annoyance or an infringement on the property rights of successful novelists;
imitation, in many cases, shaped the reception and altered the courses of
each novelist's career trajectory. It also appears that aftertexts reverse
causality: because a writer is parodied, his or her compositions are distinct
and distinguished; because a writer is imitated, that writer is considered
original. A seminal argument can be found in Edward Young's 1759
pamphlet *Conjectures on Original Composition*. While the existence of
"illustrious Examples" may "*engross, prejudice*, and *intimidate*" the latter-
day writer, Young also suggests that originals themselves are productive:
"an *Original* author ... will probably propagate a numerous offspring of
Imitators, to eternize his glory."[172] Joel Weinsheimer, in an article on
Young's thesis, finds that a work of art "is not original until it originates,
and what it originates are imitations. The originativity of the original
depends on its being imitated, and so disseminated, by readerly
writers."[173] By this view, aftertexts that mimic, in some fashion, *Oliver
Twist* (1837–39) or *Adam Bede* (1859) do not diminish or deplete their
sources; rather, these reproductions make the originals *original* in that they
originated something. Further, as will be seen, Charles Dickens, Edward
Bulwer, and George Eliot were not passive witnesses to such aftextual
attentions. The manner in which these three authors responded to their
respondents will be charted in the following chapters. There is often
a blurring between source and aftertext: sequels to *The Pickwick Papers*
seem designed to lure readers into mistaking one object for another;
reviewers of Bulwer's fiction frequently imitate the style they profess to
disdain. I argue that anonymous, hackneyed, and unoriginal writers are

part of the literary history from which they have long been excluded; they shaped that literary history and influenced – in a seeming reversal of cause and effect – three iconic novelists of the nineteenth century.

So why Dickens, Bulwer, and Eliot? Other writers were certainly subject to nineteenth-century imitation. Captain Frederick Marryat's "naval fictions were much emulated in the 1830s by a number of other authors who were also Captains," and Ainsworth's *Jack Sheppard* (1839) prompted a "Jack Sheppard mania," with works including *Eventful Life and Unparalleled Exploits of Jack Sheppard* and *Eventful Life and Unparalleled Exploits of the Notorious Jack Sheppard* (both 1840).[174] It should be noted that Sheppard was an historic figure, so facsimiles of his story in print and on the London stage were not strictly a response to Ainsworth's imaginative achievement. Beyond Marryat and Ainsworth, Benjamin Disraeli's *Coningsby* prompted William North's *Anti-Coningsby; or, The New Generation Grown Old* (both 1844), and Lewis Carroll's *Alice's Adventures in Wonderland* (1865) inspired theatrical, musical, visual, and prose recapitulations. The Brontë sisters might seem to have offered tempting possibilities for would-be imitators, but Patsy Stoneman finds that there were "no derivations of *Wuthering Heights* before the 1880's."[175] *Jane Eyre*, first published in 1847, was produced on stage in the late 1840s and 1850s, and Stoneman identifies a number of fictions that draw on Charlotte Brontë's novel, such as Julia Kavanagh's *Nathalie* and Dinah Maria Craik's *Olive* (both 1850).[176] Charlotte herself framed the writings of her sisters, Emily and Anne, by reconstructing their achievements through prefaces and new editions of the works of Currer, Ellis, and Acton Bell. Of course, Emily and Anne, then deceased, could not respond.[177]

Yet in the cases of Dickens, Bulwer, and Eliot, the production of aftertexts was more intense, immediate, and sustained. The aftertexts analyzed in the subsequent chapters meet two criteria: temporal and generic. In terms of the first, the aftertexts discussed are roughly contemporary with their sources (or, in the case of some serialized novels, precisely concurrent). The aftertexts appeared during the lifetimes of the originating authors, when the publishing and cultural conditions of the source-text still prevailed and that text itself was a current work and not an historical artifact or "classic." This temporal limitation thus excludes reworkings that are retrospective, written decades or perhaps a century later. The second criterion is to focus (as much as possible) on works of prose – that is, publications that draw closest to the imaginative medium used by Dickens, Bulwer, and Eliot. It is certainly true that Victorian dramatists were among the most aggressive of literary borrowers, and this study will occasionally venture into theatrical terrain. Nevertheless, a stage adaptation of a novel constitutes a change of medium – a medium with its own history, traditions, and pragmatic contingencies.

One other pattern emerges that makes the aftertexts of Dickens, Bulwer, and Eliot especially important to literary history. These texts, to varying degrees, usurp authorial identity: the stable, autonomous author is tested by acts of literary theft and identity theft. All three cases involve questions of names and nomenclature. Charles Dickens found that his early pen-name Boz was refashioned into Bos and Poz and Quiz; Edward Bulwer Lytton felt threatened when his wife published novels under her married name – *his* name – Bulwer Lytton; and there were deceptive authors who claimed to be George Eliot or, less plausibly, Adam Bede.

The aftertextual authors in the pages that follow are thus "other" to three popular writers of the nineteenth century; they are counterfactuals; their work, counterfictions. Thomas Peckett Prest, Rosina Bulwer Lytton, Joseph Liggins, and Edith Simcox, among others, prove, in this account, to be alternate versions of Dickens, Bulwer, and Eliot: the lesser-known writers are iterations of what might have been. They are thus the shadowy twin to some major novelists, the secret sharer, who knows something about the originating author that he or she may not know about him- or herself. Once that knowledge is revealed, the originating author is obliged to deny it, reckon with it, or outmaneuver it. Through imitation and identity theft, aftertexts inform literary history and the construction of authorship; they helped to shape the nineteenth-century canon that in turn denied them admission. Neglected, plagiaristic texts illuminate the process by which an individual authorial voice emerged amid an echo chamber of competing, imitative voices.

CHAPTER ONE

The Pickwick Phenomenon

There never was a writer except Dickens.

– Max Beerbohm

John Sutherland has called *The Pickwick Papers* "[t]he most important single novel of the Victorian era."[1] His point is compelling, except that *Pickwick* is not "Victorian," and it is not a "novel." *The Posthumous Papers of the Pickwick Club* began publication on 31 March 1836, when William IV was on the throne, and it continued to appear, in monthly shilling numbers, through 30 October 1837.[2] Fourteen of its twenty numbers thus appeared during William's reign, so *Pickwick* is, at best, 30 percent Victorian. Further, early reviewers did not identify *Pickwick* as a novel. The *Morning Chronicle* described it as "a magazine consisting of only one article," and *Chambers's Edinburgh Journal* found it to be "a series of monthly pamphlets."[3] Even Dickens himself, in July 1837, when *Pickwick* was approaching its conclusion, could mention the forthcoming *Barnaby Rudge* as "my first Novel."[4] In the twentieth century, George Orwell noted that *Pickwick* is "not a novel," and G. K. Chesterton, famously, deemed it "something nobler than a novel."[5] One could further quibble with Sutherland in that he calls *Pickwick* "single." A work that appears in twenty numbers (sold as nineteen) is, to a certain extent, multiple. In the 1847 preface, Dickens refers to "these Pickwick Papers."[6] *Pickwick* was indeed multiple, and it was a multiplier: in the 1830s and 1840s, it produced a multiplicity of variants – prose imitations, stage adaptations, extra illustrations, and consumer products.

Whatever *Pickwick* was, it was more than a book; it was a phenomenon, a mania.[7] "Nothing like it had ever happened before," claims biographer Edgar Johnson.[8] Writing just after the Second World War, Clifton Fadiman employs a military metaphor: "For the first time since 1066, England was conquered – by a fat man in gaiters, attended by a cockney."[9] Amy Cruse puts the case more modestly: "Plump little Mr. Pickwick went everywhere."[10] Hyperbole reigns in discussions of *The Pickwick Papers*. It is "unprecedented," "an unexampled phenomenon," and "the most sensational triumph in nineteenth-century publishing."[11] Percy Fitzgerald, who wrote or edited seven books on the subject, contends that "there is a regular 'Pickwick' literature."[12] Hammond Hall adds that no other novel "has called forth so large a bibliography."[13] That was in 1899.

Beyond bibliography, the phenomenon manifested itself in Pickwick hats, canes, gaiters, and figurines. The "Penny Pickwick" cigar was apparently popular with cab drivers.[14] By October 1837, the *Quarterly Review* could state, "Pickwick chintzes figured in linendrapers' windows, and Weller corduroys in breeches-makers' advertisements; Boz cabs might be seen rattling through the streets."[15] It is indicative of the Pickwick phenomenon that this report on reproduction was itself reproduced – that is, plagiarized – by Fred G. Kitton, in his 1886 book *Dickensiana*.[16] Plagiarism is, in a sense, infectious: reproduction reproduces itself. Dickens's book generated imitations, imitations of imitations, and imitations *within* imitations. On the back cover of the Pickwickian publication *Effingham Hazard, the Adventurer*, A. Thorn advertised something called "Pickwick Sauce," "for enriching soups, gravies, and all kinds of made dishes."[17] The same merchant bought advertising space in a similar monthly serial, *The Queerfish Chronicles*, to market "Thorn's Potted Yarmouth Bloaters." This advertisement includes a warning: "The Proprietor, being aware of several spurious compositions that are daily offered to the public, under the name of Potted Bloaters, begs them to observe his signature, ALEX. THORN, on the side of the pot, without which it cannot be genuine."[18] Thorn's problem was not very different from Dickens's: "spurious compositions" deceive the unknowing buyer, and only the "signature" of an author can distinguish the "genuine" from the spurious.[19] Incidentally, these bloaters were sold in pots, with labels on the side – an image that evokes Dickens's childhood labor in Warren's Blacking warehouse.

The first Pickwick plagiarist was Samuel Pickwick, Esquire. If to plagiarize is to steal someone's words, then that is precisely what Mr. Pickwick does as soon as his peregrinations begin, in chapter 2. Sam Pickwick listens with astonishment to an account given by a cabman (whose name, symmetrically, is Sam). As the narrator relates, "Mr. Pickwick entered every word of this statement in his note-book."[20] It may be recalled that the age of the cabman's remarkable horse is forty-two – the mirror image of Dickens's age at the commencement of *Pickwick*: twenty-four. A horse locked into the perpetual motion of a cab is not unlike Dickens's commitment to the procrustean bed of monthly shilling numbers for the upcoming months (and years). Plagiarizing Mr. Pickwick is, in turn, echoed by Count Smorltork, a traveler who records and corrupts language in *his* notebook.[21] Later, *The Pickwick Papers* offers yet another double: a "scientific gentleman" who is both "elderly" and "a bachelor." Struck by the "phenomenon" of Mr. Pickwick's lantern, this gentleman pens a scientific paper (422–423). In short, *Pickwick* itself models the reproducibility that would soon become a publishing sensation.

Pickwickian aftertexts arrived as early as 1837, when *Pickwick* was still appearing monthly. The first stage play that can be confirmed is *The Pickwick Club; or, The Age We Live In!*, by Edward Stirling; it premièred on 27 March.[22] In May, Alfred Crowquill (a pseudonym used by Alfred Forrester) offered *The Pickwickians*, a series of forty colored plates, published, like *Pickwick* itself, in monthly numbers (through November).[23] *Pickwick* was such a success that London publishers imitated its *form*: serialized narratives, published weekly or monthly, in paper wrappers. John Sutherland notes that "there was a rather desperate attempt to crack the formula and identify the active ingredients in Boz's appeal."[24] He mentions that alliteration was thought to have held the key; hence *Charley Chalk, David Dreamy, Pattie's Pictorial Periodical*, and *Valentine Vox, the Ventriloquist*.[25] This last was, according to the *Operative*, "another attempt to share in the glory and profits enjoyed by the redoubtable Boz."[26] An Irish publisher offered to print Charles Lever's *The Confessions of Harry Lorrequer* "in monthly numbers with illustrations like the 'Pickwick.'"[27] John Bowen might be unsurprised that Dickens's book inspired such an array of spurious compositions, since "[m]uch of *Pickwick Papers* is about imposture." Winkle, Snodgrass, Stiggins, and Jingle are all, to some degree, frauds.[28]

While the Pickwick phenomenon was intense, it was not the first occasion on which Dickens's writing was pilfered by denizens of Grub Street. The earliest of his sketches, "A Dinner at Poplar Walk," appeared in the *Monthly Magazine*, in December 1833; one week later it was pirated by the *London Weekly Magazine* (formerly bearing a more forthright title, the *Thief*).[29] Dickens's first book, *Sketches by Boz* (1836), was succeeded by *The Sketch-Book by "Bos,"* published by Edward Lloyd.[30] Michael Hancher recently reprinted what might be Dickens's earliest published piece of imaginative writing, an 1832 fictional letter to the *Athenaeum*, entitled "Merry Christmas to You; or, Wishes Not Horses." Signed by "C.D." and not by Charles Dickens or Boz, this holiday offering was itself pirated more than once.[31]

The newspaper the *Thief*, in its first issue, claimed, as a form of justification, "We only steal from them what they have stolen from others."[32] Indeed, *The Pickwick Papers*, as was recognized at the time, is a work of creative recombination. The *Athenaeum*, in an oft-quoted formula, observes, "The Pickwick Papers, in fact, are made up of two pounds of Smollett, three ounces of Sterne, a handful of Hook, a dash of grammatical Pierce Egan . . . served with an original *sauce piquante*" (note that only the *Pickwick* sauce is original).[33] One could further mention the influence of Fielding, Oliver Goldsmith, the performer Charles Mathews, and the vaguely forgotten adventures of Robert Smith Surtees's Jorrocks and William Combe's Doctor Syntax. Perhaps inevitably, Dickens earned the title of plagiarist: the *Quarterly Review*, for instance, accused him of borrowing from Washington Irving.[34] One important precursor was Pierce Egan. His *Life in London* was published in twelve monthly numbers, from 1820 to 1821, with plates by Robert Cruikshank. This work, which introduced the world to Tom, Jerry, and their friend Bob Logic, spawned its own phenomenon, with hats, coats, pantaloons, and "[n]o less than sixty-five separate publications."[35] Egan wrote an autographic sequel, which J. R. Harvey cites as another possible source. After passing through a place called Pickwick, the three companions join "the fat Knight," Sir John Blubber, "a retired, wealthy citizen," who agrees "to participate in all their adventures in the country."[36] Even small details in Dickens's work may have predecessors. A forerunner to the memorable (and contested) artifact "BILLST | UM | PSHI | S. M. | ARK" (105) can be found in the eighteenth-century *Grub-Street Journal*, which records an amusing inscription, discovered in Kent: "KEE | PONT | HISS | IDE."[37] And Robert Douglas-Fairhurst notes that Dickens may have self-plagiarized. *Pickwick*'s frame recalls the 1835 sketch "Passages in the Life of Mr. Watkins Tottle," in which a man leaves behind posthumous "papers" to be edited by Boz.[38]

Pickwick also resembles the tale collection *One Thousand and One Nights* in that Dickens's book is a story about stories. One narrative frames another, and narration is interrupted by anecdotes and songs. Chesterton argues that Dickens "tries to tell ten stories at once."[39] Indeed, the Pickwick phenomenon also partakes of this narrative proliferation. "It became the kind of event in culture about which everyone seemed to have a story," explains Steven Marcus.[40] One narrative that attaches itself to *Pickwick* is that of its origin – in John Bowen's terms, the book's "messy birth."[41] Dickens himself reconstructed the birth in his multiple prefaces, with varying degrees of honesty.[42] Peter Ackroyd commences the familiar tale: on 10 February 1836, "William Hall called upon Dickens at his lodgings in

Furnival's Inn."[43] Chapman and Hall needed someone to supply text to accompany hunting and fishing illustrations by Robert Seymour. After just one number of *Pickwick* was published, Seymour fired the contents of a shotgun into his chest (his final sporting scene), and Dickens took control.

Seymour proceeded to plagiarize *Pickwick* – from beyond the grave. *Seymour's Sketches, Illustrated in Prose and Verse* (1838–39) are truly posthumous papers. This work is not identified in Elliot Engel's bibliography; yet it is precisely what *Pickwick* was supposed to be: monthly numbers of humorous illustrations by Robert Seymour, appended by letterpress from an eager hack – in this case, Alfred Crowquill (aka Alfred Forrester). Unlike Dickens, Crowquill was "ready and willing to write up to Seymour's designs," argues Joseph Grego. "It is fair to infer that the 'Nimrod Club' under Crowquill's editorship would have resembled 'Seymour's Sketches.'"[44] The work's "Address" refers to the "inimitable Originals" – thus borrowing an adjective used for Boz.[45] Intriguingly, part 5 even offers the transactions of a fictional sporting club. The narrator begins, "A club, under the imposing style of the 'Crack-Shots,' met every Wednesday evening during the season, at a house of public entertainment in the salubrious suburbs of London, known by the classical sign of the 'Magpye and Stump.'"[46] This opening catches the ironic voice of *Pickwick*'s early numbers and presents a Pickwickian club at a Pickwickian inn: a Magpie and Stump even appears in Dickens's book. Crowquill's lifeless characters include Saggers, Sniggs, and Smart. Sample dialogue: one sportsman says to another, "Sniggs, you're a true son of – a gun!"[47]

This work was possibly undertaken to raise funds for the late artist's children. But the Seymour saga did not end there; it generated yet another aftertext. In 1854, Mrs. Seymour, the former Jane Holmes, published a pamphlet entitled *An Account of the Origin of the "Pickwick Papers."* Over the years she had solicited Dickens's help for her hard-pressed family. It seems that he obliged her only once, in 1845, by making a contribution to a fund for her children.[48] The years waned; Seymour's posthumous fame dwindled; and his widow nursed a tremendous grudge. Jane Cohen notes the pamphlet's "excessive detail" and "hysterical tone."[49] Curiously, the widow asserts that her husband would have supplied the text of *Pickwick* himself but for a cold. Her most remarkable contention is this: "had Mr. Dickens never been born, the *Pickwick Papers* would have been written."[50] One wonders: by whom?[51] Naturally, she accuses Dickens of plagiarism and even proposes that some of his subsequent works were penned by "a Mr. Morris."[52] Dickens forcefully refuted her narrative with his own counternarratives, even until the last years of his life. Indeed, the Seymour saga indicates the power of *Pickwick*. Not only is the book an example of compulsive narrativity, it also proliferates narratives, stories about the story, texts upon texts.

In addition to the book's historical origin, it has a fictional one. On 26 March 1836, five days before the appearance of the first shilling number, the *Athenaeum* printed an advertisement (possibly written by Dickens). This notice suggests that *Pickwick* is a reproduction of an unavailable (and nonexistent) original. "The Pickwick Travels, the Pickwick Diary, the Pickwick Correspondence – in short, the whole of the Pickwick Papers, were carefully preserved, and duly registered by the secretary, from time to time, in the voluminous Transactions of the Pickwick Club."[53] According to this announcement, Boz is merely the editor, not the author. Bradley Deane notes that "the conceit was perhaps already a tired one."[54] Indeed, the guise of an editor was both a form of antiquarianism and a mode of preserving the "author" Charles Dickens for the great works yet to come. An editor is not an inspired artist but rather a literary laborer, a producer of "inventio," not "creatio." Further, the supposed existence of these "voluminous Transactions" implies a source from which more than one enterprising editor or author might draw inspiration.

Critical writings on Pickwickian aftertexts are not voluminous. The most sustained examinations are Louis James's *Fiction for the Working Man, 1830–1850*; Mary Teresa McGowan's 1975 PhD thesis; and John Sutherland's chapter, "Dickens's Serializing Imitators," in his book *Victorian Fiction*. Yet all three are somewhat limited by a taxonomic approach. While James allows that his working-class publications are "*literature*," I will assert that each Pickwickian aftertext is a form of literary criticism.[55] As Paul Davis argues, "Every new edition, adaptation, parody, or sequel derives from an implicit critical perspective."[56] Anonymous and pseudonymous publications such as *Posthumous Papers of the Cadgers' Club* and *Pickwick in America* – the seeming detritus of literary history – will each offer a *reading* of Dickens's text.

Yet one is inclined to ask: what were these writers thinking? Occasional instances of direct address offer some insight. In a dedication to *The Penny Pickwick*, its editor writes, "[I]f it be urged that he has intruded upon the ground of another, he humbly submits, that every author has a right to a popular subject."[57] In other words, *The Pickwick Papers* somehow belongs to the public, by virtue of its popularity. In a preface to a volume edition, this particular plagiarist suggests that his motives are not mercantile but altruistic:

> it occurred to us that while the wealthier classes had their Momus, the poor man should not be debarred from possessing to himself as lively a source of entertainment and at a price consistent with his means; we therefore took upon ourselves that arduous but cheerful task.

He goes on to claim a weekly sale of 50,000 copies.[58] Besides such formal statements, *Pickwick* aftertexts often seem aware of their secondary status. Doubles, doppelgängers, echoes, revenants, and scenes of imitation feature in many of the narratives – that is to say, they trope themselves. An aftertext entitled "The Marriage of Mr. Pickwick" suggests that it "seems to be the destiny of great men to raise up a host of imitators."[59]

And what did Charles Dickens think of all this? Shouldn't he ask, with Sam Weller, "Ain't nobody to be whopped for takin' this here liberty, Sir?" (375). Given the mass of *Pickwick*-inspired material, Dickens's reaction was muted at first. One explanation is that he was inordinately busy during his *Pickwick* period, from 1836 to 1837: writing plays and sketches, producing the third volume of *Sketches by Boz*, committing novels to John Macrone and Richard Bentley, editing *Bentley's Miscellany*, beginning *Oliver Twist*, and mourning his sister-in-law Mary Hogarth. Surrogates sometimes entered the fray on his behalf. Leigh Hunt, in the *Town*, calls *The Penny Pickwick* "one of the most impudent plagiarisms that was ever attempted."[60] In fact, Chapman and Hall, believing that their valuable literary property was threatened by this work, tried to restrain its publication. The Vice-Chancellor heard their complaint on 8 June 1837. For the plaintiff, the legal counselors were Knight-Bruce and Bacon; for the defense, Wigram and Walesby[61] – Dickensian names for a Pickwickian case. Chapman and Hall's counsel insisted that *The Penny Pickwick* was a "fraudulent imitation calculated to deceive a portion of mankind." The Vice-Chancellor, Sir Lancelot Shadwell, decided against Chapman and Hall because only "the grossest ignorance and unobservance," he said, could mistake *The Penny Pickwick* for *The Pickwick Papers*.[62]

By reading ephemera such as *The Penny Pickwick*, this chapter expands our notion of the literary *work* (following Tanselle and McGann's use of the word) to include not only *Pickwick*'s monthly numbers, the first volume edition, the Cheap Edition, and the Charles Dickens Edition, but also jest books, songbooks, extra illustrations, allographic sequels, adaptations, and imitations. The focus will be on print material produced when the Pickwick phenomenon was at its peak, from 1837 to 1842. In

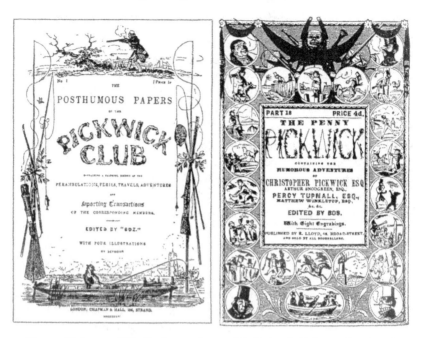

Figure 1 Title page of *The Posthumous Papers of the Pickwick Club*, no. 1 (April 1836)
and title page of *The Penny Pickwick*, part 18 (c. October 1838)

particular, I will examine two kinds of aftertexts: "club imitations," which
revive the abandoned frame of the Pickwick Club, and "prostheses," a term
I will use for texts that expand *Pickwick* beyond the limitations set by
Dickens's narrative. In each instance, an aftertext presumes to be the book
that Dickens was going to write, meant to write, advertised in the pro-
spectus, or neglected to write; these texts capture possible *Pickwicks* that
never were but might have been. They are thus counterfactual or, better
still, counterfictional. In some cases, Mr. Pickwick travels abroad – to the
United States, France, or India – whereas Dickens's Mr. Pickwick does
not. Other texts replace Mr. Pickwick with a neo-Pickwick, such as
Matthew Magnumfundum or Sir Peter Patron. Sometimes, the intended
audience appears to be lower or higher than the readership of *The Pickwick
Papers* – attempts to debase or elevate, to democratize or correct.

George Saintsbury writes, "There is no book like *Pickwick* anywhere; it
is almost . . . worth while to read the wretched imitations in order to enjoy
the zest with which one comes back to the real, though fantastically real,
thing."[63] It is a truism that Dickens's imitators reify the Inimitable

Dickens. Yet many of the aftertexts, rather than slavishly following a predecessor, seem strangely liberated: it is as if Dickens stole Promethean fire, and his imitators shared, briefly, in the glow.

***

Anything unique is at risk of vanishing: we make a twin.

– Hillel Schwartz

The Pickwick Papers is to some extent a misnomer. It is unusual for a literary work to gain esteem under a title other than that which its creator proposed (although *Gulliver's Travels* comes to mind). According to Percy Fitzgerald, the renaming of Dickens's novel "shows the hold the Book has on the affections of the public."[64] Of course, titles of works from the nineteenth century and earlier are often curtailed: we readily recognize *The History of Tom Jones, a Foundling* and *The Expedition of Humphry Clinker*. One could shorten *The Posthumous Papers of the Pickwick Club* to *The Posthumous Papers* or, alternatively, *The Pickwick Club* (the latter appears in Dickens's 1836 contract with Richard Bentley and on the bindings of some collected editions).[65] But *The Pickwick Papers*, with its changed word order, prevailed.[66] That *Pickwick* has become "Papers" and ceases to be a "Club" elides an important aspect of the narrative. Kathryn Chittick, writing on the early career of Dickens, makes the counterclaim that "Pickwick was a 'club,' not a story."[67] Indeed some of the earliest imitations of *The Pickwick Papers* foreground the club aspect.

I will focus on three works that Elliot Engel identifies as "Club Satires."[68] They are *Posthumous Papers of the Wonderful Discovery Club* (1838), *Droll Discussions and Queer Proceedings of the Magnum-Fundum Club* (1838), and *Posthumous Papers of the Cadgers' Club* (1837–38). Since their satirical content is limited, I will rechristen this batch "club imitations." These were not the only publications of this type. Louis James identifies others, such as *Major Rudbank at Home and Abroad*; "The Bachelor Club," which was serialized in a periodical called *The Odd Fellow*; and "The Dutchy Club," in *Lloyd's Penny Weekly Magazine*.[69] William Miller mentions yet another club imitation, *The Queerfish Chronicles, Forming a Correct Narrative of Divers Travels, Voyages, and Remarkable Adventures, That Have Come under the Notice of the Queerfish Society*.[70] Nevertheless, I will retain focus on Engel's trio. They are superficially similar and independently printed publications (like *Pickwick* itself) – that is, not in magazines. The three works all underscore the club aspect that *Pickwick*'s shortened title discards. In fact, *Pickwick* and these imitations partake in the phenomenon of British club organization and homosocial grouping in the eighteenth and early nineteenth centuries.

As an old joke has it, if two Englishmen landed on an uninhabited island, their first order of business would be to form a club.[71] Marie Mulvey-Roberts and Peter Clark have written on the development of the British club system in the eighteenth century. Clark describes clubs as "private associations, overwhelmingly male, meeting on a regular, organized basis, mostly in public drinking-places."[72] There were perhaps 25,000 such clubs in the eighteenth-century Anglophonic world.[73] Mulvey-Roberts claims that clubs "corresponded to virtually every sort of pleasurable activity" and notes the existence of the Sublime Society of Beef-steaks, the Roaring Boys, and the Mohocks.[74] She ventures that the eighteenth-century club could be seen as an alternative to family and country and "a secular substitute for the church": "what the club system offered was compensation for that which might be missing in everyday life."[75] As Kathryn Chittick observes, "Men in clubs are forever boyish and can remain so because privileged."[76] It might seem odd that heterosexual men would be so keen to exclude the company of females, but Mulvey-Roberts explains that "the appeal of homosociality, or socialising with the same sex, lies in the potential for transgressive behaviour."[77]

Besides satirizing clubs, *Pickwick* inspired a few. In December 1837, Dickens acknowledged the Edinburgh Pickwick Club as "the first society of its kind, established North of the Tweed," which suggests that there was already at least one such club to the south.[78] In April 1838, he apologized to the secretary of another real-life Pickwick Club for missing its anniversary dinner (he was preoccupied with *Oliver Twist* and *Nicholas Nickleby*).[79] By the twentieth century, Dickens-inspired clubs continued to bloom, such as the Eatanswill Club, the short-lived Boz Club, and the long-lived Dickens Fellowship.

It is precisely this phenomenon that the three club imitations reflect. Superficially, *The Wonderful Discovery Club*, *The Magnum-Fundum Club*, and *The Cadgers' Club* are almost identical. Each was issued as an eight-page penny weekly with cramped, double-column print and one or two crude illustrations. Four weekly numbers of each could then be stitched into a thirty-two-page monthly number with an illustrated wrapper, at 4d. each. *Pickwick*, costing a shilling a month, was thus three times as expensive. The club imitations are either anonymous or pseudonymous; *The Magnum-Fundum Club* is credited to Quiz and *The Wonderful Discovery Club* to Poz. All three pursue the alliteration suggested by Dickens's title: we meet Pater Patron, Matthew Magnumfundum, and Jeremiah Jumper.

Like the first half of *Pickwick*, the club imitations are relatively plotless. Intriguingly, all three of these works are incomplete – the occupational hazard of the serializing author. (Even the worst three-volume novel is a finished work of art – albeit a blighted one.) When *The Cadgers' Club* ceased publication, on 22 March 1838, it offered its readers an "Address" blaming "the sudden dissolution of the august *Society of Cadgers*, and the stoppage of their private documents."[80] The "Editor of The Wonderful Club papers" reports that "more important claims upon his time imperatively command him for the present to desist."[81] In contrast, *The Magnum-Fundum Club* just stops. The financial model for such publications may have been Lord Brougham's *Penny Magazine*, launched in 1832, and *Chambers's Edinburgh Journal*, which sold for one-and-a-half pence. As Louis James explains, "The eight pages could be printed as one sheet on a hand-press," and "the income of one issue paid for the printing of the next."[82] It is reasonable to guess that three club imitations failed to earn back their costs and therefore ceased publication.

Mary Teresa McGowan argues that these imitations offer only "slight acknowledgement of their association with *Pickwick Papers*."[83] The connection to *Pickwick* is in truth much stronger: the club imitations amplify and accentuate aspects of *The Pickwick Papers* in terms of style (hyperbole, periphrasis) and representation (conviviality, grotesquerie, and heterogeneity). In so doing, these aftertexts illuminate how some of the earliest readers read *Pickwick* when the book's popularity was at its apex.

Each club imitation aims at a slightly different segment of the middle- to lower-middle-class reading public. *Posthumous Papers of the Wonderful Discovery Club*, "Formerly of Camden Town, Established by Sir Peter Patron, Edited by Poz," is pitched, relatively speaking, at the highest. "[F]or the intelligent is our work published," claims the narrator, who then offers a Latin motto (32). Throughout, he exerts himself to quote Shakespeare, John Dryden, and John Lyly. Of the four clubs (including Pickwick), the Wonderful Club is the only one with a titled person as its head. A retired saddle-maker, "having leisure to cultivate the mind" (4), Sir Peter Patron may have been inspired by Sir Peter Laurie.[84] Louis James argues that the satire here is aimed at "the pretentions to culture of tradesmen who had risen in the world."[85] The Wonderful Club attempts to make and disseminate discoveries, and somewhat late in its run, it launches a corresponding branch, which was the premium mobile in *Pickwick*.

According to David M. Bevington, by December 1836, "the fiction of a posthumous history ... all but disappeared" from *The Pickwick Papers*;

yet in 1838, this aspect formed the core of all three club imitations.[86] The
"editor" of *The Wonderful Discovery Club* says that he "has in his possession
four four-bushel stacks full of papers, which detail the discoveries of The
Wonderful Club" (32). This fictional source, an earthy iteration of
Pickwick's mythical "Transactions," permits the editor to indulge in
Pickwickian moments of limited omniscience, as when he cannot determine whether a meeting took place at the Mother Red-cap or Black-cap.
More importantly, *The Wonderful Discovery Club* captures the hyperbolic
voice of *Pickwick*'s narrator. The reader of this imitation encounters the
"extraordinarily unprecedented club" – quite a claim for an obviously
derivative work – and Sir Peter brazenly boasts that "we shall possess
more valuable information than was ever to be found in the famous
Alexandrian library, or in any modern library" (4–5). Later, Sir Peter
asks, "[S]hall not my name go down to posterity to be remembered as
long as the wonders we record shall excite the attention of after ages?" (22).
In the event, the Immortal Sir Peter's posterity lasted for three monthly
numbers.

Beyond hyperbole, *The Wonderful Discovery Club* accentuates three
other aspects of *The Pickwick Papers*: its "low" status (with attention to
matters of the body and slapstick), its prison motif, and its interpolated
tales. Samuel Pickwick's body suffers indignities: he is carried in
a wheelbarrow, hurled over a wall, locked in the pound. Sir Peter Patron
also suffers bodily when he is attacked by a swarm of bees and endures
many stings – as the caption to a drawing puts it, "The Stings and Arrows
of Outrageous Fortune" (27). Just as Pickwick finds himself frequently
trapped and later imprisoned in the Fleet, the Wonderfulites land in prison
in the very first monthly number: "buried alive," moans Sir Peter (15). Club
members undergo further bouts of incarceration, and the prison motif even
infiltrates the book's prose: "The suburban villa in possession is but
a prison-house" (4). Lastly, the interpolated, or "introduced," tales in
Pickwick are an idiosyncratic feature, so it is not surprising that two of
the club imitations employ the same device. Given the reduced scale of *The
Wonderful Discovery Club*, it makes do with long anecdotes, rather than
titled interpolations. In keeping with Dickens's tales, these anecdotes
emphasize the gothic and violent aspects of life that are excluded from
the main narrative's sunnier vision. Both *Pickwick* and *The Wonderful
Discovery Club* thus, in modern parlance, outsource their darker energies
to these peripheral regions. One Captain Bodabie tells the Wonderfulites
a gruesome tale of self-mutilation among the "Mussulmans" (78). Another
anecdote tells of a servant who kills his master and is haunted by the crime.

It is perhaps a piece of intellectual honesty that *The Wonderful Discovery Club*, an imitative work, includes representations of doubles and imitations within its pages. On the night of a Wonderful Club meeting, another club convenes: "a society of mechanics," led by Mr. Heartless (12). He raises the spectre of a French invasion; and when the police try to arrest his band, he directs the officers to the Wonderful Club. Later, as Sir Peter's organization prospers, the club's efforts are duplicated across England and France, and transactions from other clubs are then quoted in the text. Indeed, Dickens in 1836 introduced an idea that was highly reproducible – a work of art in the age of mechanical reproduction – with *Pickwick*'s "unique existence" subsumed by "a plurality of copies."[87]

The shortest of the three club imitations, *Droll Discussions and Queer Proceedings of the Magnum-Fundum Club*, seems to have expired after thirty-two pages. As such, it partakes of poetic compression and contains more Pickwickian matter per square inch than its competitors. Its characters are tradesmen, modestly middle class: a linen-draper, a typographer, an attorney. Their names are overdetermined, like those in a Restoration comedy. Mr. Scribbleton acts as secretary; Mr. Guzzleton is a wine-merchant. At the center stands the club's president, Mr. Matthew Magnumfundum, whom McGowan describes as "a retired admiral, whose name indicates the possession of a very large posterior."[88] An obvious Pickwick stand-in, Magnumfundum is described as a "being of such preposterous magnitude and rotundity" with "a very capacious receptacle for turtle soup."[89]

Even more so than *The Wonderful Discovery Club*, *Magnum-Fundum* is forthright about its imitative status. At the start, the narrator admits that "the glorious achievements which 'Boz' has recorded of the Pickwickians, gave rise to the foundation of the Magnum-Fundum Club" (2). The cleverness of this conceit is that it is not the pseudonymous author but the members of the Magnum-Fundum Club who are the copycats; he is merely their editor and scribe. Mr. Magnumfundum plainly states, "I altogether disclaim all such anti-Pickwickian sentiments" – which is to say that he supports only Pickwickian (or *Pickwick*-inspired) sentiments (3).

To begin at the beginning, the long-winded opening sentence is worth quoting in full for its parade of Pickwickian (and Dickensian) motifs:

> The glimmering landscape was fading on the sight – the stars were peeping through the cloudless atmosphere of a March evening – the muffin man's bell jingled its wintry chime upon the air – the gas had begun to display its

> impertinent glare in the streets of the Metropolis – and, amidst the intense cold of a frosty night, the miscellaneous multitude passing to and fro resembled so many locomotive engines blowing off the steam from their mouths and nostrils, ere they were laid up for the night – the itinerant potatoe [*sic*] merchant, with brazen lungs, was proclaiming to his customers that his belly-balls were "all hot" – the coaches were rattling over the London stones; and one amongst them, driven with more than ordinary speed, the "Red Rover," arrived at the "Bell Inn." (1)

The initial clause is a reversal of *Pickwick*'s famous opening ("The first ray of light which illumines the gloom" [1]). Here we are at the close of day, not its commencement. The mention of a "March evening" is a nod to *Pickwick*'s first shilling number, which was published on 31 March 1836, and the undated number of *Magnum-Fundum* may have been issued around March 1838. As in many of the *Sketches by Boz*, the unnamed city is merely the "Metropolis." As in Dickens's imagery, humans appear to be machines ("locomotive engines"), and the inanimate is animated ("impertinent" gas). This long and highly paratactic opening concludes with a stage-coach, associated, as it was for Dickens, with speed; and the conveyance, like the sentence, finally arrives at a Pickwickian inn with a cheerful name, the "Bell." In the thirty-one pages that follow, *The Magnum-Fundum Club* continues to echo *The Pickwick Papers* in terms of style, an emphasis on conviviality (read: "drunkenness"), and an uncanny focus on Dickens's singular obsessions.

Considering the authorial voice of *The Pickwick Papers*, Louis James writes that "Dickens at times echoes Egan's periphrastic, Latinate style."[90] Garrett Stewart refers to "[c]ircumlocution, verbal excess, and indirection of every kind."[91] *The Magnum-Fundum Club*, as an imitative work, perfectly captures this prolixity. An early speech by one Mr. Bowsprit abounds in Johnsonian polysyllables: "meritorious," "harmonious," "eulogium," "mellifluous" (4). Mr. Magnumfundum employs periphrasis when he states, "Scarcely have seven suns revolved in their diurnal march" (15). Another temporal passage is conveyed with "Time trundled on his wheel with unusual rapidity" (15) (which may also contain an allusion to *Pickwick*'s strangely silent Mr. Trundle). Instead of guzzling wine, we find characters "having drunk unsparingly of the juice of Tuscan grape" (6), and an urn (supposedly once used by Aeneas) becomes a "repository for *lotium*" (27). As in *The Wonderful Discovery Club*, some of the discourse reaches for the hyperbolic ("ever glorious name" and "sacred place" [15]). *The Magnum-Fundum Club* even makes an argument for Latinate suffixes when Mr. Quibble insists that *-um* and *-us* endings are superior to the unclassical -*k* – perhaps a sly suggestion that a Magnum-Fundum is better than a Pick-wick (2).

Some early readers of *The Pickwick Papers* objected to its vulgarity ("all very well – but . . . damned low") and its countless scenes of drinking.[92] Mulvey-Roberts explains that this was inseparable from the British club system: "getting inebriated was a popular pastime for clubmen."[93] *The Magnum-Fundum Club*, naturally, reproduces *Pickwick*'s focus on conviviality – and its results. The members of the club consume Mr. Pickwick's favorite potation, brandy and water. After one club meeting, the narrator observes that "the remainder of the evening would be spent in conviviality" (5). The incessant alcohol consumption often leads to dancing, singing, and general chaos. In many illustrations, the characters are depicted as tumbling, crashing into one another, or landing on their magnum-fundums. In this way, *The Magnum-Fundum Club* descends from the supposed respectability of its tradesmen characters to something topsy-turvy and carnivalesque. The first illustration sets the leitmotif: a portly man topples over, thus upsetting a table with paper and ink and breaking a wine bottle – a scene of writing merged with Dionysian disorder. A later illustration is pure chaos: a teapot explodes, and men tumble over each other. *Magnum-Fundum* is also alert to the aftereffects of drink. The eponymous hero samples Dr. Humbug's Universal Vegetable Pills as a hangover cure, and a morning-after scene finds the indisposed clubmen disturbed by the clanging of a bell.

Even an idle reader picking up a stray monthly number of *The Pickwick Papers* would notice the work's comical-bombastic style and its characters' thirst. What is most fascinating about *The Magnum-Fundum Club* is that it cannily (or uncannily) identifies some of the more subterranean elements of Dickens's work. To begin with, Matthew Magnumfundum has "a timber leg"; countless jokes and pratfalls follow as a result (1). As John Carey argues, "Dickens' most popular lifeless bit is the wooden leg, about which he has a positive obsession."[94] In *Pickwick* this motif is muted: readers learn about a wooden-legged man named Thomas Burton, and Sam Weller refers to "number six, with the wooden leg" (91).[95] Although this obsession becomes manifest only with the later novels, Carey points out that the wooden-leg bit appears in Dickens's earliest extant letter. "I am quite ashamed I have not returned your Leg," writes the young Dickens, using a slang term for *lexicon*. "I suppose all this time you have had a *wooden* leg."[96] Anny Sadrin agrees that Dickens is drawn to "fragmented people."[97] In *The Magnum-Fundum Club*, the hero, rather than walking, "stumped up towards the platform" (3). On one occasion he removes his prosthesis and uses it as a gavel; on another "he seemed to forget that one of his legs was born in the forests of America" (9). Of course, the wooden leg partakes of some of the aforementioned chaos: it flies into a fire, and it catches a lady's dress. Nor is Matthew Magnumfundum alone in his disability: "forty or fifty wooden-legged sons of Neptune" stump into a tavern (20).

More surprising is *Magnum-Fundum*'s attention to one of Dickens's closest-held obsessions: Warren's Blacking, where he was employed as a manual laborer soon after his twelfth birthday. McGowan argues that knowledge of this incident is "based on later biographical information" unavailable to readers (and writers) in 1838.[98] But there it is. A character named Mr. Jinglescansion (perhaps derived from *Pickwick*'s Mr. Jingle) is a "verse manufacturer to Warren and Co., Strand" (5). As Rosemarie Bodenheimer observes, "[S]ly references to poets who wrote for Warren's Blacking crop up frequently in Dickens's early works."[99] Jinglescansion, who is more a poet than a confidence-man like his near namesake, sings a sample of his versification: "Say it shines like a tub / Of Warren's jet blacking" (7). In another instance, Mr. Sloshsquosh sings "some of those elegant stanzas inserted in the Morning Chronicle by Warren and Co., 30, Strand" (5). This last is a double-Dickens reference: both to Warren's, where Dickens worked as a child, and to the *Morning Chronicle*, where he worked as an adult. Robert Douglas-Fairhurst points out that in fact "there were two 'Warren's' warehouses within shouting distance of each other."[100] Dickens labored at the *other* one, the plagiarist, with the imitative address: Warren's Blacking, 30, Hungerford Stairs, Strand. Regardless, McGowan insists that these references "cannot be other than accidental."[101] But the question remains: did the author of this penny weekly *know the truth*? It is possible that *Pickwick* was so potent to its earliest readers that they intuited some of Dickens's secrets.

The last of the three club imitations was actually published first. *Posthumous Papers of the Cadgers' Club* probably began in December 1837, a month or so after the conclusion of *Pickwick*. If there is a class hierarchy among the three club imitations, then *Cadgers' Club* is the bottom. A *cadger*, according to the *OED*, is "[o]ne who goes about begging or getting his living by questionable means." Thus, rather than merchants and retired tradesmen, the Cadgers' Club is composed of "expert rogues" who dupe the public, such as "sailors who had never seen the sea," "soldiers who had never been in any regiment," and blind beggars with perfectly good vision (3–4). The Cadgers' Club is unusual in its inclusion of female members: mudlarks, match-sellers, and some who beg with hired infants. Edward Ward, the club collector, notes a predecessor for such a society in a "Buttock Ball," in which "Bullies, Libertines and Strumpets" dance together.[102] There is a travelogue aspect to *The Cadgers' Club*, as the narrator observes: "we shall have occasion to give the most minute detail, of every haunt, rookery, corner, and retreat" (22). This draws the work away from *Pickwick* and closer to the investigations of Henry Mayhew or the bourgeois pastime of slum-sightseeing. The leader of the Cadgers, Jeremiah Jumper, is a professional crossing-sweeper (unlike the less fortunate Jo). Because Jeremiah speaks with the cockney diction of a Weller, it is as if Tony Weller, instead of Mr. Pickwick, were the protagonist: a perfect piece of topsy-turvydom.

Comparison to *The Pickwick Papers* is not avoided but forcefully argued in the pages of *The Cadgers' Club*. "The magnanimous, all-learned, and indefatigable Mr. Pickwick had already opened the channels of enterprise and learning, by founding his immortal Club," writes the narrator. Describing the Pickwick phenomenon, he continues, "[T]he public seized upon the idea with avidity, and it was truly remarkable to see the extraordinary effect it had upon all classes of society; clubs sprang up in every direction" (2). He goes on to mention societies of dustmen, chummies, and scavengers. But the assumption was that none could have a Samuel Pickwick at the fore. "[W]eak notion! ridiculous thought!" cries the narrator. "Not many months were suffered to pass by, ere there was another luminary ordained to break forth in the hemisphere of sublunary wisdom" (2). Jeremiah Jumper is described as "the indescribable, the incomparable rival to the all-powerful Mr. Pickwick!" (4). (Although "incomparable," here the author makes a comparison.) Further, like the opening of *The Pickwick Papers, The Cadgers' Club* employs an image of light; we learn that the club "first shed the glorious effusion of its light and wisdom upon the *lower* world" – "lower" in that it is terrestrial but also lower in terms of social status (2). Referring so directly to his or her source, the narrator of *The Cadgers' Club* is all confidence: this work "will even eclipse, it is expected, the most distinguished history of the transactions of 'The Pickwick Club'" (1) – note the preference for a *Pickwick Club* and not *Papers*.

As the previous quotes indicate, hyperbole is central to the Pickwickian style of *The Cadgers' Club*. "The scene which follows will never be surpassed," writes the narrator (11). Another moment is described as "one of the most animated scenes that probably was ever witnessed, Almack's must have sunk into insignificance before it" (7). Jeremiah Jumper earns "unqualified admiration, veneration and esteem," and the hyperbole even infects the chapter headings (3). One promises that "[t]he interest of this most interesting of all interesting narratives rapidly increases" (9). The author seems to believe that saying something makes it so. His use of hyperbole verges on the mock-heroic, as he deploys lofty terms to discuss figures who are decidedly low. One example is when an injured club member pens a subliterate challenge to Jeremiah. A "grimy-faced boy" hands Jeremiah the "greasy and dirty paper." The narrator quickly heightens the scene with the following: "The renowned hero of these pages unfolded this elegantly written and indicted epistle" (19). Related to the trope of hyperbole is the narrator's use of adynata at moments when fantastic proceedings defy his descriptive powers. The narrator says that "we, even *we*, who wield so powerful a pen, despair of being able to do ample justice" to a particular scene (3). In the next weekly number, the narrator demurs, "We shall not seek to pourtray [*sic*] in language, what was done by the industrious jaws of every one at the table" (14). In *The Cadgers' Club* reading of *Pickwick*, everything must be taken to the extreme.[103]

Like *The Wonderful Discovery Club* and *Magnum-Fundum*, *The Cadgers' Club* is more than a stylistic imitation of *The Pickwick Papers*. Indeed, *The Cadgers' Club* draws attention to *Pickwick*'s grotesquerie and heterogeneity as well. In terms of the former category, readers recall that Matthew Magnumfundum has a wooden leg. Jeremiah Jumper has two such appendages, on the theory that two wooden stumps are twice as funny. With "a hump upon his back like Aesop," Jeremiah dances on his two wooden legs (which must be difficult); the accompanying illustration is decidedly grotesque (3). In the first weekly number, one of Jeremiah's artificial legs gets stuck in the floor; the following week finds him accompanying a tune by pounding "his wooden pin" (15). Further, the Cadgers' society includes a man of African descent named Black-Berry, who is "minus one eye and a leg" (10). The grotesquerie is developed further in the description of his wife: "Bearing a squint, the loss of half her nose, and being *rather* dirty, Mrs. Berry was a most fascinating woman!" (16). Naturally, Jeremiah is attracted to her, and the love-triangle leads to a battle between the cadging cripples. Louis James remarks that *Pickwick* "expresses violence only indirectly."[104] Not so *The Cadgers' Club*. It revels in the scene: "There is not a more curious and interesting display, than a fight between two wooden legged men" (17). Ultimately, both resort to detaching limbs to use as weapons. In his best mock-heroic vein, the narrator boasts, "[D]readful was the strife" (18).

Besides this grotesquerie, *The Cadgers' Club* also exploits its predecessor's heterogeneity – that is, its inclusion of poems and tales. This peculiar structural feature has disturbed more than one reader of *Pickwick*. Yet Robert L. Patten argues that the interpolations have a predecessor in Cervantes, and Philip Rogers suggests that the tales "protect Pickwick from the terrors that obsess [Dickens's] darker imagination."[105] *Cadgers'* first interpolation is "The Cadgers' Song," which asserts that everyone cadges now and then: boys, girls, lawyers, bishops, Members of Parliament (15).

In the third weekly number, the reader encounters the first interpolated tale, "The Autobiography of 'Scapegrace Jack.'" His narrative, which begins sixty years ago (like *Waverley*), is a chilling account of poverty and crime; and it consumes more than one night in the telling, just like another *Pickwick* predecessor, *One Thousand and One Nights*. Indeed, *Cadgers'* narrator notes that "interest ... could not have been surpassed even by the relation of the far-famed *Arabian Nights*" (43). *The Cadgers' Club*, however, fails to maintain the Pickwickian balance between the main narrative and the interpolations, and the tales dominate the last three-fourths of the published numbers.[106] Louis James bemoans that the author "lost his distinctive bite" because the tales descend "to the level of any Newgate Calendar account."[107] He thus misses what is fascinating about "Scapegrace Jack": with it, *The Cadgers' Club*, an imitation of *Pickwick*, suddenly becomes *Oliver Twist*. Little Jack is "alone and friendless" in the world, like little Oliver (30). Jack meets a man in the Brownlow/Cheeryble mold, "kindly, benevolent, and charitable" Mr. Hoare, as well as a band of gypsy thieves and not one but *two* Fagins, a Jewish couple named Mr. and Mrs. Bunckey (29). They run a brothel, which may clarify the ill-defined profession of Nancy. In short, to at least one plagiarist, it was no longer enough to simulate *The Pickwick Papers*. If Dickens had moved on to his next serialized story, so could this author.

There are other ways in which the three club imitations deviate from Dickens's Ur-text. Each concerns a different era. *The Wonderful Discovery Club* takes place in 1808, much earlier than *Pickwick; The Cadgers' Club*, set "ten years ago" (2), is nearly contemporaneous with *Pickwick*'s supposed date; and *Magnum-Fundum* is Victorian (a fireworks display reads "Long Live Victoria" [23]). Further, the three works de-emphasize Sam Weller, who often dominates the stage adaptations of 1837. Although Matthew Magnumfundum has a cockney servant named Sam Snubnose, he is not prominent in the text.

In the 1837 preface to *Pickwick*, Dickens refers to "the machinery of the club," which he "gradually abandoned."[108] *Fraser's Magazine for Town and Country*, in an 1840 review, reiterates this language and agrees, "The machinery of the club was indeed very hackneyed, and it soon became excessively wearisome."[109] The club imitations, on the other hand, seize the club aspect; they do not dismiss it as a booster rocket that can be discarded en route to glory.[110] Aftertexts such as these presume to be narratives that Dickens forgot to write or could have written. While the club authors may not be brilliant writers, they are excellent *readers*. Each of their readings of *The Pickwick Papers* foregrounds aspects of the work's style and content. Published in the first year after *Pickwick* completed its serial run, the club imitations are among the most extensive first responses to Dickens's breakthrough work: they help us to see *Pickwick* as its early audiences did. However, the imitations also veer into representations of sexuality and racism that seem, in a word, un-Pickwickian. In this way, these publications are typical of the larger body of *Pickwick* aftertexts. Just when an imitating author appears most keen to replicate Dickens's charm, the author suddenly leads us somewhere different, darker, surprising, or strange.

***

Whatever is felicitously expressed risks being worse expressed.

– Isaac D'Israeli

Will the perennial bachelor Samuel Pickwick ever marry? Will he travel abroad? Will he die? Will he be mistaken for a lunatic and locked in an asylum? These and other questions remain unanswered by *The Posthumous Papers of the Pickwick Club*. Into this narrative void hastened a league of imitating authors, with imitative names such as Bos and Poz and Quiz; they knew the answers and were keen to share them in exchange for shillings and pence. While the club imitations fabricate something new out of a borrowed cloak, other aftertexts are more wilfully plagiaristic. They are *Pickwick* branded – that is, they trade on obviously derivative titles, such as "An Omitted Pickwick Paper" – and they pilfer characters, ideas, and plotlines from Dickens's book.

I have christened this second batch "prostheses" – artificial extensions to the *Pickwick* corpus. Pickwick prostheses make available aspects of the original that are omitted, muted, implied, curtailed, forgotten, repressed, or secreted to distant corners. They interpret and interpenetrate with *The Pickwick Papers* and stand, alongside the club imitations, among the earliest and most vivid responses to Dickens's text. Two categories emerge: works that retain the Pickwickian innocence and those that draw on darker, hidden energies and discover instances of anti-Semitism, racism, and sexual desire.

By way of introduction to the prostheses, it will help to foreground a specimen from the field. *The Penny Pickwick*, by "Bos," may or may not be the best of the lot, but it is certainly the longest; it was published weekly, from 1837 to 1839, and was gathered into twenty-eight monthly parts. It will be recalled that this work earned the wrath of Dickens's allies and an aborted legal action on the part of his publishers. The defendant in the case, Edward Lloyd, a bookseller and eventually a publisher, maintained offices in Wych Street and, later, Broad Street, Bloomsbury. He paid his literary laborers very little: sometimes 10s. for the contents of an eight-page weekly number.[111] By this reckoning, a worker might receive £2 a month, in contrast to Dickens's £14 3s. 6d. (for fewer pages) in the original agreement for *Pickwick*.[112]

One of Edward Lloyd's most prolific authors was the inimitable Bos. His collected works include *The Sketch-Book by "Bos," The Penny Pickwick, Oliver Twiss, Nickelas Nickelbery,* and *Mister Humfries' Clock*.[113] By general consensus, Bos is taken to be the nom de guerre of Thomas Peckett Prest, "a shadowy figure," according to Mary Teresa McGowan.[114] In April or May 1838, while *The Penny Pickwick* was still appearing weekly, Prest began *Pickwick in America*, which was published from 1838 to 1839.[115] It has also been suggested that Prest is the anonymous author of *Posthumous Papers of the Cadgers' Club*. So it is possible that he generated two *Pickwick* imitations simultaneously for most of 1838 and some of 1839. Dickens, we recall, wrote only one *Pickwick* at a time. For his service to literature, Thomas Peckett Prest "died a pauper in a cheap lodging house."[116]

Like the club imitations, *The Penny Pickwick* was offered weekly, in eight-page numbers, with double-column print and two illustrations; later, the work was issued in two volumes with a revised title, *The Post-Humourous Notes of the Pickwickian Club*. Bos deviates from Boz in that the principal characters' names are vaguely corrupted. Christopher Pickwick leads Arthur Snodgreen, Percy Tupnall, and Matthew Winkletop. Mr. Pickwick's trusty servant is one Samivel Veller. Jovial Mr. Wardle, for instance, appears as Mr. Warner, of Mushroom Hall, Violet Vale. Mrs. Bardell is transposed to Mrs. Pardell; Mrs. Rogers becomes Mrs. Dodgers; Cluppins is Tuppins; and Raddle is Faddle. Mr. Jingle is absent from the proceedings, presumably replaced with Simon Shirk (aka Horatio Brutus Guff), who speaks in broken, Jingle-like utterances.

Appropriately, for a work that is so double-voiced, *The Penny Pickwick* is itself filled with doubles and replicas. On one occasion the narrator admits that his text is merely the copy: "The annexed speech is but a phantom of that splendid harangue" (126). *The Penny Pickwick* also reproduces the Pickwick phenomenon itself. For instance, the Royal George is redubbed the Pickwick Arms, and tradesmen offer Pickwick hats and "Patent Double-Sighted Pickwickian Spectacles" (124) ("double-sighted" here is an apt term). More significantly, Christopher Pickwick, that doppelgänger to his namesake Samuel, is often mistaken for others within the pages of *The Penny Pickwick*. Bos's Mr. Pickwick is chased by two men who believe that he is an escaped lunatic. In the echo chamber of Bos's universe, one of the pursuers is even named Sam. The image of a Pickwickian loon roaming the English countryside is an inspired metaphor for a *Pickwick* imitation. In any case, the forces of law/social control pursue and then incarcerate the errant being. Once imprisoned, Christopher Pickwick is about to receive shock treatment when the "shocking mistake" is suddenly rectified and the real lunatic captured (23).

Repetition forms an important part of Bos's elongated art. Nearly two hundred pages later, Christopher Pickwick is mistaken for one Humphrey Crisp, who abandoned his wife and six children (not unlike Jinkins, Tom Smart's rival, in "The Bagman's Story"). Pickwick reads the description of Crisp in a posted notice – "sixty years of age, rather stout, bald of head," plus green spectacles and "black cloth gaiters" – and he experiences the uncanny.[117] "What a strange thing!" he remarks (192). Three officers find the anti-Crisp and arrest him. When Pickwick insists that he is Pickwick, the officers laugh: "Pickwick! ha! ha! a very good name to adopt!" (194). In other words, Christopher Pickwick, like an imitating author, is stealing someone else's name.

But this was only one of many Pickwick prostheses. The effort of all these works is to extend *The Pickwick Papers* beyond the already copious limits that Dickens offered the world from 1836 to 1837. Each prosthesis marks an intervention, a coming-to-terms with that which Dickens had wrought. Some texts insist on extending Mr. Pickwick into the past and the future. For a novel published over twenty months, with many instances of what David M. Bevington dubbed "Seasonal Relevance," *Pickwick* is strangely atemporal. The very first sentence mentions "that obscurity" which shrouds "the earlier history" of the book's hero (1). Philip Rogers pursues this notion and argues that "Pickwick represents a triumph over time." Indeed, Mr. Pickwick lacks "relations that link him to the past"; he has no nephew Fred and no Cheeryble brother.[118] Steven Marcus agrees that "Pickwick is a man without a history, created, as it were, entirely in the present."[119] In W. H. Auden's famous essay on the novel, he notes, "In our minds Mr. Pickwick is born in middle age with independent means."[120]

The *Pickwick* prostheses disagree. Either they misunderstand Dickens's purpose in concealing Pickwick's past or they wilfully ignore this choice in an attempt to make the protagonist more palpable, more subject to the laws of biography and biology. *The Penny Pickwick* informs its readers that Christopher Pickwick's ancestors were "mercantile men" (96) and that they hailed from Guzzelton, England (112). "I had the distinguished honour to serve in the Guzzelton Royal Volunteers, in 1804," announces the *Penny* Pickwick. Bos is alert to the novelty of the occasion: "This was the very first intimation that Mr. Warner, or any of the Pickwickians, had received of Mr. Pickwick's military exploits" (158). In "Winkle's Journal (Omitted in *The Pickwick Papers*)," which was published in the *Metropolitan Magazine*, in 1838, readers learn that Pickwick received a gentleman's education. Both he and Winkle "conversed in Latin and Greek" while reposing in the Angel Inn, Oxford. Their Greek is a bit rusty, as Winkle admits: "Mr. Pickwick and myself had quite forgotten that mellifluous language."[121]

But the question that most piques the Pickwick prostheses is, of course: where did Samuel Pickwick get his money? George Orwell notes that Pickwick "had 'been in the city,' but it is difficult to imagine him making a fortune there."[122] Rather, we can imagine him giving one away. Percy Fitzgerald mentions that Pickwick was "an export merchant apparently" but cites no evidence for this.[123] *The Penny Pickwick* offers another possible profession for its Pickwick, Christopher, when Rosa Dupps (the Rachael Wardle figure) threatens to expose him as "A BODY SNATCHER!" "How did you get your wealth, sir?" the woman demands. "[R]ecall the silent graves, robbed of their ghastly tenants!" (94). Bos's subsequent aftertext, *Pickwick in America*, suggests that Pickwick (now Samuel once again) is a colonist of sorts. The narrator boasts that he or she has access to information that "escaped the notice of the former clever historian of this distinguished gentleman."[124] Indeed, Pickwick owns property in the United States that "devolved to [him] on the death of his father" (2). It also escaped the notice of Boz that Samuel Pickwick ever had a father. All these prostheses delineate Pickwick's emptied-out past and link him to inexorable time.

Corresponding to Samuel Pickwick's obscure past is his cloudy future. Anny Sadrin argues that "Pickwick has no future; except, of course, the simplest of futures, which is death."[125] Such a suggestion contradicts

Dickens's triumphant opening sentence, which introduces "the immortal Pickwick" (1). Yet the prostheses attempt to make the immortal mortal; drawing Mr. Pickwick closer to the race of ordinary men narrows the gap between an emulating author and Charles Dickens. "Mr. Pickwick's Hat-Box," which appeared serially in *The New Monthly Belle Assemblée*, in 1840, offers a dose of mortality. This work opens with "the decease of … Mr. Pickwick."[126] In the next installment, a quasi-literate "correspondent" counters that Pickwick is still alive and cites "Master humfrey's klok" as proof (Dickens reintroduced Pickwick in *Master Humphrey's Clock*, in May 1840). The editor of the "Hat-Box" refers his correspondent to "Johnson's Dictionary for the word 'posthumous'" and argues that Master Humphrey does not indicate when exactly "Mr. Pickwick paid him a visit."[127] In "Hat-Box," the Pickwickians proceed to ransack the earthly remains of the late Pickwick, in a mode that anticipates the death of Scrooge, also without issue, in the vision of the third Christmas spirit (although the affect is reversed). "Mr. Tupman seized his defunct leader's coat, Mr. Winkle his long-to-be remembered tight unmentionables, Mrs. Bardell rushed to secure Mr. Pickwick's shirts (being that article of apparel which is placed the nearest to the heart)."[128] This scene also suggests the efforts of Dickens's literary successors, who divest *The Pickwick Papers* for their own use and benefit.

Other visions of Pickwick's future appear in Percy Fitzgerald's *Pickwickian Studies* and the anonymous work *Pickwick in India*. Fitzgerald, besides writing multiple books on *Pickwick*, felt compelled to generate his own prosthesis on the subject of Pickwick Yet To Come. Upon retirement in Dulwich and the demise of his eponymous club, Samuel Pickwick joins yet another society, the "Dulwich Literary and Scientific Association."[129] "Literary" is a telling term in that, after the publication of *The Pickwick Papers*, Dickens's hero is a creature of literature as well as science. At one meeting, the inevitable Mr. Blotton makes an appearance and disputes with his old nemesis – an example of eternal recurrence. But Fitzgerald's primary aim is to illustrate the death of Pickwick. Unlike the ignominious affair in "Mr. Pickwick's Hat-Box," Fitzgerald's version is a glorious coda: "The funeral *cortège* left the Dell at ten o'clock, and was one of the most striking displays of public feeling that Dulwich has seen for many years."[130] In contrast, *Pickwick in India* awards its hero a harsher end. This prosthesis appeared from 1839 to 1840, in the *Madras Miscellany*, a title that recalls *Bentley's Miscellany*. After seven installments, the serial abruptly stopped and left its protagonist literally at sea. A later note informs the concerned reader that "Mr. Pickwick *has* been devoured by a Shark!"[131] That Mr. Pickwick, who consumes so much in the course of his peregrinations, ends his immortality as luncheon for a carnivore is, somehow, apt. However, the note qualifies that "the Shark is but a figurative one."[132]

Besides representations of Pickwick's past and future, the prostheses also contain alternate versions of the self. These redescribe not only Mr. Pickwick but other characters as well. Some of these rewrites are subtle shifts, mere emendations. For instance, *Pickwick*'s Sam Weller is assigned no particular age, but *The Penny Pickwick*'s Samivel Veller is twenty-four (Dickens's age at the commencement of his book). Further, Sam Weller's initial employer, the White Hart, "used Day and Martin" for blacking (92); Samivel Veller, in contrast, "gave the indifferent boots an indifferent dash of Warren's" and later insists, "[N]othing but Varren's unadulterated" (86–87). Samivel, unlike Samuel, thus evinces a preference for a brand with strong Dickensian connotations. Augustus Snodgrass, in *The Pickwick Papers*, is ostensibly a poet, but the reader is spared his poetic effusions. Seizing this opportunity, several prostheses quote directly from Snodgrass's poetry. In George W. M. Reynolds's *Pickwick Abroad; or, The Tour in France*, Snodgrass is something of a plagiarist as well; he drafts Pickwick's life and adventures into a *Pickwickiad*, "in twenty cantos written" (re: twenty monthly numbers).[133] Sometimes, the alternate versions of the Pickwickian selves are not merely different but better – removed from Regency roughhouse and elevated to Victorian virtue.[134] In "An Omitted Pickwick Paper," published in an American gift annual, Samuel Pickwick and Tony Weller are discovered walking from church.[135] While Mr. Stiggins's flock attends chapel, no one in *Pickwick*, it seems, ever goes to a *church*. Further, in "Noctes Pickwickianae" (1840), Reynolds casts the lot of imbibing Pickwickians as teetotallers, whereas temperance, in *Pickwick*, is associated with the hypocrisy of Stiggins ("all taps is vanities" [482]).

Of course, alternate versions of Pickwick himself appear in many prostheses. The genial old man turns nasty, vengeful, ambitious. In *The Penny Pickwick*, he pursues an opportunity to stand for Parliament and is "dazzled by the prospect of becoming an M.P." (113). He stands as a liberal against the Tory, Sir Gregory Graspall. Yet Pickwick's politics are ineffable: "we cannot say whether he was radical, whig, conservative, or destructive; but we are inclined to think he must be a beautiful combination of all four" (122). Fortunately, he loses the election, or Thomas Peckett Prest would have been obliged to start yet another serial, "Pickwick in Parliament." Further, distinctions between Pickwick and his fellow corresponding members blur. At times he transforms into a Winkle-like coward, in particular when challenged to a duel. In *Pickwick in America*, he flees rather than run the risk of killing his opponent, and in *The Penny Pickwick*, on the way to the field of honor, he complains of the cold air and suddenly limps with gout.

All of these examples are relatively benign. The Pickwick prostheses are more instructive and their readings more pointed when they animate the darker energies of Dickens's text and illuminate absences. Call it the return of the repressed: the seemingly un-Pickwickian trinity of anti-Semitism, racism, and sex.[136] There is an element of topsy-turvy at work – a dose of Bakhtinian "carnival laughter."[137] *The Penny Pickwick*, for instance, turns the noble fool Samuel Pickwick into the ignoble fool Christopher Pickwick. But the prostheses also offer, in many cases, working-class read-ings of a middle-class text. To turn Dickens's novel into a penny serial or theatrical production increases its access to a wider public – and to that public's tastes and cultural biases. When the price point shifts from a shilling to a penny, the number of potential readers expands; cheaper publications may then exploit the (presumed) prejudices of their working-class audiences. The efforts of Bos, in particular, seem to want to ascribe lower-class foibles to the bourgeoisie. A banker may be "intoxicated" and a pauper "drunk," but they both have the same blood alcohol level.

Anti-Semitism might seem an unlikely feature to find in the descendents of *Pickwick*. Is it a random mutation? In fact, this feature derives from the repressed Jewish origins of Samuel Pickwick. When Dickens "thought of Mr Pickwick," he may have been referring to an actual person.[138] Moses Pickwick was a "celebrated coach proprietor," who later owned the White Hart Hotel in Bath.[139] Percy Fitzgerald quotes a Mr. Peach who lived in that city and claimed that the Pickwicks "must have been a Jewish family."[140] Peach's evidence is mainly the family's preference for Biblical names: Moses and Eleazer, his grandfather. (Not to mention Samuel.) Legend held that Eleazer was a foundling, picked up in the village of Wick, hence "Pick-Wick."[141] Fitzgerald confuses the legend by stating that it was the *grandson* who was the foundling, although Fitzgerald may have con-flated Moses of Bath with Moses of Egypt.[142] Furthermore, the name Moses Pickwick would have doubly signified for Charles Dickens. Besides the acoustic connection between *Dick*ens and *Pick*wick, young Charles ascribed to his brother Augustus the nickname Moses ("in honour of the *Vicar of Wakefield*," according to Forster). Through childish jesting, "Moses" became "Boses," which was adopted into Dickens's pseudonym, Boz.[143] So when Dickens thought of Moses Pickwick, he thought of a successful, possibly Jewish businessman for whom he would have had at least linguistic affection.

George Orwell, writing in 1939, when one would have been sensitive, argues that Dickens "shows no prejudice against Jews."[144] At least in *Pickwick*, references to Jews are few and innocuous. In chapter 2, the narrator quotes from the notebook of Samuel Pickwick and finds "soldiers, sailors, Jews, chalk, shrimps, officers, and dockyard men" (11). Leo Hunter later reports that "Solomon Lucas the Jew in the High Street, has thousands of fancy dresses" (149). Again relying on Old Testament names, Percy Fitzgerald suggests that Solomon Pell, Tony Weller's legal friend, "was likely a Jew solicitor."[145] Memorably, Moses Pickwick himself is represented in his namesake novel. When Sam is affronted to find "Moses" attached to the "magic name" Pickwick on the Bath coach, the very next Wellerism a telling one: "as the parrot said ven they not only took him from his native land, but made him talk the English langvidge artervards" (374). This is a parable of the immigrant, the exotic outsider (such as an eastern European), who must learn English and assimilate. Later, Sam complains to Mary that he has been "walkin' about like the wanderin' Jew – a sportin' character you have perhaps heerd on" (417). So here the Jew is associated with perambulating, that favorite Pickwickian pastime, and he is a sporting character as well, a fitting figure for the "Sporting Transactions" of the Pickwick Club.

Imitations of *The Pickwick Papers* exploit the novel's Jewish undercurrent in unsurprisingly crass ways. A standard riff in nineteenth-century comedy seems to be the Jewish figure breaking the rules of *kashrut* and consuming pork. In "Winkle's Journal," a Welshman tells an anecdote of two Jews who try bacon; heaven responds with violent thunderclaps (168–169). *Sam Weller's Budget of Recitations* includes a poem entitled "Jewish Mutton." An accompanying illustration depicts a Jewish-looking waiter serving "Roast Pork" to a black-bearded Semite, who smiles in anticipation.[146] One theatrical version of *Pickwick* adds a Jewish reference not found in the original. Mrs. Bardell's attorneys, Dodson and Fogg, are affiliated with no particular religious group; yet in T. H. Lacy's *The Pickwickians; or, The Peregrinations of Sam Weller*, Mr. Pickwick bemoans that "[a] couple of roguish lawyers, of the Jewish tribe, have got hold of her and persuaded her to commence proceedings."[147] Typically, *The Penny Pickwick* descends to the lowest level. The narrator refers to Holywell Street as "[t]hat dirty receptacle for old clothes, old books, impudent Jews, and indefatigable 'barkers!'" Further, "Jews are perfect savages in their anxiety to do business at any place" (108–109).

If the Jew is the other to the European Christian, then a non-European is subject to more prejudice. The club imitations offer some examples. When Sir Peter Patron and his Wonderful Club members are set upon by the police, he remarks on the swarthy "complexion" of the newcomers and asks, "Are we in Algiers?" (11). An angry Black-Berry, in *The Cadgers' Club*, is described uncharitably as a "black pudding in revulsions" (16). Imitative Wellerisms also take up the theme, as in this example from *Pickwick Abroad*: "as the vite man said to his-self ven he got among the selvidges vich made a fire to eat him."[148] *The Penny Pickwick* delights in a grotesque description of Christopher Pickwick's seventy-year-old servant, a black man named John White:

> His skin was a beautiful Day and Martin hue, his nose, upon moderate calculation, measured eight inches across – entirely monopolized the extent of his face. . . . Beneath his nose was a gap – we cannot call it a mouth . . . this awful cavern was environed by two immense rolls of flesh – which nature had probably intended for lips . . . (6–7)

While the anti-Semitism of the prostheses can claim at least a possible Pickwickian provenance, such "comedy" as the above seems far from Dickens's work. Certain intervening culture-texts may be responsible. In 1836, T. D. Rice presented the character Jim Crow in London, and it was a popular success.[149] By 1837, William Thomas Moncrieff's play *Sam Weller; or, The Pickwickians* allowed its title character to sing the song "Jim Crow," not to advance the narrative, but simply because the number was a specialty of the role's performer, W. J. Hammond.[150]

For obvious reasons, *Pickwick in America* offers the most robust array of Pickwickian racism. Besides the shallow laughter derived from stereotypes, this prosthesis is compelling in that it offers African-American doubles to elements in Dickens's book. Sam Weller meets his counterpart in a boots figure named Sambo. According to Sam, Sambo "gets his livin' by aggrawatin' boots an' shoes into a polish equal to his own phiz" (78). This last bit of whimsy suggests physiognomy as well as the *Pickwick* illustrator Hablot K. Browne (aka "Phiz"). The fat boy, Joe, finds a fat facsimile of himself in an African-American waiter named Maximilian Jupiter: "he was in fact, a second edition, (*black letter* edition,) of that ponderous and somniferous juvenile!" (33). Further, like some of Dickens's imitators, African-American businessmen employ elevated, polysyllabic terms. "[D]irty shops and cellars" are rechristened "Emporiums" or "Establishments" (102). Because Prest was ignorant enough to fail to notice that slavery was illegal in New York State by 1838, a delegation of black men calls upon "Mishter

Pickvicky" to assert their rights (230). Pickwick's compassionate speech in response borrows abolitionist language ("are we not all brothers"), and he grants the petitioners £20 (231). Yet in *Pickwick in America*, as in the America of the 1830s, the issue was unresolved.

It can certainly be argued that the racism found in these prostheses ranges beyond Dickens's original and owes more to the wider culture's stereotypical assumptions and modes of "ethnic" humor. In the case of *Pickwick* and sex, the situation is more imbricated. To begin with, for a protagonist in an English novel, Samuel Pickwick is strangely uninterested in courtship. Such a function is outsourced to his fellow corresponding members: Tupman, Winkle, and Snodgrass. Indeed, the late chapters of *Pickwick* evolve (or devolve) into Roman New Comedy; obdurate fathers (and brothers) stand in the way of true love, and love prevails. (Note that the name of forbidding Mr. Winkle, Senior, appears on a brass plate "in fat Roman capitals" [538].) In terms of Mr. Pickwick and sex, the experts agree: "Sex, for example, is no temptation for him"; "even sexual love is almost outside his scope"; one finds "the almost complete extinction of sex."[151] Then there is Peter Ackroyd's pithy summary: "No sex."[152] Appropriately for a novel thus scrubbed of romantic affect, the female characters appear as "predatory spinsters" and "husband-hating wives"; there is a "deep anxiety about sexuality."[153] Samuel Pickwick would rather go to *jail* than enjoy the nuptial favors of Martha Bardell.

There is a counterview to this. Fitzgerald asks, "[W]hat is the chief note of this immortal work? *Kissing*."[154] He argues that Mr. Pickwick "seized every opportunity of kissing the young ladies."[155] John Glavin offers a more nuanced observation: "repeatedly, Pickwick blunders into erotically pregnant situations."[156] In Eatanswill, Pickwick is mistaken for a voyeur. "Putting on his spectacles to look at a married 'ooman!" wails an alarmed bystander. Another complains of his "vicked old eye," as if Pickwick were a cyclops, capable of seeing only one thing, through monocular vision (131). Fitzgerald suggests a Freudian reading of Pickwick's nocturnal encounter with Miss Witherfield.[157] In looking for his watch, the old bachelor is really looking for something (or someone) else. Once entrapped with the lady in the double-bedded room, "[i]t was quite impossible to resist the urgent desire to see what was going forward. So out went Mr. Pickwick's head again" – thus piercing the membrane of the bed curtains (233).

If sex in *Pickwick* is a loaded but unfired pistol, then the Pickwick prostheses pull the trigger. Samuel Pickwick must learn about human fallenness from his more-knowing servant; Christopher Pickwick needs no such instruction. In *The Penny Pickwick*, he plays the conventional lover to the widow Rosa Dupps and asks, "But what are roses compared to the blossom of your lovely cheeks ... ?" (50). In a most un-Pickwickian manner, he competes with his friend Tupnall for the widow's affections. The narrator reports that "the too fascinating Pickwick had completely clouded all [Tupnall's] prospects of bliss!" (40). Dickens's Pickwick, who "burst like another sun" (5), is recast as a cloud. A hundred pages later, Christopher Pickwick again turns sexual aggressor – now with a married woman, Mrs. Charlotte Squib, wife of the editor of the Guzzelton *Mercury* (a revision of Winkle's tangle with Mrs. Pott). Unlike Boz's Pickwick, who would not endure the artifice of fancy dress, Bos's Pickwick attends a masquerade as Cupid. He points his arrow towards Mrs. Squib, who is in the guise of Pysche (Prest's consistent spelling). "Cupid and Pysche found themselves alone!" (154). Nestled in a bower, they kiss and are discovered. The result is a lawsuit in which Mr. Squib claims damages of £2,000. It is a fascinating rewrite of the Bardell case. Dickens's character is sued for what he does not do (marry his landlady); Prest's is called to account for what he *does*.

Other prostheses also make available the subterranean sexuality of *The Pickwick Papers*. In *Pickwick in America*, the hero pursues adultery once more: he "felt himself in love to the eye-brows with the wife of another man!" (72). The Miss Witherfield encounter is then reworked in a way that reveals the sexual longing implicit in the original. Resting in bed, Pickwick sees a ghost enter his room. "[D]etermined to fathom the awful mystery," he follows the spirit and grabs it – only to find himself embracing the married woman of his desire, Mrs. Major Peterkin Mucklebuddy (93). (She is prone to sleepwalking.) What is an unfortunate error in Dickens's account becomes a moment of wish-fulfillment. In another aftertext, *The Magnum-Fundum Club*, Matthew Magnumfundum romances two ladies at once. Caught in this "duplex courtship," he considers suicide (11). Non-Pickwick characters are also sexualized. The Stiggins figure in *The Penny Pickwick*, named Smirkins, boards with Mrs. Veller and craves more than her pineapple rum. We find the good lady "embraced by Smirkins, who was imprinting a thousand sweet 'kisses of peace' upon her lips!" (173). Mr. Veller disposes of his faithless bride by selling her to Smirkins "for two and sixpence," plus expenses (179) – a moment that anticipates Thomas Hardy's *The Mayor of Casterbridge* (1886).

George W. M. Reynolds presents a more wholesome vision. In "The Marriage of Mr. Pickwick," which appears in *Master Timothy's Book-Case* (1842), Pickwick indeed gets married. This narrative finds a young lady separated from her friends one night. When a policeman seizes her for walking the streets unchaperoned, Pickwick intervenes and is arrested himself. Again, the Bardell plot is inverted: Reynolds's hero is punished for aiding, rather than abandoning, a female. Chaste Pickwick is soon aflame with desire: "his imagination conjured up, amid his slumbers, the graceful form and fascinating countenance of Miss Teresina Hippolyta Sago."[158] After improving his relations with her family, he proposes to the twenty-year-old girl: "I have decided upon a step which I ought to have taken twenty years ago!"[159] (At which point she would have been zero years old.) Even more inappropriately, on the wedding day, Pickwick wishes that he married "some thirty years previously" (she would have been negative ten).[160] While inept at mathematics, Reynolds generates a Pickwick that Dickens did not foresee: the bourgeois house-husband.

In other instances race impinges on Pickwickian sex, and gender boundaries are tested. *Pickwick in America*'s Mr. Tupman fancies a "brown lady," and we find him "in the very act of forcibly purloining from her chocolate phisiognomy [*sic*] a delicious kiss" (39). So Tupman's sexual exploits now raise questions of miscegenation, rape, and possible cannibalism (since her "chocolate" is "delicious").[161] The Miss Witherfield fiasco, a favorite among imitating authors, is revisited several pages later. Sleeping in a hotel, Pickwick is attacked by a rat, and he runs into another room, where he finds himself in the presence of a "hideous, fat, unwieldy black lady" (52). She screams at the intrusion and loses consciousness. The gentleman tries to restore her and "bathe[s] her dark temples with a basin of water" – an exchange of fluid that suggests sexual contact (52). But the interracial affairs that are merely suggested here are fully developed in *The Penny Pickwick*. John White, the black servant, loves Betty Bodger, the "red-armed, scarlet-faced maid of all work" (32). Yet it is not their different races, but age that is the impediment. Betty argues that "ve are both on us too YOUNG to marry yet" (34), although we learned that John is seventy. Later, when she relents, Bos allows the interracial marriage to proceed.

Finally, the subtext of an all-male club, with its "potential for transgressive behaviour," is made manifest in a few of the prostheses.[162] In *Pickwick Abroad*, Tupman confesses to (again) falling in love. His leader asks if the object is "female sex." "'What other sex would you have me select?' exclaimed the astonished Mr. Tupman."[163] "Winkle's Journal" holds one answer. This anonymous work offers a gay reading of *The Pickwick Papers*. Winkle, narrating his own story, seems attracted to a lively newcomer named Springer. Winkle "found his dancing perfection"; "I made up my mind that if I danced, I would dance opposite Mr. Springer" (172). During the figures, Mr. Winkle ignores his ostensible, female partner, whom he dismisses with the cognomen "Terpsichore"; and he admits, "I was too busy watching the manoeuvres of the officers" (173). Winkle avoids dancing with a number of aggressive Irishwomen, and he somehow ends up on the floor with Samuel Pickwick. Miss Janette scolds Winkle "for being 'so naughty a boy'"; undisturbed by this critique, he pays more attention to the Marquis of Worcester, whom Winkle describes as "handsome as the statue of Apollo" (175). Winkle is finally compelled to take a turn with Mrs. Fitzherbert O'Toole: "I suffered myself to be conducted to the sacrifice" (175). Dancing with a female, he is now clumsy. "I fell flat on my waistcoat and nose" (176) – that is, the crushed nose of sexual impotence. Pickwick demands that Winkle return home and "expose" himself no more (176). By delineating Winkle's perspective, this brief work reinterprets his character and suggests something about the nature of homosociality.

Like the devil, who can quote scripture for his own ends, the Pickwick prostheses offer sometimes radical revisions of Dickens's work. They uncover the *Pickwick* that they want to read or need to believe or desire. The trajectory is often one of elevation or degradation. In Reynolds's hands, alcoholic Pickwickians turn water-drinkers, and a wayward bachelor eases into marriage. Prest's work draws closer to Bakhtin's notion of "grotesque realism." An already-earthy text is made more so; in Bakhtin's terms, "it is a transfer to the material level, to the sphere of the earth and body."[164] Pickwick prostheses defamiliarize; they alienate and estrange. Despite such interventions, the prostheses profess continuity with *The Pickwick Papers*. They fill temporal gaps; they are the stories that Boz forgot to relate.

***

> Why, having the book in good readable type, turn it into these hieroglyphics? Who wants to read the story in that shape? or why?
> – Percy Fitzgerald

While publishing *The Penny Pickwick*, Edward Lloyd announced a new work, *Lloyd's Everlasting Entertainments; or, Pickwickian Shadows*.[165] It is uncertain whether this publication ever appeared.[166] I want to submit this bibliographical oddity – flickering between existence and nonexistence – as a metonym for the Pickwick phenomenon. The title is perfect. To begin with, *Lloyd's* is possessive; the work is not Boz's or Dickens's. *Everlasting* suggests the golden goose, the perpetual productions that can be derived from a Pickwickian original. *Entertainments*, of course, recalls *The Arabian Nights' Entertainments* – a *Pickwick* predecessor and itself the epitome of ceaseless storytelling. Lastly, *Pickwickian Shadows*: to some extent, all the aftertexts discussed above are Pickwickian Shadows – insubstantial, evanescent, dying in the light.

To conclude this chapter, I want to query some causes of the Pickwick phenomenon. Serial publication certainly played a role. Luisa Calè reminds us that *Pickwick*, in its first appearance, was a disaggregated book: each separate number begins with advertising pages, then illustrated plates, then the text.[167] Further, as Clare Pettitt observes, "[T]he reading public were encouraged to engage in the experience of assembling the 'story' themselves, part by part."[168] The aftertexts took this logic one step further and generated their own Pickwickian publications. Briefly, I will sketch two possible causes for this proliferation: *Pickwick*'s fairy-tale quality and its non-teleological nature.

Discussions of folk and fairy tales pervade readings of *Pickwick*. Edgar Johnson submits that the novel is a "realist fairy tale," and Louis James mentions "the fairy-tale world of the guinea-laden good uncle."[169] Chesterton makes the case that *Pickwick* is representative of what he calls "older literatures" – that is, "folklore."[170] *The Pickwick Papers* employs many European fairy-tale elements: character types such as heroes (Pickwick) and false heroes (Jingle) and generic elements such as Max Lüthi's "Depthlessness" and "Abstract Style."[171] *Pickwick* also resembles the eastern folk narratives contained in *The Arabian Nights*. Unlike in a modern novel, "[c]omplexity of character is achieved through repetition, shadows, duplication, collage."[172] Steven Marcus finds this motif in *Pickwick*, and Rosemarie Bodenheimer agrees that different aspects of a character might appear in more than one figure.[173]

But *Pickwick* draws closest to oral narrative due to its method of composition. As John Butt and Kathleen Tillotson argue, "Through serial publication an author can recover something of the intimate relationship between story-teller and audience."[174] A serialized story can respond to stimuli from its readers: sales figures, newspaper extracts and reviews, and anecdotal evidence can all lead a writer in one direction or another. Further, Kenneth Carlyle Thompson maintains that enthusiastic adapters transformed Dickens's literary text into something closer to orality.[175] As *Pickwick* approximates oral culture, it becomes another tale type, like "Cinderella" or "Sleeping Beauty," to be told and retold, round the fire, in the mechanics' institutes, or in the pages of a penny publication.

Equally important is the novel's non-teleological nature.[176] All books, good or bad, end – sometimes with the protagonist's death, sometimes with the author's (recall that Dickens, Thackeray, and Elizabeth Gaskell all left unfinished novels). That *Pickwick* was published in twenty monthly numbers was an arbitrary decision; it could have been ten or twelve or twenty-four numbers, like Thackeray's *Pendennis* (1848–50) and *The Newcomes* (1853–55).[177] *The Penny Pickwick* reached No. 28. Indeed, *Pickwick* could have just gone on and on, even beyond its creator's death. As a successful periodical, it might have been continued by Wilkie Collins or Charles Dickens, Jr. Chesterton asserts that "'Pickwick,' properly speaking, has no end – he is equal unto the angels."[178]

Besides the questions of when and whether a book ends, there is the corresponding issue of whither it all tends. If you do not have a goal, you can never get there. The Pickwickians, it seems, "never had a very clear reason for going anywhere."[179] Robert Douglas-Fairhurst suggests that "the pleasure of the journey is far more important than its final destination."[180] Recent work by Jonathan Grossman refers to the "seemingly aimless aim of stage-coaching around."[181] One of his insights is that "Pickwick's traveling around this stage-coaching network has been his purpose."[182] That is to say, Mr. Pickwick's goal is *motion itself*: always going, never getting there. *Pickwick* properly has no end and the Pickwickians no end in sight because of the publication's unusual genesis. This is the book that Dickens did not mean to write. It was a job, undertaken for money, while he planned the important novels he would one day compose for John Macrone and Richard Bentley. Since Dickens had no destination in mind, *Pickwick* approaches "something like pure writing"; he "let the writing write the book."[183] The structure is entirely open-ended. Any character can appear and take control of the proceedings (Jingle, Bob Sawyer, Mr. Pott). Every day begins afresh, with a newly risen Pickwickian sun. Because of the open-ended, non-teleological nature, any number of writers could wrest these characters into sequels, spinoffs, and further adventures. And so they did.

This chapter has considered a number of Pickwickian aftertexts published during and just after *Pickwick*'s initial serial run. In so doing, the chapter exerts itself to expand the literary *work* that is *The Pickwick Papers* to include aftertextual production – that is to say, the work done by *Pickwick* (generating aftertexts) and the work to *Pickwick* (their literary-critical evidence). Further, it should be clear that any reader approaching *Pickwick* today suffers an epistemological problem: he or she knows too much. It was only in retrospect that *The Posthumous*

Papers of the Pickwick Club became "*The Pickwick Papers*," a "novel," "by Charles Dickens." To readers in 1836 and 1837, Boz was one of many striving writers in the metropolis; the literary sweepstakes had not yet been won or lost. The aftertexts saw *Pickwick* as a mode, a formula, an invitation to invent *Pickwick*-like publications. As such, these aftertexts serve as counterfactuals, visions of what might have been. Some flourished, such as *The Penny Pickwick*, despite Chapman and Hall's demand for an injunction. Others floundered. As a final counter-*Pickwick*, consider *Effingham Hazard, the Adventurer*, which began publication in 1838. Yet another shilling monthly with green paper wrappers, *Effingham Hazard* exemplifies the fragility of this form of publication; after four monthly numbers, it vanished. The first number was published by Edward Ravenscroft, of Tooks Court, Chancery Lane. But by the second number, Ravenscroft's name on the cover was replaced by Foster and Hextall, of 268 Strand. By the fourth and final number, only John Foster remained. It may be a coincidence that a man named John Foster (not John Forster) was also the supposed inspiration for Samuel Pickwick's costume and girth; according to Chesterton, this Foster was "a corpulent old dandy . . . who wore tights and gaiters and lived at Richmond."[184]

Effingham Hazard in its very first number promises not to plagiarize: "we are not going to become poachers in the manor of 'Pickwick.'"[185] This image suggests eighteenth- and nineteenth-century copyright debates, in which literary property was sometimes termed a "manor," but the clause also includes a pun on *manner* – as in the manner of *The Pickwick Papers*. The first monthly number goes on to explain its wariness of potential legal action for poaching on Dickens's manor: "much as we appreciate the excellent writings of that author, we are not going to be pounced on by the Lord Chancellor for piracy, with the fear of four-and-twenty-Chapman-and-Hall-power in our eye, by way of prosecution."[186] In short, this anonymous author seems aware of *The Penny Pickwick* case, which took place less than two years earlier. He imagines Dickens's publishers, Chapman and Hall, as a telescope, with penetrating powers.

Despite this caution, *Effingham Hazard* ended up in Chancery. The plaintiff was not Chapman and Hall but rather the work's beleaguered author, a Mr. Macleath. He was engaged by Ravenscroft to write and provide illustrations, at a rate of £2 for the first monthly number and £4 for the second.[187] In February 1839, as a newspaper reported, "Mr. Knight Bruce [*sic*] applied for an injunction to restrain the defendant, a publisher and bookseller, from printing and publishing the third monthly number of a periodical entitled, 'Everingham [*sic*] Hazard,' a work of similar nature to

'Nicholas Nickleby.'"[188] It seems that Ravenscroft refused Macleath's work for No. 3. The publisher then hired someone else to perform the task, and Macleath sought the injunction, on the premise that *he* was being imitated. Because of the legal fracas, *Effingham Hazard* No. 4 failed to appear in March. But the fourth number did surface, it seems, on 1 April, with a "NOTICE" from its publisher explaining its previous "non-appearance": "Certain parties interested in the suppression of the above Work ... obtained an Injunction in the Court of Chancery to restrain the publication," but the injunction was dissolved on 26 February.[189] This victory, however, was fleeting. *Effingham Hazard* No. 4 proved to be the last of the novel-in-progress; "it sank without a trace."[190] A few days before the injunction was lifted, Edward James Ravenscroft appeared on the list of insolvents.[191] His assets were to be sold at auction, on 15 April, by Fletcher and Wheatley, and the firm's advertisement refers to "Ravenscroft's Works, privately printed," as if the failed publisher were somehow elevated to the status of author, with collected "Works" to his name.[192]

Such is the rule of literary history. Some aspirants become Charles Dickens, buried in Westminster Abbey and university curricula; others become Edward Ravenscroft, insolvent, sold at auction (not at Sotheby's or Christie's), unmourned and unremembered. It is a caution that perhaps more Pickwickian aftertexts could have heeded. Macleath would not be the last literary professional to seek redress from the law, and Ravenscroft would not be the last to find himself in Chancery.

CHAPTER TWO

Charles Dickens and the Pseudo-Dickens Industry

... there never were such books – never were such books!
                                                    – *Nicholas Nickleby*

The word *Dickensian* is older than the *OED* records. From 1881, eleven years after Charles Dickens's death, the dictionary cites an *Athenaeum* review, which describes the American journalist and humorist Bret Harte: "He has a touch of Dickens in his style; he has trained his imagination to walk with a Dickensian gait; he observes with a Dickensian eye."[1] While the *OED* concedes that the awkward coinage *Dickenesque* and the cheerier *Dickensy* appeared earlier (in 1856 and 1859, respectively), the more familiar *Dickensian* is older still. Surprisingly (or perhaps unsurprisingly, given the Bret Harte example), the word was first deployed to describe not the writings of Charles Dickens but rather an imitation thereof. An anonymous plagiarism of Dickens's weekly periodical *Master Humphrey's Clock* (1840–41) used the adjective *Dickensian* in 1840, in a twopenny newspaper, the *Town*. This paper quarrels with "Mr. Pickwick's Tale," a legend interpolated into *Master Humphrey's Clock* and told by Mr. Pickwick, who suggests that the name of Will Marks's lover is lost. The anonymous author in the *Town* protests, "This is wrong. Her name was Maria Page, as has already been said four times in this beautifully, needlessly circumfuse paragraph, of Dickensian verbosity."[2] So *Dickensian* first referred to an imitative text; further, the adjective modifies the noun *verbosity* – a trait that emulators of Dickens's fiction found themselves able to reproduce.[3]

But the *Town* was only one of many spurious bursts of Dickensiana that bloomed in the years after Dickens triumphed with *Pickwick*. By 1839, the *Morning Post* could refer to "Pickwick Periodicals," and an advertisement in James Grant's *Sketches in London* (itself inspired by Dickens's first book, *Sketches by Boz*) offers a list of "Light Reading &

Books in the Pickwick Style," including *Pickwick Abroad* and *Paul Periwinkle*.[4] While the Pickwick phenomenon was underway, Dickens did not remain idle, nor did his copyists. As he followed *Pickwick* with *Oliver Twist*, *Nicholas Nickleby*, and *Master Humphrey's Clock*, opportunistic publishers proffered works such as *Oliver Twiss*, *Scenes from the Life of Nickleby Married*, and *Master Timothy's Book-Case*. Robert Douglas-Fairhurst observes that, for Dickens, "these unauthorized literary add-ons and knock-offs meant that his identity as a writer was now in serious danger of drifting away from his control."[5]

The aftertexts themselves are often out of control, marked by a tendency to stray. An ostensible *Oliver Twist* devolves into *Pickwick*; plagiarisms of *Nicholas Nickleby* echo *Oliver* or *Sketches by Boz*. The interpenetrations of the various epigones recall G. K. Chesterton's classic statement on Dickens's art: "Strictly, there is no such novel as 'Nicholas Nickleby.' There is no such novel as 'Our Mutual Friend.' They are simply lengths cut from the flowing and mixed substance called Dickens – a substance of which any given length will be certain to contain a given proportion of brilliant and of bad stuff." Chesterton's image thus allows the possibility of intertextual straying, as he playfully suggests: "There is no reason why Sam Weller, in the course of his wanderings, should not wander into 'Nicholas Nickleby.' There is no reason why Major Bagstock, in his brisk way, should not walk straight out of 'Dombey and Son,' and straight into 'Martin Chuzzlewit.'"[6] Steven Marcus discovers this in practice: "Sam Weller has in *Oliver Twist* become the Artful Dodger, who possesses all of Sam's coolness and wit, but who exists on the margins of society."[7] Indeed, both the Dodger and Dick Swiveller, in *The Old Curiosity Shop*, seem to audition for the Weller role. Dick also recalls Mr. Pickwick's legal troubles when the young man avows, "There can be no action for breach, that's one comfort."[8] The United Metropolitan Improved Hot Muffin and Crumpet Baking and Punctual Delivery Company, in the first number of *Nicholas Nickleby*, evokes some of the leaden humor in the first number of *Pickwick*, and John Bowen finds that *The Old Curiosity Shop* repeats motifs from *Nickleby*, such as "a foolish relative," "a country school," "travelling showmen," and "monstrous villains."[9] Daniel Quilp, like Fagin and Miss Knag, compulsively rubs his hands together and is himself reproducible; he "glanced upward with a stealthy look of exultation that an imp might have copied and appropriated to himself."[10]

What emerges in these early works is a kind of Boz brand, and a single word encapsulates the brand: *Dickensian*. Various attempts have been made to define this brand, which Robert L. Patten describes as an "illustrated serial representing contemporary middle- and lower-middle-class life, chiefly about London, and narrated with humor, sympathy, and more than a modicum of distancing coolness and irony." Intriguingly, he adds that it "could be imitated."[11] Helen Small defines the synonym *Dickensese* as "performative excess, *faux* Cockney and the deliberate use of comic circumlocution or failed elevation of the manner of speech."[12] Discussing Dickens's language, Garrett Stewart identifies "[h]eavy-handed comparison, strident parallelism, deliberate contortions of idiom, rampant neologism, extended metaphor, phantom puns."[13]

In the nineteenth century, imitators of Dickens captured this essence, the quality soon known as *Dickensian*. While not always superlative writers, they were attentive readers, and they stood alongside periodical reviews and newspaper extracts among the earliest and most vivid responses to the rise of Dickens the novelist in the 1830s and 1840s. These aftertexts capture a piece of art in motion – a bird in flight – and make its features apprehensible. In other words, something that is not-Dickens helps us see with greater clarity that which is Dickens, Dickensian – itself an ambiguous term that refers to works that are produced by Charles Dickens as well as qualities that are typical of his writing. This chapter looks beyond the Pickwick phenomenon (discussed in Chapter 1) and situates Dickens in the historical context of his many plagiaristic successors, who destabilized and reified his authorial identity in its formative years.

The chapter offers two arguments. One, a reading of aftertexts of Dickens's novels, with emphasis on variations on *Nicholas Nickleby*, illuminates our understanding of the term *Dickensian*, around the time that it entered the English language. Two, I show that Dickens, rather than ignoring the gadfly, responded to the onslaught by changing his narratives and altering his forms; he even imitated *Pickwick* in *Master Humphrey's Clock* to prove, paradoxically, that he was inimitable. To conclude the chapter, I will consider a final test case: the piracies that appeared in *Parley's Illuminated Library* and the resulting dispute in the Court of Chancery. I will read the available legal evidence for the insight it offers into the practices of nineteenth-century literary imitation and evaluate the impact of domestic piracy on Dickens's novel then in progress, *Martin Chuzzlewit*.

***

... for one original writer, that appears in the republic of letters, there
are five hundred copyists and compilers.

– William Kenrick

In early 1838, Charles Dickens sent his publisher Richard Bentley two
imitations of *Oliver Twist*, both entitled *Oliver Twiss*. "The vagabonds
have stuck placards on the walls – each to say that *theirs* is the only true
Edition," Dickens complains in a letter.[14] What is most striking about
Oliver Twiss is that there were two of them, one imitative work redupli-
cated by another – perhaps an instance of polygenesis. Around
December 1837, Edward Lloyd began to publish *Life and History of
Oliver Twiss*, edited by "Bos."[15] Like *The Penny Pickwick* and the club
imitations, it was issued as an eight-page penny weekly with double-
column print and woodcuts. Weekly numbers were also stitched together
into thirty-two-page monthly parts, sold at 4d. The second weekly number
dropped the words "Life and History," and the publication then continued
under the banner *Oliver Twiss*. By 1839, the volume edition offered a new
title, *The Life and Adventures of Oliver Twiss, the Workhouse Boy*, and
a preface, dated 22 August, which boasts that "the sale of our work has
been enormous." The preface also complains that "[c]heap periodicals have
been started in every direction," without acknowledging that Lloyd was
responsible for many of them.[16]

Thackeray called Lloyd's publication "a kind of silly copy of Boz's
admirable tale."[17] Sue Zemka, in one of the few pieces of critical writing
on Bos's *Twiss*, refers to "minimal description, lots of action, and the barest
skeleton of a plot."[18] She makes the canny point that Thomas Peckett Prest
(aka Bos) was obliged to reach for a dramatic climax every eight pages (in
contrast to Dickens's more leisurely thirty-two pages); thus, that which
happens in *Oliver Twist* happens more frequently or hyperbolically in
Oliver Twiss. In Bos's more compressed narrative space, everything occurs
in a "moment."[19] Further, Zemka identifies a bleeding of formal boundaries: deeply unsentimental, the plagiaristic *Oliver Twiss* is "parodic by
default."[20]

The other *Oliver Twiss* appeared in January 1838: *Oliver Twiss, the
Workhouse Boy*, edited by Poz. This incomplete work survived for only
four eight-page penny numbers, which were also stitched together into
a 4d. monthly. Poz's *Oliver Twiss* dubs itself, on its title page, "[a]n original
satirical work."[21] Naturally, its publisher, James Pattie, resented the existence of a competing *Oliver Twiss*. In a notice "To the Public," appearing
on the back of the monthly issue, the publisher of Poz's *Twiss* proceeds to

lambast the opposition. Pattie claims that his *Twiss* appeared two days earlier than Edward Lloyd's: 2 January versus 4 January.[22] Pattie also brags, disingenuously, "This work is entirely original." The notice proceeds to effect product differentiation by referring to Bos's work as "vulgar and common-place rubbish"; "slang and cant phrases please the ignorant, but any one, possessing an atom of intellect, will discover, in any twenty lines, the satirical point and interest of this publication."[23] It should be noted that the dispute is between two publishers; mere authors (Bos or Poz or Boz) are never mentioned.

As the available sample of Dickens material grew, his successors were able to judge with greater acuity that which is Dickensian. There is an inevitable slippage; just as Chesterton proposed the notion of intertextual straying, these aftertexts merge and mingle their sources. Bos's *Oliver Twiss*, like Nicholas Nickleby and Nell Trent, falls in with a traveling performer, and a relative of Nickelas Nickelbery (in a *Nickleby* aftertext) owns "a tremendous snuff-box, resembling a juvenile coffin" – perhaps borrowed from Mr. Sowerberry.[24] Iterations of *Pickwick* are pervasive. Many characters attempt Wellerisms, and Newman Noggs, in a *Nickleby* stage adaptation, sounds rather like *Pickwick*'s Mr. Jingle: "Come with me to the city – a counting-house – kind masters – best place in the world!"[25] Further, Robert Douglas-Fairhurst reminds us that Dickens's "fiction teems with surrogate selves"; one manifestation is the compulsive replication of Charleys and Dicks: Charley Bates, Mr. Dick, Doubledick.[26] Thus, Bos's *Oliver Twiss* offers the character Knowing Dick, and the police arrest someone named Lucifer Dick. In *Scenes from the Life of Nickleby Married*, Sir Mulberry Hawk flees to an inn, where he re-experiences Mr. Pickwick's memorable misadventure in the double-bedded room. The baronet is appalled to find himself in bed with a ship's African cook: Black Dick.

Derivations of *Nicholas Nickleby* are instructive, in part because it "consolidate[s] the impressive qualities of the two novels that preceded it."[27] The most audacious *Nickleby* aftertext is *Nickelas Nickelbery, Containing the Adventures, Mis-adventures, Chances, Mis-chances, Fortunes, Mis-fortunes, Mys-teries, Mis-eries, and Mis-cellaneous Manoeuvres of the Family Nickelbery*. The author was the inevitable Bos. There is something Dantesque in the life of Thomas Peckett Prest, compelled by economic necessity or some mimetic muse to imitate one Dickens book after another – *Sketches by Boz, Oliver Twist, Nicholas Nickleby* – in smaller fragments and for less pay. Like his *Penny Pickwick* and *Oliver Twiss*, *Nickelbery* was issued as an eight-page penny weekly, published by Edward Lloyd, from 1838 to 1839.

NICKELAS

NICKELBERY

EDITED BY "BOS."

Mr. Whackem Speres' Academy, Ruminby Lodge, Yorkshire.

The impossibility of Nickelas being able to return to London if was ever so anxious, unless he travelled it on foot, came to his mind with such force that he could scarcely restrain his regret within the bounds of reason. By degrees, however, his feelings became more calm;—he thought upon the many promises his uncle had made to provide for Flora and her mother if he endeavoured to do his best in the situation he had procured for him; and should he bv any rash and hasty step plunge those he so fondly loved into misery? No, he would not!—Besides, perhaps after all, things might not turn out so bad as he had anticipated at Ruminby Lodge; perhaps they were not actually so discouraging as his distempered mind had made them appear; and it was his duty to combat with sorrow manfully, when it was to secure the comfort and ind-

No. 11.

Figure 2 The first page of the eleventh penny weekly number of *Nickelas Nickelbery* (c. June 1838), by "Bos" – a penname used by Thomas Peckett Prest, the most persistent of Dickensian imitators

In a moment that is perhaps unprecedented in the annals of imitation, Bos's first weekly number of *Nickelas Nickelbery* appeared on the same exact day as the first monthly number of *Nicholas Nickleby*, 31 March 1838 (the second anniversary of *Pickwick*). As a result, for at least eight pages,

Prest was compelled to plagiarize a work that he had not yet read. Louis James finds that "'Bos' clearly did not know what he was imitating," and Michael Slater agrees that the author was "forced to pad out his pages as best he could."[28] Periphrasis, repetition, legalese, negation, and tautology are among the strategies Bos deploys to spin his narrative without committing himself too deeply. It is worth quoting the impossible opening sentence in full:

> The Biographer of Nickelas Nickelbery does not find himself placed in the same awkward position as Lord Byron declared himself to be at the commencement of "Don Juan," viz. *in want of a hero*; on the contrary, he happens to be in possession of such a hero as no other historian, he is confident, ever found himself in possession of before; and as it is a generally received opinion, that it is rather necessary in commencing the memoirs of any extraordinary individual, or peculiar character, to begin the commencement with the beginning of such narrative; we shall not take upon ourselves to depart from that good and rather sensible rule; nay, so impressed are we with the truth and justness of this axiom, that we are resolved, in this biography not only to commence with the very commencement of the beginning of our hero's life, but to take many steps in a retrograde motion, and bring to light the whisperings of report concerning his ancestors; for they being probably directly or indirectly, concerned, accessory to, and instrumental in his forthcoming, must indisputably claim a niche in the undying pages of this incomparable history. (1–2)

In other words, this is going to be a very long book.

Since *Nicholas Nickleby* was not yet available, Bos slips into his hyperbolic Pickwickian style (he wrote more than one *Pickwick* imitation).[29] He promises "a history that should totally eclipse either Roman, Grecian, English, Eastern, or any other history that has ever been written, conceived, published, or promulgated" (2). As if more padding were needed, Bos proceeds to list several places where the Nickelbery family did *not* live. Because he must have gathered that the Yorkshire schools play some role in the forthcoming novel by Boz, Bos informs his readers that the Nickelbery family was "situated in Yorkshire" (3). He resorts to tautology ("most houses are constructed, built, and appropriated for the purposes of being inhabited" [3]) and periphrasis (a barber is referred to as "this expert mower of the grizzly chins of the unwashed members of society" [4]). Intentionally or otherwise, Bos channels his anxiety about the work he is supposedly imitating and the general excitement that would likely greet Dickens's latest by depicting the neighborhood gossip surrounding the family Nickelbery. Bos mentions the "universal and incurable epidemic of rabid curiosity" and "the reserved and mysterious manner in which that ancient family had latterly conducted themselves" (4) – as if scolding Dickens for withholding the pages of *Nickleby*. By the end of the first number, Bos allows that Mrs. Nickelbery might be pregnant, thus the hint of the possibility of the birth of the hero – that is, Bos in a most *Tristram Shandy*–like mode.

By the second and third weekly numbers, Bos caught up to Boz, and the resulting narrative is, for James, "the closest of the Dickens plagiarisms up to this date."[30] Reaching a somewhat expedited conclusion on page 342, *Nickelbery* accounts for a little less than half of Dickens's narrative. It is therefore a *Nickleby* without the Cheeryble brothers ("those pot-bellied Sir Charles Grandisons of the ledger and day-book") and without the tepid love affairs enjoyed by the hero and heroine.[31]

Nickelas Nickelbery is not quite a piracy, and it is not quite a plagiarism, which makes it representative of the formal instability exhibited by such aftertexts. Fred G. Kitton describes it as "parodying the whole of the story and characters under slightly altered names"; readers meet Whackem Speres, Mr. Crumples, Miss Cragg, and Snikes.[32] Bos is careful to paraphrase Dickens's text, as if wary of committing wholesale plagiarism.[33] To cite one of many examples, Boz's Nicholas "threw himself on the bed, and turning his face to the wall, gave free vent to the emotions he had so long stifled";[34] Bos's Nickelas "threw himself upon his coarse pallet, and burying his face in his hands, gave free indulgence to the violence of his agitation" (235). Bos is typical here of imitative Dickenses, with a use of multisyllabic words ("upon" for "on," "pallet" for "bed," "indulgence" for "vent"). Also, the addition of "coarse" and "violence" color the original scene: a sullen moment in *Nicholas Nickleby* is made more so, its condition worsened and made manifest.

Despite the ineptitude and occasional errors in Bos's book, *Nickelas Nickelbery* proves a subtle text as well.[35] It captures the willful innocence of Dickens's narrative voice, its insistence on not-knowing.[36] For example, when *Nickelbery*'s Whackem Speres returns from a tavern, "he was according to custom so mysteriously excited" (125).[37] Further, Bos's text illuminates Dickensian undercurrents, such as anxiety about cannibalism.[38] The unfortunate pupils at Ruminby Lodge (Bos's version of Dotheboys Hall) are described as so malnourished that "one cannibal could not have found meat sufficient upon all their bones to make him a luncheon" (86). But *Dickensian* is more than a motif; it is a mode of perception.[39] By reading Dickens carefully, Bos, like Bret Harte some years later, "observes with a Dickensian eye." *Nickelas*

Nickelbery illuminates absences and fills some gaps in Dickens's work. For instance, in *Nicholas Nickleby*, the landlord at the tavern near Portsmouth is not described. But in Bos's version, the landlord "was a dingy, red-nosed looking man, and was contemplating a number of hieroglyphics in chalk behind the door and rubbing his hands in a thoughtful manner" (244). This landlord sounds very much like a Dickens "type," and the "hieroglyphics" evoke the not-knowing perspective of his narratives in that a text appears illegible. What is more, like Fagin, Miss Knag, and Quilp, the landlord occupies himself by "rubbing his hands."

Bos is also alert to the structuring principles of Dickens's narratives. In the sixth weekly number of *Nickelas Nickelbery*, published after only two monthly parts of *Nicholas Nickleby* had appeared, Nickelas is introduced by his uncle, Roger, to the Yorkshire schoolmaster, Speres. Shortly after, Nickelas, in a soliloquy, states that his uncle "certainly must have some secret on his mind, and with which I am in some manner connected" (44). One page later, Speres comments, "The boy grows amazingly!" to which Roger replies, "Hush!" Bos, at this early stage, intuited a connection among Ralph Nickleby, his nephew, the schoolmaster, and an unnamed boy. As Dickens planned his novels with greater care, hidden connectivity became increasingly important, such as the revelation that Smike is Ralph Nickleby's son. However, Bos's conjectures are not infallible. At the end of his narrative, he reveals that Snikes is not Roger's son but only the victim of his treachery.

Scenes from the Life of Nickleby Married, in contrast, benefitted from the completion of Dickens's serial. Published in 1840, in 6d. parts with imitative green wrappers, *Nickleby Married* is the work of "Guess" – alerting us to the possibility that it is anyone's guess – and the illustrations are credited to "Quiz," recalling Dickens's frequent collaborator Phiz. In the book's preface, the author claims that a "friend" proffered the notion of producing a sequel to *Nicholas Nickleby*. "I liked the idea, and as the mine had been abandoned by the discoverer, I conceived that it lay fairly open to any person who might feel the inclination to work it."[40] This image suggests that Dickens's novel is a natural resource and transforms the book into something like the "Transactions of the Pickwick Club," from which more than one narrative can be drawn. Yet the narrative that follows this preface is something of a misnomer: there are almost no scenes from the life of Nickleby married.

Like *Nickelas Nickelbery*, *Nickleby Married* imitates Dickens at the stylistic level. Guess employs periphrasis (a lawyer is described as "an aspirant to the dignity of that learned profession, of which a member eats his way to the bench" [337]), but he excels at occultatio: "It would be useless to enumerate the good things that were said or eaten on that night" (15).[41] Later, an entire scene is rendered through that which the narrator does not describe:

> We mean not to dwell upon the rarity of the viands or the excellence of the wines, nor to relate how Pyke, after dinner, in the paroxysm of a Champagne fever, kissed Miss Pullman, and how Miss Pullman was so indignant that she said nothing about it . . . These and numerous other little incidents, which varied the amusements of the party until the London steamer lay alongside Hungerford Stairs at ten o'clock at night, we leave to the imagination of the affable and ingenious reader. (396–397)

This Dickensian passage naturally terminates at a Dickensian address: Hungerford Stairs, where Charles Dickens worked at Warren's Blacking warehouse as a child.

Indeed, *Nickleby Married* assimilates more than Dickens's style; it also seems to capture some of his obsessions and anxieties. Adelina Gambroon is the nouveau-riche widow of a tailor. With her new paramour, Sir Mulberry Hawk, and other elegant companions, she enjoys a pleasure outing, in which she suddenly re-encounters friends from her plebeian past – namely, the Kenwigs family and Mr. Lillyvick, gorging themselves in a picnic. Sir Mulberry's faction enjoys the widow's embarrassment as if it were a performance; "Pyke and the others, nearly smothered by endeavouring to suppress their mirth, were stuffing their pocket-handkerchiefs down their throats" (393). Mrs. Gambroon extracts herself and drags Sir Mulberry away "until they had fairly got out of sight and hearing of her humble friends" (395). "Panting from loss of breath and ready to sink with shame, Mrs. Gambroon made some sort of a confused apology to her aristocratic friends." She confesses, "I have befriended these poor people as far as I could, and now they're so grateful that its [sic] quite distressing" (396). Mrs. Gambroon ascended the social heights only to be rudely reminded of her roots.

Other characters in *Nickleby Married* also experience Dickens-like revenants or reveries. Newman Noggs might seem a surprising contender for a Dickens stand-in, except that he is an iteration of the hero, that other N. N., Nicholas Nickleby. The misfortune of Newman, once a gentleman and now a new man, anticipates that of Nicholas, the son of a gentleman but compelled to work. Robert L. Patten insists that "Newman Noggs's history is absolutely crucial to *Nickleby*."[42] In *Nickleby Married*, Newman

Noggs indulges in Dickens's pastime of walking the city at night. Newman "felt a strange pleasure in gliding into Golden Square after dusk, and standing opposite the house where Ralph Nickleby resided, and recalling the scenes he had witnessed" (203). The house, now unoccupied, is thought to be haunted. Newman, in this instance, becomes a ghost himself, haunting his past. He finds the brass plate with Nickleby's name "corroded by time" – an image that suggests the loss of identity, tantamount to Bos or Guess effacing the name of Boz. Compulsively, Newman polishes the plate "as if it had been his daily employment for the last twenty years" (205). Newman is then compelled to enter the house by the serial novelist's stock-in-trade, "curiosity" (203).

He glances at an unfinished letter on Ralph's desk, and the novel suddenly anticipates Dickens's autobiographical fragment, with its recollection of the blacking warehouse: "even now, famous and caressed and happy, I often forget in my dreams that I have a dear wife and children; even that I am a man; and wander desolately back to that time of my life."[43] Here is *Nickleby Married*: "As Newman examined at the window the well-known characters, he could with difficulty persuade himself that the events of the last ten years had not been a dream – that he was not still the broken-down drudge of the usurer" (208). This author so completely absorbs his source that he foreshadows something that Dickens had yet to write. Newman then explores the rest of the house with a "candle stuck in an empty blacking bottle" (209) – the perfect Dickensian light source.[44]

***

That book you recite, O Fidentinus, *is* mine. But your vile *re*-citation begins to make it your own.

– Martial

Mid-nineteenth-century copyright law offered little protection against such creative interventions: any enterprising author could compose his or her own *Pickwick, Twist*, or *Nicholas Nickleby*. To an extent that has yet to be fully explored, the advent of these imitators altered the direction of Dickens's career and imprinted themselves in his fiction, as early as *Oliver Twist*. Monica F. Cohen investigates some of this terrain in an article, "Making Piracy Pay: Fagin and Contested Authorship in Victorian Print Culture." She finds in Fagin "a figuration of the nineteenth-century literary pirate" and observes that "this struggle for Oliver's soul occurs as a struggle for controlling the ownership of his story."[45] Similar observations appear in Robert L. Patten's *Charles Dickens and "Boz": The Birth of the Industrial-Age Author*. In Patten's reading of *Oliver Twist*, literature and theft intertwine, and Oliver "experience[s] what it is like to be an author plagiarized."[46] Yet neither Cohen nor Patten situates *Oliver Twist* in the larger context of the Pickwick phenomenon.

The first theatrical productions based on *Pickwick* premièred in London on 27 March and 3 April 1837.[47] In the May 1837 installment of *Oliver Twist*, written during the month of April, Oliver first encounters the criminal-world figures of Jack Dawkins (The Artful Dodger) and Fagin. This might be a coincidence, but the fact remains that just as Dickens's earlier narrative was pilfered by hack playwrights, he plunged little Oliver into a den of thieves. Furthermore, weekly numbers of Bos's *The Penny Pickwick* first appeared in or around May 1837. Chapman and Hall attempted to restrain publication and failed on 8 June 1837. It is in the next installment of *Oliver Twist* (July 1837), possibly written during that same month of June, that Mr. Brownlow is robbed of his pocket-handkerchief and Oliver arrested for the theft.[48] Brownlow first appears "in a bottle-green coat with a black velvet collar, and white trousers."[49] In other words, his color scheme is that of the monthly parts of *Pickwick*: green wrappers, black ink, and white pages. Naturally, Brownlow is robbed at a book-stall while he intensely peruses a volume; he even manages to steal the book in an act of absentmindedness.

In short, just as Dickens's first great triumph was poached by unscrupulous authors of the day, he generated a narrative about thieves, loss of identity, and the struggle among a group of father/authors – Bumble, Fagin, Brownlow, Monks, and, to a lesser extent, Gamfield and Sowerberry – to determine the fate of the legal entity known as Oliver Twist (and perhaps *Oliver Twist*). Further, the handkerchief stolen from Mr. Brownlow is the perfect image for the plagiaristic process: a sheet pilfered from someone is then unwritten ("the marks shall be picked out with a needle," Fagin explains).[50] Once the author's autograph – or monogram – is effaced, the sheet can be sold afresh. In this manner, an imitating author can unwrite Dickens's narrative and market it as something new. Patten observes that "[t]he connections between handkerchiefs and publications were widespread."[51] For instance, the *Athenaeum*, addressing copycat theatrical managers, snarls, "[K]eep your hands from your neighbours' pockets."[52] Cohen cites the handkerchief motif in one of Dickens's earliest brushes with piracy: when his story "The Bloomsbury Christening," published in April 1834, was exploited six months later as a stage farce, now entitled *The Christening*, Dickens lamented, "[M]y handkerchief is gone."[53] John O. Jordan, in "The Purloined Handkerchief," proposes a similar analogy: "I believe that the idea of the handkerchief as a printed document or text is implicit in the novel."[54] Further, Jordan states that Oliver is himself "a purloined handkerchief circulating through the text."[55] Thus, Oliver Twist, like *Oliver Twist*, is an article of property on which others can indite their own texts. As an orphan, Oliver is disinherited – that is, alienated from his name and his birthright, like a piece of literary property divested from its author and progenitor.

If the issue of plagiarism is encoded in *Oliver Twist*, it became explicit with the publication of *Nicholas Nickleby*. In the *Nickleby* "Proclamation," of 28 February 1838, Boz complains that "some dishonest dullards, resident in the by-streets and cellars of this town, impose upon the unwary and credulous, by producing cheap and wretched imitations of our delectable Works."[56] It is unclear how many credulous nineteenth-century book buyers actually purchased a faux-Dickens by mistake. As free-standing penny publications, *Oliver Twiss* and *Nickelas Nickelbery*, for example, did not command much comment in the press. Yet in one newspaper, the former is wrongly attributed to Dickens: Boz is called the "author of the celebrated Pickwick Papers, life of Oliver Twiss, and Adventures of Nicholas Nickleby."[57] Another newspaper refers to "the sinister leer and whine of 'Old Fagin' the Jew, in 'Oliver Twiss.'"[58] Yet in *Oliver Twiss*, by Bos, the equivalent character is named Solomons.[59] These instances may represent typos, but they could indicate misattribution – a blurring between Dickens and not-Dickens.

In the pages of *Nickleby*, the author directs his fury at one target in particular, the playwright William Thomas Moncrieff, author of *Sam Weller; or, The Pickwickians*. *Nickleby*'s fifteenth monthly number (June 1839) chastises "a literary gentleman ... who had dramatised in his time two hundred and forty-seven novels as fast as they had come out – some of them faster than they had come out." Nicholas scolds the dramatist, "[Y]ou take the uncompleted books of living authors, fresh from their hands, wet from the press, cut, hack, and carve them to the powers and capacities of your actors, and the capability of your theatres ... all this without [the author's] permission, and against his will."[60] This attack may have been prompted by Moncrieff's latest, *Nickleby and Poor Smike; or, The Victim of the Yorkshire School*, which premièred on 20 May 1839. It was not the first stage adaptation of *Nickleby*-in-progress, but Moncrieff, unlike Bos, guessed Smike's parentage and revealed it prematurely.[61]

Because Dickens's "delectable Works" proved so imitable, the author found it necessary to twist or swivel away from his competitors. The year 1839 marked a transition. Both *Pickwick Abroad* and Bos's *Oliver Twiss* were published in volume form; thus, ephemeral aftertexts earned the distinction of bound books. In July, Dickens proposed a new work that would defy his imitators. Recalling the neglected club frame from *Pickwick*, he imagined "a little club or knot of characters" that would gather around a clock-case, a literal magazine or storehouse holding manuscripts.[62] In place of Mr. Pickwick and his companions Snodgrass, Tupman, and Winkle, Dickens offers Master Humphrey and *his* three friends: "a bizarre distortion of the Pickwickians," according to Marcus.[63] Dickens even planned to "reintroduce Mr. Pickwick and Sam Weller," to spite the Pickwickian pretenders and to show that he alone knew how to animate these beloved characters.[64]

Despite the obvious retread, Dickens was "consciously seeking a new direction."[65] He altered his format: the green covers replaced with white, the dimensions slightly larger, the page count shorter, and the price now 3d. Patten suggests that the new serial's mode of weekly publication was designed to outpace any imitating "play, parody, or sequel."[66] With *Master Humphrey's Clock*, which began publication in April 1840, Dickens splits the narration into multiples: Master Humphrey and his friends will each, in turn, read a manuscript to the club. So in place of a single authorial voice, there is a form of multiple authorship – that is, more for a bold plagiarist to master. In a letter to illustrator George Cattermole, Dickens makes his intentions clear: "my object being to baffle the imitators and make it as novel as possible" (although perhaps not a *novel*). He demands secrecy from his correspondent, otherwise "there would be fifty Humphreys in the field."[67]

Mary Teresa McGowan concedes that Dickens "had the plagiarists generally in mind," but this does not go far enough.[68] *Master Humphrey's Clock* was Dickens's revenge. Within the text, Master Humphrey's club is imitated by "Mr. Weller's Watch," a collection of servants who replicate the tale-telling evenings of their masters. In the fifth weekly number, Samuel Pickwick enters the new serial; many readers assumed that this marked a failure of invention. John Ruskin asked a correspondent, "Can it be possible that this man is so soon run dry . . . ?"[69] The *Monthly Review* argued that characters from *Pickwick* emerged in *Master Humphrey's Clock* "in order to save that new work from absolute ruin."[70] Yet the plan to reintroduce *Pickwick* characters was there from the start. Samuel Pickwick's first appearance, as described by the narrator, Master

Humphrey, clarifies the rhetorical point: "I condoled with him upon the various libels on his character which had found their way into print. Mr. Pickwick shook his head and for a moment looked very indignant, but smiling again directly, added that no doubt I was acquainted with Cervantes' introduction to the second part of Don Quixote, and that it fully expressed his sentiments on the subject."[71] These "libels" are publications that wrested Samuel Pickwick into imitative narratives or allographic sequels. Cervantes also suffered the theft of his literary property, to which part 2 of *Don Quixote* was in part a response, as Genette explains: "we owe the continuation written by Cervantes himself to the counterfeit one by Avellaneda."[72]

But *Master Humphrey*'s most inspired attack on the plagiarists appears in the form of little Tony Weller, grandson to the coachman. This infant phenomenon pretends to smoke and drink; he "pinches his little nose to make it red"; and he "actually winked upon the housekeeper with his infant eye, in imitation of his grandfather."[73] Like a professional impersonator, Tony can perform different figures. His grandfather boasts, "He's even gone so far as to put on a pair o' paper spectacles . . . and walk up and down the garden with his hands behind him in imitation of Mr. Pickwick."[74] Paper spectacles make a telling detail: Tony sees through paper, as does an imitating author.

"[N]obody much liked the idea of a miscellany," contends John Bowen.[75] The *Sunday Times* described the new publication as "what the public neither expected nor desired."[76] If Dickens thought that the form of *Master Humphrey's Clock* was one that no other writer could – or would want to – emulate, he was deceived. Frederic Fox Cooper dramatized the new serial in May 1840. George Reynolds, progenitor of *Pickwick Abroad*, asserted that "[t]he plan upon which *Master Humphrey's Clock* is built is bad," yet he proceeded to replicate it with his own publication, *Master Timothy's Book-Case*.[77]

Bos's contribution to the *Master Humphrey* literature is *Mister Humfries' Clock*. The monthly wrapper bears the title *Mister Humfrie's Clock*, and the 1840 volume edition adds a subtitle, "A Miscellany of Striking Interest." At ninety-two pages, it is, like many cheap serial narratives, an unfinished symphony. "MISTER HUMFRIES' CLOCK has, for the present, *stopped*," admits the preface.[78] Just as Dickens changed his publication format with *Master Humphrey*, so Bos rethought his own format: the double-column text of *The Penny Pickwick*, *Oliver Twiss*, and *Nickelas Nickelbery* was replaced with more-humane single columns. Bos also ventriloquizes the melancholic tone of his source; Louis James finds that the "writing is comparatively sober and literary."[79] But ingrained habits are hard to break. "The very commencement of the beginning" recalls Bos's typical palaver.[80] The highlight is the grandson to Ephraim Veller, "little Ephy," who imitates his grandsire by "drinking an' smokin' as nat'ral, as if he had been hinookylated for 'em," according to the elder Ephraim. "Now ain't Eppy grand-daddy!" cries the child: an imitation of an imitation.[81]

More eccentric is "Master Humphrey's Turnip, a Chimney Corner Crotchet," published in the *Town* (it was this work that used the word *Dickensian* in 1840). The credited author is Poz, a pseudonym favored by the class of pseudo-Bozes. Poz is also the author of *Posthumous Papers of the Wonderful Discovery Club*, "An Omitted Pickwick Paper," one of two works entitled *Oliver Twiss*, and something called *The Nickleby Papers*, but there is no evidence that they are the same person.[82] "Master Humphrey's Turnip" begins, "The reader must not expect to know where I live" – a direct plagiarism from *Master Humphrey's Clock* – but continues, "for it has been wisely observed, that the publication of one's address is a notice to creditors."[83] A *turnip*, it turns out, is slang for a watch, and this one seems to be stolen. The narrator, Master Humphrey, is a flâneur, a petty thief, and a Boz-like observational journalist:

> I have been led into the habit of assigning a character to every person I meet in the streets. Between Charing-cross and Temple-bar, or between the latter and St. Paul's, I can act one of the best dramas ever imaginable ... I can make it grave or gay, comic or tragic, farcical or melo-dramatic, long or short, just as the humour suits me.[84]

This sounds like Dickens's compositional method: to roam the streets of London and envision characters everywhere. The passage also suggests Dickens's flair for theatre, generic flexibility, and capacity to deliver installments of the appropriate length. This narrator merges his identity with that of Dickens to such an extent that he claims that Charles Dickens is stealing from *him*. "There are, at present, tales printed and published in this town, which, in some respects, are imitations of my own peculiar style."[85]

The aftertexts considered in this chapter thus far – *Oliver Twiss, Oliver Twiss, Nickelas Nickelbery*, and more – indicate the hold that Dickens's early creative output had on some of its earlier readers. They in turn created their own Dickensian texts, at the moment when that word entered the English language, and these aftertextual productions, to some extent, define the parameters of that which is Dickensian, perhaps as much as any book by Dickens himself. By assuming names such as Bos and Poz and

Guess, these pseudonymous authors align themselves with Dickens's nom de plume, Boz – in other words, they imitate both his writings and his literary identity. Yet this phenomenon was not the discovery of some latter-day critic. As the *Nickleby* "Proclamation" and *Master Humphrey's Clock* show, Charles Dickens was well aware of some of these aftertexts. Though they infuriated their creator and kidnapped – that is, plagiarized – the children of his fancy, they also made apprehensible aspects of his literary achievement. The novelist would soon decide that it was not sufficient to "write back" at these imitative successors in the pages of his fiction. Instead, he would pursue legal options.

***

... when Boz meddles with law, he is always unfortunate.

– Fraser's Magazine

Aftertexts such as *Scenes from the Life of Nickleby Married* and "Master Humphrey's Turnip" are forms of creative appropriation: Bos and Guess and the authors named Poz reworked Dickensian elements to generate their own, Dickens-like texts.[86] But the novelist was also subject to less imaginative forms of borrowing: publications that reprinted his texts, in whole or in part, without sanction. Such publishers tend to earn the metaphorical title of pirate because they, like legendary pirates on the high seas, pilfer from others.[87] While many scholars have discussed Dickens's quarrel with the American pirates and his demand for international copyright protection, fewer have investigated the role played by domestic pirates, such as the publishers of *Parley's Penny Library* and its successors. In the 1840s, *Parley's* printed unauthorized condensations of *The Old Curiosity Shop, Barnaby Rudge* (1841), *The Pic-Nic Papers, American Notes* (1842), and *A Christmas Carol* (1843). This last resulted in an 1844 Chancery case, in which Dickens, for the first time, sought legal redress from those who offered "cheap and wretched imitations of [his] delectable Works."[88]

Dickens's dispute with the United States is a well-documented episode, and there is little need to rehearse it here. But one point is worth addressing. His complaint against American piracies was not merely a matter of money, despite what some commentators may have claimed. He was distressed by the loss of authorial control: literary copyright implies the power to determine *when* and *by whom* and *under what circumstances* a text may be printed. Dickens argued that his writings could appear "cheek by jowl, with the coarsest and most obscene companions" – that is, he objected to the context in which his work was placed, such as in a "vile, blackguard, and detestable news-paper" fit only "for a water-closet door-mat."[89] In a letter to Lord Brougham, Dickens protests:

> Any wretched halfpenny newspaper can print [an author] at its plea-sure – place him side by side with productions which disgust his common sense – and by means of the companionship in which it constantly shews him, engenders a feeling of association in the minds of a large class of readers, from which he would revolt, and to avoid which he would pay almost any price.[90]

Indeed, Dickens does not lament lost income but rather claims to be willing to pay in order to spare his writings exposure in such "wretched" publications. There is a sense of shame in this complaint; he is concerned with "the minds of a large class of readers." It is the "companionship," the "association" with the low, the vulgar, the pennies and halfpennies, that so wounds him.

One of the most persistent offenders was *Parley's Penny Library; or, Treasury of Knowledge, Entertainment and Delight*; its successor publica-tions include *Parley's Illuminated Library* and *The New Parley Library*. I will consider the piratical efforts of *Parley's* as another form of aftertext and another front in Dickens's battle to assert authorial identity and establish control over his career. In January 1844, *Parley's Illuminated Library* printed "A Christmas Ghost Story," a transparent reduction and reproduction of *A Christmas Carol*.[91] It is worth noting that Dickens, a staunch advocate of copyright, did not bother to thus protect his first Christmas Book until the arrival of the pirated version. On the day after its unwelcome appearance, Dickens wrote to his solicitor, Thomas Mitton, "First, register the copyright as mine."[92]

Parley's began as a penny weekly, in 1841, and it eventually claimed sales of 50,000 to 70,000 copies (which places its gross weekly income over £200).[93] It was "nominally published by John Cleave," whom Clare Pettitt describes as a "working-class radical."[94] He also published *Cleave's London Satirist, and Gazette of Variety*, a four-page newspaper, which sold for a penny and was soon renamed *Cleave's Penny Gazette of Variety*. In 1837 and 1838, the newspaper pirated passages from Dickens's early works, often on the front page. With a certain sense of fairness, Cleave also reprinted excerpts from works that plagiarized Dickens, including *The Penny Pickwick* and *Pickwick Abroad*.[95] As Thackeray quipped, "[T]here are thieves, and other thieves who steal from the first thieves."[96] Although John Cleave's name appears on the title page, *Parley's* was actually

produced by Richard Egan Lee and John Haddock. In 1842, they advertised their printing business (aptly situated in Craven-yard) in the pages of
the *Times*. The advertisement stresses that as "steam machine printers and
stereotypers," Lee and Haddock excel at reproduction and can generate the
equivalent to a *Times* newspaper in thirty hours.[97]

Every few months the weekly issues of *Parley's* were gathered into
volume form and sold for a shilling. An "Address" in the ninth such
volume promises condensations of "costly works" valued at "One
Hundred Guineas ... divested of all their book-maker's verbiage, and
thereby calculated to save *time* as well as money."[98] The term "book-
maker" is telling. There is no author whose literary property is violated;
"book-maker" suggests a craftsman, making but not writing books (again,
"inventio" but not "creatio"). Later, the editors cheerfully note that in
a tale from Alexandre Dumas, "tiresome description and profitless dialogue
will be confined to the limits of readible [*sic*] intelligibility."[99] Dickens, of
course, had already been thus pruned. The first volume contains condensed versions of two of his novels, *Barnaby Rudge* and *The Old
Curiosity Shop*, as well as a tale, "The Lamplighter's Story."[100] *Parley's*
third volume brazenly misquotes the *New Monthly Magazine* of
January 1842 with a piece of hyperbole: "In the first volume of 'PARLEY'S
PENNY LIBRARY' we have the whole of the labour of Charles Dickens for
the last three years, together with that of several other authors of celebrity,
and all at the trifling cost of one shilling!"[101] As insurance, the first volume
includes a dedication "TO THE LIVING SHAKESPEARE, CHARLES
DICKENS."[102] In the event, the living Shakespeare was not mollified. He
complained to Thomas Noon Talfourd, "The fellow who publishes these
Piracies hasn't a penny in the World; but I shall be glad to know, at your
convenience, whether the Law gives us any means of stopping him
short."[103] No action, however, was taken.

Perhaps the piracies are meant to be exonerated by a frame narrative of
middle-class gentility and moral-precept usefulness. Readers learn that
Mr. Parley is a "gentleman of fortune," and his children have plain
English names: Edward, Henry, Jane, Emily. The girls are educated by
a governess, Miss Worthington, and the boys return from "a distant
boarding-school" for the Christmas holiday (2). What follows is
a bourgeois vision of limitless time and leisure for reading and studying –
"amusement and rational recreation," as Mr. Parley dubs it (3). He is an
idealized father/teacher/raconteur/literary advisor. Like a latter-day
Scheherazade, Mr. Parley is a narrative machine; he has a story for every
occasion. "I happen to have in my journal a tale which very closely applies

to present circumstances" is a typical remark (24). The family is eventually joined by his brother, Uncle Peter, a name that suggests the influence of the American writer Samuel Griswold Goodrich; he published a series of books for young people under the pseudonym Peter Parley. Dickens himself met Goodrich in the United States and referred rather testily to "Peter Parley" as "a scoundrel and a Liar."[104] The network of exchange includes George Mogridge, who also borrowed the name Peter Parley and, in 1833, began writing as Old Humphrey, a genial character who may have inspired Dickens when preparing *Master Humphrey's Clock* (although Robert L. Patten locates the name's origin in Thomas Humphreys and Son, clockmakers of York).[105]

Master Humphrey's Clock is remembered today as the launching ground of *The Old Curiosity Shop* and *Barnaby Rudge*; Dickens himself referred to *Master Humphrey's* framing material as "one of the lost books of the earth."[106] But in 1841, when the periodical was Dickens's latest, *Parley's Penny Library* promised that it would be "ANALYTICALLY REPRODUCED" – a curious phrase that indicates both a piracy and a précis (iv). Louis James claims that working-class readers turned to *Parley's* because it was cheaper than Dickens's serial and "easier for them to read."[107] Mrs. Parley recounts "the story about the little girl and her grandfather, which she correctly cites as "'The Old Curiosity Shop,' in 'Master Humphrey's Clock.'" Yet she avers that it is "my own version of the story, from memory" (13). The possessive often creeps into Mrs. Parley's language: "my narrative" and "my story" (196). She effects the role of a serializing novelist and assures her listeners that the "story would rather gain than lose interest by well-timed interruption" (19). *Parley's* analytical reproductions resemble the Lambs' retellings of Shakespeare and twentieth-century *Reader's Digest* condensations.[108] For instance, most of *Curiosity Shop*'s chapter 8 is reduced to a single sentence, whereas the death of Nell is quoted verbatim.[109] In some ways Dickens's narrative is "Victorianized": Quilp's sexual advances on little Nell are gone, as is the club-foot endured by each Mr. Garland; and the masculine features and attainments of Sally Brass are omitted (she is no longer "a kind of amazon at common law").[110] What is most striking is *Parley's* repurposing of the original novel. The insulting remark – "you're a uglier dwarf than can be seen anywhers for a penny"[111] – is quoted (and quietly corrected) with emphasis added, in order to instruct young Edward in "the cruelty and folly of ridiculing deformity" (50). *Parley's Penny Library* reads *The Old Curiosity Shop* not as it is but as the middle classes might want it to be: sentimental, edifying, and short.

The penny weekly relaunched itself in 1843 with a slightly larger format and an increased price (2d.) as *Parley's Illuminated Library*. Like the troubled provenance of the name "Parley," this revised title may owe a debt to Douglas Jerrold's *Illuminated Magazine*, which also began in 1843. On 19 December, Chapman and Hall published *A Christmas Carol. In Prose. Being a Ghost Story of Christmas*, in one volume, price five shillings. It is intriguing to consider that Dickens may have had *Parley's* in mind when he named Scrooge's late business partner, Jacob Marley. *Marley* may be that which is designed to mar (to ruin or injure) a *Parley*. The editors of the penny periodical certainly grasped the phonetic echo. Once the legal battle was enjoined, an article noted, "Since we have not been suffered to see or hear of Marley's ghost, a visitation at this time from that of Mr. Parley may have the same effect."[112]

Beyond the pages of *Parley's*, the *Carol* was usurped by a number of literary opportunists. The *Liverpool Albion* pirated the text as a Christmas offering on 25 December. Three stage adaptations appeared simultaneously, on 5 February 1844. C. Z. Barnett's version, which premièred at the Surrey, for some reason changes the name of Scrooge's former love: Belle is now Ellen (thirteen years before Dickens met Ellen Ternan).[113] The Adelphi production, by Edward Stirling, served a real goose and plum pudding on stage each night for verisimilitude.[114] Dickens attended one performance in February and subsequently wrote, "Oh Heaven! if any forecast of *this* was ever in my mind!"[115]

Prose adapters were no less assiduous than their stage brethren. Some publications merely copy the *form* of Dickens's Christmas Books: small volumes offered for holiday gift-giving and decorated with gold, red, green, or blue. Others rework Dickensian motifs. *The Yule Log, for Everybody's Christmas Hearth*, from 1847, introduces a working-class miser, Abel Chumps, who spurns Christmas in order to spare the expense of hosting a party. In a long dream sequence, he grows rich but loses his family in the process. The most compelling of the various *Carol* variants is probably *Christmas Shadows: A Tale of the Times*. "D. Cranch, Outfitter" is a Scrooge-like clothing manufacturer who pays his female employees as little as eight pence a day (approximately four shillings a week); his clerk, Taplely Tuff, earns 12s. 6d., which is less than Bob Cratchit's 15 bob a week.[116] Early on, Cranch, like Dickens, suffers at the hands of imitators. The clothier develops an advance in the field of advertising, namely, to turn his entire house into a giant billboard – a literal manifestation of household words. "[A]s he was unable to take out a patent for his great advertising discovery, he found, to his grief and sorrow, two or three days afterwards, that [his competitors] had followed his example."[117] Even Cranch cannot gain an edge over the competition without copycats plundering his invention. Ultimately, the miser is redeemed, through the intercession of goblins, not unlike those who visit Gabriel Grubb, in *Pickwick*, and Trotty Veck, in another Dickens Christmas Book, *The Chimes* (1844).

But the imitation that summoned the novelist's wrath and prompted five Chancery suits was "A Christmas Ghost Story." On Saturday 6 January 1844, the sixteen pages of *Parley's Illuminated Library* offered what seems to be the first half of a condensation of *A Christmas Carol*. The condenser, uncredited in *Parley's*, is Henry Hewitt, who performed the same function for *The Old Curiosity Shop* and *Barnaby Rudge*.[118] He called himself "Joint Editor" of the periodical and earned a salary of roughly a pound a week, five shillings more than that of Bob Cratchit, who first appears in Dickens's book employed in a similar act of literary labor, "copying letters."[119]

A typical assumption regarding working-class publications such as *Parley's* is that they degraded and coarsened their sources: "the pirates vulgarized the language in their retelling to make it more suitable for common readers."[120] In fact, "A Christmas Ghost Story" moves in the opposite direction; Hewitt attempts to elevate or poeticize the original through periphrasis, alliteration, and the use of multisyllabic words when one syllable will do. He referred to his mode as "a more artistical [*sic*] style of expression."[121] The result is a narrative that is at once shorter and more long-winded. In keeping with this air of gentility, "A Christmas Ghost Story" opens with epigraphs, those telltale signs of learning deployed by Walter Scott and James Fenimore Cooper but almost never by Dickens. In fact, the "Ghost Story" displays five epigraphs; three are from Shakespeare, although a line from *As You Like It* is wrongly attributed to *The Winter's Tale*. Further, each page of the "Ghost Story" is framed with an elaborate border of marginal poems and aphorisms.

Following the insights of Genette's *Paratexts*, Michael Hancher focuses on the marginalia, the threshold of the *Parley's* narrative. "The marginal poems that frame 'A Christmas Ghost Story' have a doubtful relevance to the text, but they have an independent interest," he writes.[122] Yet his relative neglect of the actual piracy typifies the critical disregard suffered by Dickens aftertexts. E. T. Jaques admits, "I cannot imagine anyone caring to read Hewitt's 'reorigination' for the pleasure of it," and Michael Patrick Hearn refers, dismissively, to "the pedestrian opening of the pirated version."[123] Yet "pedestrian" does not begin to describe the mad, grandiloquent, overwrought, and infuriating opening sentence of Henry Hewitt's version. Recall the pungent first sentence of *A Christmas Carol*: "Marley was dead: to begin with."[124] Now compare the opening of "A Christmas Ghost Story":

> Everybody, as the phrase goes, knew the firm of "Scrooge and Marley;" for though Marley had "long been dead" at the period we have chosen for the commencement of our story, the name of the deceased partner still maintained its place above the warehouse door; somewhat faded, to be sure, but there it was; and consequently the survivor, Scrooge, was addressed, both personally and by letter, sometimes as Scrooge, and sometimes Marley; but that mattered nothing; the old sinner answered as promptly to one name as the other; when his interest was concerned, they were alike to him; but, if solicited as Mr. Marley, to subscribe to a charitable fund – to afford relief to the widow and the orphan – to pluck something of the sharpness of cold and hunger from those on whom the fangs of Poverty had fixed until, like the iron of the captive's chain, they "entered into the soul," – if, as Mr. Marley, Scrooge were invited to such a feast of benevolence, such an exercise of humanity, to which he professed no claim, and of feelings which he avowedly despised, the greedy, grinding, grasping, griping, old miserly miscreant, would chillingly reply, that *he* was not Mr. Marley, and that *he* had something better to do than to waste time, which was the same as money, on farther explanation![125]

Halting, qualifying, battered with commas and inverted commas, this opening nonetheless compresses much of the first stave of the *Carol* into one, admittedly awkward, sentence. There is an anxiety at work here: the author aims for elegance but overreaches. The opening words are particularly revealing: "Everybody, as the phrase goes, knew the firm ..." "Everybody knows" is a favorite phrase of Thackeray's: examples from *Vanity Fair* alone include "an honourable and lucrative post, as everybody knows"; "If success is rare and slow, everybody knows how quick and easy ruin is"; and "Everybody knows the melancholy end of that nobleman."[126] It is a peculiar phrase, because if everybody knows something, why say it? There is of course an implied irony: "Everybody knows" suggests that some people – who are not "Everybody" – do *not* know. Now in Hewitt's version, we find the past tense with an interruption: "Everybody, as the phrase goes, knew ..." Since "Everybody knew" is thus a commonplace, one of the things that everybody presumably knew is the phrase "Everybody knew." Notice what comes next: "Everybody, as the phrase goes, knew the firm of 'Scrooge and Marley' ..." Why is it everybody knew the firm of Scrooge and Marley? Because it appeared in print, on 19 December 1843, in *A Christmas Carol*, which sold thousands of copies. It is a common trope among imitations of Dickens to admit to their secondary status: everybody knows this thing already, yet here I am writing another version.

Taking a cue from the *Carol*, this long sentence emphasizes the interchangeability of Scrooge and Marley.[127] Their dual identity reproduces the doubling of *A Christmas Carol* and "A Christmas Ghost Story." "[W]hen his interest was concerned' – that is, when there is money to be made – Hewitt's Scrooge, like the publication, is happy to be mistaken for another. The opening also demonstrates Hewitt's attempts at literary adornment; he adds alliteration not found in the original. Dickens's Scrooge is "a squeezing, wrenching, grasping, scraping, clutching, covetous old sinner!"[128] Hewitt substitutes a collection of *g*'s and *m*'s: "greedy, grinding, grasping, griping, old miserly miscreant." Overall, *Parley's* Scrooge is meaner – in several senses of the word – than the original. The imitative Scrooge contemplates lowering Bob Cratchit's salary to 12s. 6d. or 10d. a week; and when the clerk asks for a one-day Christmas holiday, his employer in fact reduces his pay to 12s. Whereas Dickens's Scrooge takes "his melancholy dinner in his usual melancholy tavern," Hewitt's dines in a "dingy hole," which must be worse (246).[129] And Scrooge's immortal phrase, "Bah! Humbug!," is rendered as "Psha!," which is shorter but not better (243).

Some of the rewrites in *Parley's* seem arbitrary. Mysteriously, Fezziwig is changed to Fuzziwig. Perhaps this is a transcription error, or perhaps it is a jolt of originality, a dollop of humor: "fuzzy wig" is a more obvious formulation. In the pages of *Parley's*, the Fuzziwig family is made Pickwickian – that is, they attain Pickwickian girth not granted by Dickens's text. "In came Mrs. Fezziwig, one vast substantial smile," writes Dickens. "In came the three Miss Fezziwigs, beaming and loveable."[130] Compare this to Hewitt's version: "Mrs. Fuzziwig, whose vast rotundity of figure, in open rivalry of that of her jovial husband, was made up of one unmistakable and substantial smile." Further, we find that the three "Misses Fuzziwig" are "plump, pleasing, promising girls" – they are well-fed and alliterative, with Pickwickian *p*'s (251). While much of "A Christmas Ghost Story" contracts the original book, in the case of the Fuzziwigs, it is literally an expansion: an instance of an imitative author turning a predilection for jolly, overweight people into a rhetorical principle.

Other alterations inject the maudlin sentiment of which Dickens is often accused and less often culpable. Here is the *Carol*: "Alas for Tiny Tim, he bore a little crutch, and had his limbs supported by an iron frame!"[131] But Hewitt's Tiny Tim is "a poor sickly little cripple" (255): "Alas, for the poor child! He carried a little crutch in his feeble hand, and his limbs were supported by an iron apparatus contrived by the mechanician" (256). Hewitt's version is 50 percent longer; it adds a "feeble"; replaces "frame" with the multisyllabic, Latinate "apparatus"; and for some reason cites the authorship of this apparatus in the form of "the mechanician."

Michael Hancher notes that "A Christmas Ghost Story" removes "extended scenic description" and the narrator's first-person interruptions to the story. On the latter feature, he notes, "*A Christmas Carol* is about Boz almost as much as it is about Scrooge."[132] But the *Carol* was not by Boz; in fact, according to its title page, it is "By Charles Dickens." It is worth noting that this Christmas Book was the first of Dickens's major fictions to be thus attributed in its initial mode of publication; *Pickwick, Oliver Twist, Nicholas Nickleby,* and *Master Humphrey's Clock* were all ascribed to Boz during serial publication and then later claimed by Charles Dickens in volume form.[133] The unnamed narrator is an intrusive presence in the pages of the *Carol*; it is as if Dickens were shaking off the mantle of pseudonymity and laying claim to his own story. For instance, when the Ghost of Christmas Past compels Scrooge to witness the happy, married life of his lost love, the narrator suddenly inserts himself into the proceedings: "What would I not have given to be one of them! Though I never could have been so rude, no, no! I would n't for the wealth of all the world have crushed that braided hair, and torn it down; and for the precious little shoe, I would n't have plucked it off, God bless my soul! to save my life."[134] The long digression that continues from there is absent from "A Christmas Ghost Story," an instance of severing the creator from his work.[135] It is *A Christmas Carol* without the *I* who tells the tale and longs to join the festivities.

At the end of sixteen pages, "A Christmas Ghost Story" leaves its readers mid-sentence – "all was eager expectation;" – no full stop (256). But before the second half could grace the world of letters, fate intervened. Dickens received a copy of the "Ghost Story" on its publication day, Saturday 6 January. On Sunday he instructed Thomas Mitton to seek an injunction.[136] In a piece of fairy-tale coincidence, Sir James Lewis Knight-Bruce, who was Chapman and Hall's counsel in the 1837 *Pickwick* case, now sat as Vice-Chancellor; he granted the injunction on Wednesday

10 January. So the second half of the "Ghost Story," scheduled for Saturday 13 January, never appeared. In the extant copy available at the Bodleian Library, there is a sixteen-page gap in the numbering (257 to 272).[137] During that same January week, Dickens initiated five Chancery suits, one against the perpetrators of *Parley's* (Lee and Haddock) and the rest against booksellers that sold the publication (George Berger, William Mark Clark, John Cleave, and William Strange).[138] Michael Patrick Hearn notes the irony that "the sentiments of good-fellowship and mercy, the tone of *A Christmas Carol*," were not extended to the publishers who chose to reprint those sentiments for profit.[139] The four booksellers acquiesced and eventually compounded. But Lee and Haddock decided to fight.

One question needs to be asked: why did Dickens respond so sharply in the case of the *Carol* when in earlier instances he was merely aggrieved? Some might reply that *A Christmas Carol* was written for money. But it is also true that Dickens's previous books were written for money; for instance, he received a monthly stipend from Chapman and Hall for *Pickwick*, *Nickleby*, and *Master Humphrey's Clock*. I want to suggest that the distinction with the *Carol* was not that the writer was paid but that he was *paying*. For the Christmas Book, he chose to become something of a self-publisher; he paid costs and utilized the resources of Chapman and Hall and their printers. Dickens thus looked to be compensated from the profits. In an oft-cited letter to John Forster, Dickens confesses that he "had set [his] heart and soul upon a Thousand, clear."[140] Lee and Haddock's piracy jeopardized Dickens's share of the proceeds. In other words, when the novelist first undertook legal action against an imitator, it was not as an author whose imaginative terrain had been trampled but as a publisher whose copyright was threatened.

Another possibility is offered by Paul Davis: the pirates of *Parley's* may have conjured memories of "Dickens's secret past" – that is, his degradation as a child laborer at Warren's Blacking. Davis argues, "Venal, vulgar, and greedy men, Lee and Hewitt held up an ugly mirror to the profession of authorship, and by bringing themselves forward as his literary collaborators, they suggested to Dickens that writing was not the way to escape the humiliating association of the blacking factory."[141] The argument, of course, recalls Dickens's dispute with the American pirates, their "wretched halfpenny newspaper," and the "companionship" that the novelist heartily disavowed.[142] This last term also appears in Dickens's autobiographical fragment, when he describes the trials of his early years: "No words can express the secret agony of my soul as I sunk into this

companionship."[143] Rosemarie Bodenheimer makes the connection explicit: "I have come to believe that Dickens's memories of Warren's were of
a piece with his responses to his American critics."[144]

Davis's reading recalls the experience of the Lord Mayor elect, in the first
tale to appear in *Master Humphrey's Clock*. A merchant, who rose from
poverty and obscurity to great wealth, is about to be named the Lord Mayor
of London. On the eve of his installation, "when it might least have been
expected," a ghost of his past returns, one Joe Toddyhigh.[145] They were boys
together at Hull, where they shared pennies and crusts of bread. Joe went to
sea, and the now-wealthy citizen went to London; over the years they lost
touch. Rather than feel joy at the reappearance of his old friend, the Lord
Mayor elect is distressed: "It's very inconvenient. I'd sooner have given
twenty pound – it's very inconvenient, really."[146] Recall that Dickens, in
his letter to Lord Brougham, claims that he "would pay almost any price."
Lee, Haddock, and Henry Hewitt can be read as real-life incarnations of Joe
Toddyhigh; the piratical publishers and their ready hack are the shadowy
other to the literary profession as experienced by Dickens. *Parley's* was issued
weekly for a penny; *Pickwick* and *Nickleby* sold monthly for a shilling. When
he first undertook *The Pickwick Papers*, a monthly serial, Dickens was
warned that it was "a low, cheap form of publication."[147] So it is possible
that he saw Lee, Haddock, and Hewitt as a rejected part of the self –
counterfactuals – that which might have been, had things turned out
differently, had Chapman and Hall not appeared, like the benevolent
Cheeryble brothers in *Nicholas Nickleby*, to invite the young Charles
Dickens to compose text for a comic monthly.[148]

Whether the motivation was economic or a more ineffable psychohis-
torical one, the result was Dickens in Chancery. Legal historian Augustine
Birrell explains that after England's first copyright law, "proceedings in
Chancery became the rule" for cases of infringement.[149] The evidence
produced for this case offers one of the rare instances in which imitators
of Charles Dickens articulate and justify their modus operandi. The
defendants submitted five affidavits, including one from publisher
Richard Egan Lee, one from adapter Henry Hewitt, and one from illustrator George Stiff. The final two deponents are noteworthy because they
were not directly involved in "A Christmas Ghost Story" and seem to have
served as expert witnesses, *avant la lettre*. George Mudie proffered his
credentials, with thirty years of "literary pursuits" and the capitalized title
of "Author."[150] Perhaps Mudie was chosen because his name recalled
Mudie's Select Library, which opened in 1842.[151] The last deponent is
something of a Boz/Bos doppelgänger: Edward Leman Blanchard, not to

be confused with Dickens's friend Samuel Laman Blanchard. As a sometime employee of Lee and Haddock, E. L. Blanchard was not exactly impartial. He earned roughly 10s. each to reduce novels such as Edward Bulwer's *Eugene Aram* (1832) for the pages of *Parley's*.[152]

The affidavits are at times disingenuous, and they repeat, sometimes verbatim, phrases from each another. Collectively, they present five key arguments tendered by Lee and Haddock in defense of their literary practice:

No. 1. In the words of Richard Egan Lee, "[N]o complaint has at any time been made by any . . . authors of this Deponent's treatment of their works."[153] Lee supplies a list of the writers so abridged. In the punctuation-free style of a Chancery affidavit, the list appears to be one titanic, multi-headed, multi-titled author: "Joanna Baillie Mrs. Gore Captain Marryat Sir Edward Lytton Bulwer Lord Byron Messieurs Moore Lockhart Campbell Cooper James Warren."[154] *Parley's* printed without permission extracts and condensations from their writings, without a stir.

No. 2. Nor did Charles Dickens complain when four of his earlier works were poached by *Parley's*. Henry Hewitt claimed that William Hewitt, his son, delivered the first volume of *Parley's Penny Library* (with the "LIVING SHAKESPEARE" dedication) to Dickens as a Christmas present in 1841. By coincidence, William Hewitt was not present in London to testify in 1844.[155] Dickens denied receiving the gift but admitted that he may have forgotten it or burned the offending volume.[156]

No. 3. The different price points indicate different audiences; therefore, *Parley's* was not stealing readers but rather providing a boon to "the humbler classes" who "have neither the time nor money to expend upon large and high priced works."[157] George Mudie concurred that the readers of the twopenny periodical were "a totally different class." *Parley's* was thus "a benefit upon society"; E. L. Blanchard echoes the phrase.[158]

No. 4. Recapitulations of Dickens increase his renown. According to Hewitt, "Such abridgments materially augmented the sale of the original works."[159] Of course, he and his co-deponents offered no evidence. The American pirates made a similar claim in 1842 and suggested that Dickens owed his dissemination to the *lack* of an international copyright agreement; in the words of the *New World*, a plagiarizing newspaper, such was "the secret of his wide spread fame."[160]

And, last, No. 5. Dickens is a plagiarist, too. Hewitt and Blanchard cite Washington Irving as a source for the *Carol*.[161] Incredibly, Hewitt suggests that Dickens found "the germ of more than one of his productions" in the pages of *Parley's*.[162] Lee is more specific. He notes that Hewitt's "The Last of the Lamplighters" contains a comment that Dickens excels at "expressing dreamy and shadowy indistinctness."[163] This observation, made in the context of a Dickens imitation, was alleged to have inspired *A Christmas Carol*. Dickens, of course, survived such charges of plagiarism, and R. H. Horne defended the novelist by insisting, "He is not an imitator of any one."[164]

The Vice-Chancellor found that "A Christmas Ghost Story" was "a mere borrowing" and "not a legitimate use."[165] On 18 January 1844, the counsel for the defense moved to lift the injunction, but the Vice-Chancellor refused. "The pirates are beaten flat," Dickens exclaimed in a letter.[166] Ultimately, he prevailed, but the victory was "emphatically a Pyrrhic one."[167] As his legal counsel prepared to claim damages, Lee and Haddock quietly retreated and turned up on the list of bankrupts, by 23 February.[168] By May, Dickens gave up the "Ghost" and had to absorb hundreds of pounds in legal fees.[169]

* * *

Everything appears to be somebody else's.

– *Martin Chuzzlewit*

To conclude this chapter, I want to consider the *Christmas Carol* case in the context of Dickens's wider career. He may have dropped his Chancery suit in 1844, but he did not let the matter drop entirely. A pair of articles appeared in his journal *Household Words*, and, as Michael Hancher argues, "[T]he triumph of *Bleak House* was born in the disaster of *Dickens v. Lee* and related legal actions."[170] E. T. Jaques concedes that Dickens "found the experience useful," and the *Times Literary Supplement* concurs: "All those who know their 'Bleak House' know that Dickens did not love the Court of Chancery."[171] Some critics have complained that *Bleak House* (1852–53) was anachronistic: its condemnation of Chancery was already out of date. Of course, the novel is set in an earlier period, and Dickens's direct experience took place the decade before. Further, William S. Holdsworth explains that "as the Chancery Commission of 1850 proved, much remained to be done."[172] While Dickens's case was not as protracted as that of *Jarndyce and Jarndyce*, he nevertheless learned the lesson that Richard Carstone fails to heed: "it is better to suffer a great wrong than to have recourse to the much greater wrong of the law."[173]

Fewer commentators have connected the *Carol* case with Dickens's novel then in progress, *Martin Chuzzlewit*, which was published in monthly numbers, from January 1843 to July 1844.[174] While many have noticed that Dickens sent young Martin to America in part to settle some scores and in part to work off unused material gathered for *American Notes*, it is also the case that *Martin Chuzzlewit* discovers a scourge closer to home and is deeply concerned with originality, unoriginality, and spurious creation.[175] Larisa T. Castillo demonstrates the novel's attention to "intellectual property and plagiaristic activity," but she does not mention the plagiarisms that stalked Dickens's success from 1837 to 1844.[176] *Chuzzlewit*, on the other hand, is highly attuned to imitation and imitators. When the novel's Tom Pinch visits the bookshops of Salisbury, he enters "a trying shop":

> where poor Robinson Crusoe stood alone in his might, with dog and hatchet, goat-skin cap and fowling-pieces: calmly surveying Philip Quarll and the host of imitators round him, and calling Mr. Pinch to witness that he, of all the crowd, impressed one solitary foot-print on the shore of boyish memory, whereof the tread of generations should not stir the lightest grain of sand. (54)

Philip Quarll is the hero of Peter Longueville's *The Hermit* (1727), an imitative successor to Daniel Defoe's ever-popular *Robinson Crusoe*. That Defoe himself rallied for copyright protection makes the reference even more pointed. That Robinson Crusoe is described as "poor" suggests his isolation but also his impoverishment at the hands of literary thieves.[177] A "foot-print" is of course one of the quintessential images in Defoe's novel, and Pinch is called on to observe that Crusoe's callow imitators – those successive "generations" – etch no such footprints in the sands of memory.[178]

Indeed, the issue of spurious creation is so integral to *Martin Chuzzlewit* that it informs three of the signature characters in the book: Montague Tigg, Sarah Gamp, and Seth Pecksniff. Montague Tigg turns himself into a new character, christened Tigg Montague. It is a piece of finite imagination worthy of the finite talents of Thomas Peckett Prest, who, writing as Bos, exchanged Samuel Pickwick for Christopher Pickwick, Oliver Twist for Oliver Twiss, and Rudge for Budge.[179]

Mrs. Gamp, too, is a kind of author; she generates an interlocutor for herself named Mrs. Harris. In the tenth monthly number, the narrator reveals "that she was a phantom of Mrs. Gamp's brain – as Messrs. Doe and Roe are fictions of the law" (304). In other words, Mrs. Harris is a fictional character (created by a fictional character). Reproductions of Mrs. Gamp also circulate through the text. For services rendered she sometimes earns a new edition of her "very rusty black gown," which she then sells, so that "the very fetch and ghost of Mrs. Gamp, bonnet and all, might be seen hanging up, any hour in the day, in at least a dozen of the second-hand clothes shops about Holborn" (236). Thus, purchasers could acquire a second-hand Gamp, just as they could a second-hand Dickens in the pages of a penny serial.

But *Chuzzlewit*'s premier progenitor of spurious creation is architect and land surveyor Seth Pecksniff. While remembered as a consummate hypocrite, Pecksniff is also "the novel's great perverter of originality."[180] Gerhard Joseph mentions "the silence on the subject of International Copyright law in *American Notes* and *Martin Chuzzlewit*" and argues that the topic is embedded in the Pecksniff narrative.[181] Like a latter-day Sam Weller or Dick Swiveller, Pecksniff speaks in quotations and borrowed aphorisms; he was "fuller of virtuous precept than a copy-book" (10). From the first monthly number, Pecksniff's mode of verbal replication is apparent:

> "A gentleman taken ill upon the road, has been so very bad up-stairs," said the tearful hostess.
> "A gentleman taken ill upon the road, has been so very bad up-stairs, has he?" repeated Mr. Pecksniff. "Well, well!"
> Now there was nothing that one may call decidedly original in this remark ... (25)

Later:

> "He is better, and quite tranquil," answered Mrs. Lupin.
> "He is better, and quite tranquil," said Mr. Pecksniff. "Very well! ve-ry well!"
> Here again, though the statement was Mrs. Lupin's and not Mr. Pecksniff's, Mr. Pecksniff made it his own and consoled her with it. It was not much when Mrs. Lupin said it, but it was a whole book when Mr. Pecksniff said it. (25)

Pecksniff thus figures the pseudo-Dickenses – Bos, Poz, Guess, and so on – who take possession of someone else's sentiments and make a "whole book" out of them.

In January 1844, the month of "A Christmas Ghost Story" and the Chancery lawsuits, the thirteenth monthly number of *Martin Chuzzlewit* appeared. It is in this number that young Martin and Mark Tapley return to England and encounter Pecksniff's greatest act of plagiarism yet. A schoolhouse, designed by Martin during his time as Pecksniff's pupil, is about to be erected. Pecksniff is on hand for the ground-breaking ceremony as architect and author. In Phiz's drawing, the hypocrite grasps an architectural sketch; bold letters proclaim it to be the work of "PECKSNIFF." Martin expresses some of the anguish that Dickens must have felt when the alchemy of his literary creations was tempered by the baser metals of Bos and others. "I invented it," Martin says of the grammar-school. "I did it all. He has only put four windows in, the villain, and spoilt it!" (415). The four windows may represent the corrupting interpolations of Dickensian aftertexts: four vantage points in (or out of) a literary construction that spoil the view. Ever philosophical, Mark sums up the situation perfectly: "Some architects are clever at making foundations, and some architects are clever at building on 'em when they're made" (416).[182]

That same month, Dickens considered reprinting – that is, pirating – Lee and Haddock's Chancery affidavits and "sewing them up with *Chuzzlewit*."[183] Although he never pursued this curious plan, it suggests that the *Christmas Carol* case was sewn up, at least in his mind, with his latest novel, and it indicates the extent to which the issues of piracy and plagiarism were linked to his own imaginative art. At a time when copyright did little to protect authors from derivative and plagiaristic works, Dickens sought to prove, in fact and in law, that he was indeed Inimitable.

Early imitations of Dickens's fiction illuminate that which is Dickensian – stylistic, formal, even subterranean elements. These strange and rarely read aftertexts improve our understanding of one of the era's foremost figures; they convey, in vivid detail, the Dickens that so enchanted his contemporaries. Of course, the novelist himself could hardly relish the phenomenon. Powerless against the legal free-for-all, he threatened the pirates, redirected his narratives, and altered his modes of publication. Yet in *Nicholas Nickleby*, there appears the possibility of solace. The protagonist gains employment with the Cheeryble brothers and assists Tim Linkinwater, who both generates and treasures the firm's books, which he has kept with meticulous care for nearly forty-four years. Tim observes that Nicholas excels at imitation: "His capital B's and D's are exactly like mine." Encouraged by the advent of this literary clone, Tim is pleased that his life's work will somehow survive him, and he imagines his own posthumous papers with a bit of verbal repetition: "The business will go on when I'm dead as well as it did when I was alive – just the same; and I shall have the satisfaction of knowing that there never were such books – never were such books!"[184]

This "business" would go on for other Victorian novelists as well. Although Dickens inspired a wide range of aftertextual productions, he was not alone, as subsequent chapters will show. Dickensian aftertexts, despite their mercantile intentions and dubious ethics, approach his work with a sense of joy, a compulsive need to prolong the entertainment. But in other cases, imitative authors sought disenchantment; their aim was to wound, to parody, as Edward Bulwer Lytton would find out.

CHAPTER THREE

Parody; or, The Art of Writing
Edward Bulwer Lytton

Our names are not settled till our death.

– Ernest Maltravers

After finishing *Great Expectations*, in June 1861, Charles Dickens visited
Knebworth, the family estate of his friend and fellow author Edward
Bulwer Lytton. The famous (or notorious) result of this encounter was
that Dickens changed the ending of his novel prior to its publication in *All
the Year Round*. Upon sending the last installment of the serial to Bulwer
Lytton, Dickens wrote, "I hope you will like the alteration that is entirely
due to you."[1] While the story of Bulwer Lytton's intervention has
prompted countless responses from Dickens scholars since it was first
revealed, fewer have connected this act of revision with Bulwer Lytton's
redrafting of his own texts.[2] Over several decades, he rewrote some of his
earlier novels in response to critical disapproval. In the case of Edward
Bulwer (later Lytton), parodic aftertexts redirected a major Victorian
career.[3] In what looks like an example of reverse causality, aftertexts,
which came after, may have influenced their sources.

This chapter analyzes Bulwer's prose style and the ways in which it was
imitated, interrogated, and parodied by his contemporaries. The assault
began in the 1830s, when anonymous contributors to *Fraser's Magazine for
Town and Country* made "Bulwer-baiting" a popular pastime.[4] In these
aftertexts, boundaries among criticism, fiction, and parody begin to blur, as
ostensible works of criticism slide into parody and parody offers doses of
insightful critique. Ever-sensitive, Bulwer proffered his theories of fiction
in order to exculpate his often ridiculed literary practice. David Masson
praised this aspect of Bulwer's achievement: "of all British novelists, he
seems to have worked most conscientiously on a theory of the Novel as
a form of literature. This, indeed, may be the very cause of his versatility."[5]
It is also possible that Bulwer's theoretical writings were not the cause but
rather the result of his novelistic practice: a retroactive defense against

parodic aftertexts. Indeed, the "work" of Edward Bulwer, now often neglected or misunderstood, is better reckoned if it includes these after-textual productions. Parody, in short, shaped the career of a best-selling novelist and is a key for readers who hope to fathom his seemingly unfathomable books. Through the correcting lens of aftertexts, readers can perceive his writing with greater clarity.

Bulwer was a prolific, almost inexhaustible, author, who wrote fiction, criticism, poetry, drama, and works of history and sociology. It can be argued that he gave his contemporaries what they wanted: "no one can please the multitude without a considerable portion of power of some sort," conceded the *Spectator*.[6] This chapter foregrounds the fiction produced during his first decade or so as a professional writer (1827 to 1838), when audiences first encountered the assertive Bulwer voice and antagonists made sport of it. From a commercial vantage point, he was undoubtedly successful. For *Pelham*, which Henry Colburn published in 1828, Bulwer was paid £500; for *The Disowned* (appearing in 1828 but bearing a publication date of 1829), Bulwer earned £800; and for the 1829 historical novel *Devereux*, £1,500.[7] *Pelham*, in particular, won critical praise. "It is written by a man who can be both witty and wise, a just and well instructed thinker, a shrewd and exact observer, carrying with his lightest observations a substratum of sound philosophy," claimed the *Examiner*, which proceeded to offer a collection of apposite quotations, or "PELHAMIANA," over the course of two articles.[8] By 1832, Bulwer's latest, *Eugene Aram*, led the *Monthly Magazine* to compare Bulwer favorably with Walter Scott and James Fenimore Cooper: "As a novelist he ranks with the highest."[9]

But there was another view, commenced in the 1830s and carried throughout and beyond Bulwer's lifetime, that he was a charlatan and a very bad writer. This view was consecrated in the twentieth century, with the foundation of a "bad" writing contest in his name.[10] Bulwer's style, which provoked such critical vitriol over so long a period, is now sufficiently obscure that it requires historical reconstruction. A Knebworth domestic servant referred to the master's "attacks of fluency" (meaning *pleurisy*): an inspired malapropism.[11] In 1859, the *National Review* scolded the novelist: "where one word would express his idea most exactly, he uses another because it is more uncommon, more pretentious, more good-looking."[12] Another reviewer describes Bulwer's "affectation, grandiloquence, inordinate love of apostrophe."[13] Michael Sadleir, in his biography, notes the "turgidity," "rhetorical digressions," and "excessive information" in the novels.[14] Thomas Babington Macaulay put the case thus: "His taste is bad."[15]

The style was in some ways atavistic; Bulwer practiced what Demetrius referred to as the "elevated" or "eloquent" style.[16] In particular, Bulwer deployed the "periodic sentence," as exemplified by Renaissance and neoclassical writers, including Samuel Johnson. The periodic sentence suspends meaning through hypotaxis, a series of dependent clauses. The effort is to recreate, in English, the structure of a classical sentence (warning: it is not always successful). Aristotle claims that such a sentence needs a beginning and an end and "must be completed with the sense"; Demetrius, citing an example from Thucydides, finds that "the historian hardly allows a pause to himself or to the reader."[17] Now consider the following sentence from Bulwer's 1833 novel *Godolphin*:

> On his way home, as the stars (that night had been spent in reading) began to wink and fade, he crossed the haunted Almo, renowned of yore for its healing virtues, in whose stream the far-famed *simulacrum*, (the image of Cybele,) which fell from heaven, was wont to be loved with every coming spring; and around his steps, till he gained his home, were the relics and monuments of that superstition which sheds so much beauty over all that, in harsh reasoning, it may be said to degrade; so that his mind, always peculiarly alive to external impressions, was girt, as it were, with an atmosphere favourable both to the lofty speculation and the graceful credulities of romance.[18]

Perhaps unsurprisingly, Bulwer's son, writing a biography of his late father, found himself on the defensive: "Magniloquence is sometimes the natural language of magnanimity."[19]

Paul Clifford may have the best-known opening of all the world's unloved books: "It was a dark and stormy night." But those seven words are merely the beginning of a much longer sentence: "It was a dark and stormy night; the rain fell in torrents – except at occasional intervals, when it was choked by a violent gust of wind which swept up the streets (for it is in London that our scene lies), rattling along the housetops, and fiercely agitating the scanty flame of the lamps that struggled against the darkness."[20] In this case, the sentence is more circular; it concludes with the "darkness" with which it began. It could be further noted that the famous opening is in fact only one variation on a motif that Bulwer frequently employed. In *The Disowned*, published two years before *Paul Clifford*, the narrator reports, "It was an evening of mingled rain and wind"; later, "It was a night of uncommon calm and beauty"; and finally: "It was a stormy and fearful night."[21] Subsequent chapters in *Paul Clifford* offer more variants: "It was a frosty and tolerably clear night" (309) and "The night was frosty and clear" (402). *Eugene Aram*, published two years after *Paul Clifford*, informs readers that "It was a broad and sunny noon."[22] Eugene himself seems to have read Bulwer's earlier narrative, for he explains to Madeline that "robbers generally choose these dark, stormy nights for their designs" (2:123).

Of all the elements of Bulwer's style, the most obvious (and frequently mocked) is his use of Excessive Capitalization. In *Paul Clifford*, one character remarks, "Melancholy ever cronies with Sublimity, and Courage is Sublime" (148). In *Ernest Maltravers*, an internal dialogue takes place between "Conscience" and "Philosophy and Pride"; appropriately, the book's protagonist aspires to "the Beautiful, the Virtuous, and the Great."[23] During dinner, Eugene Aram chats about "the Eternal and all-seeing Ruler of the universe, Destiny, or God" (1:66); courting Madeline, he refers to "Nature," "Wisdom," "Fate," "Past," and "Prophets of our Future!" (2:63–64). Contemporary reviewers were quick to notice the affectation; for instance, the *Westminster Review* observes, "[H]is philosophy consists in beginning certain words with capital letters which nobody else would think of thus honouring."[24] Again, the eighteenth century provided a model for Bulwer's personification of certain nouns, and Sadleir cites the schoolmaster T. R. Hooker as an influence on his pupil in this regard.[25]

An analysis of Bulwer's writing could mention hyperbaton ("Return we ourselves to Lucy") and apostrophe (such as Algernon Mordaunt's evocation of "Beautiful Night!").[26] In the sketch that follows, I will focus on three rhetorical tropes: sententia, periphrasis, and paradiegesis. Reviewing Lord Lytton's career in the year of his death, the *Cornhill Magazine* observed that "[h]is moral is not embodied in his work, but exhibited with all the emphasis of sententious aphorisms." Further, "[t]he writer is evidently determined that we shall not overlook his claims to be a teacher to mankind."[27] The narrator of *Paul Clifford* announces, "Love refines every roughness; and the truth which nurtures tenderness is never barren of grace" (237). A nugget from *The Disowned* is more political: "In England, not to be rich is not to be virtuous. Poverty is a crime."[28] By 1859, the *National Review* could argue that "a treasury of the author's wisdom" might be drawn from the pages of his novels.[29] In fact, *A Lytton Treasury*, *The Bulwer Lytton Birthday Book*, and *The Wit and Wisdom of Edward Bulwer Lord Lytton with Impressive Humorous and Pathetic Passages from His Works* all rise to the challenge.[30]

In addition to sententia, periphrasis is a hallmark of the windy Bulwer style. As early as 1834, the *Literary and Theological Review* could exclaim, "His volubility is astonishing."[31] Where one word might suffice, Bulwer

uses three, four, seventeen. Rome is "that immortal city, along the Appia
Via"; a policeman is "one officer in the preventative service"; a prostitute is
"one of those unfortunate women, who earn their polluted sustenance by
becoming the hypocrites of passion"; and pickpockets are "those mercurial
gentry who are afflicted with the morbid curiosity to pry into the mysteries
of their neighbours' pockets."[32] When time passes, the narrator of *The
Disowned* mentions "thirty-two legitimate revolutions of the sun" (as
opposed to illegitimate revolutions).[33] Rather than merely "strong," Paul
Clifford is

> a man in whom a much larger share of sinews and muscle than is usually the
> lot even of the strong had been hardened, by perpetual exercise, into
> a consistency and iron firmness which linked power and activity into
> a union scarcely less remarkable than that immortalised in the glorious
> beauty of the sculpted gladiator. (335)

It should be noted that this fifty-five-word description appears, disruptively,
in the middle of a fight scene. Outside of his fiction, Bulwer could be equally
verbose. Sir Frederick Rogers, commenting on Bulwer Lytton's work in
Parliament, observed that "Sir Edward writes perfect volumes of minutes."[34]

Joining *sententia* and *periphrasis* is *paradiegesis.* The *Literary and
Theological Review* argues that Bulwer's narrator "is continually stepping
on the stage, prompting, assisting, and occasionally officiating in toto."[35]
Expressing impatience, the *Monthly Review* warns that "[a] novel is taken
up ninety-nine times out of a hundred, not only by young ladies, to get to
the end of it without being interrupted by impertinencies – by any thing
which obliges the reader to stop and inquire."[36] *Eugene Aram*, among the
early novels, is especially paradiegetic. Sadleir argues that with the narrative
of this eighteenth-century scholar-murderer, the novelist "was tempted to
out-Bulwer Bulwer."[37] Late in the second volume, the narrator muses, "It
is precisely at this part of my history that I love to pause for a moment;
a sort of breathing interval between the cloud that has long been gathering,
and the storm that is about to burst" (2:247). Note that in this interruption,
it is "my history" – that is, the narrator's, not that of the eponymous hero,
Eugene Aram. And if there were any lingering doubt about who this
narrating *I* actually is, he sometimes chimes in with personal anecdotes.
After gypsies make an appearance in the third volume, the narrator
reminisces, "When I was a mere boy, and bent on solitary excursion over
parts of England and Scotland, I saw something of that wild people" (3:11).

This trope bears some structural resemblance to the more-familiar free
indirect discourse – the merging or intermingling of more than one voice

or perspective. Rather than a character penetrating the space of narration, in paradiegesis it is the author or some other narrative or narrator. Bulwer's use of this trope suggests that he was a witting participant in his style and not an obtuse blunderer: paradiegesis implies control, the power to arrest, redirect, or reflect on a narrative. Moreover, Bulwer, like the person who makes self-deprecating remarks to disarm an opponent, could readily identify his literary deficits, for instance, in *The Disowned*: "These digressions and egotisms will be the ruin of my book!"[38]

Thus, readers and reviewers in the late 1820s and early 1830s found themselves confronted with a big, new authorial voice – sententious, periphrastic, and prone to rhetorical flights and displays of erudition – a profound moralist or a shady charlatan. Either way, here was an alarmingly successful voice in the marketplace of fiction.

***

Genius makes many enemies.

– Eugene Aram

Wherever there is a popular novelist, there is a critic training his or her sights on the target. The literary assault on Edward Bulwer arrived early and lasted long. When his fourth novel, *Devereux*, appeared, the *Athenaeum* chided the writer's "ignorant dogmatism and school-boy conceit," "indescribable impertinence," and "ostentatious theories" with "truisms for their premises, and for their conclusions blunders."[39] In 1832, Bulwer's works were compared unfavorably with *Zohrab the Hostage*.[40] By 1846, the *Morning Chronicle* could discern "a hero of the Lyttonian order" and "the prodigious pomposity of his language."[41] After the novelist's death, in 1873, the *Cornhill* could still complain of characters "apostrophising the heavenly bodies, and talking sham philosophy about the true and the beautiful."[42] Such attacks are perhaps inevitable, as the *Westminster Review* explains: "satirists, caricaturists, and critics feel that the successful are their fair game – their legitimate subjects."[43]

But what is most remarkable about the critical reaction to the works of Edward Bulwer is that journalists and other commentators, consciously or unconsciously, frequently imitated the style they professed to disdain. Bulwerese is an illness, and it is contagious. For example, one twentieth-century biography opens with a sentence that could have been composed by the master:

> The old-fashioned synonym for the novel – the *romance* – is specially applicable to the prose fiction, mastery in which forms the most enduring

Figure 3 William Makepeace Thackeray, pictorial capital for chapter 13,
"Sentimental and Otherwise," in *Vanity Fair*, no. 4 (April 1847). Self-regarding
George Osborne here resembles contemporary caricatures of Thackeray's rival and
friend Edward George Earle Lytton Bulwer Lytton

title to popularity not only of Edward Bulwer, the first Lord Lytton, but of
those among his contemporaries who were, like him, the literary descen-
dants of Sir Walter Scott.[44]

As late as the 1970s, when his hold on the imagination had certainly faded,
at least one critic writing on Bulwer could still fall prey to Bulwerian
capitals: "the World," "Blood," "Wit and Fashion."[45]

The phenomenon did not require a retrospective view or a long gesta-
tion period. The *Edinburgh Review*, taking up *Eugene Aram* after failing to
notice some of the earlier novels, slides into emphatic Bulwerese: the book
"made it seem as if the Genius of Romance had snatched the pen of History
for a moment."[46] A *Times* review of *Ernest Maltravers* begins to recount the

narrative thus: "One stormy night a young traveller ..."[47] Bulwer appended the three-volume *Maltravers* with another triple-decker, *Alice; or, The Mysteries*, in 1838. In a *Times* review of the sequel, the reviewer upbraids the loquacious novelist and, in so doing, approximates the prolixity of the original: "it appears that the first thousand pages were only half-sufficient to describe the actions, and passions, the philosophy, the morals, the politics, the poetics, and the thousand varieties of sentiment and adventure which our interesting young moralist was to experience in the course of his journey after the truth."[48] This reviewer uses copia to approximate the copiousness of the novel in question, and the repetition here of "thousand" suggests the perpetual narration of *One Thousand and One Nights*.

Sometimes the line between the critic and his subject vanishes altogether. A purported review turns into imitation; imitation veers into parody. In 1843, the *Westminster Review* noticed a collected edition of Sir Edward Bulwer's writings (thus far) and reprimanded the author with some of his own ostentatious capitals: "In Art there are two inseparable things – the Real and the Ideal – which he seems to have severed." The review continues with a jumbled discourse that could have been lifted from the pages of *The Disowned* or *Eugene Aram*:

> By the Real we mean conceptions of Life viewed in reference to Truth: by the Ideal, conceptions of Life viewed in reference to Art. Truth and Art do not differ. Art is Beautiful Truth. Express the result of Evidence, and you have Truth. Represent your conceptions of the Beautiful, and you have Art. Delineate Truth, the delineation is the Real: portray Beauty, and the portraiture is the Ideal. The Ideal is Artistic Reality. Let it not be dreamed that Genius is restrained by being Chained to Reality.[49]

Is this a parody? The rest of the article is rather earnest. It is possible that the unnamed reviewer is fighting fire with fire and employing Bulwerian prose to disprove the novelist's conceptions of art using his own terminological and stylistic tools – as Sadleir put it, to out-Bulwer Bulwer. The lines that usually demarcate forms of writing – criticism and parody, for instance – begin to blur. Contemporary reviewers of Bulwer veered into the parodic, and they used parody, wittingly or otherwise, in order to form critical judgments.

Arthur Quiller-Couch, in his foreword to a 1912 parody collection, argues "that Parody must be a form of Criticism, and may be enlightening as it is vivacious," and Richard Poirier agrees: "Parody has always had the function of literary criticism."[50] Moreover, parody is "the watchdog of national interests" and "tends to be the watch-dog [sic] of established forms, a correction of literary extremes."[51] In these terms, Bulwer's fiction of the 1830s *was* extreme and needed the "correction" of self-appointed critical watchdogs. As Linda Hutcheon explains, "[P]arodies were used in English literature as a means of control of excesses in literary fashion."[52] A trick of the parodist (like that of the caricaturist) is to seize on an obvious excess, to repeat and amplify it, to make it emblematic of the whole, in a form of synecdoche. The process recalls Henri Bergson's theoretical writings on comedy: "To imitate any one is to bring out the element of automation he has allowed to creep into his person."[53] Just as imitators of Dickens seized on (and defined) the Dickensian, parodists of Edward Bulwer isolated moments when the novelist was being most Bulwer-like, most automated in his arrangement of literary tropes.

Besides the intentional or unintentional reproduction of Bulwer's style in reviews, formal parodies flourished from the 1830s onward. Walter Hamilton, the editor of a six-volume collection of parody, finds that "Lord Lytton's poetry does not appear to have offered much temptation to the parodists, probably because none of it became truly popular."[54] Bulwer's novels, on the other hand, *were* popular with contemporary readers (and parodists). In fact, when Hamilton describes parody's targets in his introduction, it sounds as if he is summarizing the critical charge against Bulwer's fiction: "stilted language," "grandiloquent phrases," "poverty of ideas," "sham sentiment," and "mawkish affectations."[55] Parody, in Hamilton's terms, seems to have been born to analyze and disinfect the prose of Edward Bulwer.

The most persistent and virulent attacks on the novelist came from *Fraser's Magazine for Town and Country*, a Tory monthly launched in February 1830. *Fraser's* was the brainchild of William Maginn, an Irishman, educated at Trinity College, Dublin, who previously contributed to the *Quarterly Review*, the *Literary Gazette*, and other journals. In his way, Maginn was as prolific as Edward Bulwer.[56] *Fraser's* was published by James Fraser but, confusingly, it was named for Hugh Fraser, who supplied the financing.[57] Gordon N. Ray calls the periodical "an avowed imitation of the famous *Blackwood's Magazine*."[58] Each monthly issue was usually 126 pages of double-column print. Miriam Thrall, in her history of *Fraser's*, notes that it was a forerunner to *Punch* (founded in 1841). Despite *Fraser's* comic thrusts, however, she finds a "dogged conviction" underneath the "levity."[59] Starting with the third issue (April 1830), *Fraser's* began its anti-Bulwer campaign. The novelist himself later referred to "a kind of ribald impertinence offered, so far as I can remember, to no other writer of my time."[60]

Fraser's deployed articles, reviews, fictional letters, the memoirs of a footman, and overt parodies in order to rib and ridicule Edward Bulwer. As in the case of some of the previously mentioned parodic reviews, there was a blurring of boundaries: a review turns parodic, and a parody delivers a cutting critique. Bulwer's first appearance in the magazine was in a list of Fraserian bugbears: "Robert Montgomeryism, Lytton Bulwerism, Colburn and Bentleyism, and Jeremy Benthamism."[61] Bulwer, at this stage, was thus associated with his publishers, Henry Colburn and Richard Bentley (during their short-lived partnership); indeed, *Fraser's* refers to "the Colburn and Bentley school of novel-writing."[62] While ostensibly reviewing another novelist, an anonymous contributor stops to praise *Pelham* ("full of light and pleasant writing").[63] But the review also attacks one of Bulwer's favorite devices, sententia, and accuses him of plagiarism. "Many aphorisms are undoubtedly set forth in the novel," but the reviewer is willing to show that they were lifted from "Rochefoucault's [*sic*] *Book of Maxims* and Colton's *Lacon*."[64]

The volubility of the novelist was addressed two months later, in an article entitled "Mr. Edward Lytton Bulwer's Novels; and Remarks on Novel-Writing." According to this piece, Bulwer could "produce a volume a month with perfect ease, till appetite were dulled and the sense palled with repetition."[65] Parodically or otherwise, this article uses Bulwerian hyperbaton ("turn we to *Paul Clifford*").[66] Further, it mentions the satirical portrait of renegade journalist Peter Mac Grawler (Bulwer inserts the space) as the novelist's attempt "to take his revenge of *Blackwood's Magazine and of ourselves*."[67] Keith Hollingsworth argues that Bulwer caricatured the Irishman Maginn as the Scotsman Mac Grawler; both were sometime schoolmasters, both perpetually low in funds.[68] This same lengthy article also offers one of *Fraser's* many diatribes against "puffs," positive critical comments inserted in friendly or publisher-owned journals. The reviewer quotes Colburn and Bentley puffs indicating that Bulwer's latest is an improvement over its predecessors. In particular, the novelist seems to be cured (at least for the moment) of paradiegesis: *Paul Clifford*, one puff pronounces, "admits of no digression or grave reflection."[69] Nonetheless, Bulwer's tautological style is mocked in a piece of parody: "If we would walk, we must have legs, though exercise be requisite to give facility to walking."[70] Note that this sentence begins with "walk" and ends with "walking" – the ABA pattern suggests that the axiom is walking in circles.[71]

"Epistles to the Literati. No. I" takes the form of a fictional letter to "E. L. Bulwer" from the pseudonym "Robin Roughhead."[72] In November 1831, Bulwer took over the editorship of Colburn's *New Monthly Magazine*; entering *Fraser's* territory, he was subject to a fresh attack. The letter suggests that Bulwer was out of his depth: while novels are easy, magazines are hard. In making this case, Roughhead offers a prescription for writing fashionable novels (of which *Pelham* is an example): "all that is required is a tolerable acquaintance with footmen and butlers, which can be easily picked up by any ingenious gentleman who will feed these functionaries a few pots of ale, reinforced by an occasional half-crown."[73] The "Epistle" turns personal when it provides an anecdote about Bulwer's brother Henry and calls him "BRANDY BULWER."[74] Parody also appears. The letter ventriloquizes Edward Bulwer and makes him apostrophize the press: "Puff me, O thou *Times*! Extol me, Black of the *Chronicle*! Be merciful to me, O *Examiner*! Look with compassion upon me, man of the *Globe*!"[75] Bulwer, as depicted by *Fraser's*, is callow, craven, and focused on worldly success.

Even Thomas Carlyle joined the Fraserian merriment. The long-lived Scottish writer might have seemed a natural ally to Bulwer, influenced as they both were by German thinkers and prone as they both were to capitalization and the collation of multiple voices. Margaret F. King and Elliot Engel find "the Carlylean romantic hero" represented in Bulwer's novels of the 1830s, although their reading does not take into account stylistic similarities.[76] Bulwer himself may have noticed an affinity. As editor of the *New Monthly* (a post he held until August 1833), he sought contributions from the older writer. However, in a letter, Carlyle refers to Bulwer as "the Mystagogue of the Dandiacal Body"; and in another letter, he is more cutting: "The Pelham-and-Devereux manufacture is a sort of thing which ought to be extinguished in British Literature" – "manufacture" of course suggests something inartistic and mechanical.[77] While resistant to Bulwer's courtship, Carlyle contributed to *Fraser's Magazine*: his *Sartor Resartus* appeared there anonymously, from 1833 to 1834. As if in keeping with house policy, the author parodies Bulwer in a chapter entitled "The Dandiacal Body," which identifies someone named "*Pelham*" (that is, Edward Bulwer) as the "Teacher and Preacher" of the fashionable set. The chapter goes on to quote "Seven distinct Articles," a comic echo of the thirty-nine articles of the Christian faith. The word "Articles," it should be noted, puns triply on articles of faith, articles of clothing, and articles produced for periodicals.[78] In the view of *Sartor Resartus*, like that of its host magazine, Bulwer was vain, superficial, dandiacal.

But the two most vigorous attacks during the early flowering of anti-Bulwerism are probably "Autobiography of Edward Lytton Bulwer, Esq." and "Elizabeth Brownrigge." Both published anonymously, they are likely the work of William Maginn.[79] The first of these aftertexts is a striking example of the formal hybridity that occurs so frequently in writings on Bulwer. The occasion was an article in the May 1831 *New Monthly*, "Living Literary Characters, no. V. *Edward Lytton Bulwer*."[80] Like much nineteenth-century journalism, this piece appeared anonymously, but *Fraser's* was quick to assume that Bulwer (a contributor but not yet editor) wrote the pages under the veil of anonymity. Bulwer, according to *Fraser's* reading of the *New Monthly*, has eclipsed Voltaire, Oliver Goldsmith, and Henry Fielding; *Fraser's*, to the contrary, backs "Anne of Swansea" against the upstart novelist.[81] Further, "Autobiography of Edward Lytton Bulwer, Esq." makes an early use of the adjective *Bulwerian* – "Bulwerian maxims" (i.e. sententia) and "Bulwerian writings" – almost a decade before the first appearance of *Dickensian*.[82]

The centerpiece of the *Fraser's* riposte is a series of direct quotations from the *New Monthly* article; in *Fraser's*, verbatim quotation becomes a form of parody. A new context changes or rearticulates a piece of text. The effect is similar to that of a passage in Jorge Luis Borges's "Pierre Menard, Author of the Quixote": two selections are placed in proximity, one from Cervantes's *Quixote* and one from Menard's.[83] They are literally the same, but the narrator reads them differently because of their different sources.

Fraser's offers a series of numbered categories, such as "*Mr. Bulwer upon himself in general*."[84] Each is then followed by direct quotation from the *New Monthly*. The result is a Lytton treasury of extracts (before the late Victorians and Edwardians took up the task). Under category no. 2, "*Mr. Bulwer's opinion of 'Weeds and Wild Flowers,' 'The Rebel,' and his first prose work, 'Falkland,'*" *Fraser's* quotes the *New Monthly* thus: "Each of these productions bears the same stamp – the broad arrow of genius. But they were too selfishly beautiful."[85] Sometimes the greatest parody is the thing itself. Category no. 6 is "*Mr. Bulwer's parallel in the manner of Plutarch, between Pelham and Devereux*." And here is the *New Monthly*: "It is curious to mark the likeness of position and the dissimilarity of character between Pelham and Devereux."[86] At this point *Fraser's* adds a direct parody: "It is curious to mark the likeness of position and the dissimilarity of character, between Charles Wright and Edward Bulwer."[87]

Thus, the novelist is compared to a professional puffmonger. *Fraser's* goes on to quote the *New Monthly*'s opinions on the press ("The truth is, we have no great literary Review") and on fellow authors ("Who shall deny that the great body of critics are made up of unsuccessful writers?").[88] It is a fascinating performance. In this aftertext Bulwer is made to look pompous, buffoonish: a perfect self-parody.

Of course, there is the possibility that *Fraser's Magazine* was wrong in its attribution and that "Living Literary Characters" was not the work of nemesis Edward Bulwer. The *Fraser's* article deems it to be an "Autobiography," as if wishing it were so, when in fact it may simply be "Biography." *The Wellesley Index to Victorian Periodicals* suggests that Letitia Elizabeth Landon is instead the author of the *New Monthly* article.[89] If so, her work suggests the contagion that is Bulwerese: to write about Edward Bulwer is to write like Edward Bulwer. *Fraser's* thus quotes an imitation in order to parody the source.

"Elizabeth Brownrigge," in contrast, is a formal parody of Bulwer's writings, in particular the Newgate-scented *Eugene Aram*, which appeared earlier the same year.[90] Elizabeth Brownrigg (without the final *e*) was, like Aram, an historical figure; she was hanged at Newgate in 1767. Further, Elizabeth, as depicted in *Fraser's*, is a female Eugene: a philosopher, a paragon, a murderer. Hollingsworth finds that the parodic story "imitat[es] *Aram* closely at a hundred points."[91] The *Fraser's* narrative is framed by another fictional letter, from an unnamed author who wants to emulate Bulwer's novel in order to succeed in fiction. "I have been taught by *Eugene Aram* to mix vice and virtue up together in such an inextricable confusion as to render it impossible that any preference should be given to either" (67).

Periphrasis, naturally, is prominent in the parody that follows: Queen Elizabeth I is referred to as "the virgin daughter of the eighth Henry" (69), and doctors are called "three eminent disciples of Esculapius" (136). The magazine wields a form of mock-sententia, with such allusive and empty wisdom as "It is not more certainly true, that 'nothing can come of nothing,' than that 'something always comes of something'" (136). A good example of paradiegesis occurs in the second part of the story: "I need not remind my antiquarian readers, that while in the benighted days of the eighteenth century no mantua-maker had yet advanced so far in the march of intellect as to approach the discovery of a reticule, the lap-dogs of those times were small, and the pockets were capacious" (132). Besides these three tropes, "Elizabeth Brownrigge" exploits hyperbaton ("Young they were ... Beautiful they were" [74]) and Bulwer's cumbersome dialogue tags ("ejaculated the uxorious apothecary" [77]).

Bulwer was not alone among the heirs to Walter Scott in producing variously anachronistic or hypercorrect historical fiction; yet in "Elizabeth Brownrigge," Bulwer is taken to task with parodic statements such as "It was somewhere about twelve o'clock on a fine, bright, sunny day, 25th of June, 1765" (70). Elizabeth dates a letter "*July* 1, A.D. 1765, N.S." (140) – as if it could be B.C. Her lover, with the suitably grand name of Alphonso Belvidere, is himself, conspicuously, "editor of a new monthly magazine" (74). *Fraser's* captures the pretentious talk of Bulwer's young lovers when Alphonso cries, "Why interdict my tongue from delivering the sentiments which are prompted by the warm, fresh-springing, and genuine emotions of my soul?" (75). But the sternest parody is reserved for Elizabeth herself. When an angry mob accosts her for murdering her apprentices, Elizabeth muses philosophically. The only thing worse than a soliloquizing fictional character is one who soliloquizes when others are near.

***

Who can keep quiet when the tarantula bites him?

– Edward Bulwer Lytton

The Fraserian view of Bulwer was one that few writers, thus afflicted, would enjoy, and the situation was exacerbated by the novelist's sensitivity. In his memoirs he admits, "Always throughout my career, I have been too thin-skinned and sensitive."[92] Wounded, Bulwer built a defense in his fiction and non-fiction. As Macaulay asked him in 1842, "What writer's place in the estimation of mankind was ever fixed by any writings except his own?"[93] Bulwer was determined to fix his own place by mounting – in various places and by no means consistently – his theories of the novel.

Stray remarks in the early fiction show the extent to which Bulwer felt obliged to respond to the negative criticisms he undoubtedly read. Apropos of nothing, characters articulate theories of literature, settle scores with the novelist's enemies, consider or pursue careers as writers, or suddenly recall a literary anecdote. *Godolphin* refers to "the thorns that beset the paths of literature" (87). In *The Disowned*, characters disapprove of both satire and parody. Talbot says, "Satire is a dwarf, which stands on the shoulders of the giant Ill-Nature." Another character remarks, "Pooh, a parody is no criticism: one might make a duck-pond out of a fountain."[94] In other instances, narrators praise the Bulwerian style that reviewers found so tiresome. According to *Paul Clifford*, a novelist is one who "spin[s] forth, in prolix pleasure, the quiet yarn of his entertainment" (449). Another narrator remarks that "[i]n the components of the novel we study mankind – in the soliloquy we study man."[95] Clearly, Bulwer was not slow to praise his own periphrasis and paradiegesis.

The second volume of *The Disowned* opens with a dialogue between a "bookseller" and "a friend of ours" (possibly Edward Bulwer). The bookseller advises the friend, who is a writer, to employ more dialogue in his fiction: "we want a little conversation in fashionable life – a little elegant chitchat or so . . . we must have something light, and witty, and entertaining."[96] Later, the narrative stops so that Talbot can explain why, unlike the publisher's unnamed "friend," he did *not* pursue a literary career. "Those terrible feuds – those vehement altercations – that recrimination of eloquent abuse, which seem inseparable from literary life, appear to me too dreadful for a man not utterly hardened or malevolent, voluntarily to encounter. Good Heavens! what acerbity sours the blood of an author!"[97]

In *Paul Clifford*, the hardened and malevolent do pursue the field of letters; indeed, literature and crime frequently intermingle. At the age of sixteen, Paul himself is an "embryo rogue," although he has pretentions to poetry (52). Before pursuing a career as a robber, he falls under the tutelage of Peter Mac Grawler, editor of the satirically named *Asinaeum*, "which was written to prove, that whatever is popular is necessarily bad" (22). Bulwer satirizes William Maginn and others in the critical fraternity with the amusing lessons that Mac Grawler provides. The tutor offers a taxonomy of nineteenth-century reviewing: the "slash," the "plaster," the "tickle." To slash a work, "you must cut up your book right and left, top and bottom, root and branch" (56). Mac Grawler also improvises parodic representations of periodical reviews. Here is his example of "the encouraging tickle": "Although this work is full of faults; though the characters are unnatural, the plot utterly improbable, the thoughts hackneyed, and the style ungrammatical; yet we would by no means discourage the author from proceeding" (56). The "facetious tickle" seems to have Edward Bulwer in mind: "Some fine ladies think him a great philosopher, and he has been praised in our hearing by some Cambridge Fellows for his knowledge of fashionable society" (56–57). Mac Grawler also instructs his young charge in the art of choosing extracts, which requires reading at least a few pages of the work in question. When Paul begins his apprenticeship as a periodical writer, completing assignments subcontracted to him by Mac Grawler, the tutor keeps 75 or 100 percent of the earnings. The young man soon turns to a life of crime, which is more remunerative.

Elsewhere in *Paul Clifford*, writing and criminal activity are closely linked. The eminently quotable Augustus Tomlinson offers various aphorisms such as "All crime and all excellence depend upon a good choice of words" (109) and "Knave I am, and knave I must be to the end of the chapter!" (329).[98] Even in Paul's career as a highway robber, the link continues. "On this paper you will see your destinations fixed," Paul explains to his crew; now his writing indicates locations for criminal pursuits (206). When robbing a gentleman who is low on cash, Paul agrees to accept a cheque for fifty guineas. The narrator then explains that Paul "was searching in his pockets for writing implements, which he always carried about him" (150). Paul, the aspiring poet turned thief, never goes to work without pen and paper.

As the Mac Grawler episode shows, Bulwer, the subject of so many parodies, could himself produce parody on occasion. Like Mac Grawler, he generated a parody of literary criticism when, perhaps unethically, he reviewed his own novel.[99] *Godolphin* was published anonymously, and the June 1833 *New Monthly Magazine* discusses it in an anonymous article, attributed to Edward Bulwer. The review emphasizes the mystery of the novel's authorship: "'Godolphin' is the work, to all appearance, (for the author is unknown,) of an idle but cultivated person of genius."[100] The reviewer refuses to guess the writer's gender and suggests, misleadingly, that the work could be "by two hands, or by an unpracticed novelist."[101] The notion of "two hands" is striking because it suggests collaboration or a single person who is ambidextrous; in parody, one writes as the parodist and as the parodee at the same time, as if with two hands. Further, the article suggests that *Godolphin* emulates the novels of Edward Bulwer: "The style of the work is an evident imitation of that of a certain author whose novels have been popular beyond their merit; but this is only a style of words and aphorisms, – the style of mind is essentially different."[102] Thus, the anonymous author of *Godolphin* is able to replicate the verbal style of the novelist but not his essence. In short: Bulwer, in a parodic review of Bulwer, accuses Bulwer of plagiarizing from Bulwer.

He parodies the more slashing type of critique in an unpublished review of *The Vicar of Wakefield* (1766), written as if by a hard-hitting contemporary. "Dr. Goldsmith is a writer not without some merit," Bulwer begins, in typical magazine style.

> His compilations deserve the praise of industry; and although, from the total want of philosophical arrangement and accurate research, they can never become authorities with the learned, nor even useful as books of reference

for readers of maturer years, they have a certain ease of style which will adapt them to the comprehension of the young; so that, with the corrections of a careful preceptor, they may serve as elementary manuals for children between the age of eight and twelve.[103]

In other words, Goldsmith's eighteenth-century classic is suitable as a schoolbook for a ten-year-old. Then the critical knife plunges: "A sense of the duties we owe to the public alone compels us to expose the false sentimentality, the monstrous absurdities, the pernicious moral of a book that, under the popular garb of fiction, might otherwise steal its poisonous way to the domestic hearth, to demoralise our sons and corrupt our daughters."[104] Bulwer's own son found this parody to be a *"jeu d'esprit,"* but the harshness suggests that Bulwer was exorcising demons of the periodical variety.[105]

Another formal experiment – and another dose of parody – appears in the preface to the second edition of *The Disowned*. It is a proto-postmodern dialogue between an unnamed "Author" and his fictional character Henry Pelham. The Author wants to sever himself from his creation: "I will give notice of lawful separation, and become henceforth answerable for no sins but my own."[106] Pelham, ever insouciant, offers his creator advice on novel-writing and proceeds to model the fashionable and historical forms. For the fashionable novel, he advises: "Have bustle, black ringlets, fighting, moon light, a waste moor, a ruin, two or three witty fellows in low life, a fascinating villain, who is very pale – no villain has a colour – all dialogue, even if it be, 'How do you do?' and 'Pretty well.'"[107] And here is Pelham's parody of historical fiction: "It was the 1st of April, 1774–5, or 6 . . . when the hands of the old Dutch clock, with a black face and red fingers, pointed to twenty-one minutes before twelve, that youthful Anabotomas Micklethwayte mounted his bay gelding."[108]

As Bulwer's ability to reproduce the style of hack journalism or historical fiction suggests, imitation stands at the center of his literary practice and theory. In childhood he imitated *Reliques of Ancient English Poetry* (1765), and he recalled his youthful experience of poets he admired: "I marvelled, and I mimicked."[109] In *A Word to the Public*, the 1847 pamphlet that defends his fiction against journalistic attacks, he plainly states, "I cannot claim the merit of originality."[110] R. H. Horne faults Bulwer for his studied style: "He constructs upon system, rather than upon sensation; and works by model, and with little help from instinct."[111] Bulwer happily agreed: "*art* does not come from inspiration."[112] For his first full-fledged novel, *Pelham*, he "had studied with no slight attention the great works of [his] predecessors, and had sought to derive from that study rules and canons to serve [him] as a guide."[113] In Bulwer's economy, reading turns into writing, as he explains to John Forster in an 1838 letter: "Not a subject to be found, though I have read for it like a tiger."[114] Similarly, Ernest Maltravers, a version of the novelist, "read till he became inspired."[115] Bulwer perhaps took this system too far when he exploited *Tristram Shandy* in *The Caxtons* (1848–49) and *My Novel* (1850–53), which Thompson Cooper calls "direct and poor imitations of Sterne for which Lord Lytton had not the requisite humour."[116] Cooper's critique fails to consider that Bulwer may have been channeling *Tristram Shandy* for years: the paradiegesis, the classical erudition, and the prolix nonsense all owe a debt to Sterne. In the words of the *Cornhill Magazine*, Bulwer was "ingenious at restoring the old."[117] To some extent, this was his strength: drawing on classical and eighteenth-century predecessors and distilling them into the popular forms of the day, such as fashionable, Newgate, and historical fiction. That Bulwer, always ready to restore the old ("inventio" rather than "creatio"), was himself the source of so many aftertexts should not be surprising.

Yet in some ways, this consummate nineteenth-century writer was at odds with his own era. In an 1827 letter to his mother, he explains, "I must write for the many, or not at all."[118] A Bulwer article entitled "The Knowledge of the World in Men and Books" suggests that a writer must capture "the feelings of the herd."[119] His letters to his son, who published poetry under the pseudonym Owen Meredith, are among Bulwer Lytton's clearest statements on the art of writing. The father tells the son to employ "[b]road effects, opinions, humours, feelings, thoughts that every man in Oxford St. knows."[120] In an 1862 letter, Bulwer Lytton writes, "[Y]ou should study the *popular*."[121] An earlier letter cautions his son about which writers to emulate: "don't study Shakespeare. His form is too contagious." Instead, Bulwer Lytton recommends non-English writers: "the poets of other tongues help us to originality" – that is, translation reduces the risk of plagiarism.[122] When Robert Lytton was in fact accused of plagiarism, his father took the occasion to expound on his principles: "Borrowing is a beauty of scholarship and taste, and can't be done too largely. All great poets do borrow in proportion to their own wealth. Dryden has observed in one of his prefaces, that the sole condition of borrowing is to improve what you take."[123] Thus, Bulwer reiterates the Romantic claim that mastery over materials is essential. Earlier, *The Disowned* made a similar claim: "imitation, if noble and general, ensures the best hope of originality."[124] Despite the caveat to avoid Shakespeare, he was one of Bulwer Lytton's two main sources, according to his memoirs. From Shakespeare, the novelist gained "a desire to investigate the strings of passion and analyse the human heart." From Euripides, Bulwer Lytton learned "a tendency to arrest narrative, often to the injury of its dramatic progress, by moralising deductions and sententious aphorisms."[125] That is to say, the tropes that so exercised his critics were not stylistic missteps but the essence of his art.

Although aiming for popularity, Bulwer often took a dim view of contemporary readers, as in his 1833 sociological work *England and the English*. "Writings addressed to the multitude must be clear and concise: the style of the present day has therefore gained in clearness what it has lost in erudition."[126] It is a revealing claim. Clearness stands in opposition to erudition, as if they were antithetical terms. Verging on self-parody, Bulwer continues, "A numerous audience . . . have no toleration for the didascalic affectations in which academicians delight."[127] Bulwer's use of the eloquent style, which was often parodied or abandoned by other mid-Victorian writers, opposes Demetrius's "plain" style – in Bulwer's book, this is discovered in the "plainness" of "the modern style"; because of the diffusion of periodical literature, he says, "style will become less elaborate and polished."[128] Bulwer the critic thus proves to be fully aware that the fulsome style of Bulwer the novelist will not be welcomed by all readers. As Leslie Mitchell argues, he "wrote for an audience whose taste he despised."[129]

Bulwer's clearest statement on his theories of the novel appears in a November 1832 article in the *New Monthly*. In contrast to the preface to *The Disowned*, here Bulwer finds no separation between an author and his or her writings. He mentions Dante, Voltaire, and Johnson and says that "to name them is enough to remind the reader that if he would learn their characters, he has only to read their works."[130] In other words, the name of the author is a metonym for the publications. This theory helps to justify Bulwer's extreme sensitivity: an attack on a novel was tantamount to an attack on the self. Ultimately – and defensively – Bulwer develops a Platonic theory of fiction. Somehow, a great writer is above or beyond his works. "He will die, and leave only a thousandth part of his wealth to Posterity"; furthermore, authors "can never perfect their own numberless conceptions."[131] The novelist's son reinforces this argument: "Every great author is greater than his greatest book."[132] *Blackwood's Edinburgh Magazine*, articulating the darker view, found that Lord Lytton "was always attempting a task far beyond his powers."[133] Indeed, this Platonic theory of literature was self-serving and a perfect excuse for a writer, such as

Edward Bulwer, who was prone to ruinous interpolations. He argues that when critics scold and parodists parody, they are attacking only incarnations of the work, not the thing itself. The Ideal ever stands beyond the reach of the Actual, and the versions of *Paul Clifford* or *Eugene Aram* that were printed by Colburn and Bentley are merely shadows on the cavern wall.

***

> What is self? A thing that changes every year and month. The self of last year has no sympathy with the self of the one before.
>
> – Edward Bulwer

This chapter has presented a view of Bulwer's style that might suggest that it was unchanging over time. Such was not the case. First editions of Bulwer's works appeared over six decades, and John Sutherland refers to him as a nineteenth-century version of Zelig.[134] Woody Allen's 1983 film presents a human chameleon, who always turns up at important historical junctures and absorbs the personae of those around him. Similarly, "Bulwer could be half a dozen kinds of novelist" – fashionable, historical, Newgate, science-fiction, and so on.[135] It was not only his imitators and parodists who could replicate a style. As early as 1830, the *Athenaeum* found that Bulwer wrote like whoever he was reading last: "he quite forgoes personal identity." He "is on one page a Bolingbroke, on the next a Bentham, on the third a Fielding, and so on."[136] The *Dublin Review* later referred to "the impersonation of scholarship, philosophy, taste" – that is, the novelist offered imitations of the genuine article.[137] In the late 1840s, Bulwer Lytton willfully changed his style and format. After a career as a three-volume novelist, he published *The Caxtons, My Novel,* and *What Will He Do with It?* (1857–59) serially, in *Blackwood's Edinburgh Magazine.* The journal would later remark that "he was fresh enough after twenty years of incessant toil to evolve a new style" (even if it owed a debt to Sterne).[138]

Beside the fact that Bulwer may have been dodging the darts of his aftertexts, this changeability suggests a certain restlessness. "He is determined to be what he is not," urges the *National Review*, "and his readers suffer for it."[139] The novelist may have fancied himself a poet who slummed it in prose. "Alas! what existence can be more unfulfilled, than that of one who has the soul of a poet and not the skill?" asks *Godolphin* (290). *Fraser's Magazine* agrees that Bulwer followed the wrong profession: "I think you are a deserving young person, whom nature intended for a footman, and pity you accordingly, in having missed your vocation."[140] In the 1830s, Bulwer was successful but nervous that the end was near: "the public, I fear, will get weary of my name."[141]

To this there was an obvious solution, in the form of his changing signature – E. L. BULWER, E. B. LYTTON, LYTTON – winning scorn from his enemies and confusion from posterity. Rosina Bulwer Lytton took especial delight in renaming her onomastically slippery husband: Sir Plagiary Puff, Sir Reptile Bulwer Lytton, Sir Liar Coward Bulwer Lytton, Sir Liar Coward Swindler, and Sir Liar Coward Janus Plagiary Allpuff Edward Bulwer Lytton.[142] She was not alone in playing this game; the *Westminster Review* cheerfully christened him "Sir Multiform Success, Bart., M.P."[143] And in an apparent error, Marie Mulvey-Roberts cites *"Letters of the Late Bulwer Bulwer"* – a variant on Humbert Humbert, lover of Lolita.[144]

The shifting Bulwer/Bulwer Lytton persona was further destabilized by parodic aftertexts. His publications themselves were not immutable; stung by critique and spurred by a changing identity, he was an active reviser of earlier texts. After reading a negative review of his 1846 novel *Lucretia*, Bulwer Lytton wrote to Forster, "[I]t is well that I should know the truth – in order to guide me."[145] In an 1852 preface to *The Disowned*, Bulwer Lytton claims to have "lightened the narrative of certain episodical and irrelevant passages, and relieved the general style of some boyish extravagances of diction"; *Eugene Aram* underwent a similar purge of "certain verbal oversights and defects in youthful taste."[146] Indeed, the novelist changed the plot of the latter book in an 1849 edition: Eugene is no longer a cold-blooded murderer but merely an accomplice. Anthea Trodd demonstrates how parody directly impacted subsequent editions of *Eugene Aram*.[147] Parody, in this case, not only imitated but also altered the original text: an example of reverse causality, a confusion of causes and effects. Edward Bulwer Lytton, in the words of *Ernest Maltravers*, "was like a beauty who had seen a caricature of herself."[148]

His baronetcy and newfound dignity as a landowner certainly played a role. What was amusing to the rising young novelist offended the baronet. *Godolphin* is a clear example; in an 1840 edition, Sir Edward rewrote Mr. Bulwer. Satirical references to the aristocracy are softened; the word *aristocratic* is sometimes replaced with "polite" or "polished."[149] Sir Edward was also less tolerant of some of the younger man's affectations and solecisms. Two lovers "blent for ever" (220) are now "blended"; a "*sçavant*" (11) becomes "a *savant*"; and "charlatanries" (22) resolve to "charlatanism."[150]

Thus, aftertexts changed the course of Bulwer's career and drove him to purify, retrospectively, earlier efforts for inclusion in collected editions under the more esteemed names of Bulwer Lytton or Lord Lytton. Bulwer's response to the critical and parodic onslaught, whether in his fiction or non-fiction, articulates his theories of literature and marks a stage in the transition from the early, inchoate, pre-Victorian novel of the 1820s and 1830s – the fashionable, historical, and Newgate varieties – to the pruned mid-century realism of Elizabeth Gaskell, Anthony Trollope, and George Eliot. Bulwer's endurance and superhuman volubility in the face of cackling parodists, however, have not earned him a place in the pantheon of the frequently reprinted. The author himself would not be surprised. He told Laman Blanchard that "prose is a very doubtful material for the artist to leave behind – its colour soon fades and its texture rots."[51] Despite this skepticism, Bulwer's work proved to be a stimulus for two of his contemporaries, who developed their novel-writing skills by producing aftertexts based on the fiction of Edward Bulwer. One was William Makepeace Thackeray, who later befriended the target of his jests; the other was Rosina Wheeler, who was married to it.

CHAPTER FOUR

Thackeray versus Bulwer versus Bulwer: Parody and Appropriation

> ... the way to perfection is through a series of disgusts ...
> – Walter Pater, *The Renaissance*

Parody degrades, but it also generates. As Edward Bulwer discovered, parodic aftertexts can guide their sources, to correct stylistic foibles or to seek new narrative modes. In the words of the 1885 *Saturday Review*, parody can serve as "a chastener and instructor."[1] Christopher Stone remarks, "Parody of the dead is static ... you will not help that author to see himself as the world sees him; and this you must do if you are going to cure him of his faults."[2] Further, parody can be generative for the parodist as well as the parodee. Many writers launch their careers by writing, at first, like someone else. A literary style can be a school, a discipline, an apprenticeship of sorts: Arthur Quiller-Couch commended parody as a practice for the young, "breaking their teeth upon literature."[3] Richardson's *Pamela* was famously skewered by Fielding's *Shamela*, and Richardson himself noted the debt: "The Pamela, which he abused in his Shamela, taught him how to please."[4]

In the nineteenth century, there were at least two novelists who developed their narrative voices by parodying the style of Edward Bulwer. While Dwight Macdonald argues that "[m]ost parodies are written out of admiration rather than contempt," it is clear that William Makepeace Thackeray and Rosina Bulwer Lytton, for varying reasons, resented the Bulwerian voice that they inhabited.[5] Both began their novel-writing careers by writing *out of* and *against* the excesses of Bulwerese. Rosemarie Bodenheimer acknowledges that parodists might be attracted to and repelled by their targets: "Parody says, 'I simultaneously rely on and ridicule this language.'"[6] Indeed, the best parodists identify with their targets in some way. From the parodee's point of view, such identification threatens a loss of authorial identity: if someone else can write the way I do, who am I? For the parodist, there is the risk that close identification with a source leads to a form of literary confinement – recall Seamus Perry's observation that style can be "a sort of prison."[7] Nevertheless, Stone finds that "the best parodists, like the best translators, refuse to be hampered and enslaved by their originals."[8] While most readers like to imagine a translator as somewhat obligated to his or her source, the notion that a parodist has free rein is compelling. Margaret A. Rose, drawing on Harold Bloom's terminology, calls parody "a form of 'strong reading.'"[9] The extent to which Thackeray and Rosina Bulwer Lytton would prove to be Bloomian "strong poets" (albeit writing prose) is a question to which this chapter is addressed.

As the previous chapter indicated, *Fraser's Magazine* was the site of many Bulwer parodies in the 1830s; for the anonymous contributors, including William Maginn, these exercises were passing amusements, predicated on puncturing the balloon of supposed greatness. However, for William Makepeace Thackeray, an early contributor to *Fraser's*, these periodical squibs formed something of an education. William Maginn left the *Fraser's* fold in 1836, and the anti-Bulwer campaign was subsequently marshaled by Thackeray, Maginn's ally and sometime collaborator. To begin with, Thackeray was an expert parodist; Thrall argues that "he sedulously imitated William Maginn."[10] According to the *Times*, "If imitation were the highest kind of art Mr. Thackeray would be the first of living artists."[11] In *Fraser's*, Thackeray scorned and frequently parodied the writings of Edward Bulwer. The attack was not personal. Years later Thackeray explained, "[W]hen I used to lampoon a certain Bulwer, I had never seen him but in a public place, and had no kind of animosity to him."[12] But in another sense, the attack was entirely personal. G. K. Chesterton describes Thackeray thus: "Whenever he sneers it is at his own potential self."[13] J. G. Riewald argues that a parodist must "'identify' himself with the parodee's work"; "impersonation" is required.[14] Thus, there is a kind of identity theft at play.

Superficially, William Thackeray and Edward Bulwer share some biographical affinities. Both went up to Cambridge; both were subject to dominant mothers; both endured unfortunate marriages with Irishwomen; both were well-born but compelled to write for money. In brief, Thackeray could reasonably fear that he would become the next Edward Bulwer. "If I don't mind I shall be setting up for an unacknowledged genius, & turn as morbid as Bulwer," Thackeray wrote to his friend Edward FitzGerald.[15]

Like other writers and reviewers in the 1830s, Thackeray was critical of the overripe Bulwer style. Gordon N. Ray finds that Thackeray "was always on the lookout for traits of snobbery, meanness, and humbug" and that he had a "spontaneous revulsion for Bulwer's artificiality, pretentiousness, and morbidity."[16] In another letter, Thackeray writes, "[T]here are sentiments in his writing w[hich] always anger me, big words w[hich] make me furious, and a premeditated fine writing against w[hich] I cant [sic] help rebelling."[17] Trodd adds that Thackeray "found it useful to confront himself with a type of the Bad Novelist" (more capitalization).[18] Of course, he could have sharpened his novel-writing skill against another target – Theodore Hook or Ainsworth or Dickens – and Thackeray indeed parodied a number of contemporary authors. But the Bulwer imitations are especially potent and frequent: it is as if Thackeray were exorcising a part of himself – the bad novelist that he feared he might be or could become.[19]

Furthermore, the early novels of Edward Bulwer are at times Thackerayan. "Vanity of vanities! What have I acquired?" asks the hero of *Falkland*.[20] The narrator of *Godolphin* comments, "My God, what a strange life this is! what puppets we are!"[21] Almost a hundred pages later, one of the characters finds herself in a state of Thackerayan malaise: "Constance, Countess of Erpingham, was young, rich, lovely as a dream, worshipped as a goddess. Was she happy? and was her heart wholly occupied in the trifles that surrounded her?" (102). Unsurprisingly, Thackeray's early reading of Bulwer's novels fueled his own ambitions. In 1829, he found *Devereux* less effective than *Pelham* and *The Disowned* and foresaw himself one day composing a novel: "I could write as good a one myself."[22] Three years later, in his diary, he recorded that he "was much disappointed" with *Eugene Aram*. "The book is in fact humbug, when my novel is written it shall be something better I trust."[23]

In essays and other periodical writings, Thackeray lambasts Bulwerian excess and, in so doing, begins to formulate his own novelistic voice. The 1837 *Times* review of *Ernest Maltravers* is attributed to Thackeray, and it includes a vivid passage that shows the writer discovering one of his indelible images, one used less than a decade later to frame *Vanity Fair*. The reviewer refers to Bulwer's characters as "puppets" and continues, "in the guidance of his puppets and the action of his drama his head is always peeping over the barrier, like that of the proprietor of the show, in the comedy of *Mr. Punch*. Like a schoolboy with a new book, in every page of his we find scrawled the eternal name of Edward Bulwer."[24] This "proprietor of the show" would soon become *Vanity Fair*'s "Manager of the Performance."[25] Thackeray's narrator plays puppet master as well, and the novel memorably concludes, "Come, children, let us shut up the box and the puppets, for our play is played out."[26] Further, the *Times* review accuses Bulwer of scrawling his name on every page, which reflects some of the complaints about his paradiegesis. Ironically, the "eternal name of Edward Bulwer" would soon change, to Sir Edward and other variants.

With his writings for *Fraser's* and later for *Punch*, Thackeray parodies Edward Bulwer and shapes his own authorial identity. *The Yellowplush Correspondence* appeared in *Fraser's*, with some irregularity, from November 1837 to January 1840. Taking its cue from the December 1831 issue, which indicated that an "acquaintance with footmen and butlers" was required to write fashionable fiction, *Yellowplush* is supposedly the memoir of an ambitious footman, Charles Yellowplush, related in his unique orthographic style.[27] Bulwer is a target as early as the second monthly installment. "Does BULWER," asks Yellowplush, "for instans, know any think of fashnable life?"[28] In the seventh installment, Bulwer enters the proceedings and introduces himself as "Sawedwadgeorgeearlelittnbulwig." Quickly, he corrects himself: "Sawedwad – no, I mean *Mistaw*edwadLyttnBulwig."[29] This is, of course, a topical reference to Bulwer's recent elevation to a baronetcy. Indeed, Yellowplush associates authorship with self-invention. Bulwig's friend Dionysius Lardner (variously "Larner," "Larder," etc.) can deem himself a doctor; Bulwer can be made a baronet; and other published authors are spurious captains or countesses. Naturally, the Bulwig character (occasionally "Bullwig") speaks in parodic Bulwerese, with classical allusions and arrogant hyperbole ("I have gazed with the eagle eye on the sun of philosophy, and fathomed the mysterious depths of the human mind").[30]

The Yellowplush Correspondence concludes with "Epistles to the Literati. No. XIII," a successor to the 1831 "Epistle." In a December 1839 letter, Thackeray reports, "I have just turned off a thundering article against Bulwer."[31] The *Spectator* agrees: "As a piece of criticism it is sound and searching."[32] After Yellowplush and a friend see Bulwer's 1839 drama *The Sea-Captain; or, The Birthright*, they decide to write letters to each other on the subject. Yellowplush sends his letter to Bulwer himself. It opens "Honrabble Barnet!" and compares the author-footman to the author-baronet. "We are but tradesmen," both writing for "*l'argong, gelt, spicunia.*"[33] Ultimately, the letter claims that the sensitive baronet has not the "*staminy*" for pugnacious battle with the rough-and-tumble *Fraser's* crew (72). In particular, the letter takes issue with Bulwer's preface to the fourth edition of *The Sea-Captain*, which begins, "No one can be more sensible than I of the many faults and deficiencies to be found in this play."[34] Yellowplush scolds, "You shew that the play must be bad, and *then* begin to deal with the critix for finding folt!" (73).

After a lull, Thackeray resumed the anti-Bulwer charge in the pages of *Punch*. He had reread *Eugene Aram*, and the experience "reawakened" his "revulsion," according to Gordon N. Ray.[35] *Punch's Prize Novelists* appeared in installments, from April to October 1847. In addition to Bulwer Lytton, Thackeray took on Benjamin Disraeli, Catherine Gore, G. P. R. James, Charles Lever, and James Fenimore Cooper. The parodist also included a parody of himself – a perfect Thackerayan gesture. He wanted to imitate Charles Dickens, but Bradbury and Evans, the publishers of *Punch* as well as *Dombey and Son* (then appearing monthly), probably did not want to offend their prize novelist. While Disraeli and Lever were wounded by Thackeray's literary squibs and Dickens noted "the absurdity and injustice of being left out," the most deleterious of the parodies is "George de Barnwell, by Sir E. L. B. L. B B. L L. B B B. L L L., Bart."[36] Thackeray had finished this parody by January 1847, the month in which *Vanity Fair* made its first appearance. In a letter written that same month, he boasts that George Barnwell "will quote Plato and speak in Big Phrases."[37] Remembering *Punch's Prize Novelists* five years later, a *Times* reviewer found that "Mr. James, Mr. Disraeli, and Sir Edward Bulwer Lytton looked rather more original and like themselves than in their own works" – a fascinating suggestion that a parody is more "original" than its source, as if G. P. R. James and the rest merely imitated Thackeray's comic iterations.[38]

In "George de Barnwell," Thackeray, writing as Bulwer Lytton, proves a master of sententia: "Figs pall; but O! the Beautiful never does! Figs rot; but O! the Truthful is eternal" (5). The *Punch's* narrator is also periphrastic ("the fragrant potage that mocks the turtle's flavour") and enthralled by capital letters (3). For example, the parody opens, "In the Morning of Life the Truthful wooed the Beautiful, and their offspring was Love" (1). Later, George is referred to as "Refined," "Gentle," "Loving," "Beloved," "Poet," and "Sage" (12). Beyond these affectations, Thackeray captures Bulwer's tedious repetition. In *Eugene Aram*, a chapter bearing the subtitle "The evening before the trial" begins, "It was the evening before the trial."[39] Likewise, the first chapter of "George de Barnwell," entitled "Noonday in Chepe," opens by telling us "'Twas noonday in Chepe" (2). Other tautologies are readily available to the narrator of "George de Barnwell." For instance: "In Kingly and Heroic ages, 'twas of Kings and Heroes that the Poet spake" (2). Further, that which should be simple grows eminently complex. Consider this description: "'Twas Cocoa – and that nut the Cocoa-nut, whose milk has refreshed the traveler and perplexed the natural philosopher" (3).

Fittingly for a work in which one writer writes as another, identity is slippery in "George de Barnwell." The hero's lady love is variously called Ellinor, Emily, and Adelaide. The historical setting is similarly inexact: "an indefinite period of time between Queen Anne and George II" (6). Likewise, formal boundaries blur once more. The parodic narrative drifts into plagiarism when the murdering George announces that he is "ridding the world of a sordid worm" (11). Thackeray's footnote proclaims, "This is a gross plagiarism: the above sentiment is expressed much more eloquently in the ingenious romance of *Eugene Aram*" (11). Once more, a work of parody easily slides into plagiarism, and the self-aware parodist makes a joke out of this very instability: to parody Edward Bulwer is, to some extent, to plagiarize, to steal from his writing.

Further, *Punch's Prize Novelists* is inextricably linked to *Vanity Fair*, Thackeray's best-known work and the one on which his modern reputation rests. The novel's second monthly number, which was published two months before the first *Punch* installment, offers a dress rehearsal for the subsequent parodies. The *Vanity Fair* narrative is reimagined in various novelistic styles; for example, the characters are ennobled, as in fashionable fiction: Lord Joseph Sedley, the Marquis of Osborne, Lady Amelia. The parody continues in a cancelled passage (removed in the 1853 edition), in which Thackeray ridicules Ainsworth, G. P. R. James, and the memorable, circular (ABA) opening of *Paul Clifford*:

> The night was dark and wild – the clouds black – black – ink-black. The wild wind tore the chimney-pots from the roofs of the old houses and sent the tiles whirling and crashing through the desolate streets. No soul braved that tempest – the watchmen shrank into their boxes, whither the searching rain followed them – where the crashing thunderbolt fell and destroyed them . . . Horrible night![40]

Although this extensive literary jest was excised from later editions of *Vanity Fair*, its place in the novel's genesis indicates the extent to which parody and authorial impersonation loomed large in Thackeray's development as a novelist. That it was removed suggests that parodying Bulwer was something of a booster rocket, no longer needed once Thackeray himself was launched as a Victorian novelist.

Two years after the appearance of "George de Barnwell," Thackeray changed his tune. He regretted "pelting at that poor old Bulwer."[41] It should be observed that Sir Edward Bulwer Lytton had called on Thackeray one month earlier. By 1853, Thackeray could write to his former punching bag, "I ask pardon of the author of *The Caxtons* for a lampoon which I know he himself has forgiven, and which I wish I could recall."[42] Note that Thackeray refers to "the author of *The Caxtons*" and not the author of *Eugene Aram* or, for that matter, Bulwer or Bulwer Lytton. An identity shift is once again clear. During the same summer of this apology, Thackeray was again emulating Bulwer Lytton, not in order to ridicule but to produce one of the novels of his maturity. Employing a technique "borrowed from Pisistratus Bulwer," Thackeray planned to narrate *The Newcomes* from the perspective of his fictional character Arthur Pendennis.[43] According to its title page, Bulwer Lytton's *My Novel; or, Varieties in English Life* is the work of Pisistratus Caxton. By writing as Pendennis writing as Bulwer Lytton writing as Pisistratus writing *My Novel*, Thackeray claimed, "I shall be able to talk more at ease than in my own person."[44] It is only by being – or writing like – someone else, it seems, that Thackeray can feel like himself.

In short, Thackeray appropriated the Bulwer style in order to mock it and in order to develop and distinguish his own novelistic voice. After his success with *Vanity Fair*, Thackeray rose to "all but at the top of the tree," in his own estimation, in open rivalry with leading light Charles Dickens.[45] The parodies that propelled the career of Thackeray the anonymous and pseudonymous journalist were less important to Thackeray the Victorian novelist; in fact, he could jettison Bulwer-tinted material from *Vanity Fair* in the 1853 reprint. Thackeray, it seems, escaped the confinement of the byzantine Bulwerian style and succeeded as a novelist in his own right. Others were less fortunate.

***

     ... one hates to be a mere echo.

– Rosina Bulwer Lytton

Jane Welsh Carlyle referred to the life of Rosina Bulwer Lytton as "a bad dream, or a Balzac novel."[46] A quick sketch of this life provides some useful context. Born Rosina Anne Doyle Wheeler, in 1802, she married Edward Bulwer, in 1827. They had two children, Emily Elizabeth and Edward Robert. The marriage was an unhappy one; Bulwer was cruel and physically attacked his wife on more than one occasion. He also openly courted another woman. In 1836, Mr. and Mrs. Bulwer formally separated: the pivotal event in her long life. According to their descendent David Lytton Cobbold, this was the start of "forty years of bitter trench warfare."[47] In 1838, Bulwer removed the children from Rosina's care – a horrible blow to her, to which a husband was entitled under English law. He paid his wife an annuity of £400, which was a pittance compared to the baronet's eventual wealth as landowner and author. He made infrequent payments, and she fell into debt.

For the remaining decades of Rosina's life, her husband systematically persecuted and tormented her. She tried to seek redress in the courts, but a wife could not sue without her husband's consent (which he was unwilling to grant). Various spies were employed (including John Forster), and Rosina claimed that a "vulgar old woman" once tried to poison her soup in the Welsh village of Llangollen.[48] While in Paris, Rosina was harassed by two men, Lawson and Thackeray, who attempted to bribe witnesses (including Rosina's maid) and sought evidence of adultery that Bulwer could use to secure a divorce.[49] In the small world of Victorian literature, Thomas James Thackeray was a distant relation of the novelist; educated at Eton and Cambridge, Tom "followed no profession" and was himself a sometime author.[50] In 1851, Rosina threatened to disrupt the performance of her husband's play *Not So Bad as We Seem; or, Many Sides to a Character*. She was to disguise herself as an orange seller and pelt the invited audience, including Queen Victoria, with rotten eggs. (This never happened.) In 1858, Rosina publicly humiliated her husband at the hustings during a parliamentary election for Hertford. She scolded him before the gathered audience, and he ran from the scene. According to Helen Small, "Mr Brooke's unhappy experience at the hustings in Middlemarch was nothing compared to what Bulwer-Lytton [*sic*] went through."[51]

Victorian husbands had a remedy for errant or disobedient wives.[52] Four days after the hustings, Rosina was interviewed by Hale Thompson and other medical men. They decided that she was not insane. She subsequently wrote five distempered letters to Thompson, and he changed his diagnosis.[53] (It was only on the page that he found her to be unstable.) Rosina was incarcerated in a lunatic asylum, run by Robert Gardiner Hill, from 22 June to 17 July 1858. Since she was literate and had allies, the story of her wrongful incarceration made the local newspapers and the *Daily Telegraph*; the ensuing scandal compelled Bulwer Lytton to relent. In October, he renegotiated the terms of their separation, and her annuity was increased to £500.[54] When Rosina read Wilkie Collins's *The Woman in White*, in 1860, the story was eerily familiar. She reported to a friend that Sir Percival Glyde and Count Fosco were "mere suckling doves" compared to her villainous husband.[55] An uneasy stalemate between husband and wife continued until their deaths; they never divorced. When her grandson happened upon a cache of her vindictive letters, he described it as "a drawer full of dead wasps."[56]

All of this would be history or biography if it were not the case that Rosina Bulwer Lytton was also a professional novelist. In this career choice, she clearly emulated her husband. Marie Mulvey-Roberts, one of the few literary critics to investigate this career, argues that Rosina "decided to take a leaf out of his book by becoming a writer of fiction."[57] In 1827, Bulwer's own allowance was reduced by his mother because of his unsanctioned marriage to Rosina Wheeler. He then turned to writing and produced *Falkland, Pelham, The Disowned*, and *Devereux* in quick succession. In 1838, Rosina, separated from her husband and children and reduced in means, sought similar emolument from her writing. In an 1840 preface, she defiantly states, "[A]s I merely write for bread, I shall continue to write, and to publish what I do write."[58] This was a consequence that Bulwer feared, even during their happy courtship. In the midst of a playful letter, he turns earnest and demands, "I beseech you to tell me expressly and explicitly whether you have any Author-designs, and whether you intend to turn Love and Literature into Manuscripts and Money. I want very much to have a clear and definite answer to this inquiry."[59] His use of hendiadys ("expressly and explicitly," "Love and Literature," et al.) suggests the emphasis intended: it seems clear that Bulwer did not want his future wife to follow his profession.

Yet mimicry was one of Rosina's distinguishing traits. In her memoirs, unpublished during her lifetime, she explains:

> I was a born mimic, and for my further misfortune was endowed, as most mimics are, with a terribly keen sense of the ridiculous, and once knowing a person's peculiarities, I could not only imitate their face, voice, and gestures, but could extemporise whole scenes of adventures for them, and furnish dialogues of what they *would* have said had they been placed in such circumstances.[60]

The references here to "adventures" and "dialogues" suggest a future novelist, one who produces narrative based on sets of "circumstances." Rosina's biographer calls this mimicry "her dangerous gift."[61] Further, Isaac D'Israeli reminds us that parody "strongly resembles mimicry."[62] Mulvey-Roberts shows that Rosina "found in her husband's novels material with which she could develop her talent for pastiche and parody."[63] In her novels, published between 1839 and 1871, Rosina frequently parodies Bulwer's style, and the forms she undertook reproduce his formal variety: the silver-fork novel, historical fiction, and the mystical or supernatural. Her professional earnings were respectable, if not as great as her husband's, with initial payments of £300 for her first novel and £400 for her second.[64]

There is a view, promulgated to a large extent by her own grandson, that Rosina was as a shrew or a succubus, a woman "unhinged," and her husband's "most implacable enemy and bitterest traducer."[65] But there is a countervailing view that she was actually a canny professional. She saw that Bulwer's novels rewarded him handsomely, and she essayed to crack the code and reproduce some of his formal elements. In the early (and happy) years of their marriage, Rosina had unequaled access to Bulwer's processes and procedures; it seems that she served as a kind of literary assistant or agent – his John Forster or G. H. Lewes. In 1830, she wrote to William Jerden, editor of the *Literary Gazette*, to see if he had received a copy of *Paul Clifford*.[66] In 1832, she wrote to Richard Bentley to check on the reviews for *Eugene Aram*.[67] According to Jane Preston, Bulwer kept his wife "fully occupied with time-consuming, exacting research for his novels."[68] Rosina told a friend, "I have been studying the Newgate Calendar to help Edward with 'Paul Clifford.'"[69] Having absorbed her task, she could later refer to "black, atrocious, Newgate-looking weather."[70] By 1835, when their marriage was in jeopardy, Bulwer told Rosina how she might salvage the situation: "if you could learn to make my occupation yours."[71] And so she did – only more than he had ever imagined.

Rosina Bulwer Lytton imitated her husband's style, erudition, obsessions, and, for obvious reasons, his name. Leslie Mitchell avers that Rosina "hated taking the name Bulwer or Lytton ... because it symbolized the smothering of one personality by another," and Mulvey-Roberts remarks that Rosina was drawn to the "analogy with slavery" and "slaves who took on the names of their masters."[72] Indeed, in 1851, Rosina complained to her husband, "I am branded with the name of the most contemptible villain in Europe."[73] Nine years later, after more than two decades of separation, she could still find herself "in a cruelly false position, hampered by a beggarly title."[74] If the name was such a loathsome burden, why not change it – at least on the title pages of her works?

In this regard, Rosina proved quite clever: her name was a marketing tool. In 1839, she wrote again to Richard Bentley, now on her own behalf, to negotiate the rights to her first novel, *Cheveley; or, The Man of Honour*: "you are aware that a Book by me just now is a very good speculation." Further, she noted that "the additional circumstance of its being opposed – or prosecuted" would be a "guarantee for an enormous sale."[75] By 1851, she could write in a similar manner to another publisher, William Shoberl, "[M]y books are a very good speculation to any publisher, as the *name* alone sells them, and they have a certain sale in the provinces of the three kingdoms, and a great one in America."[76] Unhappy with the feeble launch of a later novel, ironically entitled *Very Successful!* (1856), she planned to "open a public subscription" to sell the book with her "*name*" (Rosina's emphasis).[77] Perhaps growing tired of this tactic, by 1860 she wanted to publish a one-volume collection of essays "under the name Robert Denham."[78]

Naturally, Rosina's name was a point of contention between her and her lineage-loving husband. When *Cheveley* won critical praise, Bulwer was furious and called it "wretched trash" and its author one "whose only distinction is the name she bears."[79] When he was created a baronet, he did not want his estranged wife to achieve the title of Lady Lytton Bulwer. She replied in the sharpest terms to one of his advisors:

> It is not in the power of Sir Edward Lytton Bulwer or his bran new Brummagen Title, to deprive me of the name I have the misfortune – and the disgrace to bear – unless I can succeed in ridding myself of it by a Divorce, which I shall endeavour to do – he is Gazetted as "Edward George Earle Lytton Bulwer" and without an Act of Parliament he cannot waive his Christian name.[80]

Note her absorption of his capital letters. This comment also proved prescient. In 1844, after succeeding his mother to the Lytton estate, Bulwer legally changed his surname to Bulwer Lytton. A lawyer working for the baronet told Rosina that Sir Edward did not want his wife to take on the new moniker but rather "restrict herself to Bulwer."[81] Rosina, ever recalcitrant, did not oblige him. She was soon sending and receiving letters as Lady Lytton, and her next published book, *Memoirs of a Muscovite*, appeared that same year, as the work of "Lady Bulwer Lytton." In fact, Rosina, with perfect precision, kept in step with Bulwer's shifting and ever-ennobled name: Mrs. Edward Lytton Bulwer, Lady Lytton Bulwer, Lady Bulwer Lytton. Her final book, *Shells from the Sands of Time*, published three years after his death, is attributed to "The Dowager Lady Lytton."

In other words, Rosina Bulwer Lytton was, to some extent, an identity thief. More unnervingly, she was her husband's doppelgänger, the secret sharer, a part of the self that he firmly rejected, which returned, again and again: the uncanny. Bulwer Lytton frequently hindered his wife's writing career and threatened potential publishers. His reasons were threefold. First, the less her financial means, the greater his power to suppress her. Second, Bulwer Lytton wanted to be the only Bulwer Lytton in fiction – an issue of competition or product differentiation. The third reason was that Rosina's works (especially early on) served to ridicule the

Bulwers and the Lyttons. She could wound and mock and ridicule and parody the great Bulwer – and in his own name.

Others, such as Maginn and Thackeray, certainly reprimanded Bulwer and parodied his ostentatious writing, often anonymously or pseudonymously. But when composed by a Bulwer or a Bulwer Lytton, the parody could be even more cutting. Rosina, with unequaled access, "had a thorough knowledge of his weaknesses."[82] Their grandson later wrote that "she was continually wounding him where he was most sensitive."[83] Mulvey-Roberts agrees that Rosina "taunted him mercilessly by targeting his greatest vulnerabilities – his family name, career, and reputation."[84] It is illuminating that Mulvey-Roberts considers Bulwer Lytton's name, of which he was so proud, to be a vulnerability. Rosina herself wrote to a friend, "Exposure is the only thing that complex monster dreads."[85] Chris Baldick, in his book on *Frankenstein*, explains that the earlier sense of a monster as a moral aberration "persist[ed] into the nineteenth century."[86] Just as Frankenstein and his Monster became confused in the popular imagination, both Bulwer and Rosina could reasonably have considered each other to be the monster in their long-lasting quarrel.

***

I shall be ridiculed, lampooned! I, the head of the Mowbrays!
                                                – *Not So Bad as We Seem*

Rosina proved to be an incisive reader of her husband's works. Four years after their separation, she wrote an unsigned two-part review of Bulwer's poetry for the *Dublin University Magazine* (perhaps only a little less ethical than Bulwer reviewing Bulwer in the *New Monthly*). "But it is in point of *style* that we have always considered Bulwer most faulty," says Rosina. She calls him "the Euphuistic novelist," who spews "mawkish affectation of philosophical sentiment."[87] Like other reviews, this one dissects Bulwer's hyperbolic style: "Were he to describe a shower, it would be lavender water. Every tree is a weeping willow, or a cedar of Libanus. His sunsets are topazes and rubies."[88] Rosina seems particularly nettled by the author's excessive paradiegesis. In his poetic drama *Richelieu*, she says, Bulwer "checks every moment at small prettinesses, as a child on its way to school loiters over every daisy in its path."[89] As in some other reviews of Bulwer, Rosina shows that direct quotation can foreground unintentional self-parody: "Debarr'd the *Actual*, we but breathe a life / To the chill marble of the *Ideal*."[90] Finally, she herself provides a parody of Bulwer's writing, thus blurring once again the boundary between sober criticism and parodic assault. Replacing Richelieu's France with her native Ireland, Rosina offers a speech for a Mr. O'Connell: "I am an Irishman – I must love – debarred the Domestic, I must have recourse to the Political."[91] This parody holds satiric content as well; Rosina knew at least one person who had abandoned the felicities of domestic life for a public career as author and parliamentarian.

It was not simply that Rosina Bulwer, once separated from her husband, turned to writing to supplement a meagre and irregular income. When she became an author, she wrote *about* Edward Bulwer; she wrote *as* Edward Bulwer; she absorbed, ridiculed, and parodied her husband and his work. He was her *bête noire* and her inspiration, an inalienable part of her existence. On one occasion Bulwer threatened her in a letter: "Tremble! while I write you are in my power!"[92] That is to say, his writing (of letters or of fiction) holds her enthralled, enslaved; as long as he is writing, she cannot escape that writing. Of course, this quotation from her estranged husband was reported by Rosina herself, so there is some instability of voice. Was Bulwer parodying himself? Or is this Rosina's satirical iteration of a typical Bulwerian threat? In her first published piece of fiction, "Artaphernes the Platonist; or, The Supper at Sallust's," set in republican Rome, Edward Bulwer is front and center. Not incidentally, this short story, drenched in the pseudo-antiquarianism of Bulwer's 1834 novel *The Last Days of Pompeii*, appeared in April 1838, in *Fraser's Magazine for Town and Country*.[93]

Parody is forceful in "Artaphernes the Platonist." It reproduces the awkward *in medias res* opening of Bulwer's novel ("Ho, Diomed, well met!") with "Ho, noble Brutus, well met!"[94] Elsewhere, the story exploits Bulwer's love of apostrophe. Asteria, the mistress to Artaphernes, apostrophizes her lover's wife, "Oh! happy, happy Charmion!"[95] Imitation also plays a role in the story. After Artaphernes leaves his mistress's company, a Roman, named Lepidus, calls on her. Asteria proceeds to mock Artaphernes for the newcomer's entertainment "by exaggerated imitations of his pompous way of speaking, and feigned decorum of manner"; this performance recalls Rosina's skill at impersonation.[96]

Besides parodic content, the story has satirical intentions towards its subject. Artaphernes the Platonist is a version of Edward Bulwer the Platonist. The Greek protagonist seems to be something of a Victorian writer of miscellany (although living in the first century B.C.). At one point he must "shut himself up, to finish an essay he was writing upon female education."[97] Lest readers miss the point, the first page of the story informs them that "he had forestalled the principle of the political economists of the nineteenth century."[98] The portrait is not a flattering one. Artaphernes is cheap – he never gives dinners; he gives nothing but advice. Moreover, he is not a hero of the ancient world but a hypocrite, a dissembler, and one of the co-conspirators in the assassination of Julius Caesar. After the murder, Artaphernes flees Rome with his mistress and leaves Charmion and their two children to be trampled to death by the vengeful mob. According to David Lytton Cobbold, Bulwer was "enraged" by the story.[99]

But "Artaphernes" was only the first arrow in Rosina's quiver. After she failed to secure the imprint of her husband's sometime publishers Colburn and Bentley, now themselves uncoupled, her 1839 novel *Cheveley* was published by Edward Bull (whose name suggests a curtailed version of Edward Bul-wer).[100] Mulvey-Roberts argues that with this first major work Rosina "resolved to capitalize on the miseries of her marriage."[101] Indeed, the novel "proved the *succès de scandale* Rosina had hoped for," and it went through "three editions in six months."[102] An 1839 review in the *Athenaeum* found "considerable power and feeling" in *Cheveley*; further, its "writer has a keen sense of the humorous."[103] The reviewer also observed the novel's protofeminist leanings. According to *Cheveley*, Englishmen expect women to be "imitations of automatons," and the novel anticipates Bulwer's reaction to a writing Rosina: "the world cannot be large enough for them both, any more than two suns can shine in one hemisphere."[104]

Cheveley accomplishes some of its effects by parodying the imitable style of Edward Bulwer. Rosina was such an expert mimic, in training since childhood, that she could write as her husband, as in this bloated Bulwerian description:

> there is to me an indescribable charm in the calm, the quiet, the soft, the cultivated, and, above all, the home look of English scenery, which neither the gorgeous and Belshazzar-like splendour of the East, the balmy and Sybarite softness of the South, the wildness of the West, nor the frozen mighty magnificence of the North, can obliterate or compensate for. (128)

This narrator refers to something "indescribable" and then goes on to describe it in a systematic (and alliterative) fashion. Further, *Cheveley* reproduces Bulwer's preferred trio of tropes. Sententia: "in order to appreciate wit, a person himself must possess it" (11). Periphrastically, the novel refers to "the watchmaking city of Geneva" rather than, simply, Geneva (11). And after a paradiegetic digression on women's rights in Britain and France, the novel resumes course with one of Bulwer's favorite formulations: "But to return: Herbert Grimstone had had the satisfaction . . ." (115).

Throughout, *Cheveley* displays excessive erudition, another attempt to out-Bulwer Bulwer, to show that he was not unique in his access to a font of impertinent information. Mulvey-Roberts, who edited a modern edition of the novel, counts 1,400 "cultural, social and political allusions and quotations."[105] The title page includes epigraphs from Wordsworth and Erasmus (the latter in Latin and French). The very first sentence of the novel refers to Pythagoras, Plato, and St. Paul; and it quotes, without attribution, Thomas Middleton, St. Augustine, and Coleridge (7). Another passage, in a jumbled mélange of liberal education, cites Voltaire, Orpheus, Mozart and Rossini, Talleyrand and Machiavelli, St. Catherine and St. Teresa, and, for good measure, the ballerina Marie Taglioni (11).

In addition to playfully parodying the faults in Bulwer's style, *Cheveley* directly confronts his family and its honor. In this *roman à clef,* Bulwer, the author of *Paul Clifford,* appears as Lord De Clifford; Bulwer's brother Henry is now Herbert Grimstone (although attributes of both Henry and Edward appear in the two representations). The eldest of the three Bulwer brothers, William, seems to have escaped Rosina's wrath.[106] Their mother, born Elizabeth Barbara Warburton-Lytton, is now Elizabeth Barbara Langton, who married a Colonel Grimstone (i.e. Colonel [later General] Bulwer). Rosina noticed that her preening mother-in-law would say "vaustly" instead of *vastly,* so the woman's fictional counterpart claims to be "*'vaustly'* fond of dogs in general" (38).[107] Other Lytton/Langtonisms include "hort" for *heart* (67). Even Thackeray falls under Rosina's satiric eye. A potential ally with a literary opponent in common, Thackeray destroyed any chance of amity when, after reading Rosina's manuscript, he told James Fraser not to publish *Cheveley.*[108] So Thackeray appears as Major Nonplus, and his portrayal anticipates his own Becky Sharp: he is "one of those clever managing mortals" who lives "with little money or credit" (15).[109]

Of course, the ridicule reserved for Lord De Clifford is harsher: "Nature seemed to have given him a sort of rag-bag of a mind, made up of the strangest and most incongruous odds and ends possible," which the narrator refers to as "the 'Penny Cyclopaedia' printed upside down" (31). Alluding to *The Last Days of Pompeii,* a character named Mademoiselle d'Antonville wishes that Lord De Clifford "had perished in the destruction of Pompeii, and then he could not have prosed her to death as he was doing" (60). This amusing remark indicates Bulwer's extreme volubility, and the phrase "prosed . . . to death" suggests novel writing and readers prosed to death by three-volume novel after three-volume novel. Lord De

Clifford, for his part, snaps at one point: "Ridicule is not an argument" (42–43).

The identities of Bulwers and Lyttons, of Grimstones and De Cliffords are expertly blurred in one early passage. Herbert Grimstone is described as "the most imitative of his imitative race" (91). Readers learn that his cousin is a successful author, and Herbert occasionally meets a student who asks if Herbert is related to the "great" Grimstone. "To which Herbert modestly replied that *he* was the great Grimstone! Great was the poor student's delight," the narrator relates (91). Thus, imitative Herbert Grimstone, a version of Henry Bulwer and Edward Bulwer, pretends to be his own talented cousin. The implication could be that Edward Bulwer was happy to be mistaken for Henry or that Henry accepted applause intended for his fiction-writing brother. In any case, Herbert Grimstone soon believes the lie and decides to turn author.[110]

Rosina's first novel, with its talent for parody and veiled slander, was itself the subject of another parody, *Lady Cheveley; or, The Woman of Honour*. It is an anonymous, fifty-six-page pamphlet, published in 1839. The preface faults *Cheveley* for its "mawkish philosophy" and "stilted sentiment," phrases that resemble terms used in critiques of Bulwer's writings.[111] Was *Lady Cheveley*'s author identifying weaknesses in *Cheveley* or in the works that it imitated?

Lady Cheveley is a poem, in heroic couplets and two cantos. Intentionally or otherwise, the poet at times versifies in a Bulwer-like vein: "It is an English home . . . Old Time sits brooding 'neath its hoary walls" (32); "Art and Nature there go hand in hand!" (33). But the poem's main function is to abuse Rosina Bulwer. It mounts an argument with which her husband would have agreed: Rosina, by writing *Cheveley*, took advantage of a surname she professed to dislike. "She felt the magic influence of a name," sings the poet (38). "She shone / With the reflected lustre of his own" (39). Further, as others have observed, "[S]he knew how best / To wound so sensitive, so proud a breast" (31). While Rosina Bulwer remains discreetly unnamed, the poet offers a hint with the phrase "no roseate blossoms smiled" (48). The poem's subtitle claims that it is "A New Version of Cheveley, the Man of Honour," but it is more a work of literary criticism or revenge, perhaps at the hand of Bulwer or a member of his family.[112]

This poem was itself the subject of a satiric attack, in a sixty-six-page pamphlet, *Cheveley's Donkey; or, The Man in the Ass's Hide*, from publisher James Pattie. In an opening letter to the author of *Lady Cheveley*, *Cheveley's Donkey* takes issue with the earlier publication for daring to "tarnish the family name."[113] In the doggerel verse that follows, *Cheveley's Donkey* generates a fable-like account of a Bulwer-like family. Miss Betty (probably Elizabeth, Bulwer's mother) marries Cheveley (Bulwer's father); the couple produces two children, Ned and Harry (reversing the birth order of Henry Bulwer and his younger brother, Edward). The poem soon loses track of its characters, meter, and rhyme scheme, and its impact on the Rosina–Edward feud was probably negligible. Still, the fact that Rosina's version of an Edward Bulwer novel, *Cheveley*, produced two scurrilous pamphlets – all three appearing in 1839 – demonstrates the self-multiplication of Victorian aftertexts.

Her second novel, *The Budget of the Bubble Family*, appeared in 1840. Despite the pathetic outline of her life, Rosina's "gift was for comedy, not tragedy."[114] Having exorcised some demons with *Cheveley*, Rosina now had fun at the expense of the Bulwers (or Bubbles). A bubble is an apt satiric image – smooth, shiny, empty, and always ready to burst. The novel's first sentence is consummate Bulwerese, tortured and digressive:

> At an epoch like the present, when the political hemisphere of Great Britain is dazzling the world with its brightness, owing entirely to those stars of the Bubble Family which now sway its destinies – it would be superfluous, if not impertinent, to descant, physiologically, or even historically, upon their well-known attributes; suffice it to say, that they have been from time immemorial *Whigs* – a term in itself comprising, and implying that love of civil and religious liberty, which makes men Arians, or any-thing-Arians, as occasion, or that most colossal of Whig bulwarks, expediency, may require. (1:1)

Here the narrator promises not to "descant," as Bulwer might do, and then does so anyway. Also note the "bulwarks" at the end: a slight hint at the target of this windy parody.

As Dickens took delight in coining names like Gummidge, Creakle, and Pinch, so Bulwer had a predilection for fulsome, polysyllabic names: Ernest Maltravers, Vavasour Mordaunt, Clinton L'Estrange, Latimer Highclerc, Kenelm Chillingly.[115] Rosina, in *The Budget of the Bubble Family*, generates a few Bulwer-worthy names: Sir Headworth Clavering, Lord Mornington, Horace Stewart Vernon. Lady Annette Lovell takes the surname of Paul Clifford's alias, and the novel simulates Bulwer's pretentions to ancient lineage with the appearance of a painting of "Bubelus, King of Rome – no doubt the founder of the family" (1:85).

Sympathy is now granted to the Bulwer stand-in, Cecil Bubble Howard. He considers pursuing a career as a writer and thinks to himself, "[W]hen one sees the trash that sells, I am sure I could write" (1:120–121). By the third volume, however, he knows "that success, not merit, is the test that wins popular applause" (3:54). Cecil does not suffer boredom but rather "toedium vitae" (3:194), and a dining room is decorated in purple and "Pompeian red" (1:92). Cecil, like Artaphernes the Platonist, exploits the consolations of philosophy. When a servant presents Cecil with some bills, the narrator offers a parodic glimpse of Bulwerian rationalization: "but query, did Bishop Berkeley, or Kant, ever pay a bill? – No – Q.E.D. – or they never would have raved the anti-reality nonsense they did" (1:16). Cecil, like a Bulwer protagonist, is pretentious even when (or especially when) he is talking to himself.

Young lovers, when declaring themselves, quote Dryden and Jonson, as young lovers must, and Rosina has so absorbed Bulwer's obsessions that she describes her hero and especially her heroine as Bulwerian paragons. Madeline, in *Eugene Aram*, has a complexion that is "translucently pure and soft" and "teeth whiter than pearls" (1:16). *Godolphin's* Constance is found to have a "white, round, dazzling arm," "the most dazzling teeth," "a bust of the most dazzling whiteness," and "a foot, whose least beauty was its smallness" (60–61). Godolphin is equally drawn to Lucilla Volktman, not least because "her hands and feet were small to a fault" (116). *Fraser's Magazine* picked up on this motif: Elizabeth Brownrigge's coloring is that of "transparent whiteness of the purest alabaster."[116] But *The Budget of the Bubble Family*, if possible, exceeds the hyperbole of these examples. Here is the object of Cecil's affection, Theresa Manners:

> her skin was dazzlingly white, with polished, satiny surface; the shape of her face, which was a perfect oval, was almost as beautiful as the features of which it was composed; her lips were literally like twin cherries, and the teeth within them were so white and fairy-like, that they looked as if the blossoms had still lingered with the fruit . . . (1:97)

Later, the narrator continues: "her hands were as beautiful as any hands need be, being small, with long taper fingers, yet plump and dimpled, of an ivory whiteness without, while pink, as though tinged with henna within" (1:100).

The level of detail is maddening here: can this information contribute to the reader's knowledge of the character? To some extent, Rosina displays the habits of a three-volume novelist, filling the wide-margined pages with alabaster pearls. But she is also parodying a three-volume novelist; she subjects Bulwer's quirks and obsessions to the glare of the operating theatre. Early on, in a paradiegetic passage, *The Budget of the Bubble Family* attacks the Bulwer school of unrealism, hyperbole, and paragon.

"I make housemaids and helpers speak like housemaids and helpers," the narrator insists, "and not like shepherdesses out of Arcadia, and philosophers from Utopia" (1:66–67). In this regard, Rosina's second novel points towards mid-nineteenth-century domestic realism, as practiced by authors such as Gaskell and Trollope.[117] Yet Lucille P. Shores finds Rosina to be "out of tune with her times," and Mulvey-Roberts, perhaps Rosina's staunchest modern defender, decries the novels as "tedious, repetitive, and histrionic."[118] Rosina, like Bulwer, could not keep herself in check. In the midst of almost any narrative, the lamented tale of Rosina Bulwer Lytton asserts itself, like a revenant or a mournful refrain.

Memoirs of a Muscovite, published in 1844, seems to be a departure of sorts. It is a first-person narration, told from the perspective of a thirty-four-year-old Russian man. He skims through Europe and meets fashionable persons, with names such as "Madame A——" and "Julia L——p."[119] But in the second volume, the story of Rosina returns in the form of "poor Lady Craven."[120] One character disapproves of this lady for writing without her husband's consent. Another character champions Lady Craven: "had she money enough to live without, I'm very certain she would never write a line, but ... she has not (for four hundred a year is rather a scanty pittance for a gentlewoman)."[121] The husband, Sir Augustus Craven, prevents Lady Craven from bringing a trial (as Bulwer did). The narrator, however, notes that Lady Craven "wrote books without the slightest allusion to her husband"[122] – a statement that cannot be said of Rosina Bulwer Lytton.

Twelve years later, in *Very Successful!*, the Rosina story emerges again. This time the Bulwer figure is Sir Janus Allpuff, who is fifty but looks eighty. Unrelated to the narrative, one character explains that Sir Janus is "not content with having hunted his unhappy wife nearly to death, and reduced her to the lowest ebb of pecuniary destitution from defending herself against his infamous conspiracies"; no, he "also prevents her in every way from earning her bread."[123] The lamentable leitmotif sounds again in the third volume, when other characters resume the tale. "Sir Janus Allpuff's victim wrote her first book for bread," but "Colburn had refused it." A gossipy version of Rosina's experiences follows, with references to William Maginn, Gore House, and "the —— administration" (under which "baronetcies were cheap").[124] Even in Rosina's most autobiographical novel, *Miriam Sedley*, which recounts her youth in Ireland, the novelist cannot help but tell her tale in Bulwer Lyttonian terms: "It was a dark and stormy night at the end of August. The wind was sending forth those mysterious wailings, which are alternately like the low, hollow moan of

Warnus Court, the Seat of Lieut. General Sir Gregory Kempenfelt, Bart., G.C.B.

Figure 4 An illustration produced for Rosina Bulwer Lytton's 1856 novel *Very Successful!* This grand estate evokes Knebworth, the ancestral home of her husband's family, and the titled name Lieutenant General Sir Gregory Kempenfelt recalls Sir Edward Bulwer Lytton, a baronet at this time

suppressed suffering, and the loud frantic shriek of insanity which the lower orders of Irish conscientiously believe to be the howling of the Banshee."[125] If this is parody, it is not particularly droll. Bulwer's famous opening is now associated with screaming, insanity, and Ireland. Even Rosina's early years, before she met Edward Bulwer, are infected by his language and imbued with her later suffering.

But the most curious of Rosina's novels is probably *The Peer's Daughters*, published in 1849. By this point the assimilation of identity seems to be complete. The main function of this novel is not to mock her husband or parody his style; now Rosina writes *as* Bulwer Lytton. She is like the actor who forgets that he or she is playing a role or a liar so accustomed to the fib that the boundaries between truth and falsehood vanish. *The Peer's Daughters* is a crossbreed of three of Bulwer's fictional modes: the historical, the fashionable, and the supernatural. For the last, Mulvey-Roberts calls the book "a less successful version of his occultist master-piece *Zanoni*," which appeared in 1842.[126] But there are different kinds of success. As an act of novel-length literary impersonation, *The Peer's Daughters* has few peers. For admirers of the occult, there is Comte de Saint Germain, who may or may not be over 900 years old (his memories date to around 807 A.D.). He offers the Bulwerian hero, noble Raphaël Valasquez, the gift of immortality and an asp ("Here ... take the OPHIDIAN").[127] One phantasmagoric evening they meet the shades of Julius Caesar, Antony, Cleopatra, Shakespeare, and Bianca Cappello (the subject of Rosina's third novel). Saint Germain believes that some element called "primary matter" exists through all time; only the forms change (1:98). It is not clear whether this is parodic Bulwer nonsense or legitimate argument, but it is a reasonably good analogy for a theory of aftertextuality. An originating author – say, a Dickens or a Bulwer – creates literary works composed of this "primary matter" that is then reworked by aftertextual writers; thus, there is no imitation, only recombination.

In *The Peer's Daughters*, Rosina so perfectly embodies Bulwer's compulsions and obsessions that she seems to see with his eyes. Recall that *peer* is a social relationship, an honorific (Edward Bulwer Lytton joined the peerage in 1866), and a verb – to peer into something. When Saint Germain is described, the narrator sees the character through the lens of Bulwer's oral fixation: "Nothing could exceed the freshness and brilliancy of his mouth and teeth" (1:45). Corella, yet another youthful paragon, is described with Bulwerian luxuriance. Her forehead is of "ivory smoothness and whiteness," and her face

> was only exquisitely fair, and of the texture of white Camelia, into which, love himself appeared to have kissed a blush. Her mouth was of that rich, ripe, cherry red, which, from the two rows of small pearl like teeth within it, gave it perfectly the appearance of that pouting fruit, surrounded by a coronal of its own snowy blossoms. (1:76)

Again, redness and whiteness and teeth (once more conveniently located "within" a mouth). Like the description of Theresa in *The Budget of the Bubble Family*, this passage can be read as parody, but in this later novel, the lines between the parodic and the genuine blur. With *The Peer's Daughters*, Rosina seems to be writing – not parodying – an Edward Bulwer Lytton novel.

By the 1850s, Rosina was at work on her memoirs, titled "Nemesis" (aka "The Nemesis"). The form is epistolary, and some of the letters are written from the perspective of Edward Bulwer Lytton. Here, in the personal space of autobiography, Rosina assimilates the view of her nemesis: an uncanny act of ventriloquism. Even when alone with her thoughts, Rosina is not alone. In one letter, writing as Bulwer, Rosina recounts when she discovered her husband entertaining his mistress, Laura Deacon – but now the point of view is reversed. "[I]t was eleven o'clock at night," the letter states.

Enjoying a cozy evening with Miss Deacon, Bulwer opens the door and sees his wife: "I was for a moment so taken aback at seeing my victim that I actually staggered." This letter employs Bulwerian affectation ("*soi-disant*" and "*en chemise*") and assumes the careless style of a silver-fork novelist, interrupted by commas and qualifications, as in Bulwer's fiction.[128]

In a later letter, Rosina, writing as Bulwer once again, imitates his tortured syntax and impersonates his debased mind. Speaking of their children, this Bulwer says that

> their too deeply injured mother's name was never to be mentioned to them, as if it had been a crime more heinous than any forbidden in the Decalogue, which, in truth, was a work of fiendish supererogation, as the mere monstrous, unnatural, and unpardonable fact of bringing up children away from a mother whose moral conduct has given no warrant for such an outrage is quite enough to erase all natural affection from their hearts . . .[129]

Later still, Rosina's version of Bulwer reflects on his wife's decision to publish: "Mrs. Bulwer was driven to commit scribbledom, a crime which, as the sequel will show, I registered a vow never to forget or forgive."[130] In Rosina's view of Bulwer's view, her professional career is a "crime" and her writing mere "scribbledom." After some twenty years of separation, Rosina's identity nearly merged with that of her husband. To write her life story, she must write as him. While Chapter 2 indicated the Dantesque life of Thomas Peckett Prest, Rosina's fate seems even more aligned to that of the dwellers in the *Inferno*: she is like a poet bound to echo through the years the one singer she most despised.

The cases of William Makepeace Thackeray and Rosina Bulwer Lytton suggest the cautionary nature of aftertextuality. Does it liberate, or does it imprison? Certainly, their different positions in Victorian Britain must be taken into consideration. Thackeray, as a man in a patriarchal society, had mobility and access that were denied to Rosina; further, she was legally tethered to an unloving and oppressive husband. Author–publisher relations could also be mentioned. Dickens, Thackeray, and Bulwer were not only productive writers; they were for the most part well served by various publishing firms. Rosina, on the other hand, made do with lower-tier establishments, such as Edward Bull and T. C. Newby, and she even attempted a form of self-publishing. With her second novel, *The Budget of the Bubble Family*, Rosina's writing approaches an independence from Bulwer's, with a wit that is very much her own; here she moves, with some hesitation, towards domestic fiction. But a lack of temperament – or talent perhaps – kept her from reaching the achievement of a mid-century realist, who could be gratefully read by later generations. Indeed, Rosina was confined by her husband's style and his narrative modes, just as he confined her in a lunatic asylum, during the summer of 1858. That same year, another writer débuted with a two-volume work of fiction. She, too, would soon be consumed by a web of aftertextuality, her authorial identity poached by opportunistic publishers and identity thieves.

CHAPTER FIVE

Being George Eliot: Imitation, Imposture, and Identity

> ... popularity, as every one knows, is the most complex and self-multiplying of echoes.
>
> *– Scenes of Clerical Life*

George Eliot might seem an unlikely candidate to endure the imitative embrace of Victorian aftertexts: her work was popular but not populist like that of the eager, early Dickens, and her style was pronounced but not overwrought like that of the parody-provoking Edward Bulwer. In the estimation of John Holloway, Eliot was a sage, and she was also an oracle quoted in Alexander Main's anthologies.[1] A sage and an oracle might well escape the mercantile instincts of Reynolds and Prest and the satirical exercises of *Fraser's* and *Punch*. Indeed, the kinds of aftertexts engendered by the successes (and failures) of Dickens and Bulwer seem, at first glance, to have neglected George Eliot. John M. Picker points out that "*Madam Bedes*" and "*Shomolas*" did not roll off the presses.[2] In the *Oxford Reader's Companion to George Eliot*, there is no entry for *imitation, parody, plagiarism, sequel*. A brief entry for "theatrical adaptations" explains that "George Eliot was emphatic in her refusal to countenance theatrical adaptations of her writings."[3] Of course, lax copyright law meant that authorial sanction was superfluous. Yet few Eliot dramatizations reached the stage during her lifetime. There was an *Adam Bede* at the Royal Surrey Theatre (1862), and *Silas Marner*, first published in 1861, inspired both *Effie's Angel* (1871) and W. S. Gilbert's *Dan'l Druce, Blacksmith* (1876). One inhibition may have been the importance of Eliot's narrative voice – calm, knowing, inclusive, analogical – and the challenge of translating that voice into a theatrical idiom. In 1884, on the occasion of another *Adam Bede* play (this one after the novelist's death), the *Daily News* observed:

> As a rule it may be said that George Eliot's novels do not offer any great inducement to the playwright for conversion to stage purposes. The great novelist's marvellous powers of analysing the mental workings of her

characters, as well as the philosophical acumen with which she was wont to play the part of Chorus in her own person, are necessarily lost once her creations are transferred in the body upon the boards of a theatre.[4]

Nonetheless, as Robert A. Colby asserts, "The great vogue of George Eliot's works in the latter half of the nineteenth century produced some curious outgrowths."[5] Picker claims that *Adam Bede, Junior* and *Gwendolen* were the only prose sequels offered while the novelist was still alive, although the former "may never have seen the light of day," which limits the anti-canon to one.[6] Leah Price casts a wider view and considers

> a series of literary doubles who appropriated [Eliot's] work throughout her career: readers who claimed to have written her work, or, conversely, who wrote sequels misrepresented by others as hers; readers who claimed to know (or to be) the originals of her characters; readers who adapted her novels for the stage; and even, more simply, readers who translated them.[7]

Unraveling some of the complexity above, this chapter investigates a few of the "Other Eliots" who haunted the writer during the first and last phases of her novel-writing career, such as Joseph Liggins, the spurious claimant to the honor of being George Eliot, and Edith Simcox, the woman who loved her. The chapter mounts two arguments. One, Eliot was infected by imitation and not immune to the circulation and appropriation of literary identity. Two, this phenomenon changed the trajectory of her career as she responded by lifting the veil, intensifying her style, and becoming "George Eliot" in word and in fact.

George Eliot may have been a sage and an oracle, but one thing that she was *not* was George Eliot. Therein the troubles began. Born Mary Anne Evans, in 1819, the future novelist variously signed or styled herself Mary Anne, Mary Ann, Marianne, Marian, Polly, and Pollian; her surnames included Evans, Lewes, Evans Lewes, and Cross. In her first published work, in the January 1840 *Christian Observer*, she signed herself M. A. E., and Simcox referred to another variant, "little Mary Evans."[8] Part of the confusion stems from her anomalous pseudomarriage to fellow writer George Henry Lewes. Kristin Brady argues that Marian Evans (to use the preferred form of the 1850s) took the name "George" because she could not legally take the name "Lewes."[9] In the mid-1850s, Evans referred to herself as Mrs. Lewes, primarily to deceive landladies, but the ruse soon ventured into fact: "My *name* is Marian Evans *Lewes*."[10] In a letter to James A. H. Murray, she insists, "I wish always to be quoted as George Eliot" and yet signs herself "M. E. Lewes."[11] Upon Lewes's death, in 1878, she legally changed her name to "Mary Ann Evans Lewes" (it seems that she was never actually Marian); and upon her marriage, in 1880, she signed herself "Mary Ann Cross."[12]

For her first major work, *The Life of Jesus, Critically Examined* (1846), her efforts as the translator of David Friedrich Strauss appeared anonymously. When she joined John Chapman's *Westminster Review*, she "stipulated that her editorial role be kept a secret." Rosemary Ashton, recounting the episode, declares that Marian Evans "enjoyed anonymity."[13] In 1856, Evans wrote to her friend Sara Sophia Hennell, "[W]e should all of us pass very different judgments now and then, if the thing to be judged were anonymous."[14] One day later, Evans began to write "The Sad Fortunes of the Reverend Amos Barton," which appeared anonymously, in *Blackwood's Edinburgh Magazine*, in January and February 1857. For her first novel, *Adam Bede*, Evans told the publisher, "I wish the book to be judged quite apart from its authorship."[15] Henry Alley argues that anonymity was not only a practice but also a theme in her fiction: "separating acts of goodness from their acknowledgment."[16] It should be noted that the name "Marian Evans" appeared in print only once, for her translation of Ludwig Feuerbach, *The Essence of Christianity* (1854). Evans, rather like Thackeray, could most comfortably be herself when she was writing as someone else.

Confusion arises when authors hide or disguise their names. In 1859, an anonymous contributor to the *Critic* asserted, "[T]he law of the land … evidently abhors anonymity."[17] Like many others, this critic conflates anonymity and pseudonymity. George Eliot, the pseudonym, first appeared in a letter to the publisher John Blackwood, on 4 February 1857, after "Amos Barton" had already appeared anonymously. Even after Blackwood was disabused of the Eliot fiction, he continued to correspond with George Eliot, "as if making it so."[18] Of course, pseudonyms are an honored literary tradition. Charles Dickens employed "Boz," and George Henry Lewes signed himself "Slingsby Lawrence" for theatrical endeavors and "Vivian" when reviewing for the *Leader*.[19] Alexander Welsh makes the canny point that all writing is, in a way, pseudonymous. "Charles Dickens" or "William Faulkner," appearing on a title page, is a verbal construct and is not the same thing as the Charles Dickens or the William Faulkner that one might meet "face to face" in Victorian England or twentieth-century Mississippi.[20] Rosemarie Bodenheimer contends that "George Eliot" "acquired a kind of independent existence."[21] Subsequent generations of readers read George Eliot in a way that they do not read Currer Bell or Michael Angelo Titmarsh, who are not the subject of biography and remain only as historical footnotes. Bodenheimer also sketches a compelling case that the rise of the pseudonym George Eliot made the domestic fiction "Mrs. Lewes" a rational possibility: "If she could be George Eliot, why not Marian Lewes?"[22]

But George Eliot, who first appeared in print as the author of the 1858 two-volume edition of *Scenes of Clerical Life*, was more than a pseudonym. It is an obvious point but worth remembering that Marian Evans gendered herself male. In the same summer that she turned her pen to fiction, Evans also wrote "Silly Novels by Lady Novelists," an essay that Gillian Beer finds "unsisterly because of its writer's refusal to acknowledge that she is also female, beset by the problems of other women writers."[23] Evans herself was sometimes described as a hybrid, "a pathological monster created by the unnatural conjunction of a masculine mind with a female body."[24] Perhaps unsurprisingly, the first readers of *Scenes of Clerical Life* and *Adam Bede* were divided on the question of gender. Thackeray and Margaret Oliphant thought that George Eliot was a man; Dickens was certain that "he" was a she.[25] A picture emerged of what George Eliot must look like: male, a Cantab, a clergyman, a father.[26] A candidate soon arose who met at least two of these qualifications (fig. 5).

It is instructive to return to Eliot's first published narrative, "Amos Barton," and trace gender signifiers used by the narrator. While Pam Hirsch finds that Marian Evans, in her fiction, "made no great effort to disguise her gender," Rosemary Ashton contends that "[t]he voice of the narrator is androgynous."[27] Barbara Hardy argues that, at least in the earliest fiction, "the voice is masculine. It is the voice of the pseudonym" (although "Amos Barton" predates the pseudonym).[28] In the case of this early text, Hardy seems closest to the truth. In the third chapter, the narrator partakes of the male gaze, as conventionally understood, with "excessive admiration for small hands and feet, a tall lithe figure, large dark eyes, and dark silken braided hair" and confesses, "You and I, too, reader, have our weaknesses, have we not?"[29] While the narrator is privy to what "every husband has heard" (43), he shies away from "women's matters that it would be impertinent for us to listen to" (36). Further, the character Mrs. Barton is something of a Marian Evans: in her skill with needle and thread, "no one would suspect the sex of the tailor" (22).

Besides the gender trouble that kept early readers guessing, George Eliot was sometimes mistaken for someone else. At different points, it was supposed that her writings were (or could have been) the work of Elizabeth Gaskell, William Makepeace Thackeray, and Edward Bulwer Lytton, who felt that Eliot's fiction partook of too much Dickens.[30] Sara Hennell wondered if Evans wrote Margaret Oliphant's *Salem Chapel*; later,

Figure 5 Anne Leigh Smith, *Popular Idea of George Elliott* [*sic*], *in the Act of Composing "Adam Bede."* Reviewers in 1859 determined that George Eliot, the pseudonym used by Marian Evans, must be a man

Thomas Hardy's *Far from the Madding Crowd* was found to contain "the ring of the wit and wisdom" of George Eliot.[31] The foregoing can be read as a somewhat confused history of Victorian fiction, but in the case of George Eliot, literary identity emerged through the medium of what it was not and who it was not, with imitation as the field, the middle distance against which novelists distinguish themselves.

Early reviewers argued that Eliot was an imitator; her chapter mottoes, for instance, echo "the style of Hooker or Burton or Sir Thomas Browne."[32] Like many mid-nineteenth-century novelists, she fell under the sway of Walter Scott and wrote out Scott narratives in her youth (a pastime also pursued by Maggie Tulliver).[33] Mary Anne Evans read Edward Bulwer's *Devereux* and some time later produced her unfinished, Bulwer-scented historical narrative "Edward Neville."[34] By 1857, John Blackwood could write to G. H. Lewes and imply that the favor was returned: readers had been attributing *Scenes of Clerical Life* to Bulwer Lytton.[35] Three years later the baronet praised *The Mill on the Floss* but qualified, "The only criticism I should here make is that now and then there is a little unconscious imitation of Dickens; not more so perhaps than so fascinating and popular a genius as his would inevitably cause in persons writing somewhat after him and resorting to somewhat the same classes of Society for characters."[36] There is an underlying melancholy to this, as if Bulwer Lytton wished that he could say that George Eliot was imitating *him*. Note that Dickens is "fascinating and popular" – qualities that may not coincide with artistic merit – and Eliot's imitation is merely inevitable for those coming "after": a fact of chronology, like midday following morning. *After*, as I indicated in the Prologue, is certainly an ambiguous term: while it may suggest artistic influence, it also implies the more aggressive notion of coming "after" someone. Further, Eliot is described as "resorting" to humble classes of persons, as if other classes were out of stock or out of reach.

In terms of literary form, the nexus of imitation and reproduction continued. Lewes proposed publishing *The Mill on the Floss* in monthly shilling numbers, Dickens's preferred mode.[37] In the event, *Mill* appeared in the same three-volume format as its predecessor, *Adam Bede*. During the 1850s, Eliot shared a publisher with Bulwer Lytton: William Blackwood and Sons. *Adam Bede* was delayed until after Christmas 1858 so that it would not usurp sales from another Blackwood holiday offering, Sir Edward's *What Will He Do with It?* In late 1849, eager to break the back of the triple-decker (with which he had been very successful), Bulwer Lytton explored the idea of publishing *My Novel* in 5s. parts, similar to French *livraisons*.[38] This did not happen. But a number of years later, Blackwood may have remembered or re-originated the idea, and *Middlemarch* appeared in 5s. numbers, between December 1871 and December 1872. Naturally, Bulwer Lytton was perturbed that he could no longer offer the world this literary novelty: "those who may follow the example are looked upon as imitators."[39]

Yet in terms of style, Eliot's connection to Thackeray's writing is stronger. A persuasive *Times* review of *Adam Bede*, attributed to E. S. Dallas, draws comparisons with Thackeray and even imitates the older writer's distinctive voice in order to make a point: "See what a monster I have painted; – I am that monster. Good friends, let us all shake hands."[40] Again, the borderline between parody and criticism blurs. Further, the reviewer argues that Eliot reverses Thackeray's moral charge; while Thackeray demonstrates that everyone is at least a little wicked, Eliot asserts that "we have all a remnant of Eden in us."[41] Intriguingly, *Adam Bede* is found to contain "a sentence which Thackeray himself may have written."[42] The *Times* then quotes two sentences:

> Before you despise Adam as deficient in penetration, pray ask yourself if you were ever predisposed to believe evil of any pretty woman – if you ever *could*, without hard head-breaking demonstration, believe evil of the *one* supremely pretty woman who has bewitched you. No: people who love downy peaches are apt not to think of the stone, and sometimes jar their teeth terribly against it.[43]

The halting construction, the direct address, the sense of shared human frailty, the awkwardness of "hard head-breaking demonstration," and the conversational "No" all evoke the author of *Vanity Fair* and *Pendennis*. Bodenheimer states that Eliot "probably learned this interruptive and confrontational technique from Thackeray," and Beer asserts that Eliot found a "model of masculinity" in his "equivocations of voice."[44] Even as late as *Middlemarch*, Eliot could offer readers a Thackerayan digression on Henry Fielding's digressions.[45] Despite these insights, however, the *Times* reviewer did not hold an answer to the question: who was George Eliot?

***

Do not guess at authorship – it is a bad speculation.

– Marian Evans

Until the end of her life, Marian Evans was haunted by the shade of Joseph Liggins. What began as an amusement became a cover story, then an annoyance, then a threat to her authorial identity, and finally a part of herself – a key to her idiosyncratic, final work.

If Evans did not want to claim the mantle of George Eliot, Joseph Liggins seemed happy to assume the role. This opaque Warwickshire man, in an act that is perhaps unprecedented, became a passive author, one who achieves renown by doing *nothing whatsoever*. In 1857 and again in 1859, rumors circulated in Evans's former county that the author of *Scenes of Clerical Life* and *Adam Bede* was Joseph Henry Liggins (note the symmetry with the name George Henry Lewes, the other man in her life at the time). Alexander Welsh claims that Liggins "shamelessly exploited the secret" and thus "became a force in literary history."[46] Bodenheimer adds that Liggins "pointed up the paradoxes of pseudonymity with a fiendish twist."[47] Susan de Sola Rodstein concurs: "Liggins filled the conspicuous gap created by Eliot's own imposture." Anyone, it seems, could potentially be George Eliot "and profit by it."[48] Various accounts indicate that Liggins, the allegedly impoverished author cheated by the Blackwoods, received charitable donations for this misfortune. Rodstein makes the parallel between author and pseudo-author explicit: "George Eliot, like Liggins, accepts money on the pretense of being someone other than Marian Evans Lewes (or even Marian Evans)."[49] Perhaps better still, one could argue that Marian Evans, like Liggins, accepted money on the pretense of being George Eliot. In 1885, a distempered reviewer, unpersuaded by the adoption of the name Lewes, argued a similar point about the confusion of identity: "It is no more true that the author of *Adam Bede* was Mrs. Lewes than that it is true that the author of *Adam Bede* was Mr. Liggins."[50]

Many writers reduce Joseph Liggins to an anecdote, a pest. "Her works deserved a better author than the unappetising if unloquacious Liggins," quips R. N. Currey.[51] Kathryn Hughes, among biographers, is unsettled, perhaps even mystified by the whole affair. Liggins "cut so shambling a figure that it is hard to believe he thought up the fraud himself."[52] The implication is that Liggins was not only not clever enough to write the works of George Eliot, he was not even clever enough to pretend that he had done so. However, it does not require cleverness for a starving man to covet or purloin a rich man's dinner.

In the various accounts of the Liggins affair, two pieces of the puzzle have always been missing. The first is why so many contemporaries believed that Joseph Liggins, of all people, was the author of *Scenes* and *Adam Bede*. Ruby V. Redinger, for instance, writes that "there is no rational explanation of why Joseph Liggins was catapulted into a brief moment of vicarious fame." Lacking a better notion (and any evidence), she supposes that Liggins was bribed into the imposture by enemies of Lewes (or Marian Evans), who wanted to expose the real George Eliot.[53] The problem with conspiracy theorists is that they always see the world as more orderly and sequential than it actually is: the truth may be messier. During the imbroglio, the *Literary Gazette* recalled the time when the fictional works of Walter Scott were still attributed to the "Great Unknown": "how many men were accused of being the author of the Waverley Novels, before the true author declared himself? And is it likely that they all denied the honour?"[54] Such comments exculpate and help to explain Liggins's behavior. Maybe he wanted to be George Eliot – at least for a while. "The payoff for Liggins was enjoyment of the glory of authorship," declares Alexander Welsh.[55] For Marian Evans, the summer of 1859 was a trial; for Liggins, it was his finest hour. The second missing piece of the puzzle is the voice of Liggins himself. "Mostly he stayed quiet," writes Hughes.[56] On record we have the comments of Marian Evans, G. H. Lewes, the Blackwoods, the press, the clergy and gentry of Warwickshire, Dickens, and Gaskell. The one voice missing is the mute, inglorious Liggins: an omission this chapter offers to remedy.

Biographical information on Joseph Liggins is fragmentary. Born around 1806, he was the only son of a prosperous baker, William, and his wife, Sarah. They lived in Attleborough, about five miles from where Mary Anne Evans was born. In 1824, the baker's son went up to Cambridge and joined St. Catharine's College but was rusticated the same year. An unpublished cache of letters reveals that three years later, Liggins and his father were still corresponding with the college. It seems there was some question about payment. S. R. Hartnell wrote to the tutor George Elwes Corrie, on behalf of William Liggins (which suggests that the baker may have been illiterate). Mr. Liggins sent a payment of £150 in January 1827 through Raine's Bank in London; "the sum remitted would have concerned his college expence," clarifies Hartnell, referring to the son.[57] Over a year later, in October 1828, Hartnell again corresponded with Corrie. By this point it is clear that Joseph Liggins has "left College."[58] Another letter in the file is from a John Newman, of 122 Regent Street, London. In 1831, he requested the address of Joseph Liggins or his father.[59] It is possible that this Newman was a tradesman to whom Liggins was indebted.

Gaps in the story can be filled in by the Reverend John Gwyther, who was a curate at Chilvers Coton, from 1831 to 1841. He may have also encountered Liggins at Cambridge; Gwyther took his BA at St. John's, in 1828.[60] He remembered young Liggins as "a spoiled child." At Cambridge, with "plenty of money" in his pocket, he "formed connexions to his disadvantage and was advised to Rusticate to save expulsion. He never returned to Alma Mater, but travelled a great deal on the Continent and having sown his wild oats was in a reforming state when I parted with him in 1836."[61] The *Manx Sun* claimed that Liggins lived on the Isle of Man around 1832.[62] He also resided at some point in Liverpool and worked for a time as a tutor, but "he appears to have stuck at nothing," according to Hirsch.[63] The 1841 census finds him back in Attleborough and living with his parents.

One myth that attached itself to Joseph Liggins is that he was a minister in the Church of England. He was "an impoverished n'er-do-well Nuneaton clergyman," "a destitute local cleric," and "an obscure Warwickshire parson."[64] Kathryn Hughes offers a correction: Liggins "had not been ordained, but he had been sent to Cambridge with that aim in mind."[65] Elizabeth Gaskell, in a letter to Harriet Martineau, offers one variation on the tale of Liggins. It was not his parents who sent him to university but "a gentleman who had noticed his talents &c."[66] This assertion makes the story a forerunner to *Great Expectations*, in which the relative of another provincial Joe gains the assistance of a generous benefactor. What is clear is that by the late 1850s, Liggins was in Attleborough and down on his luck. He "lived just a few hundred yards" from Christiana Clarke, Marian's widowed sister.[67] Whatever fortune he may have realized from his parents was squandered.

The notion that Liggins wrote *Scenes of Clerical Life* first surfaced in 1857, as "Mr. Gilfil's Love-Story" and "Janet's Repentance" appeared anonymously in *Blackwood's* (as mentioned, the stories would not be publicly attributed to George Eliot until 1858). Frances (Fanny) Houghton, Evans's half-sister, wrote in May 1857 about "a bit of intriguing local gossip."[68] Evans responded with some amusement, denied the authorship of Liggins, and let fall a misleading error by referring to her own work, incorrectly, as "Clerical Sketches."[69] On 4 July 1857, the *Manx Sun* proposed one "Liggers," "an old Cantab," as the author of *Scenes*.[70] George Henry Lewes was delighted by the attribution: "Quel nom!," he wrote to John Blackwood two weeks later. Lewes went on to suggest a parodic version of a Liggers title page: "Liggers's New Novel. / The Manx Cat. / By Joshua Liggers. / 3 vols."[71] It is curious that Lewes here christens the novelist "Joshua" since the *Manx Sun* printed only a surname. This suggests the possibility that Lewes was already aware of Joseph Liggins (through Evans's recollection) and that Lewes substituted one Biblical name beginning with *J* for another.

Marian Evans responded to this first outbreak of Liggins by changing the text of *Scenes of Clerical Life* – the earliest instance of his imposture affecting, even slightly, her literary output. In the opening of "Mr. Gilfil's Love-Story," which appeared in March 1857, there is a character named Mrs. Liggins. This may be a coincidence, or it may be a family name that Evans recalled from her early years. But in the

1858 volume edition, she quietly emended the name to "Higgins," so that the Liggins advocates could not grasp at this shred of evidence.[72] In that same year, John Blackwood encountered Charles Newdigate Newdegate, for whose family Evans's father had long worked as a steward, and Newdegate claimed to know the author, Mr. Liggers (a reappearance of the *Manx Sun*'s variant on the name).[73] Otherwise, the issue remained reasonably quiet until 1859, when *Adam Bede* was published, and the Liggins legend metastasized. By April, Evans admitted to Sara Hennell, "Mr. Liggins I remember as a vision of my childhood – a tall black coated young clergyman-in-embryo."[74] It is telling that she refers to him as a "vision," as if he were another piece of the reminiscence from which she drew some of her *Scenes of Clerical Life*. In fact, in "Amos Barton" there is a Mr. Furness, "who was plucked at Cambridge" and later "published a volume of poems" (52). "Furness" could be a homophone for *furnace*: a fiery place that evokes the warm ovens of the bakers of Attleborough. However, a little more than a week after her letter to Sara Hennell, the amusement dissipated, and Evans wrote to John Blackwood, "[T]his myth about Liggins is getting serious and must be put a stop to."[75]

A pro- and anti-Liggins campaign was waged in the press in the spring and summer of 1859. In the *Times* of 15 April, the Reverend Henry Smith Anders, one of the clergymen who rallied around Liggins, asserted in the plainest terms, "The author of *Scenes of Clerical Life* and *Adam Bede* is Joseph Liggins, of Nuneaton, Warwickshire." Anders continued, "Mr. Liggins himself and the characters whom he paints in *Scenes of Clerical Life* are as familiar there as the twin spires of Coventry."[76] Twin spires is an apt image, since it projects twinned authorship: Marian Evans and her double, Mr. Liggins. George Eliot responded rapidly, with a letter in the next day's *Times*. This letter, it seems, was actually written by Lewes; such an act of substitution implies that "George Eliot" was something of a corporate author, in whom more than one individual could participate. This George Eliot denied the authorship of Liggins yet admitted to being a pseudonym. "Allow me to ask whether the act of publishing a book deprives a man of all claim to the courtesies among gentlemen?"[77] Welsh expands on the ironies contained in this angry query: "Lewes of course knew that he was not George Eliot, knew also that George Eliot was not a gentleman."[78] Curiously, Lewes, like Evans, slightly corrupts the title of Eliot's book: *The Scenes of Clerical Life*.[79] In this case, however, such an unauthoritative slip undercuts the argument.

The issue resurfaced in June, when S. G. O. (the initials used by author, aristocrat, and controversialist Sidney Godolphin Osborne) wrote to the editor of the *Times*, in a piece granted a Scott-inspired headline, "The Great Unknown." S. G. O. misspells Eliot "Elliot," which he perhaps remembered from the aforementioned *Times* review of *Adam Bede*, and he asks for the "mystery" to "be cleared up." He demands that the Liggins claimants prove their case or "admit their *protégé* to be insane or an imposter" – a suggestive pair of choices.[80] Again, the anti-Liggins contingent returned to print, this time with a pair of letters to the *Times*, one from "WM. BLACKWOOD AND SONS" (another corporate author) and one from Eliot. The first letter states that *Scenes* and *Adam Bede* "are not written by Mr. Liggins, or by any one with a name like Liggins" – a phrase that recalls the brief heyday of Liggers.[81] The report of Liggins's ill-gained emolument had circulated by this point, and Eliot's letter states that it is "painful to me" that he should get "charitable donations" on false assertions. What follows is her dolorous stroke: "If those benevolent persons who persist in attributing the authorship of the works in question to Mr. Liggins will induce Mr. Liggins to write one chapter of a story, that chapter may possibly do what my denial has failed to do."[82] Thus, the Eliot Challenge. If you can write like George Eliot, then you may well *be* George Eliot. In the clearest terms, this letter equates literary style with identity. There is no evidence that Liggins ever accepted the challenge. But one can imagine Thackeray rising to the occasion and writing as Liggins writing as Eliot, perhaps for *Punch*.

While the tenor of the *Times* correspondence is measured and calm, the *Athenaeum*, in a trio of articles, offers a more biting tone. Just five days after the pair of letters in the *Times*, the *Athenaeum* of 11 June 1859 asked, "[W]ho *is* Mr. Liggins? Has anybody seen him the flesh? Is he a shadow like George Eliot?"[83] Again, Eliot and Liggins are twinned; each appears to be equally insubstantial. One week later, E. Nicholas, described as a student, claimed to be Liggins's only living male relative. Defending his blood relation, Nicholas equivocates a bit: "Whether or not Mr. Liggins wrote 'Scenes of Clerical Life' and 'Adam Bede' I am unable to say, but the story of 'Amos Barton' is just such a story as he could write, and there are names, characters, and scenes in it which I recognize as belonging to the district."[84] Thus, Nicholas does not deny Liggins's authorship and even avows that "he could write" such a work as Eliot's, even though the "names, characters, and scenes" belong to a geographic region, to which more than one potential Eliot would have had access.

Two weeks later, the periodical attempted to settle matters. "It is time to end this pother about the authorship of 'Adam Bede.'" By this stage, in London literary circles, it was whispered that Marian Evans, the woman who lived with Lewes, was in fact the author in question. The *Athenaeum* then surmised that the writer could be "a clever woman with an observant eye and an unschooled moral nature." Ultimately, this vigorous and mean-spirited article suggests that the authorship debacle is a "mystification" generated by Eliot and friends to promote sales of the novel. Instead of Liggins writing Eliot, now Eliot is found to have created Joseph Liggins; he is a character from her imaginative (if morally corrupt) mind. The *Athenaeum* categorizes Liggins, Eliot, and recent correspondent E. Nicholas as fictions, "seemingly a far-away echo of Sairy [*sic*] Gamp, Betsy [*sic*] Prig, and Mrs. Harris." This allusion to *Martin Chuzzlewit* implies that one fictional character (George Eliot) has imagined another for his or her rhetorical purposes, as if George Eliot were now plagiarizing Charles Dickens. The article continues, "Vanish Eliot, Nicholas, Liggins, – enter (let us say, at a guess) Miss Biggins!" This last figure obviously connotes Miss Evans. In short, the whole fiasco is merely a publisher's ploy, aimed, like the sapient pig, at "penny-paying rustics," but "no book was ever permanently helped by such a trick." The *Athenaeum*, in the end, proved to be wrong. Marian Evans became the accepted author, and Liggins receded into obscurity.[85]

All of this is a matter of existing record. The story can be gleaned from Gordon S. Haight's biography or from his collection of Eliot's letters. Other biographers nod to the narrative, and Bodenheimer and Welsh are especially perceptive. It still remains to be seen why, precisely, Liggins was taken for Eliot. This hapless soul cannot have been the *only* university-educated man in nineteenth-century Warwickshire who could have witnessed some of George Eliot's scenes of clerical life. But Joseph Liggins, the baker's son, had one qualification more, which has yet to be clearly asserted: he had literary pretensions. The scant evidence shows that he worked for a Liverpool newspaper, although it is not clear in what capacity. After the Reverend James Richard Quirk was finally disabused of the notion that Liggins was the author of George Eliot's early works, Quirk asserted that Liggins would write a book soon.[86] Indeed, the Liggins that the local busybodies latched on to was not only an available blank of a person with nothing better to do than claim to be George Eliot for a fleeting summer of reflected fame: at some point in his life, he wanted to be a writer and may have made a few attempts.

In June 1859, the *Literary Gazette* intuited the connection between the spurious Liggins claim and artistic ambition: "if a literary man, the suspicion of such an authorship might do him infinite good."[87] That is to say, a Liggins who was or wanted to be a writer had a reason to pursue the false identification; it might boost his own writing prospects. In a reminiscence in a local newspaper, almost twenty years after the summer of Liggins, an anonymous writer reiterated Liggins's pretensions to authorship. Liggins often "talked vaguely of his publishers, and was believed to be 'writing a book.'"[88] Charles Dickens, too, recalled that Liggins was or wanted to be in print. In his typical attraction-repulsion manner, Dickens wrote to G. H. Lewes, "I have a horrible and unnatural desire upon me to see Liggins: whom, I am proud to remember, I contemptuously rejected."[89] In what manner could Dickens have rejected Joseph Liggins? Possibly in his editorial capacity, if Liggins submitted an article to *Household Words*.

Beyond the impersonation of George Eliot, Liggins may also have been a forger. Evans herself heard that Liggins was showing neighbors a manuscript of *Scenes of Clerical Life*, written in his own hand.[90] Bodenheimer insists that the rumor was "never substantiated," but it was enough to disturb the actual author.[91] The very idea that Liggins was literally writing the words of Eliot (copying them out, like a plagiarist) was enough to make her, soon after, remove the veil of pseudonymity. Liggins, of course, also claimed to write *Adam Bede*, although he may not have bothered to produce a fake manuscript. Intriguingly, he claimed that he submitted the novel to the Blackwoods some ten or twelve years earlier (thus, in the 1840s).[92] This backdating follows the temporal direction of the novel's historic setting (around the turn of the nineteenth century), but it also places the "writing" of *Adam Bede* in the past, when Liggins's literary ambitions may have still been vibrant, his potential not yet dissipated. This particular lie suggests that *Adam Bede*, a piece of his forgotten "past," returned, in a sense, to Liggins, just as the ghosts of Warwickshire (including Joseph Liggins himself) descended on Marian Evans, who thought that she had escaped.

Still: why did Joseph Liggins let it be known that he was George Eliot? He may have felt that he *could have been* George Eliot, if things had turned out differently. He was born in the right place and time (Warwickshire in the early nineteenth century); he was familiar with the scenes, characters, and local legends that prompted *Scenes of Clerical Life*; he had the beginnings of the requisite education of a gentleman at Cambridge; he had traveled abroad for the broader perspectives it supposedly grants; and he even enjoyed the seeming benefit of being a man.

Even if Liggins, with his thin writing résumé, could reasonably have been proposed as the mysterious George Eliot, it is not clear who proposed it. The Ligginsites of the 1850s, such as the Reverend Quirk and Charles Holte Bracebridge, circulated the story that Liggins, like Malvolio, had the honor "thrust upon him."[93] Reticent Mr. Liggins "never asserted or denied that he was the author," which seems untenable over a two-year period.[94] Gaskell, on the other hand, heard from a local source about a dinner party in which Liggins essentially admitted to being George Eliot.[95] Various clues indicate that the legend of Joseph Liggins originated in a tavern. Kathryn Hughes relates that the would-be author was "a penniless alcoholic"; another source calls him an "oracle of the taprooms."[96] In the history of Joseph Liggins, fact and myth blend somewhat, but a pattern emerges from within the clouded recollections.

The anonymous writer for the *Literary Gazette*, using the coy indirection of nineteenth-century journalism, recounts the experience of a visitor to Aylesbury (who may be the journalist or a friend – it is never quite clear). This visitor chats with a barmaid who, belying the narrator's class prejudice, is a reader of "Maga" (the affectionate name given to *Blackwood's Edinburgh Magazine*). She recognized scenes and situations in the recently published *Scenes of Clerical Life* and insisted that "the author's name was so-and-so." The barmaid could further contend that So-and-So "certainly 'wrote things,' because he never went about without little square bits of paper and a pencil, and he was always bringing out the pencil and a square of paper and 'making a note.'" In short, this unnamed figure is figured as a writer – armed with the tools of his trade. Further, the quotations within the quotation above might indicate So-and-So's own language, especially "making a note." Not only was he a writer, he wanted other people to know it. Recalling this trip to the country, the visitor finally remembers that So-and-So was named Higgins, which he may have encountered in the 1858 edition of *Scenes*. Naturally, the visitor connects Higgins with "the fathering of the book upon Mr. Liggins," a phrase that is notable for its gender assumption.[97] So the question is this: did Joseph Liggins let it be known to an Aylesbury barmaid that he, of all people, was the author of *Scenes of Clerical Life*? Was he trying to impress her, bed her?

Another hazy version of events appeared in the 1877 *Nuneaton Observer and District Advertiser*, a local newspaper that sold for a penny. In a section headed "Rambles Roundabout," the anonymous writer recounts the Liggins story from a distance of eighteen years. Again, it seems that the authorship story was born in a pub. With hindsight, this writer allows his narrative to drift into the mythic, with a classic structure of a prodigal's return and his consequent triumph. Still, the article creates one of the clearest pictures of misty Joseph Liggins. It also accords with accounts from the Reverend Gwyther and others. "After years of wandering he returned to his native village, living a wretched aimless life, now teaching a few lads, now writing letters for ignorant villagers." This last practice finds him following in the footsteps of S. R. Hartnell, who once wrote letters for Liggins's father. The *Nuneaton Observer* paints a picture of Liggins as an intellectual bully, lording over mental inferiors at a local pub. He holds court, quotes Byron, brags about London and his travels, rolls out "some Greek hexameters," and appears "dogmatic and sententious." It is in just such a scene, with "a jug of beer" in hand, that one can imagine Liggins letting it slip that *he* was George Eliot.[98]

Besides the question of origins, the other missing piece of the Liggins puzzle is his own voice. According to the *Times Literary Supplement*, he is "the one person in the story with no recorded statement to his name."[99] In the file at St. Catharine's College, Cambridge, there is one letter from Liggins himself. It is addressed to the "Rev G. Corrie," dated 25 February 1827, and sent from an inn at Bath. I will quote the letter in full, not because it is revelatory (it isn't) but because the Man Who Would Be George Eliot has been stone silent for a century and a half.

Revd Sir,

It is to me, a matter of the greatest concern and anxiety, that I am prevented by illness, from being now at Camb—. When I left, it was with the intention, and expectation, of being able to return by the 1st Inst.

I had prepared Mr Blakelock whom I had engaged to read with [?] my examination to expect me at that time. Whether I ought to have written to you earlier than this I do not know; but I assure you I was for some time unable to write or even to move but with extreme pain. I desired Mr James one of the Surgeons who attends me to write to you which he tells me he has done. I hope his letter was satisfactory.

I will leave Bath for Camb as soon as I possibly can with safety. I hope to be able by perseverance and assiduity to recover all I have lost. I have been in many respects very remiss and culpable and more particular in my lavish expenditure of my time & money. Trust for the future I shall be more careful of both[.] My Account due to you, has been paid into the Bank of [?] & Co for you, but you have no doubt recd it er[e] this; if not, however, on application you can: 150£ was sent there for you. If you will favour me with a letter, as to what plans I must adopt, or how I must act, at the present, I shall feel myself extremely honored and obliged.

I am Revd Sir your ob^d humb^l Servant

J Liggins[100]

Here Liggins is (or pretends to be) the penitent, the prodigal son – wasteful, extravagant, ready to make amends. This confession tallies with accounts given by others. Note that in this small sample, Liggins shows a fondness for hendiadys: "concern and anxiety," "intention, and expectation," "perseverance and assiduity," "time & money," and the adjectival forms "remiss and culpable," "honored and obliged." It is a trope that expresses grandiosity, making an idea larger by compounding it, multiplying it.

His byline appeared at least once, on an 1833 pamphlet, *A Refutation of the Calumnies Circulated by the Anti-Slavery Agency Committee, against the West India Planters*, by Joseph Liggins. The editors of *The Letters of Charles Dickens* duly attribute the pamphlet to our Joseph Liggins.[101] The pamphlet is dated 30 January 1833, with an address, 37 Mincing Lane, which places Liggins in London, in near proximity to the John Newman of Regent Street who wanted his address in 1831.[102] The Liggins who emerges in the pages of the *Refutation* is difficult for a modern reader to embrace. While not exactly pro-slavery, the pamphleteer is opposed to the anti-slavery movement; he accuses its members of deception and refers to "[t]he unprincipled crusade lately waged against England's colonies and England's welfare." The author is a gradualist: he is against "*immediate*, unconditional emancipation."[103] This London-based Liggins wrote to the *Morning Post* a number of times on this subject, and he spoke at an Anti-Slavery Society Meeting on 20 July 1833. As reported in the *Morning Chronicle*, "He had himself 3,000 negroes under his care, and . . . he felt a great anxiety for their future welfare."[104] In short, this sounds like a wealthy colonist and not the baker's son; the pamphleteer must have been another man named Joseph Liggins, a double to the doppelgänger. Yet *another* Joseph Liggins, a poacher who resided in Leicestershire, was "charged with trespassing, on a Sunday, during divine service."[105] The three Ligginses here recorded – a slaver, a poacher, and an impersonator – all represent helpful metaphors for the arts of literary theft. The poacher, it seems, died in 1855, and Liggins of London in 1860; the latter's British estate was worth some £12,000.[106] Joseph Liggins, of Warwickshire, left no such wealth at his demise. In May 1872, he was taken from his home by the authorities, and he died in the Chilvers Coton workhouse.

***

... if it succeeds, I imitate it.

– G. H. Lewes, Ranthorpe

Joseph Liggins was not the only Other Eliot to stalk Marian Evans during her first flush of success. In 1859, the year of *Adam Bede*, there was a book about Seth Bede; Adam himself turned author; and Thomas Cautley Newby advertised an unofficial sequel.

To start with the first, *Seth Bede, "the Methody:" His Life and Labours; Chiefly Written by Himself* appeared in 1859. It is a forty-four-page pamphlet, which sold for one shilling. The title, at least, has authorial sanction. Chapter 1 of Eliot's novel refers to "Seth Bede, the Methody."[107] This pamphlet is an instance of the trouble with "originals" – that is, historic persons who are supposed to be the inspiration for fictional characters. Marian Evans's reminiscences of childhood inevitably recalled some of the men and women of Nuneaton and its surrounding neighborhoods. A few of them appear, in some form, in *Scenes of Clerical Life* and *Adam Bede*. The Reverend John Gwyther, for instance, has been accepted as the original of the Reverend Amos Barton.[108] Charles Holte Bracebridge, one of Liggins's staunchest advocates, finally ceded ground by September 1859 and turned his attention to tracing the sources of Eliot's imagination.[109] There is a perversity to original-hunting, as practiced by Bracebridge and others in the nineteenth century. The effort to find the "originals" of fictional characters inevitably reduces the work in question to something less original, less fictive. While the search may begin with admiration for a particular novel, the process, like that of plagiarism-hunting, diminishes the "originality" of seemingly original authors: rather than imitate other texts, these authors steal from nature.[110] One of Bracebridge's stranger ideas was that Liggins "supplied material" for Eliot, as if she could not conduct her own research. Ironically, Bracebridge, the "muddle-headed magistrate," may have himself inspired *Middlemarch*'s Mr. Brooke.[111] In the case of *Adam Bede*, three central characters have possible "originals." Adam bears traces of Marian's father, Robert Evans; Seth may have been inspired by Samuel Evans, Robert's brother; and Dinah draws on Samuel's wife. In a journal entry for the novel, written around the time of its completion, Evans asserts, "Adam is not my father any more than Dinah is my aunt. Indeed, there is not a single *portrait* in 'Adam Bede.'"[112]

The publishers of *Seth Bede, "the Methody"* disagree. Samuel Evans died on 8 December 1858. Not long before, he either sat for an interview or wrote an account, which became the source of *Seth Bede*.[113] Perhaps unsurprisingly, the pamphlet confuses identities and refers to Marian's uncle as Sam or Seth, his fictional namesake. Her aunt Elizabeth Tomlinson, who married Samuel Evans, is referred to as "Dinah ———" (16), again confusing the actual and the fictional. (Note that in the novel, Adam, the presumed Robert Evans figure, marries Dinah.) One curious sentence reads, "The 'Adam Bede' of the novelist, Seth Evans's brother, died some years before him" (37). The phrase "of the novelist" suggests a fictional character, but here Adam Bede is said to be "Seth Evans's brother," when in fact Adam is Seth Bede's brother and Robert was Samuel Evans's brother. This same confounding sentence implies that Adam Bede, a fictional character, died, which strictly speaking cannot happen. Such are the ontological disorders that arise when original hunting.

Overall, *Seth Bede* serves as an amplifying sequel to Eliot's novel. The implication is that the pamphlet has the real story: here is what the novelist failed to tell you. In this way, the little book evokes some of the unsanctioned sequels to *The Pickwick Papers*, such as *Pickwick in America* and *Pickwick Abroad*. The introduction to *Seth Bede* states, "The talented authoress of 'Adam Bede' has, under fictitious names, made known to the world the peculiar virtues and characteristics of her two uncles. No one acquainted with either of them will dispute the correctness of the descriptions. They are life-like – photographs of both" (3). Here "fictitious names" may refer to the George Eliot pseudonym as well as the cloaked character names. The mention of "two uncles," however, is an error; Robert Evans was Marian's father, not her uncle. Further, the pamphlet praises "the correctness of the descriptions," as if this were George Eliot's aim. In contrast to the "life-like," photographic quality praised in the introduction, the journal entry noted above states that the characters are not portraits.

Seth Bede is a stylistic imitation as well. The story opens in an Eliotic manner, with a wise, analogical, and Bible-infused narrator: "The death of a good man is a calamity. The loss of his influence and example in the sphere of life in which he existed leaves as it were an oasis in the wilderness to be replanted, and, however humble his lot, his departure must be mourned as that of a light withdrawn from the earth" (5). The voice here is that of the sage, the Eliotic narrator who is prone to "epigraphs and lapidary generalizations," which critics of the novels sometimes find "excessive or tautological."[14] Further, a local clergyman is described in terms that resemble one of Eliot's unreconstructed rectors, such as the Reverend Irwine; the *Seth Bede* clergyman is "one of the old class, fond of fox-hunting, and other amusements" (9). In scenic descriptions, the pamphlet reproduces Eliot's vision of a pastoral idyll, threatened but not yet ruined by inevitable progress. "Those who are familiar with the county of Derbyshire, cannot have failed to notice the extreme simplicity of the inhabitants in the more secluded rural districts, and which the great modern innovator, the rail, has not yet altered in any material degree" (7).

Like other aftertexts, *Seth Bede* slides into replicating, rather than correcting or enhancing, a charismatic original. "But marriage was far from Dinah's thoughts," the narrator explains, "her mission she considered was to minister to the wants of others in this world" (19). At times, *Seth Bede* abandons the *Adam Bede* narrative and drifts into guide-book terrain, much like various surveys of the taverns of *Pickwick* or geographical settings of Dickens's novels. The pamphlet refers to "the delightful village of Edlaston, distant about 14 miles from Derby, and three from Ashbourne" (24). Derby itself gets the travel-book treatment: "The population of the town in 1851 was 7,480 inhabitants. The church is a spacious and venerable structure, capable of seating 2,000 persons" (29). Despite the pamphlet's promise to elucidate the life of Samuel Evans, the self-confessed purpose at the end is to "have the effect of encouraging youthful Christians to imitate his example" (42). *Seth Bede* is then an imitative work promoting imitation.

As one opportunistic publisher issued a life of Seth Bede, another sold a pamphlet written by his brother. *The Natural History of Puseyism: With a Short Account of the Sunday Opera at St. Paul's, Brighton* is an undated, sixteen-page pamphlet, probably also from 1859, credited to one "Adam Bede."[115] In a preface, the fictional character, now turned writer despite his limited verbal agility, states his case: "The Author of the following pages has endeavoured to bring before the public a few of the more obvious facts connected with the pretensions of Puseyism."[116] This tract against the Tractarians then opens with a stylistic imitation but, like *Seth Bede*, soon finds mimicry too difficult or too irrelevant to the purpose at hand. Adam begins, "If there is anything that can be predicted with certainty of human affairs, it is that they are for ever fluctuating, for ever changing, and constantly in a state of ceaseless motion."[117] Here Adam, like his creator, proffers a general rule and assumes the role of the natural historian of his title. The majority of the work, however, is more fevered and hysterical in tone, with many exclamation points and a clenched, unironic dislike of Dr. Pusey and his ilk. "Mormonism and Spirit-Rapping, Puseyism and Holloway's Pills" are among modern phenomena according to this Adam Bede.[118]

Other iterations of an *Adam Bede* phenomenon arose in 1859. In an advertisement in the *Times*, a firm called Cramer, Beale, and Co. offered "SONGS from the most interesting POPULAR NOVELS of the season." Among the songs mentioned are "Dinah" and "Hetty," named for the heroines of *Adam Bede*.[119] But the work that most distressed Marian Evans was not a pamphlet or a piece of sheet music but a book, one that threatened to reproduce her own imaginative form: the novel. On 22 October, an advertisement appeared in the *Examiner* for "ADAM BEDE, JUNIOR. A Sequel." In one volume, priced at 10s. 6d., the new work from Newby was supposed to be "Just ready."[120] A week later, the *Times* carried a similar advertisement, this time for a work dubbed "A SEQUEL to 'ADAM BEDE'" and allegedly ready "in a few days."[121] On 19 November, Newby advertised his spurious sequel in the *Examiner* once more. "In consequence of the great demand for this work the day of publication is unavoidably postponed to the 26th inst."[122] Despite the enthusiasm, Graham Handley asserts that "[t]he notorious Newby did not issue his sequel ... either because of the threat of legal proceeding or because it didn't get written."[123] *Adam Bede, Junior* may be one of the world's lost books – or a non-existent one.

Still, in the autumn of 1859, Marian Evans and G. H. Lewes were concerned. He wrote to John Blackwood in October to illustrate the authorial confusion wrought by the "Blackguard" Newby:

> From two people who spoke to me on Saturday I learned that one concluded that Adam Bede Junior was by George Eliot and the other by Liggins. These ideas of course will obtain currency in the provinces, and will damage the *next* work. As the title of Adam Bede is copyright, and no one can have a right to publish a *sequel* to a living author's work surely Newby might be stopped by a letter threatening legal proceedings?[124]

Here Lewes, the consummate print-culture professional, evinces some misunderstanding of copyright law. Blackwood apparently reminded Lewes of "Pickwick Abroad and the many similar felonies on popular authors."[125] Copyright in nineteenth-century Britain, as previous chapters have indicated, did not protect novelists from imitative productions.

Dickens, pierced by plagiaristic Pickwicks and knock-off Nicklebys, took an interest in the affair. In November, he wrote to Lewes and suggested a paper in *All the Year Round* "protesting most strongly and indignantly, in the interests of Literature, against that most shameful and abominable proceeding." He wanted Lewes to write the piece: "You have the whole question at your fingers' ends." Dickens also provided an anecdote about one of Newby's salesmen who had solicited "a certain Librarian" to stock *Adam Bede, Junior*. The unnamed librarian hesitated to subscribe to such a dishonest endeavor. "'Dishonest!' says the Scavenger; 'how do *you* know by whom it's written? How do *you* know it is not by Miss Evans?'"[126] Deniability is key to Newby's approach. Readers have access to the information on the title page of a work but cannot know for certain whether the attribution is genuine or spurious. Recall that the *Athenaeum* doubted the existence of Joseph Liggins and wondered if George Eliot were nothing but a "shadow."[127] Like Liggins, Thomas Newby penetrated the gap between Marian Evans and George Eliot, between an author and his or her work.

Punch took measure of the saga of *Adam Bede, Junior* with its usual caustic wit. In "A Venerable and a Non-Venerable Bede," *Punch* "condemns spurious sequelizers and their publishers as base profiteers."[128] Mr. Punch expresses "infinite contempt" for those who manufacture reproductions of other people's works "for the sake of certain miserable shillings." According to *Punch*, Newby "does not see why something should not be done by which he may profit from the notoriety attached to the words *Adam Bede*."[129] It is curious that *Punch* stipulates "the words *Adam Bede*," as if the proposed sequel were not a sequel to Eliot's novel but merely to the two words "Adam Bede" or, more specifically, to the "notoriety" attached to those words. It could also be argued that *Punch*, in pieces such as this one, produced its own form of aftertext and profited as a result.

In the summer of Liggins and before the autumn of *Seth Bede* and *Adam Bede, Junior*, Evans, it seems, considered generating her own sequel, continuation, or spinoff to her runaway success of a first novel. In the letters there is a reference to *The Poysers at the Seaside*, another unrealized literary work. On 20 June 1859, William Blackwood wrote to his brother:

> With regard to the Poysers at the Seaside Simpson is not very anxious. He does not think favourably of it commercially. I have rather the feeling that the Poysers are so good as they stand in Adam Bede that it would be a pity to weaken the effect of that unique work by extending as it were one section of it. Altogether I doubt whether such a thing will be for the author's advantage in the end; at the same time there is no doubt it would take, and if the author is bent on it we would be wrong not to go into it heartily, but I certainly would not press it in any way.[130]

It appears that someone conceived of an extension to *Adam Bede* based on the Poyser family. This could have been an intended dramatic adaptation or a prose continuation. William Blackwood's sensitivity to the author's "bent" makes it seem that Evans was at least interested, although the idea may have been hatched by Lewes. He had theatrical experience and may have seen the potential of Poysers on the stage. However, Gordon S. Haight observes, "There is no further allusion to *The Poysers at the Seaside*."[131]

Is there a progression from *Pickwick* to *Adam Bede*, from *The Penny Pickwick* to *Adam Bede, Junior*, from *Master Humphrey's Clock* to *The Poysers at the Seaside*? In Genette's terminology, *Master Humphrey's Clock* and the would-be *Poysers* are autographic sequels – sanctioned by the original creators; *The Penny Pickwick* and *Adam Bede, Junior* are allographic – works by some other hand.[132] It should be noted that the pair of *Adam Bede* spinoffs never materialized (as far as I can tell).[133] Does this indicate a diminution in the power of aftertextuality as the century progressed? The attraction was certainly still there. Newby may simply have been unlucky or cowed, and the Blackwoods may have dodged an authorial misstep. Clearly, the bright flame of George Eliot's early fiction drew an array of moths, from the false claimant Liggins to the original-hunting Bracebridge – the uncreative and the didactic – all of whom would remain merely the source anecdote were it not the case that these Eliot aftertexts impacted her career in ways that have yet to be fully explored.

***

... heaven has taken care that everybody shall not be an originator ...

– *Middlemarch*

The unrealized *Poysers at the Seaside* was by no means Marian Evans's only response to the success of *Adam Bede* and the echoes it engendered. In a letter to Charles Bray, in November 1859, she evaluates her recent travails: "You see I am well provided with thorns in the flesh, lest I should be exalted beyond measure. To part with the copyright of a book which sells 16000 in one year – to have a Liggins, a Bracebridge, and an unknown writer of one's 'Sequel' all to one's self – is excellent discipline."[134] From 1857 to 1859, Evans experienced, in rapid progression, anonymity, pseudonymity, and the unmasking of the pseudonym. In *Silas Marner*, Godfrey Cass explains to his wife, "Everything comes to light, Nancy, sooner or later. When God Almighty wills it, our secrets are found out."[135] Even in Eliot's final two novels, reverberations of the Liggins period continue to sound. In *Middlemarch*, Mary Garth writes a book, but everyone believes that Fred Vincy is the author because "he had been to the university ... and might have been a clergyman if he had chosen" – that is, he is another iteration (albeit more agreeable) of Joseph Liggins. Similarly, Mr. Gascoigne, in *Daniel Deronda*, pens a pair of anonymous articles, which are "attributed to some one else."[136]

In the late 1850s, Marian Evans, the successful, London-based writer, may have thought that she had escaped her past. Then the Reverend Gwyther, her source for Amos Barton whom she believed to be dead, proved to be alive and keen to write letters to the Blackwoods. Liggins rose from memory to claim that the memories were his own; Bracebridge traced the originals of Dempster and Dinah Morris, among others; and *Seth Bede* offered Evans family legend to the readers of George Eliot. Rather than veer away from this vexed history – perhaps to write a novel of fifteenth-century Florence – she returned willfully to the past with her next major fiction, *The Mill on the Floss*, which many consider to be her most auto-biographical ("George Eliot's *David Copperfield*," says Haight).[137] Bodenheimer explains that *Mill* "was written during the year of Liggins"; with this novel, "George Eliot drowns not only her childhood but the whole world of her early fiction."[138] Welsh qualifies this point and makes the case that Marian Evans, the girl who lived, was a counterfactual Maggie Tulliver: "Instead of drowning with her arms around her brother, Marian Evans became an intellectual."[139] Silas Marner's past is also washed away, it seems, when he tries to locate Lantern Yard. "The old home's gone," he laments.[140]

Although Maggie and Tom in *The Mill on the Floss* recall Mary Anne and her brother, the novelist had learned her lesson; the past is now more densely embroidered, the narrative less obviously peopled with actual persons (aka originals) from among the Evans family or the neighboring ones. Nancy Henry makes a compelling case that Evans was "disillusioned" by the Liggins fiasco, and her later works grew "more complex, challenging, and allusive."[141] The authorship struggle of 1859 to 1860, in this reading, stands as a fault line separating phases in Eliot's career. After *Mill* and *Silas Marner*, "[h]er work becomes more dense and allusive, less popular, and less autobiographical."[142] It was as if Marian Evans no longer wanted to write the kind of books that Joseph Liggins could have written or Thomas Newby could have sequelized; she wanted to write the books that only George Eliot could write.

Besides the stylistic changes that gestate in this period, there are three works by Eliot in which the Liggins affair and the struggle for authorial identity ring clearest: "The Lifted Veil" (1859), "Brother Jacob" (1864), and *Impressions of Theophrastus Such* (1879). Intriguingly, these three are among her less familiar writings, deviations from the progression of the major novels, from *Adam Bede* to *Daniel Deronda*. Further, Gillian Beer discerns that Eliot uses first-person narration three times, including in "The Lifted Veil" and *Theophrastus*.[143] "Brother Jacob," although told by a wry, omniscient narrator, is closely focalized on its male protagonist. Bodenheimer adds that "[i]t was typical of George Eliot to reverse the gender when she took on the darkest and most alienated parts of herself."[144] Latimer and David Faux, in particular, animate the darker energies of Eliot's imaginative vision.

Evans interrupted work on *The Mill on the Floss* to compose the short, atypical story "The Lifted Veil." It was completed in April 1859, when she "was in the thick of the battle against the Liggins imposture," and published in the July issue of *Blackwood's*, just as her own authorial veil was lifted.[145] Lewes recommended that the name George Eliot be appended to the text, in contradiction to *Blackwood's* usual practice of anonymous contribution. His argument was that Eliot but not Joseph Liggins would create such a tale of the macabre, that "The Lifted Veil" would serve as an antibody to kill the anti-Eliot.[146] In some ways, the story depicts the reverse of its author's experience. Latimer can perceive all through supernatural ability; she feared that all would see her through the dismantling of the "Eliot" fiction: the sole object in a panopticon of literary exposure. In "The Lifted Veil," omniscience is a kind of curse – "my unhappy gift of insight," Latimer calls it.[147] As Beer argues, "[H]e cannot escape his own insight or give it any issue."[148] Further, Latimer may be Eliot's earliest vision of a Liggins figure: the non-writer, without a creative outlet for his vision, doomed to the ultimate anonymity of the ages. "I shall leave no works behind me for men to honour," he says.[149]

"Brother Jacob," written in 1860 but not published until 1864, is even more closely attuned to the Liggins narrative. Eliot tells the story not from the perspective of the thieved but that of the thief: the Liggins surrogate, a con artist and a prodigal son, who adopts another name (as Liggins adopted "George Eliot"). "Brother Jacob" marks an attempt to answer the vexing question: why did Liggins do it? David Faux, the wily hero of the tale, "yearns for adventure, accomplishment, upward mobility, wealth, impressive relations, and a new patronym."[150] As the narrator observes of David, "His soul swelled with an impatient sense that he ought to become something very remarkable."[151] Susan de Sola Rodstein calls "Liggins a prototype of the imposter David Faux," and she explains that the short story "was the first work begun after the public disclosure of [Eliot's] authorial identity in 1859."[152] Names in the story point indirectly to

Ligginsian origins. Joseph in the Bible is the son of Jacob; the short story
makes the titular Jacob not the father but the brother to the Joseph Liggins
figure, David Faux. Bodenheimer reminds us that the Biblical David was
"the clever younger son"; thus, brother Jacob "is an Esau figure."[153]
Further, David's new surname, Freely, recalls one of Evans's letters: she
retells the story that Liggins is the author of *Adam Bede* and that he "*gives it
freely to Blackwood*."[154] As Liggins was a secret sharer to Eliot's literary
production, so the brothers in "Brother Jacob" are twinned in a sense, as if
fragmented parts of one consciousness. This is why Jacob uncannily finds
David whenever he is not supposed to be found.

David travels abroad only to return somewhere that is close to home, so
close that Jacob can merely wander around and find him. Why not settle
somewhere farther off? One could similarly ask why a plagiarist chooses to
reproduce the words of another when a clearly established provenance can
expose the deception. For obvious reasons, literary history does not offer
examples of the perfect, undetected plagiarism; yet this may be because
Thomas Mallon is right when he suggests that the plagiarist wants to get
caught.[155] In Eliot's story, David, aka Edward Freely, is depicted variously
as a plagiarist and a forger. When he courts Penny Palfrey in the conventional manner, she "wondered if he had made the words of the
valentine!"[156] – that is, are the sentiments his own or borrowed? He also
forges a letter from a supposed "uncle in Jamaica" from whom he has great
"expectations."[157] Like Liggins with his manuscript of *Scenes of Clerical
Life*, Edward Freely shows the letter to his would-be father-in-law,
Mr. Palfrey. David/Edward, again like Joseph Liggins, travels overseas
and then returns to England, where he triumphs, briefly, under an assumed
name. It should also be remembered that Liggins's father was a baker.
David/Edward pursues the profession of a confectioner, one who prepares
and bakes foods for consumption by the neighborhood.

The connections among print culture, sugar, and the sources of that
sugar are quite provocative. Rodstein notes that the Sugar Equalisation
Acts reduced its price and led to the lower classes eventually consuming
more sugar than the upper classes.[158] Similar legal reform of the so-called
taxes on knowledge also placed more print matter into the hands of the
middle and working classes as the century progressed. "Silly Novels by
Lady Novelists," incidentally, connects the two forms of consumption
when it refers to literary offerings that are "a sort of medicinal sweetmeat
for Low Church young ladies."[159] For Rodstein, sugar is "the locus of an
intense moral and economic debate over slavery, emancipation, free trade,
and social definition."[160] "Brother Jacob," in fact, reproduces abolitionist

language, first in its title and then when Mr. Prettyman asks if Jacob is, in fact, Edward Freely's brother. "All men are brothers," Freely responds.[161] David/Edward, ever the hypocrite, mimics an abolitionist slogan, even though he had hoped to live in the Caribbean and lord it over the black population by mere virtue of his whiteness. His end, while not quite as ignominious as that of Joseph Liggins, is obscure: "Mr David Faux, *alias* Mr Edward Freely, had gone – nobody at Grimworth knew whither."[162]

After a burst of energy in the 1857–60 period, the cloud of Eliot imitators and imposters dispersed. It may be that Nancy Henry is correct in arguing that the "more complex, challenging, and allusive" Eliot daunted some readers and disengaged the epigones.[163] It should also be recalled that the early novels of both Dickens and Bulwer drew more aftertextual attention than the later. Dickens's works of the 1850s and 1860s elicited occasional squibs, and Bulwer's late fiction was less frequently parodied. Imitations of the novel are most sharply focused on that which is *novel*: the new authorial voice that breaks through the crowd of middling, grey, and three-volume novelists satisfied to net a modest living and drift into the backlist. So Eliot earned a period of quiescence. But in the last stage of her career, the issue resurfaced.

Her final work, *Impressions of Theophrastus Such*, returns forcefully to the subject of originality and unoriginality. It was as if Joseph Liggins, now deceased, had never gone away. The memory may have been stirred by Algernon Charles Swinburne. In 1877, he issued *A Note on Charlotte Brontë*, which praises her beyond all other "female immortals," including those who happen to be alive (read: George Eliot).[164] Confusingly, he combines Charlotte Brontë and her sister Emily by lauding the "twin-born genius" of *Jane Eyre* and *Wuthering Heights*.[165] More to the point, he accuses Eliot of plagiarizing from Elizabeth Gaskell. With a great deal of indirection, Swinburne suggests that *The Mill on the Floss* owes an "apparent amount of obligation ... to Mrs. Gaskell's beautiful story of 'The Moorland Cottage.'"[166] A mild accusation, no doubt, but it may have put Evans on the defensive.

Theophrastus, published two years later, was originally to be titled "Characters and Characteristics by Theophrastus Such, edited by George Eliot."[167] In the end, she kept the guise of Theophrastus but not that of an editor. The historic Theophrastus, a Greek, lived circa 370 to 288 B.C., and Haight notes that Evans consulted Isaac Casaubon's "edition of Theophrastus."[168] The revised title, *Impressions*, suggests print culture: both the printing press and the first, second, and third "impressions" that it produces. Nancy Henry also reminds us that "impressionism" was then a contemporary phenomenon in the visual arts.[169] In contrast to the unifying, omniscient narration of the late Eliot novels, *Impressions* offers fragments that leave it to the reader to form the whole picture. Hirsch says that Eliot "adopted the persona of an irascible middle-aged man who, unlike herself, is a failed author" – perhaps a vision of the older Liggins, withdrawn from the field and reflecting on literary lives unled.[170] Bodenheimer locates an "autobiographical impulse," especially in the first two chapters, "Looking Inward" and "Looking Backward."[171] Edith Simcox, who excelled at both, declares these chapters to be "more or less personal confession or reminiscence."[172] Once again, when writing as someone else, Eliot can most be herself.

Robert Macfarlane investigates possible sources of this surprising, final work. He mentions G. H. Lewes and Auguste Comte but neglects Marian Evans's brushes with literary imitation and appropriation.[173] Indeed, the Liggins story reappears, now years later, not as it was, but as Evans internalized it. There is a bitterness to *Impressions of Theophrastus Such*, a sense of depletion. A satire that is unfunny veers into invective. Evans, imbued as she was with nineteenth-century science, composed something of a zoology: a bedraggled parade of imitators, monomaniacs, bullies, and hacks – a funhouse full of cracked reflections. Pepin, one of the demented writers on display, believes that he is already the author of the works he only *intended* to write. Authors of the past are merely "pre-Pepinians," as if waiting for his advent.[174] Pepin (named for a son of Charlemagne who proved to be less than great) is a Liggins type, deceiving and self-deceived. Similarly, "How We Encourage Research," the third chapter, refers to people "believing that they are still what they once meant to be" (232). As I have argued, Joseph Liggins seemed to believe that he was or could have still been the writer that he had hoped to become – a George Eliot, for example.

Theophrastus is also a vision of Marian Evans herself. "[M]y father was a country parson, born about the same time as Scott and Wordsworth," the narrator informs us (35). Robert Evans was just a little younger than those writers, and it is telling that Eliot allies her father with two of her literary forefathers. The chapter goes on to explain that the Reverend Mr. Such was something of a plagiarist, since his sermons may have been "copied out from the works of elder divines" (40). Theophrastus, as an author, was in turn the victim of such pilfering. His own efforts went unnoticed, he explains, "as if they were anonymous pictures"; but "when they were appropriated by some one else they were found remarkable and even brilliant" (12). Despite this lament, Theophrastus, like the young Marian

Evans, prefers anonymity in authorship: "The haze is a necessary condition. If any physiognomy becomes distinct in the foreground, it is fatal" (21).

But the chapter that is most clearly concerned with plagiarism and appropriation is "The Wasp Credited with the Honeycomb." The image in the title finds a predecessor in "Brother Jacob." David/Edward hopes to lure his brother away from Grimworth and the confectionery shop, but "there would never be any security against his coming back, like a wasp to the honey-pot."[175] "The Wasp" chapter introduces readers to Euphorion, whose name connotes joy. He "is disposed to treat the distinction between Mine and Thine, in original authorship, as egoistic, narrowing, and low" (189). Euphorion believes in a collective consciousness and insists on "the infinitesimal smallness of individual origination compared with the massive inheritance of thought on which every new generation enters" (190). It is self-serving for plagiarists and wasps to discover that originality counts for very little and that we owe more to the "massive inheritance" of our nation or species. "The Wasp Credited with the Honeycomb" rehearses some of the familiar excuses for plagiarism, such as polygenesis and forgetfulness (197). However, the narrator drily notes that "some persons are so constituted that the very excellence of an idea seems to them a convincing reason that it must be, if not solely, yet especially theirs" (201).

This chapter contains one of Eliot's fiercest statements on the Liggins affair, twenty years after the fact – a piece of indirect autobiography filtered through the persona of Theophrastus:

> It is this foolish trust in prepossessions, founded on spurious evidence, which makes a medium of encouragement for those who, happening to have the ear of the public, give other people's ideas the advantage of appearing under their own well-received name, while any remonstrance from the real producer becomes an unwelcome disturbance of complacency with each person who has paid complimentary tributes in the wrong place. (205–206)

The bitterness is undeniable, despite the loftiness of tone. "[S]purious evidence" suggests the slenderness of the Liggins claim, and the "real producer" must be Eliot herself. But in a plagiarism narrative, sympathy quickly moves from the plagiarized to the plagiarizer. The "real producer" who points out the true authorship is something of a crank or a spoilsport, one who disturbs the "complacency" of what readers were all too happy to believe.

In its final pages, "The Wasp Credited with the Honeycomb" evolves into a fable, with various animals struggling to identify the "author" of the honeycomb. The Owl appears to be a version of Charles Holte Bracebridge or James Richard Quirk, promoting Musk-rat as the onlie begetter of the honey. The Owl "argu[es] from his particular knowledge that the animal which produced honey must be the Musk-rat, the wondrous nature of whose secretions required no proof" (207). It is telling that the Owl requires "no proof," just as Bracebridge promoted Liggins's authorship with little more than a boast. Soon, however, "the Musk-rat began to make himself obtrusive, believing in the Owl's opinion of his powers, and feeling that he could have produced the honey if he had thought of it" (207–208). Again, this perfectly captures Liggins's deception and self-deception. In the end, the Fox reveals that the progenitor is really the Wasp.

The foregoing might make *Impressions* sound like a settling of scores. But there is a generosity in Eliot's depiction of literature's scavengers and scamps. In the opening chapter, Theophrastus (sounding rather like Thackeray) declares, "Dear blunderers, I am one of you" (6). There is also at least a possibility that *Impressions of Theophrastus Such* was a response to a *Daniel Deronda* phenomenon. Like her first novel, her last attracted a variety of echoes, variants, and imitative sequels. But the affect in the later case was reversed. *Adam Bede* was a beloved text, and everyone from Joseph Liggins to Methodists to anti-Puseyites to "Paternosteric" publishers wanted a piece of its glory.[76] *Daniel Deronda*, on the other hand, is a "problem" novel. The *North American Review* of January 1877 refers to "the almost universal disappointment at the unanticipated conclusion of the story, – a conclusion which many readers have resented as though it were a personal grievance or affront."[77] Robert A. Colby finds that Eliot's last novel has "two separate audiences."[78] Readers often grapple with the book; some go further and attempt to chastise, correct, rewrite, or reduce it to its correct proportions.

One of the first writers to offer a *Deronda* aftertext was the young Henry James. His "*Daniel Deronda*: A Conversation" appeared in the *Atlantic Monthly*, in December 1876, just three months after the novel's final part was published. In a piazza one autumn, three friends with unlikely names discuss George Eliot's latest. Theodora adores it; Pulcheria is disparaging; and Constantius, who plans a career as a reviewer and novelist, is Henry James – or at least his spokesman. Constantius identifies the trouble with *Deronda*: "Roughly speaking, all the Jewish burden of the story tended to weary me."[79] He refers to this as "the cold half of the book."[80] Sententia is also an issue: "the importunity of the moral reflections." Without apparent irony, he asserts that Eliot "has chosen to go into criticism"; in fact, Marian Evans abandoned criticism to pursue a career as a fiction writer. Constantius wonders if the author were "under a sort of external pressure" to produce the book – for instance, the pressure to write another great "George Eliot" novel, a worthy successor to her achievement in *Middlemarch*.[181] Many believe that James himself produced a worthy successor to *Daniel Deronda*, namely *The Portrait of a Lady*, which was published serially, from 1880 to 1881. George Levine calls it a "conflation of the Dorothea sections of *Middlemarch* and the Gwendolen sections of *Daniel Deronda*," while John M. Picker finds that James's novel "is a reply to *Deronda*," one that removes the "bad part" – that is, it omits the Jews.[182]

To stray beyond the nineteenth century for one proleptic moment, F. R. Leavis "believed himself to be completing and perfecting the task James had begun with his review."[183] In *The Great Tradition* (1948), Leavis writes, "In no other of her works is the association of the strength with the weakness so remarkable or so unfortunate as in *Daniel Deronda*."[184] He goes on to distinguish "the good half" from "the bad half," which recalls James's "cold half."[185] Claudia L. Johnson clarifies that Leavis found the bad half of *Deronda* to be bad not because of James's "Jewish burden" but because of its artistic failings.[186] Ultimately, Leavis decided to generate a new novel by George Eliot, entitled *Gwendolen Harleth*; through "simple surgery," he could remove "the deadweight" of the Deronda narrative.[187] The Gwendolen narrative, for Leavis, "represents the great creative George Eliot" and is a "greater novel than *Middlemarch*" (he likes *great*).[188] However, the task proved difficult in reality. "[I]t is impossible to purge *Gwendolen Harleth* completely of the voluminous clouds of Zionising altruism and Victorian nobility that Daniel trails and emits."[189] Such a statement undercuts Johnson's assertion. There is more than a whiff of anti-Semitism here; the idea that Daniel "emits" something suggests an odor. One would think that a British critic writing in the years after the Second World War would have been more wary of threatening to "purge" Jews from even a literary work, and "voluminous clouds" conjure the gas chambers that were a not-so-distant memory. Picker remarks, unpleasantly, that Leavis's version was to be a "castration" or "circumcision."[190] In 1973, the Bodley Head invited Leavis to prepare his *Gwendolen* for print.[191] But for some reason, production was halted in 1976 (the centenary of *Daniel Deronda*).[192] So *Gwendolen Harleth* joins *Adam Bede, Junior* in the genre of unrealized Eliotic aftertexts.

Leavis was anticipated by a 1914 silent film entitled *Gwendolin* [sic] and by *Gwendolen; or Reclaimed. A Sequel to Daniel Deronda. By George Eliot*, published in 1878. This *Gwendolen* is an imitative sequel, like *Pickwick in America* and the proposed *Adam Bede, Junior*. Appropriately, *Gwendolen*, the novel that doubles *Daniel Deronda* (itself a bifurcated Daniel/ Gwendolen narrative), was itself doubled. Two different American publishers offered this work in the same year, with slightly different titles. *Gwendolen: A Sequel to George Eliot's Daniel Deronda* was published by Ira Bradley and Company; the aforementioned *Gwendolen; or Reclaimed* was published by William F. Gill and Company. Both firms were located on Washington Street, in Boston.[193] Gill had produced a piracy, *The Dickens-Collins Christmas Stories*, in 1876. It is thus possible that Gill, the trans-Atlantic pirate, also pirated the work of his neighbor. In any case, Gill's edition offers one feature that Bradley's does not: an author, Anna Clay Beecher. This shadowy figure may have been a relative of Harriet Beecher Stowe, a sometime correspondent of Marian Evans. It seems that no one ever disputed Beecher's authorship of *Gwendolen*, so the attribution may stand.

John M. Picker and Graham Handley castigate Beecher's *Gwendolen* in the manner that usually results when aftertexts encroach on a Victorianist's professional terrain. Robert A. Colby is gentler. He mentions that Gill's edition of *Gwendolen* was produced to look like Harper's Library Edition of the Works of George Eliot, with green covers and her signature on the binding.[194] Beyond this, Colby notes "peculiar merits of style," which one supposes is ironic.[195] Picker adds that *Gwendolen* "strikingly anticipates, in title and spirit, Leavis's century-later abridgement of *Deronda*." However, "[t]he prose of *Gwendolen* is turgid, the epigraphs by canonical authors superfluous, and the unintentional parody of Eliot's style painful."[196] As in the case of some Dickens aftertexts, opportunistic imitations earn the epithet of "parody." Picker argues that sequels usually honor an original, but *Gwendolen* "is a reproach"; it "attacks … Eliot's plot, structure, and characters, but especially her treatment of the Jewish Question."[197] Handley, more affronted still, finds the novel to be "an offence against the lasting codes of humanitarian tolerance and enlightenment by which [Eliot] wrote and lived."[198] The style, too, distresses Handley: "The author of *Reclaimed* is full of wordy sentiment, most of it incomprehensible, a mass of verbiage wrapping up spurious wisdom."[199]

Gwendolen: A Sequel (aka *Gwendolen; or, Reclaimed*) was a response to a perceived reader response. The *New-York Times* of 30 March 1880 mentions the sequel and states that "[t]he average reader demanded that Deronda should marry Gwendolen, instead of Mirah, and they have never forgiven either him or his creator for marrying the wrong woman."²⁰⁰ In this way, *Gwendolen* serves as a piece of wish-fulfillment for frustrated readers, and it anticipates twentieth- and twenty-first-century fanfiction in that one reader of *Deronda* was able to "correct" an errant creator and generate preferred narrative outcomes. Despite the promising title, Leavis would be disappointed that *Gwendolen* is not a *Gwendolen Harleth* with Deronda surgically removed or reduced to a mere advisory capacity. Rather, the sequel, at least at the start, replicates the balancing act of Eliot's novel by interweaving Deronda and Gwendolen narratives. However, as *Gwendolen* progresses, Gwendolen recedes. When she becomes the object of Daniel Deronda's search, she fades into a cipher, and we lose access to her consciousness. The double narrative then tracks Deronda and a "comic" subplot featuring Hans Meyrick. So this *Gwendolen* is not, in fact, a *Gwendolen Harleth* and could be called *Daniel Deronda II*.

The opening mimics the question posed at the beginning of *Deronda* with an overwrought and exhausting series of questions – an attempt to out-Eliot Eliot.

> What is happiness? Who can claim it as their own? What is the substance, is it material or is it fancy – a phantom which lures to pursuit, but vanishes at the touch – that attracts with its sound, and disappoints with its substance – which blossoms delight, but whose fruits destroy – a fairy myth to those who are in pursuit, and a destroying fiend to the possessed?²⁰¹

And so forth. In emulating Eliot, Beecher seems to recall the ending of *Vanity Fair* – "Which of us is happy in this world?"²⁰² – another instance of confusion among literary voices. She also channels one of America's founding documents, the Declaration of Independence, with its "pursuit of happiness." In the novel that follows, the plot is driven by the mysterious origin of a package sent to Deronda. It contains the all-important bracelet, and his attempt to solve the mystery leads to a search for Gwendolen Grandcourt. Mirah conveniently dies at the outset, and this time disgruntled readers get the ending they desire.

Eliotic elements in *Gwendolen* include secrecy, gossip, scientific observation, and attention to the workings of consciousness. As Picker mentions, Beecher consistently uses epigraphs at the head of each chapter – a practice associated with the later novels of Eliot. Beecher quotes Coleridge, Cowper, Dante, Goethe, Irving, Keats, and a number of unidentified sources. Beyond such elements, *Gwendolen* represents an attempt to replicate the authorial voice of George Eliot, a feat that Joseph Liggins and Thomas Newby only threatened to do. Eliot was noted (and disparaged) for her *sententia*, the non-narrative dollops of observation or insight that filled so many pages in Alexander Main's anthologies. *Gwendolen* offers kernels such as "When a belief is shaken, hope will clutch at superstitious signs" (35). Chapter 5 turns hyper-Eliotic when a compulsive string of sententious utterances flows from the narrator:

> In selfishness we experience the most utter destitution of the soul. . . .
> . . . where goodness and charity abound, misery cannot. . . .
> Selfishness gives nothing to cling to in adversity. . . .
> Beauty may claim admiration, graces may induce homage, character may awaken respect. The three combined may create a passion for possession. But this passion cannot be called love. Love hath a holier motive than either gain or possession. (80–82)

The author here seems to be attempting her own anthology, "Wise, Witty, and Tender Sayings of Anna Clay Beecher."

Her sequel exerts itself to recreate Eliotic passages that mirror internal processes. In chapter 5, almost nothing happens, as Gwendolen dwells upon her life thus far. Chapter 7 is similarly event-free; now the novel focuses on Deronda's inner processes. By the end he writes a letter and goes outside. Early on, *Gwendolen* in one sentence catches Eliot's narrative voice (if a bit heightened) and a reasonable facsimile of her generalizing omniscience: "His life he considered but an ephemeral scintilla in the general germination of matter, and humanity in general a contribution to the laws of nature" (108). Later: "He experienced a presentiment of a possibility – new alike to his thoughts and yearnings, yet tantalizing to his peace of mind – the possibility of love" (186). This is almost Jamesian. At least, the "presentiment of a possibility" offers the fraught hesitation of a parody of James. At times, however, this heady game gets out hand, and Beecher's narrator settles for sound over sense: "Reasoning towards a conclusion, he was still deducing probabilities from an hypothetical standpoint, which was a logic too vague for evidences of fact; such conclusions could not be of a kind as to be self-sufficient of their own quality" (242). This narrator mistakes complexity for depth.

Like some of the prose imitations of Dickens, *Gwendolen* tropes itself and makes imitation a theme. The narrator states, "Human nature is constituted upon a pattern of imitative philosophy, we take up opinions and experiences on trust, and generally without guarantee, without examining and judging for ourselves" (97). In short, we are all unreflecting copycats. Later, and unironically, the narrator dismisses the use of "textbooks" because "instead of thought inspired by the object, we appropriate the interpretation of some one else . . . we learn to imitate" (287). Clearly, Anna Clay Beecher's "text-book" was *Daniel Deronda*, which she appropriated and imitated to the best of her ability.

In a curious sequence, Hans, the artist, sneaks into the working studio of an esteemed German painter in order to peer into the master's compositional process. Hans, in this regard, is an embodiment of Beecher herself, who peers into the atelier of *her* master, George Eliot, in order to learn how to write an Eliotic novel. At this point in *Gwendolen*, the narrator inserts an unidentified aphorism: "The mind is but a barren soil; a soil which is soon exhausted, and will produce no crop, or only one, unless it is continually fertilized and enriched with foreign matter" (193). Hans finds the artist at work on a painting of Napoleon. "With a keen perceptive appreciation of an artist's vision, [Hans] saw it all, clear through the idea of the painter" (198). As a fellow laborer, Hans can see what the painter means to do, as Beecher, studying Eliot's artistic process, supposedly perceives the novel that Eliot *meant to write* but fumbled in the execution.

Beecher, however, fumbles herself in the attempt to produce a George Eliot novel. Like *Seth Bede*, the sequel drifts into travel literature as Deronda and Hans undertake a Grand Tour, and the final scene is pure melodrama, with Gwendolen dying of an unnamed fictional-character disease until she is reclaimed by her hero. At times the narrator's voice is a little too excited to be a plausible facsimile of Eliot's: "A knock at the door; a despatch, a momentary sensation of weakness came over him as if his heart stopped beating" (32). The narrator employs short, telegraphic sentences ("The full moon" [36] and "A thunderstorm arose" [38]) to create a sense of breathlessness quite removed from Eliot's detached, contemplative ideal. Ultimately, *Gwendolen* represents the revenge of the Silly Novels by Lady Novelists. It is as if the castigated Lady Novelists had rewritten *Daniel Deronda* in their own, feminized image. *Gwendolen* offers descriptions of generic beauty, scenes of illness, and tea. "It was a starlit night, such as might rival the finest ever seen," purrs the narrator (34). Beecher, in contradiction to Eliot's impulses, employs cliché ("Time will heal all wounds" [43]) and hyperbaton ("mild featured, but fading with age, is she whom she calls mother" [42]).

Finally, *Gwendolen* deviates from *Daniel Deronda* with scenes of anti-Semitism. This sequel not only feminizes but also Christianizes a secular original. To some extent, *Gwendolen* is a New Testament to Eliot's Old: the revelation of Jesus was always the missing element. In a German churchyard, Deronda literally finds Christ, as a statue: "a life-sized and remarkably life-like representation of the crucified Saviour" (152). The

Jewish storyline in *Deronda*, carefully engineered by Eliot, is now merely "a whim" and Mordecai "a fanatical dreamer" (102–103). *Gwendolen*'s narrative reverses the conversion story of Eliot's; Deronda is now reclaimed for Christianity. In this manner, Beecher solves the problem for readers, such as Constantius and Leavis, who were uncharmed by Eliot's fascination with Judaism. Deronda can return to England, marry the "right" (Christian) woman, and *Daniel Deronda* – or *Gwendolen* or *Gwendolen Harleth* – can reclaim its stature as a "Victorian" novel, domestic, uninterested in mysticism or the East, and part of a great tradition.

In its handling of the "Jewish burden," *Gwendolen* resembles another unauthorized sequel, this one a miniature, just a few pages compared to Beecher's 312-page tome. Yet both sequels dispatch with Mirah so that Deronda can marry Gwendolen. *Punch's Pocket-Book* appeared from 1843 to 1880 (dated 1844 to 1881) and sold for 2s. 6d. or 3s. 6d. The tiny volumes were designed to be personal diaries or calendars. The first half of each is filled with useful facts, such as the birthdays of the royal family, names of Members of Parliament, banking and insurance information. The latter half of each is a Lilliputian version of *Punch*, with original content and illustrations by John Tenniel, among others. *Punch's Pocket-Book for 1877*, produced in late 1876, offers its buyers "Book IX" of *Daniel Deronda*, subtitled "Tire and Side-on."[203] In two little chapters, each with an epigraph, *Punch* mocks Eliot's novel and employs stereotypical humor. Using a comic trope also found in *Pickwick* derivatives, Mirah writes to her husband, "I am lunching with Hans on pork chops and sausages."[204] *Punch* catches the ostentation of *Deronda*'s Jewish chapters, "the sands of Semitic inspirations."[205] Deronda himself begins to resemble a stage Jew in physical appearance: "his finely cut nose sensibly developing into the nobler prominence of the Judaico-Roman, his naturally undulating hair curling in sympathetic ringlets."[206] Yet it is possible that the target was not Eliot but rather the Prime Minister, Benjamin Disraeli, a frequent punching bag for the *Punch* brotherhood. By the end, Deronda decides to stand for Parliament in Buckinghamshire, Disraeli's home county.

Marian Evans in her letters does not refer to *"Daniel Deronda: A Conversation,"* *Gwendolen*, or *Punch's Pocket-Book for 1877*. By the 1870s she was perhaps above the fray, too rich and too successful to be bothered – or maybe too well guarded by Lewes in a glass menagerie of comfort and good feeling. The three Derondic aftertexts are also distinctly minor literature, and two of them were published in America. As Dickens found in the 1840s, publishers in the former colonies were keen to produce and reproduce "English" literature. A personal transformation was also at work during this period. In the late 1850s, George Eliot was revealed to be Marian Evans, the *other* Mrs. Lewes (not the one to whom he was inconveniently married). By the 1870s, Marian Evans Lewes became, to some extent, George Eliot: a self-imitation. Ruby V. Redinger argues that the novelist "grew into the name, endowing it with a personality all its own"[207] – that is, the fiction writer became her own fictional character. Eliza Lynn Linton found that Evans crafted a persona for herself, "the goddess on her pedestal," and proceeded to embody it.[208] Similarly, Rosamond Vincy, in *Middlemarch*, "was by nature an actress ... she even enacted her own character."[209]

The goddess whom Marian Evans embodied needed worshippers, and in the 1870s a coterie of young persons formed a circle of admiration around the aging novelist. Alexander Main compiled the anthologies; John Walter Cross married the widow and wrote her biography; and Elma Stuart purchased the burial plot next to Evans's to spend eternity side by side. Referring to this period, Nancy Henry describes "worshippers" and "worshipful homage"; an 1881 article mentions "worship paid at the shrine of George Eliot."[210] Bodenheimer notes that identity shift was part of the transformation, from fallen woman to goddess: "For the younger generation she was not Marian Evans, who had run away with George Henry Lewes."[211] Instead, she was George Eliot.

***

> I will take the life she points to, lose myself in it and leave a few impersonal footprints.
> – Edith Simcox

Of all the admirers who paid reverence at the Priory, perhaps none was more enamored with and fixated on George Eliot than Edith Jemima Simcox. Born in 1844, she was a contemporary of Gwendolen Harleth (who would have been twenty in 1864). The Simcox family was comfortable, upper-middle class. Simcox's two older brothers both went up to Oxford, and both became Fellows at Queen's College. Their father was George Price Simcox (yet another George). Edith, like the young Marian Evans, wrote and reviewed for London periodicals, but Edith also managed a cooperative shirtmaking enterprise, Hamilton and Company, from 1875 until 1884. She published three books in her lifetime, the last a two-volume history of ownership in the ancient world. Her name would probably be forgotten if she were not "the would-be sweetheart of George Eliot."[212]

Edith Simcox, who never married, was in love with Marian Evans, an unrequited infatuation that lasted beyond the novelist's death.

It seems that she loved the writing first. Simcox reviewed *Middlemarch* for the *Academy* and found it to be "a fresh standard for the guidance and imitation of futurity."[213] Like Evans, Simcox at first used a pseudonym: H. Lawrenny. In letters to the *Times*, she deceptively signed herself "E. J."; in the resulting correspondence, she was "'mistered' of course with success."[214] Simcox "thought she had a man's mind, and she cherished hopes of becoming an important writer."[215] This brief biographical overview should suggest that Simcox, on paper at least, had the makings of another George Eliot. Information on Simcox can be derived from her journal, "Autobiography of a Shirtmaker," held in the Bodleian Library and first published in 1998 with a more marketable title, *A Monument to the Memory of George Eliot*. The journal covers the years 1876 to 1900; roughly two-thirds of the text focuses on the George Eliot years.

Edith Simcox met her idol in December 1872, the month in which *Middlemarch* completed its serial publication. Five years later Simcox noted that 8 December 1877 was "the anniversary of the day ... when I first saw her handwriting," presumably a letter inviting Simcox to visit.[216] It is intriguing that she celebrates the day when she saw Evans's handwriting, her manuscript, not the woman herself. Simcox, in love with Marian Evans, also admired Lewes and may have been relieved by his presence, a useful impediment to uncontrolled desire. When Lewes died, rather than trying to capture the emotionally weakened novelist, Simcox, according to Ellen Bayuk Rosenman, "pulls back, refashioning her desire into an identification with Eliot."[217] It is telling that when the widow married Johnny Cross, Simcox commented, "If I ever write another book I shall dedicate [it] to the loved memory of George Henry Lewes."[218] Thus, she merges her identity with that of Marian Evans, as if honoring the memory that the widow seemed to neglect.

Simcox loved Evans and wanted, perhaps, to be her. "I have copied Her ideal of a great and good man's life, and some day before I die perhaps it may be given to me to write of Her as She would wish."[219] Copying the Eliotic ideal, Simcox of course replicates a "man's life." (The capitalization of "Her" and "She" also stresses Simcox's reverence.) Rosenman reads the story of Simcox and Evans as a bad fairy tale.[220] George Eliot is the undying mother who prevents her child from growing up and experiencing life's richness; it is a *roman* with no *bildung*.

But perhaps mother–daughter is not the right metaphor. Imagine instead a temporal one: Simcox and Evans represent different stages of existence. Simcox, like a young, aspiring George Eliot, shielded herself with a pseudonym and broke into male-dominated print culture, first with journalism, then book-length publications – just as her predecessor did. If Eliot is a version of what Simcox could have become, it is also the case that Edith Simcox is a counterfactual Marian Evans. Gillian Beer notes that, for Evans, "Simcox represented, perhaps, a road not taken, an avatar of achievements she had not pursued." What is more, Simcox's "career seemed to take up and take farther George Eliot's own early experience as an intellectual journalist and translator."[221] In this regard Edith Simcox is a different kind of Other Eliot: she is the one who does not "marry" George Henry Lewes, turn to fiction, and withdraw from the world; she is the one who writes erudite, book-length works of non-fiction; she is the independent female, living alone, yet active in achieving social justice. Perhaps this is the person that Evans saw when Edith Simcox visited the Priory: the woman that she, Mary Anne Evans of Warwickshire, could have become.

K. A. McKenzie, in his account of Simcox's life, asserts that her three published books "were written under the inspiration of George Eliot."[222] Bodenheimer uses a similar phrase and refers to works written "under the influence of George Eliot," as if she were an intoxication or narcotic.[223] *Natural Law: An Essay in Ethics*, Simcox's first book, was published in 1877. This plodding, well-researched volume reads like a George Eliot book if George Eliot had no talent. Simcox follows the practice of compulsively appending epigraphs; she quotes Spinoza in Latin, Montesquieu in French, Coleridge in English, and the *Imitation of Christ*, among other sturdy authorities. *Natural Law* is not an imitative work, although it simulates Eliot's erudition and authority of tone. Naturally, Simcox gave a copy to Marian Evans. It seems that the author waited a long time for her idol to respond and "was devastated" when that response was not forthcoming.[224] At last, Evans commented positively about the effort and suggested that her disciple "write a history of religious thought, or a natural history of Christianity."[225] What is telling about this notion is that it sounds like a project that Marian Evans of the 1850s might have pursued. *The Life of Jesus* was a recent accomplishment and "The Natural History of German Life" (1856) an even more recent title for the *Westminster Review*. In other words, she proposed that Simcox write a book that Evans herself might have created, had things turned out otherwise – had she not become George Eliot.

In 1878, Simcox told Evans her aspiration to write "a history of property." Evans "thought it was a failing" that Simcox aimed to produce a book that would be "impracticably complete."[226] That is, the author of *Middlemarch* feared that Simcox was something of a Casaubon, whose own impracticably complete work is, famously, never realized. Edith, writing as E. J. Simcox, managed to complete two plump, octavo volumes of *Primitive Civilizations; or, Outlines of the History of Ownership in Archaic Communities*, published by Swan Sonnenschein (also the publisher of Devey's *Life of Rosina*), in 1894. Although a history of property, Simcox's book does not address literary property. Haight notes that the published volumes, covering Egypt, Babylonia, China, and other ancient societies, are but "a fragment of her ambitious plan."[227]

From a literary-historical perspective, Simcox's most important book is her second. *Episodes in the Lives of Men, Women, and Lovers* was written during the last year of Evans's life and just after her death. Five chapters appeared as independent articles in *Fraser's Magazine*, in 1881, and the complete volume was published in 1882. The form resembles *Impressions of Theophrastus Such. Episodes*, as the name suggests, is not a novel but rather a sketchbook, a string of impressions told by a series of narrators. The trio of *Men, Women, and Lovers* is particular. Simcox – a tomboy as a child who wanted to be (or possess) George Eliot, who was really a woman – perhaps felt herself to be part of that third, not-quite-gendered category. The working title was "Vignettes," and many of the vignettes read like emotional autobiography. In her journal Simcox wrote, "Barring the Introduction, which amounts to little, every scrap of feeling is taken from my own experience."[228] Rosenman describes the book as "a series of dreamlike, loosely connected fictional vignettes that encode and rewrite her erotic frustrations."[229] Some of the pieces are quite modernist, at times Joycean, and Rosenman concedes that Simcox is "an experimental writer."[230] Water and drowning are never far away, and readers recall that the latter is a motif in Eliot's fiction. Simcox also employs Eliotic chapter mottoes: Burton, Fletcher, James I of Scotland. The final chapter appends a quote from the Talmud, as if replicating Eliot's late gesture towards Judaism. *Episodes* occasionally displays the Eliotic gift for sententia: "Weapons have changed since Homer, but dying is much the same as in the 'Iliad.'"[231] However, like the author of *Gwendolen*, Simcox sometimes falters into cliché, for instance: "Opportunity comes to those who know how to wait" (88).

Many of the *Episodes* rework the stimulating and vexed relationship between Edith Simcox and Marian Evans. Sometimes the narrator is male, sometimes female; sometimes lovers unite; sometimes parting is inevitable. Character names include Marian, Edith, Elma, and Johnny (Simcox claimed to have no imaginative ability). A frame story, entitled "In Memoriam" (note that Evans died two years earlier), emulates the first of Evans's published fictions, "Poetry and Prose, from the Notebook of an Eccentric." Both narratives open with a man's death and a trove of writing that subsequently becomes available. In *Episodes*, the "master" of an unnamed island dies at sea. A new master creates a tradition in which inhabitants of the island, after seven years' residence, contribute a story or recollection to a communal writing project, a "big, clasped volume, with 'Vignettes' stamped on the cover" (3). Thus, the master and his fellow authors form something of a club, or literary corresponding society, which summons memories of *The Pickwick Papers* and *Master Humphrey's Clock*. Dickens himself undertook such collaborative projects with his Christmas Stories, for *Household Words* and *All the Year Round*, for which he might provide a frame and others contribute tales. Obviously, the conceit of *Episodes* also evokes classics of group narration, such as *The Decameron* and *The Canterbury Tales*.

The eleven vignettes that follow are supposedly drawn from the master's ever-growing book. One vignette, "Love and Friendship," stands in synecdochic relationship to the whole: it is a tale of tale-telling round the fire. Like many others, this one reconfigures the Lewes–Evans ménage of the 1870s. Lewes appears as the Admiral. His wife, the Marian Evans figure, is "Madame V—," a woman in her fifties (the age at which Simcox knew the novelist). Like George Eliot, Madame is omniscient; the narrator reports, "I had nothing to tell Madame but what she had seen and knew" (190). Joining the older pair is a younger one: the unnamed male narrator and Elma (recalling fellow worshipper Elma Stuart). Madame tells the first tale of the evening, a faux historical narrative that could have been mocked in "Silly Novels by Lady Novelists" as a "*modern-antique*."[232] The Admiral's tale deals with the fantastic; it speaks of witches who can remove and hide the hearts of giants. In sharp contrast, "At Anchor" is a protomodernist short story, with an ending worthy of Joyce's *Dubliners* (1914). Reuben, an artist, perhaps like Simcox, expects his art to communicate his love to its object, "a pretty rich young woman of the gay world" (125). Despairing that his work failed to convey the intended message, he escapes to the seaside and contemplates his lamentable situation in internal monologue. Here is the last sentence: "And so he went back to the station and caught the Parliamentary train to town; and his landlady hoped he had a pleasant journey and would not fail to change his socks" (138).

Perhaps the most developed of the vignettes is "Diptych." The narrator, Arthur, animates a pair of paintings by recounting his experience of the women featured, Edith and Eleanora; each was significant in his early life. The narrator was engaged to Edith but his heterodox views of the Bible and inability to sham otherwise cost him his Anglican lover. In this regard, the young Arthur sounds like a version of Evans, whose religious doubts jeopardized her relationship with her father. The second panel depicts Eleanora, known as the "Diva," clearly a version of Eliot the sage. In a flashback to the time when he first met Eleanora, she makes pronouncements and answers his probing questions. "[P]assionate love is of no sex," the Diva proclaims (71), recalling the third category of *Men, Women, and Lovers*. Arthur resists the urge to love Eleanora, despite her wisdom and charisma. "Stay, sweet goddess, on your pedestal," he cries (77). Perhaps like Edith Simcox, Arthur prefers his love-object to remain beyond the realm of phenomena, godlike, unsullied by the messiness of desire. As the narrator of an earlier vignette states, "I saw visions and dreamed dreams, but rash mortals fare ill who would woo the very gods" (43).

Simcox inquired into purchasing the burial plot next to Evans's, in Highgate Cemetery, but Elma Stuart, as previously mentioned, snatched this piece of earth. Simcox enjoys another form of memorial, her name locked into historical embrace with that of the woman she loved, wanted to become, or be worthy of. Liggins and Simcox, in different ways and with different affect, merged their identities with that of George Eliot. So, too, did Marian Evans. The life of Edith Simcox can be read as a sequel or continuation to that of George Eliot – life as aftertext. Eliot (née Evans) was born in 1819, the year of Queen Victoria's birth, and Simcox died in 1901, as did the monarch who lent her name to the era. But the urge to reproduce and reinvent the novels of the Victorian period would not die with the queen or the sage of the Priory; in the next century there would be more aftertexts, in old media and new.

Postscript, Posthumous Papers, Aftertexts

> ... he who lights his taper at mine, receives light without darkening me.
>
> – Thomas Jefferson

The foregoing chapters have traveled the byways of literature – the neglected, the obscure, the unoriginal, and the insipid. I have recovered a number of texts that imitate the creative output of three nineteenth-century novelists. These aftertexts (as I designate them) have various aims and purposes: they denigrate the successful, capitalize on their triumphs, or associate, even obliquely, with the reigning authors of the day. Because of his immense popularity, Charles Dickens was a natural resource for after-textual authors. The most persistent Dickensian copyist of the mid-nineteenth century was Thomas Peckett Prest, but other anonymous and pseudonymous texts stalked the early career of Dickens the novelist. With his literary identity thus under siege, Dickens fought back: threatening the pirates, deriding them in his fiction, changing his publication formats, and seeking legal redress from the notorious Court of Chancery. In the case of Edward Bulwer (later Lytton), imitations were energized less by affinity than by satire and scorn. While Dickens's works were frequently plagiarized, Bulwer's were often parodied. Circumlocution, pretentious diction, and Excessive Capitalization made Bulwer's style an easy target for the parodist. But parody can also serve as a guide, an apprenticeship of sorts, and two nineteenth-century authors developed their novel-writing skills by imitating the portentous Bulwer style: William Makepeace Thackeray and Rosina Bulwer Lytton. I have also demonstrated that George Eliot's works were not immune to aftertextual attention. There were stage adaptations, song books, a proposed sequel to *Adam Bede*, and an American sequel to *Daniel Deronda*. But in the case of Eliot, it was to a large extent the Eliot persona itself that commanded emulation. Joseph Liggins and Edith

Simcox – one an imposter, the other a fan – each wanted to be or become George Eliot: life as aftertext.

Yet a study of this sort precludes the possibility of closure because the Victorian novelists are ever available for the next imaginative intervention. While the focus has been on near-contemporary after-texts, produced under the same conditions that shaped the originating fictions, aftertexts can arrive long after those conditions have faded into the past. In the latter part of the nineteenth century and in the decades that followed, echoes and appropriations of Victorian novels continued to appear. The BBC has made a mini-industry out of the nineteenth-century novel and maintained countless members of British Equity in regular employment. It would require another book (or more) to delineate all the possibilities and permutations. To conclude, however, I want to consider a few later manifestations of Victorian fiction, in print and in other media, and the resonance of aftertex-tuality in our own cultural moment.

To take one example: the Pickwick phenomenon did not die after the initial bout of productivity, in the late 1830s. Subsequent decades saw the publication of further aftertexts, such as *The Adventures of Marmaduke Midge, the Pickwickian Legatee* (undated, but probably from the 1840s). This book holds little Pickwickian relevance, except that its title character discovers that he is the nephew and heir to the late Samuel Pickwick. In Elizabeth Gaskell's *Cranford* (published in Dickens's *Household Words*, from 1851 to 1853), Mr. Brown is abstracted by the pages of *Pickwick* just before he is killed by an oncoming train. By the 1860s, four American sisters could form their own, imitative Pickwick Club in Louisa May Alcott's novel *Little Women; or, Meg, Jo, Beth and Amy* (1868–69). The twentieth century, of course, translated *Pickwick* into new media. Almost as soon as there were motion pictures, there were motion pictures based on the writings of Dickens. Cinematic versions of *Pickwick* appeared in 1912, 1913, 1921, and 1952.[1] The BBC aired a radio play, "Bardell v. Pickwick," in 1927, and a similar television play in 1938, before anyone could reasonably expect to have owned a television.[2] On the heels of Lionel Bart's *Oliver!* (1960), London saw the première of a musical *Pickwick* (1963). Epidemiology has also descried a medical condition called Pickwickian syndrome, in which overweight people have difficulty breathing. In 2015, Stephen Jarvis produced yet another Pickwickian aftertext, *Death and Mr. Pickwick*, a novel that reasserts illustrator Robert Seymour's role in the origin of Dickens's book – as one character explains, "the collaborator gets forgotten."[3]

Figure 6 Aftertexts continued to appear in the twentieth century. This "Book of the Film," a condensation of Dickens's text, was published to complement a 1952 feature film based on *The Pickwick Papers*

Of course, *Death and Mr. Pickwick* is part of a larger movement of neo-Victorianism. Allographic sequels and other counternovels forcefully intervene in beloved Victorian texts. Jean Rhys's *Wide Sargasso Sea* (1966), famously, reframes the narrative of *Jane Eyre*, and Peter Carey's *Jack Maggs* (1997) operates in a similar fashion on *Great Expectations*. On television, both Showtime's *Penny Dreadful* (2014–16) and the BBC's *Dickensian* (2015–16) offer forms of neo-Victorianism. The list goes on. Many of these aftertextual offerings reflect the sentiment pronounced by novelist Jonathan Lethem: "I like art that comes from other art."[4] To some extent, neo-Victorianism iterates twentieth-century notions of an entertainment "franchise," in which narratives are repurposed in various forms. Darren Werschler has developed a "transmedia theory," based on the notion that "storytelling now takes place across multiple media platforms."[5] David S. Roh agrees that "multiplicity is sought and desired"; he refers to "multiple versions," "multiple editions," and "multiple translations." Further, "[e]ach edition brings a slightly different perspective."[6] One can enjoy the book, the movie, the TV show, the video game, the YouTube parody, and maybe the theme-park attraction.

Victorian aftertexts look forward to another twentieth-century development: fan-produced fiction, known as fanfiction or fanfic. Readers assert themselves as collaborators, as creators, rather than as passive receptors of another's imaginative construct. Legal scholar Lawrence Lessig explains the cultural shift by introducing a pair of computing terms, "RO" and "RW": "Read/Only" and "Read/Write."[7] RO is the culture of consumption, in which professionals produce works of art, and everyone else is the grateful recipient. In RW culture, consumers play an active role: they can rewrite, remix, send up, or sample earlier works. David S. Roh makes a similar case when he distinguishes life in the computing era from that of print: "Computing, conversely, stems from a completely different culture that has built an environment that prioritizes progression, experimentation, and tinkering even after a product has been pushed out."[8] In a computing culture, version 2.0 is necessarily an improvement over 1.0. By contrast, Thomas Noon Talfourd, in the nineteenth century, argued that *King Lear* and *Clarissa* "cannot be added to meaningfully."[9] With such masterpieces of what Lessig would deem RO culture, Talfourd sees no possibility of progression. But users of the computer are familiar with system updates: presumably, things keep getting better (at least the engineers think so). Stimulated by twentieth-century advances such as Xerox technology, audiocassette and videocassette recorders, and the Internet – all of which make mechanical reproduction more widely available – RW is the culture of consumer participation and fanfiction.[10] Anne Jamison traces the notion of fanfiction to the success of that late Victorian phenomenon, Sherlock Holmes.[11] Obviously, the foregoing chapters have demonstrated that Arthur Conan Doyle's detective was not the first literary character to be thus honored.

Henry Jenkins's *Textual Poachers: Television Fans and Participatory Culture* elucidates the urge to rewrite an existing work: "Undaunted by traditional conceptions of literary and intellectual property, fans raid mass culture, claiming its materials for their own."[12] Whether the source is a British novel, such as *Robinson Crusoe* or *Oliver Twist*, or an American television series, such as *Star Trek* (1966–69 and subsequent voyages) or *Twin Peaks* (1990–91 and revivals), "fans actively assert their mastery over the mass-produced texts which provide the raw materials for their own cultural productions."[13] Recalling the title of A. S. Byatt's neo-Victorian novel *Possession* (1990), Lev Grossman argues that writers of fanfiction want to do more than read a particular work or spend time in its story-world: "fanfiction asserts the rights of storytellers to take possession of characters and settings from other people's narratives and tell their own tales about them."[14] Jamison further defines fanfiction as "writing that interrupts, reimagines, or just riffs on stories and characters other people have already written about."[15] It is telling that she refers so casually to elements that "other people have already written about," as if those "stories and characters" were found objects rather than imaginative creations wrought by an artist's labor. Jamison adds that the efforts are usually amateur – that is, produced for *amour*, not for profit – and that the writers are often categorically "other" to the mainstream: "Fanfic is disproportionately written by women, queers, and others who are underrepresented or excluded from economies of financial *and* cultural capital."[16]

One issue that remains contested is that of copyright. In Great Britain, from the nineteenth century onward, copyright expanded both temporally (longer terms) and conceptually (a greater number of protected forms). As a result, Paul K. Saint-Amour refers to "copyright creep" and the "shrinking public domain."[17] The trend is similar in the United States. The 1998 Sonny Bono Copyright Term Extension Act, named for the late congressman and singer, extended copyright once again, in part, it seemed, to protect intellectual properties about to fall into the public domain, including Mickey Mouse. But a different cultural context obtained in the nineteenth century. The novels *Cheveley* and *Gwendolen*, for instance, were commercial endeavors, offered by for-profit publishers. Such aftertexts, albeit spurious, were perfectly legal. It was the openness of eighteenth- and

nineteenth-century copyright law and the vast latitude given to condensations and adaptations that produced the cultural moment that made so
many aftertexts possible. No one, it seems, could stop Thomas Peckett
Prest from writing his own Dickensian serials, and Rosina Bulwer Lytton
could offer as many Bulwer Lyttonian novels as the market would bear.
Under the conditions of Saint-Amour's "copyright-creep," such imitative
publications may face challenges in the courts. Neo-Victorianism is perfectly safe: to produce a sequel or spinoff to a long-out-of-copyright novel
is deemed harmless in the eyes of the law. For example, Stephen Jarvis can
write *Death and Mr. Pickwick* or *Death and Mr. Scrooge* or *Death and
Mr. Dombey*, and no Pickwickian or Dickensian legatee can seek an
injunction. However, for aftertexts based on works still under copyright,
the legal free-for-all, which enriched many a publisher on Paternoster Row,
is no longer available.

There is also the issue of reception. Victorian aftertexts changed the
reception and sometimes the career trajectories of the originating novelists.
Dickens altered his publication format with *Master Humphrey's Clock*;
Bulwer rewrote some of his earlier novels; and George Eliot avoided certain
modes of reminiscence when Joseph Liggins claimed those reminiscences.
Moreover, aftertexts offer readings, and each reading informs our interpretation of a Victorian source-text: we *see* Dickens, Bulwer, or Eliot
through the lens of the works that they inspired. Further, aftertexts seem
to reverse chronology. For example, literary parodies offer a kind of
survival to works that risk being forgotten. According to Dwight
Macdonald, "[O]ne is able to reconstruct these extinct forms of life from
the single parodic bone thrown to one."[18] What is more, aftertexts change
the ontology of their sources. Once an imitation or allographic sequel is
produced, the original can then be read through the prism of the aftertext.
As Marjorie Garber demonstrates in her discussion of the "sequel-effect,"
once an aftertext appears, the source-text is forever altered.[19] We deem
a work the "original" when there is something else that is not the original.

As this study has shown, that which is original and that which is
unoriginal exist in a continuity or continuum: originating novels shape
their successors, yes, but those successors in turn shape their source
material. In some cases, nineteenth-century novelists, such as Bulwer and
Eliot, literally changed their texts in response to imitators and imposters; in
other cases, our understanding of a particular source is enriched by the
experience of its aftertexts. The imitative authors discussed in this book
were not necessarily the world's most elegant writers, but they were
excellent readers. Without access to the past century of Victorian

scholarship, these aftertextual authors perceived and distilled the essence of their sources; they were among the earliest and most insightful readers of Dickens, Bulwer, and Eliot.

In the twentieth century, careful observers, such as Sergei Eisenstein, noted that the cinema drew on the resources of the Victorian novel: see D. W. Griffith's debt to Dickens.[20] In the twenty-first century, it is not the canonical novel but its aftertextual counterpart that seems to be the clearest forerunner to our culture of sequels and reboots, of remixes and online parodies. Cinema viewers can enjoy the merits of *The Amazing Spider-Man 2* (2014), the sequel to the reboot of the film adaptation of the 1960s comic-book series. The live-action remake *Beauty and the Beast* (2017) can be faulted for its unoriginality, but its source-text, Disney's animated *Beauty and the Beast* (1991), is itself a version of a literary fairy tale, with its own prehistory in folklore. In the twenty-first century, it seems, everything is a version of something else. Belated, we are ever following after. We are living in the era of *Oliver Twiss*, not *Oliver Twist*.

This is not to say that Victorian aftertexts somehow predicted the future. Nonetheless, aftertexts produced in the mid-nineteenth century do seem more legible now. It was relatively easy for critics over the last two centuries to dismiss such publications as unoriginal and bad. In ways that perhaps could not have been apprehended earlier, imitations of Dickens, Bulwer, and Eliot did not diminish their source-texts but rather participated in their production and reception. This trio of novelists can be deemed original in that they originated something – namely, an array of aftertexts and authors seeking to replicate a literary brand. Imitation does not harm but rather qualifies and reifies the original: the reflection in the mirror proves that you are, in fact, there. Thomas Peckett Prest, Rosina Bulwer Lytton, Joseph Liggins, and Edith Simcox are counterparts to the canonical; their shadowy existence in literary memory makes the memory of some great authors burn a little brighter.

Notes

Prologue

1. W. Jackson Bate, *The Burden of the Past and the English Poet* (London: Chatto and Windus, 1971), 3–4.
2. Marilyn Randall, *Pragmatic Plagiarism: Authorship, Profit, and Power* (Toronto: University of Toronto Press, 2001), xii.
3. Solomon Lowe, quoted in Thomas Keymer and Peter Sabor, Pamela *in the Marketplace: Literary Controversy and Print Culture in Eighteenth-Century Britain and Ireland* (Cambridge: Cambridge University Press, 2005), 1.
4. "Charles Dickens in Chancery," *Dickensian* 10, no. 8 (August 1914): 216.
5. Nick Groom makes a similar case for forgery. James Macpherson, Thomas Chatterton, and William Henry Ireland form "an anti-canon" (*The Forger's Shadow: How Forgery Changed the Course of Literature* [London: Picador, 2002], 142). For more on forgers and forgery, see Anthony Grafton, *Forgers and Critics: Creativity and Duplicity in Western Scholarship* (London: Juliet Gardiner Books, Collins and Brown, 1990); Mark Jones, ed., *Fake? The Art of Deception* (Berkeley: University of California Press, 1990); K. K. Ruthven, *Faking Literature* (2001; Cambridge: Cambridge University Press, 2010); Jonathon Keats, *Forged: Why Fakes Are the Great Art of Our Age* (Oxford: Oxford University Press, 2013).
6. Margaret Cohen, quoted in Franco Moretti, *Distant Reading* (London: Verso, 2013), 45; John Sutherland, *Victorian Fiction: Writers, Publishers, Readers*, rev. ed. (Basingstoke: Palgrave Macmillan, 2006), chap. 8. Cf. Nigel Cross, *The Common Writer: Life in Nineteenth-Century Grub Street* (1985; Cambridge: Cambridge University Press, 2010), introduction.
7. Processes that might overlap with some of the forms mentioned include influence, mimesis, mimicry, impersonation, translation. For other lists of possibilities, see Michael Baxandall, *Patterns of Intention: On the Historical Explanation of Pictures* (New Haven, CT: Yale University Press, 1985), 59; Adrian Poole, *Shakespeare and the Victorians* (London: Arden Shakespeare, 2004), 2; Julie Sanders, *Adaptation and Appropriation* (London: Routledge,

2006), 3, 18. Harold Bloom's six revisionary ratios could also join the list (*The Anxiety of Influence: A Theory of Poetry* [1973; London: Oxford University Press, 1975]).

8. Gérard Genette, *Palimpsests: Literature in the Second Degree*, trans. Channa Newman and Claude Doubinsky (Lincoln: University of Nebraska Press, 1997).

9. Johann Joachim Winckelmann, quoted in Hans Robert Jauss, *Toward an Aesthetic of Reception*, trans. Timothy Bahti (Brighton: Harvester Press, 1982), 49.

10. Thomas Carlyle, *On Heroes, Hero-Worship, and the Heroic in History. Six Lectures. Reported, with Emendations and Additions* (London: James Fraser, 1841), 290.

11. I[saac] D'Israeli, "Quotation," in *A Second Series of Curiosities of Literature: Consisting of Researches in Literary, Biographical, and Political History; of Critical and Philosophical Inquiries; and of Secret History*, 3 vols. (London: John Murray, 1823), 1:75.

12. Paul K. Saint-Amour, *The Copywrights: Intellectual Property and the Literary Imagination* (2003; Ithaca, NY: Cornell University Press, 2010), 10.

13. Robert Macfarlane, *Original Copy: Plagiarism and Originality in Nineteenth-Century Literature* (Oxford: Oxford University Press, 2007), 13.

14. Richard McKeon, "Literary Criticism and the Concept of Imitation in Antiquity," in *Critics and Criticism: Ancient and Modern*, ed. R. S. Crane (Chicago: University of Chicago Press, 1952), 159.

15. Aristotle, *Poetics*, trans. Stephen Halliwell, in *Aristotle Poetics; Longinus on the Sublime; Demetrius on Style*, Loeb Classical Library (1995; Cambridge, MA: Harvard University Press, 1999), 37. See also Erich Auerbach, *Mimesis: The Representation of Reality in Western Literature*, trans. Willard R. Trask (1946; Princeton, NJ: Princeton University Press, 2003).

16. Groom, *Forger's Shadow*, 33; McKeon, "Literary Criticism," 148.

17. Groom, *Forger's Shadow*, 33.

18. McKeon, "Literary Criticism," 169. For instance, prosopopoeia (writing in character) was a rhetorical exercise.

19. Richard Terry, *The Plagiarism Allegation in English Literature from Butler to Sterne* (Basingstoke: Palgrave Macmillan, 2010), 137. *Imitation* hereafter refers to *literary* imitation and not the attempt to emulate the morals or behavior of another.

20. Henry Felton, quoted in Trevor Ross, "The Fate of Style in an Age of Literary Property," *ELH* 80, no. 3 (Fall 2013): 754.

21. Samuel Johnson, *Rambler*, no. 164 (12 October 1751), in *The Yale Edition of the Works of Samuel Johnson*, ed. E. L. McAdam, Jr., et al., 23 vols. (New Haven, CT: Yale University Press, 1958–2012), 5:107.

22. "Historical Romance. No. I. Sir Walter Scott and His Imitators," *Fraser's Magazine for Town and Country* 5, no. 25 (February 1932): 17.

23. Robert Browning, "Essay on Chatterton," in *The Complete Works of Robert Browning*, ed. Roma A. King, Jr., et al., 17 vols. (Athens: Ohio University Press; Waco, TX: Baylor University, 1969–2011), 3:165.

24. [James] Brander Matthews, "The Ethics of Plagiarism," in *Pen and Ink: Papers on Subjects of More or Less Importance*, 3rd ed. (New York: Charles Scribner's Sons, 1902), 52. This article originally appeared in 1886.

25. Zachary Leader, *Revision and Romantic Authorship* (Oxford: Clarendon Press, 1996), viii; Linda Hutcheon, *A Theory of Parody: The Teachings of Twentieth-Century Art Forms* (1985; Urbana: University of Illinois Press, 2000), 4; Ruthven, *Faking Literature*, 40.

26. Andrew Bennett, *The Author* (London: Routledge, 2005), 60.

27. Macfarlane, *Original Copy*, 6.

28. Ibid., 39.

29. Sutherland, *Victorian Fiction*, 92.

30. Tilar J. Mazzeo, *Plagiarism and Literary Property in the Romantic Period* (Philadelphia: University of Pennsylvania Press, 2007), 153, 30.

31. [Thomas De Quincey], "Samuel Taylor Coleridge," *Tait's Edinburgh Magazine* 1, no. 8 (September 1834): 510–511. Cf. Norman Fruman, *Coleridge, the Damaged Archangel* (New York: George Braziller, 1971).

32. "Literary Impostures. – Alexandre Dumas," *North American Review* 78, no. 163 (April 1854): 329.

33. Ibid., 336.

34. J. Cuthbert Hadden, "Plagiarism and Coincidence," *Scottish Review* 27 (April 1896): 339.

35. H. M. Paull, *Literary Ethics: A Study in the Growth of the Literary Conscience* (London: Thornton Butterworth, 1928), 103.

36. Thomas McFarland, *Originality and Imagination* (Baltimore, MD: Johns Hopkins University Press, 1985), 22.

37. Stephen Orgel, quoted in Christopher Ricks, *Allusion to the Poets* (2002; Oxford: Oxford University Press, 2007), 231; Macfarlane, *Original Copy*, 3.

38. Peter Shaw, "Plagiary," *American Scholar* 51, no. 3 (Summer 1982): 327.

39. Ibid., 336, 332.

40. Ralph Waldo Emerson, "Quotation and Originality," in *Ralph Waldo Emerson*, ed. Richard Poirier (Oxford: Oxford University Press, 1990), 434.

41. Shaw, "Plagiary," 330, 331.

42. Quoted in ibid., 331. For more on *The Rachel Papers* episode, see Thomas Mallon, *Stolen Words: Forays into the Origins and Ravages of Plagiarism* (New York: Ticknor and Fields, 1989), chap. 3.

43. Hillel Schwartz, *The Culture of the Copy: Striking Likenesses, Unreasonable Facsimiles* (New York: Zone Books, 1996), 315, 314.

44. "Literary Impostures," 308n.

45. Robert L. Patten, *Charles Dickens and "Boz": The Birth of the Industrial-Age Author* (Cambridge: Cambridge University Press, 2012), 171; "Literary Impostures," 308n.

46. Martial, book 1, epigram 29, in *Epigrams*, trans. D. R. Shackleton Bailey, Loeb Classical Library, 3 vols. (Cambridge, MA: Harvard University Press, 1993), 1:61.

47. Martial, book 1, epigram 52, in ibid., 1:81. The Latin text appears on 1:80.

48. Joseph Hall, quoted in Terry, *Plagiarism Allegation*, 18. This example is also cited in the *OED*.

49. Randle Cotgrave, quoted in Terry, *Plagiarism Allegation*, 19.

50. John Ash, quoted in Terry, *Plagiarism Allegation*, 4.

51. Cf. Macfarlane, *Original Copy*, 41: "a species of literary journalist which specialized in tracking down allusions, borrowings, and derivations." One forerunner is *Momus Triumphans*, which lists plays and their sources (Gerard Langbaine, *Momus Triumphans; or, The Plagiaries of the English Stage* [1687; Los Angeles: University of California, 1971]).

52. Alfred Tennyson, quoted in Paull, *Literary Ethics*, 123.

53. W[illiam] Barnes, "Plagiarism and Coincidence; or, Thought-Thievery and Thought-Likeness," *Macmillan's Magazine* 15, no. 85 (November 1866): 73; Hadden, "Plagiarism and Coincidence," 336; Harold Bloom, *A Map of Misreading* (1975; Oxford: Oxford University Press, 1980), 17.

54. "The Cry of Plagiarism," *Spectator* 66, no. 3270 (28 February 1891): 306.

55. Walter Scott, quoted in Matthews, "Ethics of Plagiarism," 25.

56. Ralph Waldo Emerson, quoted in McFarland, *Originality and Imagination*, 14.

57. Emerson, "Quotation and Originality," 427.

58. Saint-Amour, *Copywrights*, 241n37.

59. "Recent Poetic Plagiarisms and Imitations," parts 1–2, *London Magazine*, December 1823, 602–604; March 1824, 277–285. Subsequent references to this edition will be made parenthetically within the text.

60. Mazzeo, *Plagiarism and Literary Property*, 96.

61. Marcel Proust, among modern writers, would challenge the accumulative thesis presented in the *London Magazine*: "each individual starts the artistic or literary endeavour over again, on his own account . . . A writer of genius today has everything to do. He is not much further advanced than Homer" (*Against Sainte-Beuve and Other Essays*, trans. John Sturrock [London: Penguin Books, 1988], 11).

62. Alexander Lindey, quoted in Ricks, *Allusion to the Poets*, 224.

63. Saint-Amour, *Copywrights*, 19; Shaw, "Plagiary," 336.
64. Percy Bysshe Shelley, quoted in Mazzeo, *Plagiarism and Literary Property*, 132.
65. Mark Rose, *Authors and Owners: The Invention of Copyright* (Cambridge, MA: Harvard University Press, 1993), 3.
66. Ibid., 142, 2.
67. "The *Labour* of his Body, and the *Work* of his Hands, we may say, are properly his" ([John Locke], *Two Treatises of Government: In the Former, the False Principles, and Foundation of Sir Robert Filmer, and His Followers, Are Detected and Overthrown. The Latter Is an Essay Concerning the True Original, Extent, and End of Civil Government* [London: Printed for Awnsham Churchill, 1690], 245). I have modernized orthography when quoting older texts: no long *s*, no ligature.
68. Rose, *Authors and Owners*, 121.
69. Ibid., 91.
70. Ibid., 9.
71. John Sutherland, in Harold Bloom, et al., "Plagiarism – A Symposium," *Times Literary Supplement*, 9 April 1982, 414.
72. Martha Woodmansee, *The Author, Art, and the Market: Rereading the History of Aesthetics* (New York: Columbia University Press, 1994), 51.
73. William Blackstone, quoted in William Enfield, *Observations on Literary Property* (London: Printed for Joseph Johnson, 1774), 9.
74. Enfield, *Observations on Literary Property*, 10.
75. Isaac D'Israeli, quoted in Ross, "Fate of Style," 778.
76. Ross, "Fate of Style," 748.
77. Ibid., 774.
78. Adrian Johns, *Piracy: The Intellectual Property Wars from Gutenberg to Gates* (Chicago: University of Chicago Press, 2009), 45. He also qualifies that copyright did not reach "roughly its modern form" until the 1770s (109). The case of *Donaldson v. Becket*, in 1774, ended the possibility of perpetual copyright. See Rose, *Authors and Owners*, 92–103; Joseph Loewenstein, *The Author's Due: Printing and the Prehistory of Copyright* (Chicago: University of Chicago Press, 2002), 13–22. Thomas Becket variously spelled his surname with one or two *t*'s, and the case is sometimes referred to as *Donaldson v. Beckett*.
79. Johns, *Piracy*, chap. 2.
80. Daniel Defoe, "Miscellanea," *A Review of the State of the British Nation* 6, no. 129 (2 February 1710): 516, 515.
81. The full title is "An Act for the Encouragement of Learning, by Vesting the Copies of Printed Books in the Authors or Purchasers of Such Copies, during the Times therein Mentioned."
82. For more on copyright history, see Augustine Birrell, *Seven Lectures on the Law and History of Copyright in Books* (London: Cassell and Company;

New York: G. P. Putnam's Sons, 1899); Rose, *Authors and Owners*; John Feather, *Publishing, Piracy and Politics: An Historical Study of Copyright in Britain* (London: Mansell, 1994); Loewenstein, *Author's Due*; Larisa T. Castillo, "Natural Authority in Charles Dickens's *Martin Chuzzlewit* and the Copyright Act of 1842," *Nineteenth-Century Literature* 62, no. 4 (March 2008): 435–464.

83. Feather, *Publishing, Piracy and Politics*, 124.

84. Ibid., 6.

85. Daniel Defoe, *An Essay on the Regulation of the Press* (London: n.p., 1704), 20.

86. Ross, "Fate of Style," 760.

87. Philip Yorke, Lord Hardwicke, quoted in Joseph J. Beard, "Everything Old Is New Again: Dickens to Digital," *Loyola of Los Angeles Law Review* 38, no. 1 (Fall 2004): 24.

88. E. T. Jaques, *Charles Dickens in Chancery: Being an Account of His Proceedings in Respect of the "Christmas Carol" with Some Gossip in Relation to the Old Law Courts at Westminster* (London: Longman, Green and Co., 1914), 40.

89. Henry Bathurst, Lord Apsley, quoted in Beard, "Everything Old Is New Again," 25.

90. Birrell, *Seven Lectures*, 158.

91. Patten, *Charles Dickens and "Boz,"* 168.

92. "Approximately 40 reactions to *Tristram Shandy* appeared in print before Sterne's death in 1768" (Anne Bandry, "Imitations of *Tristram Shandy*," in *Critical Essays on Laurence Sterne*, ed. Melvyn New [New York: G. K. Hall and Co., 1998], 39). Titles include *The Life and Opinions of Miss Sukey Shandy, of Bow-Street, Gentlewoman. In a Series of Letters to Her Dear Brother Tristram Shandy, Gent.* (London: Printed for R. Stevens, 1760); *The Life and Opinions of Bertram Montfichet, Esq; Written by Himself*, 2 vols. (London: Printed for C. G. Seyffert, [1761]). Samuel Richardson referred to "a *Shandy*-age" (quoted in Thomas Keymer, *Sterne, the Moderns, and the Novel* [Oxford: Oxford University Press, 2002], 1). For Defoe, Swift, and Richardson, see below.

93. Genette, *Palimpsests*, 161. For Goodman the terms refer not to individual works but to art forms. The autographic are those for which there is a sharp distinction between an original and a copy (e.g. painting); the allographic are those for which that distinction is less pronounced (e.g. sheet music or photography) (Nelson Goodman, *Languages of Art: An Approach to a Theory of Symbols* [London: Oxford University Press, 1969], 113).

94. J. K. Welcher, "Gulliver in the Market-place," *Studies on Voltaire and the Eighteenth Century*, no. 217 (1983): 127n7; Carl Fisher, "The Robinsonade: An Intercultural History of an Idea," in *Approaches to Teaching Defoe's Robinson Crusoe*, ed. Maximillian E. Novak and Carl Fisher (New York: Modern Language Association of America, 2005).

95. David A. Brewer, *The Afterlife of Character, 1726–1825* (Philadelphia: University of Pennsylvania Press, 2005), 41.

96. Welcher, "Gulliver in the Market-place," 126, 134.

97. Keymer and Sabor, Pamela *in the Marketplace*, 1.

98. Ibid., 51.

99. Quoted in ibid., 61.

100. Quoted in ibid., 57.

101. Ann Rigney, *The Afterlives of Walter Scott: Memory on the Move* (Oxford: Oxford University Press, 2012), 13, 52.

102. Ibid., 51.

103. H. Philip Bolton, *Scott Dramatized* (London: Mansell, 1992), vii.

104. L. H. C. Thomas, "'Walladmor': A Pseudo-Translation of Sir Walter Scott," *Modern Language Review* 46 (January 1951): 219.

105. Seamus Perry, "Sweet Counter-Song," *Times Literary Supplement*, 20 August 2010, 4.

106. Thomas, "'Walladmor,'" 218, 220.

107. Rigney, *Afterlives of Walter Scott*, 15.

108. Bolton, *Scott Dramatized*, 345–346. The publication date of *Ivanhoe* is 1820, but it appeared in late 1819.

109. Ibid., 342.

110. [Thomas Archer], *Richard of England; or, The Lion King* (London: F. Hextall, n.d.), 36. Cf. [Walter Scott], *Ivanhoe; a Romance*, 3 vols. (Edinburgh: Archibald Constable and Co.; London: Hurst, Robinson and Co., 1820), 1:156. For Rowena, see [Scott], *Ivanhoe*, 1:73; for Alena, see [Archer], *Richard of England*, 4.

111. [Scott], *Ivanhoe*, 1:156.

112. Ibid., 1:268; [Archer], *Richard of England*, 377; [Scott,] *Ivanhoe*, 1:269; [Archer], *Richard of England*, 378.

113. [Archer], *Richard of England*, 67.

114. William Makepeace Thackeray, *Rebecca and Rowena: A Romance upon Romance*, in *The Christmas Books of Mr. M. A. Titmarsh* (London: Smith, Elder, and Co., 1879), 107. Thackeray previously sketched some ideas in "Proposals for a Continuation of Ivanhoe," a two-part article that appeared in *Fraser's Magazine for Town and Country* 34, nos. 200 and 201 (August and September 1846): 237–245 and 359–367 respectively.

115. Thackeray, *Rebecca and Rowena*, 107.

116. Ibid., 121.

117. Ibid., 126.

118. "Recent English Romances," *Edinburgh Review* 65, no. 131 (April 1837): 183. George Kitchin refers to "amateurs and bunglers who imagined that the thing could be done according to recipe" (*A Survey of Burlesque and Parody*

in English [Edinburgh: Oliver and Boyd, 1931], 253–254). The cooking metaphor also appears in "Literary Recipes," *Punch; or, The London Charivari*, 7 August 1841, 39; [W. H. Mallock], *Every Man His Own Poet; or, The Inspired Singer's Recipe Book* (Oxford: Thomas Shrimpton and Son, 1872). The latter is ascribed to "a Newdigate Prizeman."

119. Andrea Cabajsky, "Plagiarizing Sir Walter Scott: The Afterlife of *Kenilworth* in Victorian Quebec," *Novel: A Forum on Fiction* 44, no. 3 (Fall 2011): 355. In an analogue to the Waverley phenomenon, Chris Baldick makes a case for Mary Shelley's *Frankenstein* (1818) as "a modern myth" (*In Frankenstein's Shadow: Myth, Monstrosity, and Nineteenth-Century Writing* [Oxford: Clarendon Press, 1987], 1).

120. Terry Castle, *Masquerade and Civilization: The Carnivalesque in Eighteenth-Century English Culture and Fiction* (Stanford, CA: Stanford University Press, 1986), 133.

121. Ibid., 134.

122. John Feather, *Publishing, Piracy and Politics*, 123. For the eighteenth century's anticipation of some of these developments, see Welcher, "Gulliver in the Market-place," 127.

123. Brewer, *Afterlife of Character*, 78, 2.

124. Linda Hutcheon with Siobhan O'Flynn, *A Theory of Adaptation*, 2nd ed. (London: Routledge, 2013), xvi.

125. Sarah Cardwell, *Adaptation Revisited: Television and the Classic Novel* (Manchester: Manchester University Press, 2002), 13.

126. Hutcheon with O'Flynn, *Theory of Adaptation*, xiv, 4.

127. Marjorie Garber, *Quotation Marks* (New York: Routledge, 2003), 78.

128. Ibid.

129. Castle, *Masquerade and Civilization*, 133, 134.

130. Genette, *Palimpsests*, 177.

131. D. A. Miller, *Narrative and Its Discontents: Problems of Closure in the Traditional Novel* (Princeton, NJ: Princeton University Press, 1981), ix.

132. Ibid., 5, 267.

133. Thackeray, *Rebecca and Rowena*, 105.

134. There was, of course, a professional reason. For more on the longevity of the three-volume novel, see Guinevere L. Griest, *Mudie's Circulating Library and the Victorian Novel* (Bloomington: Indiana University Press, 1970), especially chap. 3. By the 1890s, this convention was dead.

135. Thackeray, *Rebecca and Rowena*, 109.

136. Hutcheon, *Theory of Parody*, 25; Dwight Macdonald, "Some Notes on Parody," in *Parodies: An Anthology from Chaucer to Beerbohm – and After* (1960; London: Faber and Faber, 1964), 557; J. G. Riewald, "Parody as Criticism," *Neophilologus* 50, no. 1 (1 January 1966): 125.

137. Margaret A. Rose, *Parody: Ancient, Modern, and Post-modern* (1993; Cambridge: Cambridge University Press, 2000), 54.

138. Fred W. Householder, Jr., "ΠΑΡΩΙΔΙΑ," *Classical Philology* 39, no. 1 (January 1944): 5.

139. Kitchin, *Survey of Burlesque and Parody*, xxii. In the United States, burlesque developed as a low form of vaudeville, sometimes incorporating striptease.

140. M. H. Abrams, "Burlesque," in *A Glossary of Literary Terms*, 6th ed. (Fort Worth, TX: Harcourt Brace Jovanovich College Publishers, 1993), 17; John D. Jump, *Burlesque* (London: Methuen and Co., 1972), 2. Abrams's statement that "parody has been the favorite form of burlesque" is typical of the confusion here (18).

141. Rose, *Parody*, 55.

142. Genette, *Palimpsests*, 89; Rose, *Parody*, 72.

143. Fredric Jameson, "Postmodernism and Consumer Culture," in *Postmodern Culture*, ed. Hal Foster (1983; London: Pluto Press, 1985), 114; David Bromwich, "Parody, Pastiche, and Allusion," in *Lyric Poetry: Beyond New Criticism*, ed. Chaviva Hosek and Patricia Parker (Ithaca, NY: Cornell University Press, 1985), 328. Foster's volume was previously published as *The Anti-Aesthetic*.

144. "John Gilpin and Mazeppa," *Blackwood's Edinburgh Magazine* 5, no. 28 (July 1819): 434. Incidentally, this was the year of Queen Victoria's birth.

145. Aristotle, *Poetics*, 35.

146. For *parode*: Rose, *Parody*, 280; for *parodia*: Genette, *Palimpsests*, 10.

147. Hutcheon, *Theory of Parody*, 32.

148. Perry, "Sweet Counter-Song," 3.

149. Genette, *Palimpsests*, 11. An early English translation attributes the latter to Homer himself (*Homer's Battle of the Frogs and Mice. With the Remarks of Zoilus. To Which Is Prefix'd, the Life of Said Zoilus* [London: Printed for Bernard Lintot, 1707]). For more on parody in antiquity, see Householder, "ΠΑΡΩΙΔΙΑ"; Rose, *Parody*, chap. 1; Simon Dentith, *Parody* (2000; London: Routledge, 2005), chap. 2.

150. John Keats recorded his reaction in a letter to his brothers: "Hone the publisher's trial, you must find very amusing; & as Englishmen very encouraging – his *Not Guilty* is a thing, which not to have been, would have dulled still more Liberty's Emblazoning" (*The Letters of John Keats, 1814–1821*, ed. Hyder Edward Rollins, 2 vols. [Cambridge, MA: Harvard University Press, 1958], 1:191).

151. Matthew Arnold, quoted in Kitchin, *Survey of Burlesque and Parody*, xix; George Eliot, *Impressions of Theophrastus Such* (Edinburgh: William Blackwood and Sons, 1879), 182.

152. John Poole, preface to *Hamlet Travestie*, in *Nineteenth-Century Shakespeare Burlesques*, ed. Stanley Wells, 5 vols. (London: Diploma Press, 1977–78), 1:5.
153. [Francis Jeffrey], review of *Rejected Addresses; or, The New Theatrum Poetarum, Edinburgh Review* 20, no. 40 (November 1812): 435.
154. Ibid., 436.
155. Review of *La Parodie chez les Grecs, chez les Romains, et chez les Modernes, Athenaeum: Journal of English and Foreign Literature, Science, the Fine Arts, Music and the Drama*, no. 2279 (1 July 1871): 12.
156. Quoted in Walter Hamilton, *Parodies of the Works of English and American Authors*, 6 vols. (1884–89; New York: Johnson Reprint Corporation, 1967), 2:103.
157. Bromwich, "Parody, Pastiche, and Allusion," 328.
158. Arthur Quiller-Couch, "Foreword on the Gentle Art," in *Parodies and Imitations Old and New*, ed. J. A. Stanley Adam and Bernard C. White (London: Hutchinson and Co., 1912), vii.
159. Dentith, *Parody*, 30. Bromwich argues that parody was a developmental stage for Austen, Thackeray, and others: "a particular stage of the maturing of a writer" ("Parody, Pastiche, and Allusion," 328).
160. Even before this number appeared, in December 1838, Dickens was identified in the press as a "parodist" ([T. H. Lister], "Dickens's Tales," *Edinburgh Review* 68, no. 137 [October 1838]: 76). For more, see Tore Rem, "Dickens and Parody" (DPhil thesis, University of Oxford, 1998); Rosemarie Bodenheimer, *Knowing Dickens* (2007; Ithaca, NY: Cornell University Press, 2010).
161. Carrie Sickmann Han, "Pickwick's Other Papers: Continually Reading Dickens," *Victorian Literature and Culture* 44, no. 1 (March 2016): 19; David S. Roh, *Illegal Literature: Toward a Disruptive Creativity* (Minneapolis: University of Minnesota Press, 2015), 4. Elsewhere, Roh uses "*extralegal texts*" to refer to fanfiction and related forms (59). For more, see Postscript.
162. Genette, *Palimpsests*, 399.
163. Robert Darnton, "What Is the History of Books?," in *The Kiss of Lamourette: Reflections in Cultural History* (New York: W. W. Norton and Company, 1990), 122. An earlier version of this chapter appeared in *Daedalus*, in 1982.
164. Michel de Certeau, *The Practice of Everyday Life*, trans. Steven Rendall (1984; Berkeley: University of California Press, 1988), 174.
165. [Jeffrey], review of *Rejected Addresses*, 436.
166. G. Thomas Tanselle, *A Rationale of Textual Criticism* (1989; Philadelphia: University of Pennsylvania Press, 1992), 27, 93. Jerome J. McGann concurs with Tanselle's terminology in *A Critique of Modern Textual Criticism* (Chicago: University of Chicago Press, 1983), 52; and *The Beauty of Inflections: Literary Investigations in Historical Method and Theory* (Oxford: Clarendon Press, 1985), 10.

167. Roland Barthes, "From Work to Text," in *The Norton Anthology of Theory and Criticism*, ed. Vincent B. Leitch, et al. (New York: W. W. Norton and Co., 2001), 1471.

168. Peter Lamarque, *Work and Object: Explorations in the Metaphysics of Art* (Oxford: Oxford University Press, 2010), 151.

169. Loewenstein, *Author's Due*, 27.

170. Alexander Welsh, *George Eliot and Blackmail* (Cambridge, MA: Harvard University Press, 1985), 35.

171. Grafton, *Forgers and Critics*, 12. For another argument in favor of the non-canonical, see Roh, *Illegal Literature*, 10–11.

172. [Edward Young], *Conjectures on Original Composition. In a Letter to the Author of Sir Charles Grandison* (London: Printed for A. Miller, 1759), 17, 68.

173. Joel Weinsheimer, "Conjectures on Unoriginal Composition," *Eighteenth Century* 22, no. 1 (Winter 1981): 66.

174. Matthew P. M. Kerr, "With Many Voices: The Sea in Victorian Fiction" (DPhil thesis, University of Oxford, 2012), 8; "William Ainsworth and Jack Sheppard," *Fraser's Magazine for Town and Country* 21, no. 122 (February 1840): 228.

175. Patsy Stoneman, *Brontë Transformations: The Cultural Dissemination of* Jane Eyre *and* Wuthering Heights (London: Prentice Hall/Harvester Wheatsheaf, 1996), 6.

176. Ibid., 18–24.

177. For example, the 1850 edition of *Wuthering Heights* and *Agnes Grey*, published by Smith, Elder, and Company.

Chapter 1 The Pickwick Phenomenon

1. John Sutherland, *The Stanford Companion to Victorian Fiction* (Stanford, CA: Stanford University Press, 1989), 506. Also published as *The Longman Companion to Victorian Fiction*.

2. Monthly numbers, like magazines, were usually available on the last day of the previous month, i.e. "Magazine Day." So the first number of *Pickwick* was officially April 1836; the last, November 1837.

3. *Morning Chronicle*, 5 October 1836, quoted in Kathryn Chittick, *Dickens and the 1830s* (1990; Cambridge: Cambridge University Press, 2009), 65; *Chambers's Edinburgh Journal*, 29 April 1837, quoted in ibid., 77.

4. Charles Dickens to Richard Bentley, 14 July 1837, in *The Letters of Charles Dickens*, ed. Madeline House, Graham Storey, and Kathleen Tillotson, 12 vols. (Oxford: Clarendon Press, 1965–2002), 1:283. Hereafter cited as *CD Letters*, followed by volume and page number. As late as 1841, he still distinguished works in monthly numbers from novels (Charles Dickens to Thomas Mitton, 30 August [1841], *CD Letters*, 2:372).

5. George Orwell, "Charles Dickens," in *A Collection of Essays* (1946; San Diego, CA: Harcourt, 1981), 65; G. K. Chesterton, *Charles Dickens* (1906; London: Methuen and Co., 1960), 95.

6. Charles Dickens, 1847 preface, in *The Posthumous Papers of the Pickwick Club*, ed. Robert L. Patten (1836–1837; London: Penguin Books, 1986), 43.

7. "No one has fully mapped the 'Pickwick phenomenon'" (John Bowen, *Other Dickens: Pickwick to Chuzzlewit* [2000; Oxford: Oxford University Press, 2003], 48n12).

8. Edgar Johnson, *Charles Dickens: His Tragedy and Triumph*, 2 vols. (New York: Simon and Schuster, 1952), 1:156.

9. Clifton Fadiman, "Pickwick Lives Forever," *Atlantic Monthly*, December 1949, 24.

10. Amy Cruse, *The Victorians and Their Books* (London: George Allen and Unwin, 1935), 159.

11. Robert L. Patten, *Charles Dickens and His Publishers* (Oxford: Oxford University Press, 1978), 45; Steven Marcus, *Dickens from Pickwick to Dombey* (1965; New York: Simon and Schuster, 1968), 15; George H. Ford, *Dickens and His Readers: Aspects of Novel-Criticism since 1836* (1955; New York: W. W. Norton and Company, 1965), 6.

12. Percy Fitzgerald, *The History of Pickwick: An Account of Its Characters, Localities, Allusions, and Illustrations* (London: Chapman and Hall, 1891), 4. Fitzgerald is the author or editor of *The History of Pickwick, Pickwickian Manners and Customs, Pickwickian Studies, The Pickwickian Dictionary and Cyclopaedia, Bardell v. Pickwick, Pickwick Riddles and Perplexities*, as well as the anthology *Pickwickian Wit and Humour*.

13. Hammond Hall, *Mr. Pickwick's Kent* (Rochester: W. and J. Mackay, 1899), 3.

14. Percy Fitzgerald, *The Pickwickian Dictionary and Cyclopaedia* (London: W. T. Spencer, [1900]), 55.

15. Review of *The Posthumous Papers of the Pickwick Club* and *Sketches by Boz*, *Quarterly Review* 59, no. 118 (October 1837): 484.

16. Kitton writes that "presently Pickwick chintzes figured in linendrapers' windows, Weller corduroys in breeches-makers' advertisements . . . Boz cabs rattled along the streets" (Fred G. Kitton, *Dickensiana: A Bibliography of the Literature Relating to Charles Dickens and His Writings* [London: George Redway, 1886], xxiii–xxiv).

17. *Effingham Hazard, the Adventurer* (London: Edward Ravenscroft; London: Foster and Hextall; London: John Foster, 1838–39), no. 4, back cover.

18. *The Queerfish Chronicles, Forming a Correct Narrative of Divers Travels, Voyages, and Remarkable Adventures, That Have Come under the Notice of the Queerfish Society* (London: B. Steill, 1837), no. 5, inside cover.

19. For more on Dickens and the spurious, see Daniel Hack, *The Material Interests of the Victorian Novel* (Charlottesville: University of Virginia Press, 2005), 39–40.
20. Charles Dickens, *The Posthumous Papers of the Pickwick Club* (London: Chapman and Hall, 1836–37), 6. Subsequent references to this edition will be made parenthetically within the text.
21. Cf. Bowen, *Other Dickens*, 79.
22. For more on theatrical adaptations of *Pickwick*, see William Miller, ed., *Catalogue of a Pickwick Exhibition* (London: The Dickens Fellowship, 1936); William Miller, *The Dickens Student and Collector: A List of Writings Relating to Charles Dickens and His Works, 1836–1945* (London: Chapman and Hall, 1946); Malcolm Morley, "Pickwick Makes His Stage Début," *Dickensian* 42, no. 280 (Autumn 1946): 204–206; H. Philip Bolton, *Dickens Dramatized* (London: Mansell, 1987); Elliot Engel, *Pickwick Papers: An Annotated Bibliography* (New York: Garland Publishing, 1990).
23. Such "extra-illustrations" were also produced by Thomas Onwhyn and Hablot K. Browne, *Pickwick*'s third and final illustrator. See Luisa Calè, "Dickens Extra-Illustrated: Heads and Scenes in Monthly Parts (The Case of *Nicholas Nickleby*)," *Yearbook of English Studies* 40, no. 1/2 (2010): 8–32.
24. John Sutherland, *Victorian Fiction: Writers, Publishers, Readers*, rev. ed. (Basingstoke: Palgrave Macmillan, 2006), 90.
25. Ibid., 91.
26. Review of *The Life and Adventures of Valentine Vox, Operative*, 5 May 1839, 11. *Valentine Vox* (1839–40), by Henry Cockton, was initially offered in monthly shilling numbers and attributed to the cheerful pseudonym Sherry.
27. J. R. Harvey, *Victorian Novelists and Their Illustrators* (London: Sidgwick and Jackson, 1970), 13. Serialized at first in the *Dublin University Magazine*, Lever's novel appeared in monthly parts, March 1839 to January 1840, with illustrations by Hablot K. Browne.
28. Bowen, *Other Dickens*, 57. Dickens, too, participated in the phenomenon by editing *The Pic-Nic Papers* (1841), a collection produced to aid the family of the late John Macrone.
29. Duane DeVries, *Dickens's Apprentice Years: The Making of a Novelist* (Hassocks, Sussex: Harvester Press; New York: Barnes and Noble Books, 1976), 41. Cf. *CD Letters*, 1:33. This tale was revised and republished as "Mr. Minns and His Cousin," in *Sketches by Boz*, Second Series (1836).
30. Also issued as *The Sketch Book by "Bos," Containing a Great Number of Highly Interesting and Original Tales, Sketches, &c. &c.* It is undated but probably 1837. In 1839, Henry Hetherington reprinted thirty-seven of Dickens's sketches in the weekly periodical *The Odd Fellow*. Hetherington later defended this practice and claimed "the right of fair quotation for editorial

purposes," thus conflating piracy and quotation (quoted in Paul Schlicke, "Dickens and the Pirates: The Case of *The Odd Fellow*," *Dickensian* 100, no. 464 [Winter 2004]: 225).

31. Michael Hancher, "Dickens's First Effusion," *Dickens Quarterly* 31, no. 4 (December 2014): 285–297.

32. "Our Leader," *Thief*, no. 1 (21 April 1832): n.p.

33. Review of *The Posthumous Papers of the Pickwick Club*, *Athenaeum: Journal of English and Foreign Literature, Science, and the Fine Arts*, no. 475 (3 December 1836): 841.

34. Dickens "too frequently condescends to be a copyist," and "The Bagman's Story," in *Pickwick*, is further "a palpable plagiarism from the 'Adventures of my Grandfather'" (review of *Pickwick* and *Sketches*, *Quarterly Review*, 497, 494).

35. Julian Franklyn, *The Cockney: A Survey of London Life and Language* (London: Andre Deutsch Limited, 1953), 18.

36. Pierce Egan, *The Finish to the Adventures of Tom, Jerry, and Logic, in Their Pursuits through Life in and out of London* (1828; London: Reeves and Turner, 1887), 46, 55, 80. Cf. Harvey, *Victorian Novelists and Their Illustrators*, 14.

37. *Grub-Street Journal*, no. 31 (6 August 1730): 1.

38. Robert Douglas-Fairhurst, *Becoming Dickens: The Invention of a Novelist* (Cambridge, MA: Belknap Press of Harvard University Press, 2011), 131. This final passage in the life of Watkins Tottle was excluded when the sketch was reprinted in *Sketches by Boz*: "He left a variety of papers in the hands of his landlady – the materials collected in his wanderings among different classes of society – which that lady has determined to publish, to defray the unpaid expenses of his board and lodging. They will be carefully arranged, and presented to the public from time to time, with all due humility by BOZ" ([Charles Dickens], "Passages in the Life of Mr. Watkins Tottle," part 2, *Monthly Magazine*, February 1835, 137). Cf. DeVries, *Dickens's Apprentice Years*, 55n20.

39. G. K. Chesterton, *Criticisms and Appreciations of the Works of Charles Dickens* (1911; London: J. M. Dent and Sons, 1933), 16.

40. Marcus, *Dickens from Pickwick to Dombey*, 16.

41. Bowen, *Other Dickens*, 49.

42. See David Parker, "The *Pickwick* Prefaces," *Dickens Studies Annual: Essays on Victorian Fiction* 43 (2012): 67–79.

43. Peter Ackroyd, *Dickens* (1990; New York: HarperPerennial, 1992), 176.

44. Joseph Grego, *Pictorial Pickwickiana: Charles Dickens and His Illustrators*, 2 vols. (London: Chapman and Hall, 1899), 1:60.

45. Alfred Crowquill [Alfred Forrester], "Address," in *Seymour's Sketches, Illustrated in Prose and Verse* (London: Published for the Proprietor, by Joshua Thompson, 1838–39), part 1, n.p.

46. Crowquill, *Seymour's Sketches*, part 5, n.p.
47. Ibid.
48. Parker, "*Pickwick* Prefaces," 71.
49. Jane R. Cohen, *Charles Dickens and His Original Illustrators* (Columbus: Ohio State University Press, 1980), 49.
50. Mrs. [Jane] Seymour, "An Account of the Origin of the 'Pickwick Papers,'" in *A Centenary Bibliography of the Pickwick Papers*, by W[illiam] Miller and E. H. Strange (London: Argonaut Press, 1936), 206.
51. William Clarke and Charles Whitehead both rejected the Chapman and Hall offer that Dickens eventually accepted. Other writers who may have been considered include Theodore Hook, Henry Mayhew, and William Thomas Moncrieff, who later wrote a *Pickwick* play, *Sam Weller; or, The Pickwickians* (Walter Dexter and J. W. T. Ley, *The Origin of Pickwick: New Facts Now First Published in the Year of the Centenary* [London: Chapman and Hall, 1936], 22–23; Grego, *Pictorial Pickwickiana*, 1:11–12).
52. Seymour, "Account of the Origin," 197.
53. Advertisement, *Athenaeum: Journal of English and Foreign Literature, Science, and the Fine Arts*, no. 439 (26 March 1836): 232. The phrase "from time to time" also appears in the similar passage in "Passages in the Life of Mr. Watkins Tottle."
54. Bradley Deane, *The Making of the Victorian Novelist: Anxieties of Authorship in the Mass Market* (New York: Routledge, 2003), 32.
55. Louis James, *Fiction for the Working Man, 1830–1850: A Study of the Literature Produced for the Working Classes in Early Victorian Urban England* (London: Oxford University Press, 1963), xi.
56. Paul Davis, *The Lives and Times of Ebenezer Scrooge* (New Haven, CT: Yale University Press, 1990), 12. Nelson Goodman also suggests that imitation acts upon its sources: "It selects, rejects, organizes, discriminates, associates, classifies, analyzes, constructs" (*Languages of Art: An Approach to a Theory of Symbols* [London: Oxford University Press, 1969], 7–8).
57. [Thomas Peckett Prest], "Dedication," in *The Penny Pickwick* (London: E. Lloyd, [1837–39]), n.p. Subsequent references to this edition will be made parenthetically within the text.
58. [Thomas Peckett Prest], preface to *The Post-Humourous Notes of the Pickwickian Club* (London: E. Lloyd, [1838–39]), 5–6.
59. George W. M. Reynolds, "The Marriage of Mr. Pickwick," in *Master Timothy's Book-Case; or, The Magic-Lanthorn of the World* (1842; London: William Emans, 1844), 521. An earlier version of this tale, entitled "Pickwick Married," was published in *The Teetotaller* in 1841.
60. Leigh Hunt, quoted in "A Preface to the Reprint of *The Beauties of Pickwick*," in *On the Origin of Sam Weller, and the Real Cause of the Success of the*

Posthumous Papers of the Pickwick Club, *by a Lover of Charles Dickens's Works* (London: J. W. Jarvis and Son, 1883), 9.

61. William J. Carlton, "A *Pickwick* Lawsuit in 1837," *Dickensian* 52, no. 317 (December 1955): 33–34.

62. "Vice-Chancellor's Court, Thursday, June 8," *Times*, 9 June 1837, 7. While the Vice-Chancellor refused to restrain the offending publication, he allowed Chapman and Hall to bring an action; it seems that they did not. Richard Bentley was more successful when he won an injunction to prevent the *Birmingham Journal* from reprinting excerpts from Dickens's subsequent book-length narrative, *Oliver Twist*, in the case of *Bentley v. Flyndell* ("Vice-Chancellors' Court, Wednesday, May 2," *Times*, 3 May 1838, 6).

63. George Saintsbury, "Dickens," in *The Cambridge History of English Literature*, Vol. 13: *The Nineteenth Century 2*, ed. A. W. Ward and A. R. Walker (New York: G. P. Putnam's Sons, 1917), 345.

64. Fitzgerald, *History of Pickwick*, 258n1.

65. Agreement with Richard Bentley, 4 November 1836, in *CD Letters*, 1:650.

66. Recall that the 1836 *Athenaeum* advertisement refers to "the whole of the Pickwick Papers."

67. Chittick, *Dickens and the 1830s*, 70.

68. Engel, *Annotated Bibliography*, 64.

69. James, *Fiction for the Working Man*, 58.

70. Miller, *Catalogue of a Pickwick Exhibition*, 34.

71. Marie Mulvey[-]Roberts, "Pleasures Engendered by Gender: Homosociality and the Club," in *Pleasure in the Eighteenth Century*, ed. Roy Porter and Marie Mulvey[-]Roberts (Basingstoke: Macmillan, 1996), 48.

72. Peter Clark, *British Clubs and Societies, 1580–1800: The Origins of an Associational World* (Oxford: Oxford University Press, 2000), 12.

73. Ibid., 2–3.

74. Mulvey[-]Roberts, "Pleasures Engendered," 48–49.

75. Ibid., 75.

76. Chittick, *Dickens and the 1830s*, 74.

77. Mulvey[-]Roberts, "Pleasures Engendered," 50.

78. Charles Dickens to William Howison, 21 December 1837, *CD Letters*, 1:346. The Charles Dickens Museum, in London, holds the minutes of one such club.

79. Charles Dickens to the Secretary of the Pickwick Club, 21 April [1838], *CD Letters*, 1:398.

80. *Posthumous Papers of the Cadgers' Club* (London: E. Lloyd, [1837–38]), n.p. Subsequent references to this edition will be made parenthetically within the text.

81. *Posthumous Papers of the Wonderful Discovery Club, Formerly of Camden Town* (London: William Mark Clark, 1838), n.p. Subsequent references to this edition will be made parenthetically within the text.

82. James, *Fiction for the Working Man*, 8. Cf. Patten, *Charles Dickens and His Publishers*, 54; Deane, *Making of the Victorian Novelist*, 35–37.

83. Mary Teresa McGowan, "Pickwick and the Pirates: A Study of Some Early Imitations, Dramatisations and Plagiarisms of *Pickwick Papers*" (PhD thesis, University of London, 1975), 477.

84. Ibid., 479.

85. James, *Fiction for the Working Man*, 59.

86. David M. Bevington, "Seasonal Relevance in *The Pickwick Papers*," *Nineteenth-Century Fiction* 16, no. 3 (December 1961): 225.

87. Walter Benjamin, "The Work of Art in the Age of Mechanical Reproduction," in *Illuminations*, trans. Harry Zohn (1968; New York: Schocken Books, 1969), 21.

88. McGowan, "Pickwick and the Pirates," 490.

89. *Droll Discussions and Queer Proceedings of the Magnum-Fundum Club* (N.p., [1838]), 1–2. Subsequent references to this edition will be made parenthetically within the text.

90. Louis James, "*Pickwick in America!*," *Dickens Studies Annual* 1 (1970): 76.

91. Garrett Stewart, *Dickens and the Trials of the Imagination* (Cambridge, MA: Harvard University Press, 1974), 55.

92. John Lockhart, quoted in S. M. Ellis, *William Harrison Ainsworth and His Friends*, 2 vols. (London: John Lane, the Bodley Head; New York: John Lane Company, 1911), 1:336.

93. Mulvey[-]Roberts, "Pleasures Engendered," 58.

94. John Carey, *The Violent Effigy: A Study of Dickens' Imagination*, 2nd ed. (London: Faber and Faber, 1991), 91.

95. Of course, a later S. W., Silas Wegg, graces the pages of *Our Mutual Friend* (1864–65).

96. Charles Dickens to O. P. Thomas, [1825–26], *CD Letters*, 1:1.

97. Anny Sadrin, "Fragmentation in *The Pickwick Papers*," *Dickens Studies Annual: Essays on Victorian Fiction* 22 (1993): 30.

98. McGowan, "Pickwick and the Pirates," 493.

99. Rosemarie Bodenheimer, *Knowing Dickens* (2007; Ithaca, NY: Cornell University Press, 2010), 68.

100. Douglas-Fairhurst, *Becoming Dickens*, 30–31.

101. McGowan, "Pickwick and the Pirates," 493.

102. Mulvey[-]Roberts, "Pleasures Engendered," 59.

103. Occultatio, a related trope, is considered in Chapter 2.

104. James, "*Pickwick in America!*," 79.

105. Robert L. Patten, "The Art of *Pickwick*'s Interpolated Tales," *ELH* 34, no. 3 (September 1967): 360; Philip Rogers, "Mr. Pickwick's Innocence," *Nineteenth-Century Fiction* 27, no. 1 (June 1962): 31.

106. A similar imbalance affects *The Queerfish Chronicles*, also a club imitation. The interpolated tales take up of the bulk of the extant numbers, and the club narrative is a flimsy pretext. On page 110, the work finally introduces a *Pickwick*-like character, "Mr Sitfall, the elder." This work expired on page 164.

107. James, *Fiction for the Working Man*, 58.

108. Charles Dickens, 1837 preface, in *Pickwick Papers*, vii.

109. "Charles Dickens and His Works," *Fraser's Magazine for Town and Country* 21, no. 124 (April 1840): 382.

110. Cf. review of *Pickwick* and *Sketches*, *Quarterly Review*, 518: "he has risen like a rocket, and he will come down like a stick."

111. James, *Fiction for the Working Man*, 33.

112. Letter from Chapman and Hall to Charles Dickens, 12 February 1836, *CD Letters*, 1:648. Dickens at first provided letterpress for twenty-four pages. After Seymour's death the monthly page count eventually increased to thirty-two.

113. Bos's *Twiss* (1837–39), *Nickelbery* (1838–39), and *Mister Humfries' Clock* (1840) are discussed in Chapter 2.

114. McGowan, "Pickwick and the Pirates," 366.

115. When published in volume form, this work gained an exclamation point: *Pickwick in America!*

116. James, *Fiction for the Working Man*, 33.

117. As Rosemarie Bodenheimer suggests, "Freud's idea of the uncanny as a return of repressed but intimately familiar material is something that Dickens knew, not in theoretical terms of course, but in experiential ones" (*Knowing Dickens*, 7). Freud's 1919 essay explains that "the uncanny is that species of the frightening that goes back to what was once well known and had long been familiar" (Sigmund Freud, *The Uncanny*, trans. David McLintock [1919; London: Penguin Books, 2003], 124). For Dickens, *The Penny Pickwick* may have seemed a species of the uncanny: his own text returned to him, now made strange by the interventions of Bos.

118. Rogers, "Mr. Pickwick's Innocence," 28.

119. Marcus, *Dickens from Pickwick to Dombey*, 25.

120. W. H. Auden, "Dingley Dell and the Fleet," in *The Dyer's Hand and Other Essays* (New York: Random House, 1962), 416.

121. "Winkle's Journal (Omitted in *The Pickwick Papers*)," *Metropolitan Magazine*, October 1838, 164. Subsequent references to this edition will be made parenthetically within the text.

122. Orwell, "Charles Dickens," 52.

123. Percy Fitzgerald, *Pickwickian Studies* (London: The New Century Press, 1899), 70.

124. [Thomas Peckett Prest], *Pickwick in America* (London: E. Lloyd, [1838–39]), 2. Subsequent references to this edition will be made parenthetically within the text.

125. Sadrin, "Fragmentation," 25.

126. "Mr. Pickwick's Hat-Box," ed. Henry Ross, no. 1, *New Monthly Belle Assemblée*, June 1840, 305.

127. "Mr. Pickwick's Hat-Box," ed. Henry Ross, no. 2, *New Monthly Belle Assemblée*, August 1840, 83.

128. "Mr. Pickwick's Hat-Box," no. 1, 305.

129. Fitzgerald, *Pickwickian Studies*, 107.

130. Ibid., 112.

131. "Preface to the Volume," *Madras Miscellany*, July 1839–March 1840 (Madras: J. B. Pharoah, 1840), n.p.

132. Ibid.

133. George W. M. Reynolds, *Pickwick Abroad; or, The Tour in France* (1837–39; London: Henry G. Bohn, 1864), 101.

134. Cf. Bowen, *Other Dickens*, 67: "a last gasp of Regency England."

135. "An Omitted Pickwick Paper," in *The Token and Atlantic Souvenir* (Boston: William D. Ticknor, 1841), 51.

136. For Freud on the return of the repressed, as it relates to the uncanny, see *Uncanny*, 147–148.

137. For more, see Mikhail M. Bakhtin, *Rabelais and His World*, trans. Hélène Iswolsky (1968; Bloomington: Indiana University Press, 1984).

138. Dickens, 1847 preface, 44. On the ambiguity of this phrase, see Marcus, *Dickens from Pickwick to Dombey*, 20.

139. Edwin Pugh, *The Charles Dickens Originals* (1912; New York: AMS Press, 1975), 85.

140. Fitzgerald, *History of Pickwick*, 14.

141. B. W. Matz, *The Inns and Taverns of "Pickwick": With Some Observances on Their Other Associations* (London: Cecil Palmer, 1921), 173.

142. Fitzgerald, *Pickwickian Dictionary*, 178.

143. John Forster, *The Life of Charles Dickens*, 3 vols. (1872–74; Cambridge: Cambridge University Press, 2011), 1:83. Ruth Richardson challenges this origin story in "'BOZ': Another Explanation," *Dickens Quarterly* 30, no. 1 (March 2013): 64–65. See also William F. Long, "'Boz': Reinforcement of the Received Wisdom," *Dickens Quarterly* 31, no. 2 (June 2014): 165–166.

144. Orwell, "Charles Dickens," 71.

145. Fitzgerald, *Pickwickian Dictionary*, 268.

146. *Sam Weller's Budget of Recitations* (London: J. Clements, 1838), 161.

147. T. H. Lacy, *The Pickwickians; or, The Peregrinations of Sam Weller. A Comic Drama, in Three Acts* (London: Samuel French, [1837]), 38.

148. Reynolds, *Pickwick Abroad*, 4.
149. Curiously, Rice was also considered to be inimitable: "He is, in fact, the only real representative of the character he professes to play that has yet appeared on the stage, and as he is the copyist of no predecessor, so will his imitators find it difficult to give any translation of his peculiarity and originality" (review of *A Flight to America; or, Ten Hours in New York, Times*, 8 November 1836, 5).
150. The song is also known as "Jump Jim Crow." In an early instance of product placement, the printed version of the play includes a note: "This song is Published with the Music, and a Likeness of Mr. HAMMOND, by Limbard & Co., 143, Strand" (William Thomas Moncrieff, *Sam Weller; or, The Pickwickians. A Drama* [London: Printed for the Author, 1837], 21n).
151. Auden, "Dingley Dell," 416; Orwell, "Charles Dickens," 98; James R. Kincaid, *Dickens and the Rhetoric of Laughter* (Oxford: Oxford University Press, 1971), 23.
152. Ackroyd, *Dickens*, 197.
153. Bowen, *Other Dickens*, 62.
154. Percy Fitzgerald, *Pickwick Riddles and Perplexities* (London: Gay and Hancock, 1912), 30.
155. Fitzgerald, *Pickwickian Studies*, 14.
156. John Glavin, *After Dickens: Reading, Adaptation and Performance* (Cambridge: Cambridge University Press, 1999), 89.
157. Fitzgerald, *Pickwickian Studies*, 15.
158. Reynolds, "Marriage of Mr. Pickwick," 495.
159. Ibid., 529.
160. Ibid., 540.
161. According to the *OED*, to *tup* means to copulate.
162. Mulvey[-]Roberts, "Pleasures Engendered," 50.
163. Reynolds, *Pickwick Abroad*, 79.
164. Bakhtin, *Rabelais and His World*, 19.
165. "The Pickwickian Advertiser," no. 6, in *Penny Pickwick*, part 8, n.p.
166. Engel, *Annotated Bibliography*, 74. Various database searches have discovered no copies. My research has led to a few other titles for which no copies can be found. They are works that were never published, are now lost, or arose from the clerical errors of bibliographers. Genette refers to "nonexistent" literary works (*Palimpsests*, 251), and for Jorge Luis Borges, "[I]t suffices that a book be possible for it to exist" (*Labyrinths: Selected Stories and Other Writings*, ed. Donald A. Yates and James E. Irby, rev. ed. [New York: New Directions, 1964], 57). Call them pseudotexts.
167. Calè, "Dickens Extra-Illustrated," 14. Unlike in a modern paperback, the illustrations were not placed near the relevant scenes; the images were, in

a sense, anachronistic or proleptic (more like previews of coming attractions).

168. Clare Pettitt, *Patent Inventions: Intellectual Property and the Victorian Novel* (Oxford: Oxford University Press, 2004), 21.
169. Johnson, *Charles Dickens*, 1:174; James, "*Pickwick in America!*," 80.
170. Chesterton, *Charles Dickens*, 68.
171. Max Lüthi, *The European Folktale: Form and Nature*, trans. John D. Niles (Philadelphia: Institute for the Study of Human Issues, 1982), 11, 24.
172. Eva Sallis, *Sheherazade through the Looking Glass: The Metamorphosis of the Thousand and One Nights* (Richmond, Surrey: Curzon, 1999), 96.
173. Marcus, *Dickens from Pickwick to Dombey*, 40; Bodenheimer, *Knowing Dickens*, 6.
174. John Butt and Kathleen Tillotson, *Dickens at Work* (London: Methuen, 1957), 16.
175. Kenneth Carlyle Thompson, "Boz and the Hacks: Literature and Social Exchange in Early Victorian England" (PhD thesis, University of Virginia, 1993), 20–21.
176. Cf. Jonathan H. Grossman, *Charles Dickens's Networks: Public Transport and the Novel* (Oxford: Oxford University Press, 2012), 70: "the extemporaneous, non-teleological concatenation of ongoing diverse activities."
177. As in the case of *Pickwick*, the last two numbers of each were published together as double numbers.
178. Chesterton, *Charles Dickens*, 65.
179. Logan Clendening, *A Handbook to* Pickwick Papers (New York: Alfred A. Knopf, 1936), 64.
180. Douglas-Fairhurst, *Becoming Dickens*, 187.
181. Grossman, *Charles Dickens's Networks*, 39.
182. Ibid., 40.
183. Steven Marcus, "Language into Structure: Pickwick Revisited," *Daedalus* 101, no. 1 (Winter 1972): 189.
184. Chesterton, *Charles Dickens*, 64.
185. *Effingham Hazard*, 2.
186. Ibid.
187. "Vice-Chancellor's Court. – This Day," *Standard*, 11 February 1839, 4.
188. Ibid.
189. *Effingham Hazard*, no. 4., n.p.
190. Sutherland, *Victorian Fiction*, 92.
191. Noted, for instance, in "London Gazette," *Morning Chronicle*, 23 February 1839, n.p.
192. Advertisement, *Morning Post*, 10 April 1839, 1.

Chapter 2 Charles Dickens and the Pseudo-Dickens Industry

1. Review of *The Complete Works of Bret Harte, Athenaeum: Journal of English and Foreign Literature, Science, the Fine Arts, Music and the Drama*, no. 2786 (19 March 1881): 390. Harte's parodies include "The Haunted Man," attributed to "Ch-l-s D-k-ns" (1867).
2. "Master Humphrey's Turnip, a Chimney Corner Crotchet," *Town*, 23 May 1840, 1245. The *Town* was published by Renton Nicholson, author of a subsequent aftertext, *Dombey and Daughter: A Moral Fiction* (London: Thomas Faris, 1847).
3. For some recent discussions of *Dickensian*, see John Gardiner, "The Dickensian and Us," *History Workshop Journal*, no. 51 (Spring 2001): 226–237; Juliet John, *Dickens and Mass Culture* (Oxford: Oxford University Press, 2010), introduction. *Dickensian* is also the title of a BBC television series.
4. *Morning Post*, 8 August 1839, quoted in Kathryn Chittick, *Dickens and the 1830s* (1990; Cambridge: Cambridge University Press, 2009), 135; advertisement, in James Grant, *Sketches in London* (London: W. S. Orr and Co., 1838), n.p. *Paul Periwinkle; or, The Pressgang*, by W. Johnson Neale, appeared serially, 1839–41. For George W. M. Reynolds, *Pickwick Abroad; or, The Tour in France* (1837–39; London: Henry G. Bohn, 1864), see Chapter 1.
5. Robert Douglas-Fairhurst, *Becoming Dickens: The Invention of a Novelist* (Cambridge, MA: Belknap Press of Harvard University Press, 2011), 308.
6. G. K. Chesterton, *Charles Dickens* (1906; London: Methuen and Co., 1960), 66.
7. Steven Marcus, *Dickens from Pickwick to Dombey* (1965; New York: Simon and Schuster, 1968), 91.
8. Charles Dickens, *The Old Curiosity Shop*, in *Master Humphrey's Clock* (London: Chapman and Hall, 1840–41), 120.
9. John Bowen, *Other Dickens: Pickwick to Chuzzlewit* (2000; Oxford: Oxford University Press, 2003), 132.
10. Dickens, *Old Curiosity Shop*, 87. In April 1840, *Fraser's* noted that *Sketches by Boz* "contains germs of almost every character Boz has since depicted" ("Charles Dickens and His Works," *Fraser's Magazine for Town and Country* 21, no. 124 [April 1840]: 381). Some early Dickens novels forecast later ones as well. A theatrical fellow in *Martin Chuzzlewit* boasts, "Pip's our mutual friend" (Charles Dickens, *The Life and Adventures of Martin Chuzzlewit* [London: Chapman and Hall, 1843–44], 339). Subsequent references to this edition will be made parenthetically within the text.
11. Robert L. Patten, *Charles Dickens and "Boz": The Birth of the Industrial-Age Author* (Cambridge: Cambridge University Press, 2012), 76.

12. Helen Small, "Dispensing with Style," in *Dickens's Style*, ed. Daniel Tyler (Cambridge: Cambridge University Press, 2013), 272n3.

13. Garrett Stewart, "Dickens and Language," in *The Cambridge Companion to Charles Dickens*, ed. John O. Jordan (Cambridge: Cambridge University Press, 2001), 138.

14. Charles Dickens to Richard Bentley, [?Early January 1838], in *The Letters of Charles Dickens*, ed. Madeline House, Graham Storey, and Kathleen Tillotson, 12 vols. (Oxford: Clarendon Press, 1965–2002), 1:350. Hereafter cited as *CD Letters*.

15. The date is cited in Louis James, "The View from Brick Lane: Contrasting Perspectives in Working-Class and Middle-Class Fiction in the Early Victorian Period," *Yearbook of English Studies* 11 (1981): 89.

16. [Thomas Peckett Prest], preface to *The Life and Adventures of Oliver Twiss, the Workhouse Boy* (London: E. Lloyd, [1837–39]), n.p.

17. [William Makepeace Thackeray], "Half-a-Crown's Worth of Cheap Knowledge," *Fraser's Magazine for Town and Country* 17, no. 99 (March 1838): 285.

18. Sue Zemka, "The Death of Nancy 'Sikes,' 1838–1912," in *Dickens Adapted*, ed. John Glavin (Farnham, Surrey: Ashgate, 2012), 411.

19. Ibid., 413.

20. Ibid.

21. *Oliver Twiss, the Workhouse Boy* (London: James Pattie, 1838).

22. Because of the inexact dating of these aftertexts, it is difficult to verify Pattie's claim. It is possible that the first weekly number of Poz's *Twiss* (2 January) appeared before the first monthly issue of Bos's *Twiss* (4 January) as Pattie suggests. But if Louis James's dating is correct, then the weekly numbers of Bos's *Twiss* appeared slightly earlier, in December 1837.

23. "To the Public," in *Oliver Twiss, the Workhouse Boy*.

24. [Thomas Peckett Prest], *Nickelas Nickelbery* (London: E. Lloyl [*sic*], [1838–39]), 10. Subsequent references to this edition will be made parenthetically within the text. Sowerberry's snuff-box is "an ingenious little model of a patent coffin" (Charles Dickens, *Oliver Twist; or, The Parish Boy's Progress, Bentley's Miscellany*, no. 3 [March 1837]: 225).

25. Edward Stirling, *The Fortunes of Smike; or, A Sequel to Nicholas Nickleby. A Drama* (London: Sherwood, Gilbert, and Piper, [1840]), 20.

26. Douglas-Fairhurst, *Becoming Dickens*, 10. For more Charleys and Dicks, see Bowen, *Other Dickens*, 38–39.

27. Marcus, *Dickens from Pickwick to Dombey*, 92.

28. Louis James, *Fiction for the Working Man, 1830–1850: A Study of the Literature Produced for the Working Classes in Early Victorian Urban England* (London: Oxford University Press, 1963), 63; Michael Slater, *The Composition and*

Monthly Publication of Nicholas Nickleby (Menston, Yorkshire: Scolar Press, 1973), 19.

29. [Thomas Peckett Prest], *The Penny Pickwick* (London: E. Lloyd, [1837–39]) and *Pickwick in America* (London: E. Lloyd, [1838–39]). As Chapter 1 indicates, *Posthumous Papers of the Cadgers' Club* (London: E. Lloyd, [1837–38]) may also be the work of Prest.

30. James, *Fiction for the Working Man*, 64.

31. "Charles Dickens and His Works," 396.

32. Fred G. Kitton, *Dickensiana: A Bibliography of the Literature Relating to Charles Dickens and His Writings* (London: George Redway, 1886), 392.

33. Douglas-Fairhurst refers to "publishers whose output trod such a fine line between paraphrase and plagiarism" (*Becoming Dickens*, 309).

34. Charles Dickens, *The Life and Adventures of Nicholas Nickleby* (London: Chapman and Hall, 1838–39), 192.

35. In the latter half in particular, page numbers, chapter numbers, and part numbers are sometimes missing or inaccurate. Furthermore, the protagonist's curious name proves difficult to spell. "NICKELA" (114) and "Niekelas" (243) appear, and the preface to the volume edition refers to "Nickelas Nickleebry" (n.p.)

36. Chesterton refers to "things, that is, that Dickens saw but did not understand" (*Charles Dickens*, 130). See also Rosemarie Bodenheimer, *Knowing Dickens* (2007; Ithaca, NY: Cornell University Press, 2010), chap. 1.

37. Cf. Dickens, *Nicholas Nickleby*, 40: "Mr. Squeers got down at almost every stage – to stretch his legs as he said, and as he always came back from such excursions with a very red nose, and composed himself to sleep directly, there is reason to suppose that he derived great benefit from the process."

38. Cf. Bowen, *Other Dickens*, 90; Harry Stone, *The Night Side of Dickens: Cannibalism, Passion, Necessity* (Columbus: Ohio State University Press, 1994), especially 81–83.

39. For Marcel Proust, "the great artist is the man capable of an original vision and capable too of imposing that vision (little by little) upon his public" (Gérard Genette, *Palimpsests: Literature in the Second Degree*, trans. Channa Newman and Claude Doubinsky [Lincoln: University of Nebraska Press, 1997], 106).

40. Preface to *Scenes from the Life of Nickleby Married* (London: John Williams, 1840), iii. Subsequent references to this edition will be made parenthetically within the text.

41. For the former, see Chapter 1. For the latter, see Matthew Bevis, *The Art of Eloquence: Byron, Dickens, Tennyson, Joyce* (Oxford: Oxford University Press, 2007), 89; Jon Mee, *The Cambridge Introduction to Charles Dickens* (Cambridge: Cambridge University Press, 2010), 33. The term *occultatio* overlaps with *apophasis* and *paralipsis* (aka *paralepsis*).

42. Patten, *Charles Dickens and "Boz,"* 223. The aftertexts agree. Edward Stirling's first dramatization casts Newman as a narrator (*Nicholas Nickleby. A Farce* [London: Chapman and Hall, 1838]), and Luisa Calè reports that Newman was the first portrait offered in *Illustrations to Nicholas Nickleby* and *Heads from Nicholas Nickleby* ("Dickens Extra-Illustrated: Heads and Scenes in Monthly Parts (The Case of *Nicholas Nickleby*)," *Yearbook of English Studies* 40, nos. 1/2 [2010]: 26).

43. Charles Dickens, quoted in John Forster, *The Life of Charles Dickens*, 3 vols. (1872–74; Cambridge: Cambridge University Press, 2011), 1:33.

44. This image also appears in [Prest], *Oliver Twiss*, 129: "A candle, stuck in a blacking bottle, gave them some light."

45. Monica F. Cohen, "Making Piracy Pay: Fagin and Contested Authorship in Victorian Print Culture," *Dickens Studies Annual: Essays on Victorian Fiction* 44 (2013): 44.

46. Patten, *Charles Dickens and "Boz,"* 173.

47. For details, see H. Philip Bolton, *Dickens Dramatized* (London: Mansell, 1987), 77–78.

48. *Oliver Twist* did not appear in June because Dickens was mourning the death of his sister-in-law Mary Hogarth.

49. Dickens, *Oliver Twist*, *Bentley's Miscellany*, no. 7 (July 1837): 8.

50. Ibid., 5.

51. Patten, *Charles Dickens and "Boz,"* 172.

52. "An Act to Amend the Laws Relating to Dramatic Literary Property," *Athenaeum: Journal of English and Foreign Literature, Science, and the Fine Arts*, no. 295 (22 June 1833): 405.

53. Charles Dickens to the Editor of the *Monthly Magazine*, [October 1834], *CD Letters*, 1:42. Cf. Monica Cohen, "Making Piracy Pay," 50.

54. John O. Jordan, "The Purloined Handkerchief," *Dickens Studies Annual: Essays on Victorian Fiction* 18 (1989): 7.

55. Ibid., 12.

56. The *Nickleby* "Proclamation," in Charles Dickens, *Nicholas Nickleby*, ed. Mark Ford (1838–39; London: Penguin Books, 1999), 780–781. In April 1838, Edward Lloyd countered with his own "Proclamation," which Louis James describes as "a very fair parody of Dickens's notice set up in identical type" (*Fiction for the Working Man*, 63). "BE IT KNOWN," the document begins, "that we alone are the accepted, authorised, able, and actual chroniclers of NICKELAS NICKELBERY" – as if there were any pretenders to the throne (The *Nickelbery* "Proclamation," in [Prest], *Oliver Twiss*, monthly part 4 [?]).

57. Advertisement, *Bristol Mercury*, 7 July 1838, n.p.

58. "Corn Law Repeal Humbug," *Northern Liberator*, 9 March 1839, n.p.

59. A name probably borrowed from Ikey Solomons, a real-life underworld figure who may have inspired Dickens's fence. J. J. Tobias disputes the connection in "Ikey Solomons – A Real-Life Fagin," *Dickensian* 65, no. 359 (September 1969): 171–175. There is also no Fagin character in the other *Oliver Twiss*, by Poz.

60. Dickens, *Nicholas Nickleby*, 477–478.

61. Edward Stirling's *Nicholas Nickleby* opened on 19 November 1838 and thus preceded Moncrieff's by six months.

62. Charles Dickens to John Forster, [14 July 1839], *CD Letters*, 1:563.

63. Marcus, *Dickens from Pickwick to Dombey*, 131.

64. Dickens to Forster, [14 July 1839], *CD Letters*, 1:563.

65. Carol de Saint Victor, "*Master Humphrey's Clock*: Dickens' 'Lost' Book," *Texas Studies in Literature and Language* 10, no. 4 (Winter 1969): 577.

66. Patten, *Charles Dickens and "Boz,"* 243.

67. Charles Dickens to George Cattermole, 13 January 1840, *CD Letters*, 2:7, 9.

68. Mary Teresa McGowan, "Pickwick and the Pirates: A Study of Some Early Imitations, Dramatisations and Plagiarisms of *Pickwick Papers*" (PhD thesis, University of London, 1975), 435.

69. John Ruskin, quoted in *Dickens: The Critical Heritage*, ed. Philip Collins (London: Routledge and Kegan Paul, 1971), 100.

70. Review of *Charles O'Malley, the Irish Dragoon*, *Monthly Review* 2, no. 3 (July 1840): 399.

71. Charles Dickens, *Master Humphrey's Clock* (London: Chapman and Hall, 1840–41), 51.

72. Genette, *Palimpsests*, 206. Part 1 of *Don Quixote* was first published in 1605, part 2 in 1615. Alonso Fernández de Avellaneda's spurious sequel appeared in 1614.

73. Dickens, *Master Humphrey's Clock*, 131, 129.

74. Ibid., 132.

75. Bowen, *Other Dickens*, 147.

76. *Sunday Times*, 28 June 1840, quoted in Chittick, *Dickens and the 1830s*, 148.

77. George Reynolds, quoted in William Miller, "G. W. M. Reynolds and Pickwick," *Dickensian* 13, no. 1 (January 1917): 10.

78. [Thomas Peckett Prest], preface to *Mister Humfries' Clock* (London: E. Lloyd, 1840), n.p.

79. James, *Fiction for the Working Man*, 64.

80. [Prest], *Mister Humfries' Clock*, 1. Perhaps it is a bit of self-plagiarism as well: "to commence with the very commencement of the beginning" appears in the opening sentence of *Nickelas Nickelbery*.

81. Ibid., 63.

82. *The Nickleby Papers*, like *Lloyd's Everlasting Entertainments; or, Pickwickian Shadows*, is another possible pseudotext. Fred G. Kitton cites the former as

"another of these wonderful complications; it was issued in penny numbers, and, although said to be stupid and dull, had a steady sale" (*The Minor Writings of Charles Dickens: A Bibliography and Sketch* [London: Elliot Stock, 1900], 240–241). I have traced no extant copies of this aftertext (or pseudotext). Intriguingly, the *Madras Miscellany* observed, in July 1839, "The Nickleby papers and the latest Magazines are perhaps the choicest treat for us Indians" (*Madras Miscellany* [Madras: J. B. Pharoah, 1840], 47). Yet this probably refers to Dickens's *Nicholas Nickleby*, merged, however, with the title of *Pickwick* and disaggregated into "papers."

83. "Master Humphrey's Turnip," *Town*, 25 April 1840, 1213. Cf. Dickens, *Master Humphrey's Clock*, 1.

84. "Master Humphrey's Turnip," *Town*, 16 May 1840, 1237.

85. "Master Humphrey's Turnip," *Town*, 9 May 1840, 1230. Thomas Mallon argues that plagiarists are frequently zealous in accusing others of literary theft (*Stolen Words: Forays into the Origins and Ravages of Plagiarism* [New York: Ticknor and Fields, 1989], 31–32).

86. Another popular variant on Boz is Buz, author of *Current American Notes* (an undated *American Notes* aftertext); *Dolby and Father; or, Incongruity* (1868); and *The Haunted Druggist; or, Bogey's Speculation* (1849). As in the case of Poz, the pseudonym may mask more than one identity.

87. Patten notes that in the nineteenth century, the terms *piracy* and *plagiarism* were "often used interchangeably" (*Charles Dickens and "Boz,"* 169). For more on piracy as a motif, see Monica F. Cohen, *Pirating Fictions: Ownership and Creativity in Nineteenth-Century Popular Culture* (Charlottesville: University of Virginia Press, 2017).

88. *Nickleby* "Proclamation," 781. On previous occasions it was Dickens's publishers, first Chapman and Hall and then Richard Bentley, who pursued legal restraint.

89. Charles Dickens to Henry Austin, 1 May 1842, *CD Letters*, 3:230.

90. Charles Dickens to Lord Brougham, 22 March 1842, *CD Letters*, 3:145.

91. Thought to be lost, this work was rediscovered in the collection of Iona and Peter Opie, in the Bodleian Library.

92. Charles Dickens to Thomas Mitton, 7 January 1844, *CD Letters*, 4:16.

93. James, *Fiction for the Working Man*, 65.

94. Michael Hancher, "Grafting *A Christmas Carol*," *SEL Studies in English Literature 1500–1900* 48, no. 4 (Autumn 2008): 814; Pettitt, *Patent Inventions*, 36.

95. "A Touching Scene. (*From the Penny Pickwick*)," *Cleave's London Satirist, and Gazette of Variety* 1, no. 2 (21 October 1837): 1; "Pickwick Abroad," *Cleave's Penny Gazette of Variety. Late the London Satirist* 1, no. 11 (23 December 1837): 1.

96. [Thackeray], "Half-a-Crown's Worth of Cheap Knowledge," 286.

97. Advertisement, *Times*, 15 December 1842, 2.

98. "Address," *Parley's Illuminated Library*, vol. 9 (London: Cleave, [1843–44]), n.p.

99. Introduction to "The Fisherman of Nisida and His Children," *Parley's Illuminated Library*, 55.

100. Based on an unproduced play, "The Lamplighter's Story" appeared in *The Pic-Nic Papers*, which Dickens edited. The first volume of *Parley's* also includes other pieces of non-fiction and fiction, including a condensation of *Valentine Vox, the Ventriloquist*.

101. Quoted in *Parley's Penny Library; or, Treasury of Knowledge, Entertainment and Delight*, vol. 3 (London: Cleave, [1842?]), v. This is almost a complete fabrication. The *New Monthly* did notice *Parley's* but called it "this most voracious parasite," which "managed to eat up his labours for the last two or three years." "Other popular writers are devoured after the same fashion . . . we trust the public will entertain a proper feeling for the plunderer, and treat his parasitical labours with the contempt they deserve" ("Notes on New Publications," *New Monthly Magazine and Humorist* 64, no. 253 [January 1842]: 158).

102. Dedication to *Parley's Penny Library; or, Treasury of Knowledge, Entertainment and Delight*, vol. 1 (London: Cleave, [1841]), vi. Subsequent references to this edition will be made parenthetically within the text.

103. Charles Dickens to T. N. Talfourd, 30 December [1842], *CD Letters*, 3:411.

104. Charles Dickens to Thomas Hood, 13 October 1842, *CD Letters*, 3:341.

105. Patten, *Charles Dickens and "Boz,"* 245. *Parley* also evokes conversation as well as the verb *parlay*, to exploit or transform something.

106. Charles Dickens, 1848 preface, in *The Old Curiosity Shop*, ed. Elizabeth M. Brennan (1840–1841; Oxford: Oxford University Press, 1999), 5. In the first edition of *A Christmas Carol*, there is an advertisement for "WORKS OF MR. CHARLES DICKENS"; *Master Humphrey's Clock* is not on the list.

107. James, *Fiction for the Working Man*, 66.

108. Cf. Hancher, "Grafting *A Christmas Carol*," 821: "an early *Reader's Digest*."

109. For the death of Nell, see Dickens, *Old Curiosity Shop*, 209–211; "The Curiosity Shop (Concluded)," *Parley's Penny Library*, 223.

110. Dickens, *Old Curiosity Shop*, 277–278.

111. Ibid., 111. Cf. "The Old Curiosity Shop," *Parley's Penny Library*, 19: "*you're an uglier dwarf than can be seen anywhere for a penny*, that's all!"

112. "A Genuine Ghost Story. (Not by Charles Dickens)," *Parley's Illuminated Library*, 301.

113. Charles Zachary Barnett, *A Christmas Carol; or, The Miser's Warning! A Drama* (London: John Duncombe, [1844]).

114. Thomas Edgar Pemberton, *Charles Dickens and the Stage: A Record of His Connection with the Drama as Playwright, Actor and Critic* (London: George Redway, 1888), 171.

115. Charles Dickens to John Forster, [21 February 1844], *CD Letters*, 4:50.

116. [W. M. Swepstone], *Christmas Shadows. A Tale of the Times* (London: T. C. Newby, [1850]), 2.

117. Ibid., 6.

118. Richard Egan Lee affidavit, 16 January 1844, in E. T. Jaques, *Charles Dickens in Chancery: Being an Account of His Proceedings in Respect of the "Christmas Carol" with Some Gossip in Relation to the Old Law Courts at Westminster* (London: Longman, Green and Co., 1914), 71.

119. Henry Hewitt affidavit, 16 January 1844, in Jaques, *Charles Dickens in Chancery*, 75; Charles Dickens, *A Christmas Carol. In Prose. Being a Ghost Story of Christmas* (London: Chapman and Hall, 1843), 6. For Hewitt's salary, see Jaques, *Charles Dickens in Chancery*, 54.

120. Paul Davis, *The Lives and Times of Ebenezer Scrooge* (New Haven, CT: Yale University Press, 1990), 47.

121. Hewitt affidavit, 75.

122. Hancher, "Grafting *A Christmas Carol*," 818.

123. Jaques, *Charles Dickens in Chancery*, 47; Michael Patrick Hearn, *The Annotated Christmas Carol* (New York: Clarkson N. Potter, 1976), 24.

124. Dickens, *Christmas Carol*, 1.

125. [Henry Hewitt], "A Christmas Ghost Story," *Parley's Illuminated Library*, no. 16 (6 January 1844): 241–242. Subsequent references to this edition will be made parenthetically within the text.

126. William Makepeace Thackeray, *Vanity Fair*, ed. John Sutherland (1847–48; Oxford: Oxford University Press, 2008), 27, 212, 828.

127. "Sometimes people new to the business called Scrooge Scrooge, and sometimes Marley, but he answered to both names: it was all the same to him" (Dickens, *Christmas Carol*, 3).

128. Ibid.

129. Ibid., 18.

130. Ibid., 59.

131. Ibid., 90.

132. Hancher, "Grafting *A Christmas Carol*," 816. In a footnote he concedes that it may be only "an avuncular avatar of Boz" (825n20).

133. *The Pic-Nic Papers*, which preceded the *Carol*, was edited by "Charles Dickens," but this work is a miscellany; *American Notes*, a travel book, is also credited to Charles Dickens. On the transition from "Boz" to "Charles Dickens," see Patten, *Charles Dickens and "Boz."*

134. Dickens, *Christmas Carol*, 69.

135. Dickens also cut this passage in the version that he prepared for public readings. See *Charles Dickens: The Public Readings*, ed. Philip Collins (Oxford: Clarendon Press, 1975), 17.
136. Dickens to Mitton, 7 January 1844, *CD Letters*, 4:16.
137. It seems that the second half was set up in type but never distributed (see Lee affidavit, 74). The printed version carries readers as far as the middle of Stave the Third in *A Christmas Carol*. *Parley's* resumes on page 273, with *Rivondi; or, The Old House in Birmingham Bull-Ring*. No author's name appears.
138. Jaques, *Charles Dickens in Chancery*, 14.
139. Hearn, *Annotated Christmas Carol*, 28.
140. Charles Dickens to John Forster, [11 February 1844], *CD Letters*, 4:42. Dickens also sought £1,000 in damages from the publishers of *Parley's* (S. J. Rust, "At the Dickens House: Legal Documents Relating to the Piracy of *A Christmas Carol*," *Dickensian* 34, no. 245 [Winter 1937–38]: 42).
141. Davis, *Ebenezer Scrooge*, 10.
142. Dickens to Brougham, 22 March 1842, *CD Letters*, 3:145.
143. Charles Dickens, quoted in Forster, *Life of Charles Dickens*, 1:33.
144. Bodenheimer, *Knowing Dickens*, 18. She writes, "All roads, it seems, lead back to Warren's Blacking" (17).
145. Dickens, *Master Humphrey's Clock*, 9. In *Great Expectations* (1860–61), Pip is embarrassed by the appearance of another provincial Joe.
146. Dickens, *Master Humphrey's Clock*, 9.
147. Charles Dickens, 1847 preface, in *The Posthumous Papers of the Pickwick Club*, ed. Robert L. Patten (1836–37; London: Penguin Books, 1986), 45.
148. On Dickens and counterfactuals, see Douglas-Fairhurst, *Becoming Dickens*. He quotes *David Copperfield* (1849–50): "the things that never happen, are often as much realities to us, in their effects, as those that are accomplished" (8).
149. Augustine Birrell, *Seven Lectures on the Law and History of Copyright in Books* (London: Cassell and Company; New York: G. P. Putnam's Sons, 1899), 102.
150. George Mudie affidavit, 16 January 1844, in Jaques, *Charles Dickens in Chancery*, 79.
151. For a thorough account, see Guinevere L. Griest, *Mudie's Circulating Library and the Victorian Novel* (Bloomington: Indiana University Press, 1970).
152. Jaques, *Charles Dickens in Chancery*, 53.
153. Lee affidavit, 72.
154. Ibid.
155. Hewitt affidavit, 76.
156. Charles Dickens to Thomas Mitton, 17 January 1844, *CD Letters*, 4:22.
157. Hewitt affidavit, 77.

158. Mudie affidavit, 80; Edward Leman Blanchard affidavit, 19 January 1844, in Jaques, *Charles Dickens in Chancery*, 82.
159. Hewitt affidavit, 76.
160. Quoted in *CD Letters*, 3:60n1.
161. Hewitt affidavit, 76; Blanchard affidavit, 82. As mentioned earlier, the *Quarterly Review*, in October 1837, cited Washington Irving as an influence.
162. Hewitt affidavit, 76.
163. Lee affidavit, 74. I have not traced this in *Parley's*. The first volume does find that "The Lamplighters' Story" is "in his very best style" (102).
164. R. H. Horne, ed., *A New Spirit of the Age*, 2 vols. (London: Smith, Elder, and Co., 1844), 1:74.
165. "Vice-Chancellors' Courts, Thursday, Jan. 18," *Times*, 19 January 1844, 7.
166. Charles Dickens to John Forster, [18 January 1844], *CD Letters*, 4:24.
167. "Dickens in Chancery," *Times Literary Supplement*, 2 July 1914, 319.
168. Noted, for example, in "From the London Gazette, Feb. 23," *Morning Post*, 24 February 1844, 7.
169. Jaques estimates the cost as no less than £500 (*Charles Dickens in Chancery*, 57); S. J. Rust claims that Dickens spent £700 ("At the Dickens House," 44). The latter amount, incidentally, is the cost of damages claimed by Mrs. Bardell in her breach-of-promise case in *Pickwick*.
170. [Alfred Whaley Cole], "The Martyrs of Chancery," *Household Words* 2, no. 37 (7 December 1850): 250–252; [W. H. Wills and Alfred Whaley Cole], "The Martyrs of Chancery. Second Article," *Household Words* 2, no. 47 (15 February 1851): 493–496; Hancher, "Grafting *A Christmas Carol*," 813.
171. Jaques, *Charles Dickens in Chancery*, 59; "Dickens in Chancery," 319.
172. William S. Holdsworth, *Charles Dickens as Legal Historian* (New Haven, CT: Yale University Press, 1928), 114.
173. Charles Dickens to John Forster, [?October–November 1846], *CD Letters*, 4:651.
174. *Chuzzlewit* prompted at least two immediate prose successors: Thomas Peckett Prest's *Sayings and Doings of the Funny Club. The Life and Adventures of Martin Puzzlewhit*, an 1843 newspaper serial, which I have been unable to locate, and *My Own Home and Fireside: Being Illustrative of the Speculations of Martin Chuzzlewit and Co., among the "Wenom of the Walley of Eden"* (Philadelphia: John W. Moore; London: Wiley and Putnam, 1846), an American "prequel," attributed to Samuel Adams Allen.
175. See, for instance, Alexander Welsh, *From Copyright to Copperfield: The Identity of Dickens* (Cambridge, MA: Harvard University Press, 1987), 30: "It is easy to feel that the Americans were the true inspiration of *Martin Chuzzlewit*."
176. Larisa T. Castillo, "Natural Authority in Charles Dickens's *Martin Chuzzlewit* and the Copyright Act of 1842," *Nineteenth-Century Literature* 62, no. 4 (March 2008), 455.

177. For more, see Carl Fisher, "The Robinsonade: An Intercultural History of an Idea," in *Approaches to Teaching Defoe's* Robinson Crusoe, ed. Maximillian E. Novak and Carl Fisher (New York: Modern Language Association of America, 2005).

178. The reference here to "boyish memory" suggests that Tom Pinch's childhood reading may resemble David Copperfield's (and Charles Dickens's) absorption of standard works of the eighteenth century.

179. For the last, see [Thomas Peckett Prest], *Barnaby Budge* (London: E. Lloyd, 1841).

180. Castillo, "Natural Authority," 456.

181. Gerhard Joseph, "Charles Dickens, International Copyright, and the Discretionary Silence of *Martin Chuzzlewit*," in *The Construction of Authorship: Textual Appropriation in Law and Literature*, ed. Martha Woodmansee and Peter Jaszi (Durham, NC: Duke University Press, 1994), 268.

182. It should be noted that Martin imitated Pecksniff during the American episode; Martin set himself up as "CHUZZLEWIT & CO., ARCHITECTS AND SURVEYORS" (Dickens, *Martin Chuzzlewit*, 287), a denomination resembling Pecksniff's business cards (10).

183. Charles Dickens to John Forster, [20 January 1844], *CD Letters*, 4:26.

184. Dickens, *Nicholas Nickleby*, 356.

Chapter 3 Parody; or, The Art of Writing Edward Bulwer Lytton

1. Charles Dickens to Edward Bulwer Lytton, 24 June 1861, in *The Letters of Charles Dickens*, ed. Madeline House, Graham Storey, and Kathleen Tillotson, 12 vols. (Oxford: Clarendon Press, 1965–2002), 9:429.

2. See Edgar Rosenberg, "Putting an End to *Great Expectations*," in Charles Dickens, *Great Expectations*, ed. Edgar Rosenberg (1860–61; New York: W. W. Norton and Company, 1999).

3. His name is a point of confusion. Is he Bulwer, Lytton, Bulwer Lytton, Bulwer-Lytton, Sir Edward, Baron Lytton, Lord Lytton? His father was a Bulwer; his mother was a Lytton. Edward George Earle Lytton Bulwer was born on 25 May 1803. In 1838, he was created a baronet and became Sir Edward Bulwer. In 1843, his mother, Elizabeth Bulwer Lytton (who inherited her father's estate, Knebworth, and reassumed her family name), died. Sir Edward inherited the estate and in turn added another Lytton to his name to become Sir Edward George Earle Lytton Bulwer Lytton. In 1866, he was elevated to the peerage, as Baron Lytton of Knebworth (hence Lord Lytton). One form not used by the novelist is "Bulwer-Lytton." (His descendents concur: "I don't believe he ever used a hyphen and we do not" [Henry

Lytton Cobbold to author, email, 27 March 2014].) This chapter attempts to employ the correct name for each epoch of the author's life (e.g. Bulwer Lytton in the 1850s) to avoid anachronism and to be alert to the impact that his ever-changing name wrought on his work. When not referring to a particular time, the chapter resorts to his name at birth, Bulwer.

4. The term appears in Robert Blake, "Bulwer-Lytton," *Cornhill Magazine*, Autumn 1973, 75.

5. David Masson, *British Novelists and Their Styles: Being a Critical Sketch of the History of British Prose Fiction* (1859; Folcroft, PA: The Folcroft Press, 1969), 228–229.

6. "Mr. Bulwer's New Novel," *Spectator* 2, no. 56 (25 July 1829): 473.

7. [Edward Robert Bulwer Lytton], *The Life, Letters, and Literary Remains of Edward Bulwer, Lord Lytton*, 2 vols. (London: Kegan Paul, Trench and Co., 1883), 2:236.

8. Review of *Pelham; or, Adventures of a Gentleman, Examiner*, no. 1076 (14 September 1828): 595–596. Continued in *Examiner*, no. 1077 (21 September 1828): 613–614.

9. Review of *Eugene Aram, Monthly Magazine of Politics, Literature, and the Belles Lettres* 13, no. 74 (February 1832): 233.

10. First held at San Jose State University, in 1982.

11. Quoted in [Victor Alexander Bulwer Lytton], *The Life of Edward Bulwer First Lord Lytton*, 2 vols. (London: Macmillan and Co., 1913), 2:493.

12. [W. C. Roscoe], "Sir E. B. Lytton, Novelist, Philosopher, and Poet," *National Review* 8, no. 16 (April 1859): 287.

13. Lewis Melville, "The Centenary of Bulwer-Lytton: May 25th, 1903," *Bookman* 24, no. 140 (May 1903): 49.

14. Michael Sadleir, *Bulwer and His Wife: A Panorama, 1803–1836*, new ed. (London: Constable and Co., 1933), 221. Previously published as *Edward and Rosina, 1803–1836*.

15. Quoted in Leslie Mitchell, *Bulwer Lytton: The Rise and Fall of a Victorian Man of Letters* (London: Hambledon and London, 2003), 93.

16. Demetrius, *Demetrius on Style: The Greek Text of the Demetrius De Elocutione Edited After the Paris Manuscript with Introduction, Translation, Facsimiles, Etc.*, trans. W. Rhys Roberts (Cambridge: At the University Press, 1902), 89.

17. Aristotle, *The "Art" of Rhetoric*, trans. John Henry Freese (London: William Heinemann; New York: G. P. Putnam's Sons, 1926), 389; Demetrius, *Demetrius on Style*, 93.

18. Edward Bulwer, *Godolphin* (1833; London: Pickering and Chatto, 2005), 118. Subsequent references to this edition will be made parenthetically within the text.

19. [E. R. Bulwer Lytton], *Life, Letters, and Literary Remains*, 2:230. The eloquent style is also the domain of Dickens's more grandiloquent characters, such as Mr. Micawber – Johnsonian English by way of John Dickens. Charles was John's son.

20. Edward Bulwer, *Paul Clifford* (1830; London: George Routledge and Sons, 1877), 13. Subsequent references to this edition will be made parenthetically within the text. This opening also inspired the Bulwer-Lytton [*sic*] Fiction Contest and its various publications, beginning with Scott Rice, ed., *It Was a Dark and Stormy Night: The Best (?) from the Bulwer-Lytton Contest* (New York: Penguin Books, 1984).

21. Edward Bulwer, *The Disowned*, 3 vols. (1928; London: Henry Colburn, 1829), 3:280, 3:299, 2:305.

22. Edward Bulwer, *Eugene Aram*, 3 vols. (London: Henry Colburn and Richard Bentley, 1832), 1:271. Subsequent references to this edition will be made parenthetically within the text.

23. Edward Bulwer, *Ernest Maltravers* (1837; London: George Routledge and Sons, 1877), 39, 96.

24. [John Robertson], "Sir Lytton Bulwer," *Westminster Review* 39, no. 1 (February 1843): 47.

25. Sadleir, *Bulwer and His Wife*, 29. Here is Hooker writing about Bulwer to the boy's mother: "He has an Emulation rarely found, and an Anxiety and Attention, and Care about his Business, very uncommon. He has physique, Force and Spirit, which defy all competition here; and all these things, so desirable, and so fitting him for a Public School, are ruin to him Here" (T. R. Hooker to Elizabeth Bulwer Lytton, 18 September 1818, quoted in [E. R. Bulwer Lytton], *Life, Letters, and Literary Remains*, 1:120).

26. E. Bulwer, *Paul Clifford*, 272; E. Bulwer, *Disowned*, 3:214.

27. [Leslie Stephen], "The Late Lord Lytton as a Novelist," *Cornhill Magazine*, March 1873, 348.

28. E. Bulwer, *Disowned*, 1:185.

29. [Roscoe], "Sir E. B. Lytton," 282.

30. Publication information appears in the bibliography. For more on the connection between such compilations and fiction, see Leah Price, *The Anthology and the Rise of the Novel: From Richardson to George Eliot* (2000; Cambridge: Cambridge University Press, 2003).

31. Edward S. Gould, "Review of the Writings of Bulwer," *Literary and Theological Review* 1, no. 3 (September 1834): 412.

32. E. Bulwer, *Godolphin*, 113; Edward Bulwer, *Pelham; or, Adventures of a Gentleman* (1828; London: George Routledge and Sons, 1877), 28; E. Bulwer, *Disowned*, 1:158; E. Bulwer, *Paul Clifford*, 31.

33. E. Bulwer, *Disowned*, 1:305.

34. Quoted in [V. Bulwer Lytton], *Life of Edward Bulwer*, 2:281.

35. Gould, "Review of the Writings of Bulwer," 412.

36. Review of *The Disowned*, *Monthly Magazine* 7, no. 37 (January 1829): 84.

37. Sadleir, *Bulwer and His Wife*, 269.

38. E. Bulwer, *Disowned*, 2:109.

39. Review of *Devereux*, *Athenaeum and Literary Chronicle*, no. 90 (15 July 1829): 433.

40. [John Gibson Lockhart], review of *Zohrab the Hostage*, *Quarterly Review* 48, no. 96 (December 1832): 394–396.

41. [William Makepeace Thackeray], review of *The New Timon*, *Morning Chronicle*, 22 April 1846, 5.

42. [Stephen], "Late Lord Lytton as a Novelist," 350.

43. [Robertson], "Sir Lytton Bulwer," 34. Or, in the words of Walter Scott, "Envy always dogs Merit at the heels" (*Tales of My Landlord, Collected and Arranged by Jedidiah Cleishbotham, Schoolmaster and Parish-Clerk of Gandercleugh*, 4 vols. [Edinburgh: William Blackwood; London: John Murray, 1816], 1:4).

44. T. H. S. Escott, *Edward Bulwer First Baron Lytton of Knebworth: A Social, Personal, and Political Monograph* (London: George Routledge and Sons, 1910), 1.

45. Anthea Trodd, "Michael Angelo Titmarsh and the Knebworth Apollo," *Costerus: Essays in English and American Literature* 2 (1974): 66–67.

46. Review of *Eugene Aram*, *Edinburgh Review* 55, no. 109 (April 1832): 214.

47. [William Makepeace Thackeray], review of *Ernest Maltravers*, *Times*, 30 September 1837, 5.

48. [William Makepeace Thackeray], review of *Alice; or, The Mysteries*, *Times*, 24 April 1838, 6.

49. [Robertson], "Sir Lytton Bulwer," 49.

50. Arthur Quiller-Couch, "Foreword on the Gentle Art," in *Parodies and Imitations Old and New*, ed. J. A. Stanley Adam and Bernard C. White (London: Hutchinson and Co., 1912), xi; Richard Poirier, "The Politics of Self-Parody," *Partisan Review* 35, no. 3 (Summer 1968): 339.

51. George Kitchin, *A Survey of Burlesque and Parody in English* (Edinburgh: Oliver and Boyd, 1931), xiii; J. G. Riewald, "Parody as Criticism," *Neophilologus* 50, no. 1 (1 January 1966): 132.

52. Linda Hutcheon, *A Theory of Parody: The Teachings of Twentieth-Century Art Forms* (1985; Urbana: University of Illinois Press, 2000), 77.

53. Henri Bergson, "Laughter," in *Comedy*, ed. Wylie Sypher (1956; Baltimore: Johns Hopkins University Press, 1980), 81.

54. Walter Hamilton, *Parodies of the Works of English and American Authors*, 6 vols. (1884–89; New York: Johnson Reprint Corporation, 1967), 5:222. Despite Hamilton's assertion, two poetic parodies of Bulwer, "A Midnight Meditation" and "On a Toasted Muffin," appear in Walter Jerrold and

R. M. Leonard, eds., *A Century of Parody and Imitation* (London: Oxford University Press, 1913).

55. Hamilton, *Parodies*, 1:1.

56. For more on Maginn, see David E. Latané, *William Maginn and the British Press: A Critical Biography* (Farnham, Surrey: Ashgate, 2013).

57. Miriam M. H. Thrall, *Rebellious Fraser's: Nol Yorke's Magazine in the Days of Maginn, Thackeray, and Carlyle* (New York: Columbia University Press, 1934), 4.

58. Gordon N. Ray, *Thackeray: The Uses of Adversity, 1811–1846* (New York: McGraw Hill Book Company, 1955), 197.

59. Thrall, *Rebellious Fraser's*, 9.

60. Quoted in [E. R. Bulwer Lytton], *Life, Letters, and Literary Remains*, 1:237.

61. "The Dominie's Legacy," *Fraser's Magazine for Town and Country* 1, no. 3 (April 1830): 318. Robert Montgomery, clergyman and poet, was the author of *The Puffiad* (1830), among other works.

62. "Dominie's Legacy," 319.

63. Ibid., 322.

64. Ibid.

65. "Mr. Edward Lytton Bulwer's Novels; and Remarks on Novel-Writing," *Fraser's Magazine for Town and Country* 1, no. 5 (June 1830): 511.

66. Ibid., 526.

67. Ibid. Emphasis in the original.

68. Keith Hollingsworth, *The Newgate Novel, 1830–1847: Bulwer, Ainsworth, Dickens and Thackeray* (Detroit: Wayne State University Press, 1963), 79.

69. "Mr. Edward Lytton Bulwer's Novels," 526.

70. Ibid., 513.

71. It also recalls the circular opening sentence of *Paul Clifford*.

72. "Epistles to the Literati. No. I. To E. L. Bulwer," *Fraser's Magazine for Town and Country* 4, no. 23 (December 1831): 520.

73. Ibid. Also the price of *Fraser's*.

74. Ibid., 525.

75. Ibid., 521.

76. Margaret F. King and Elliot Engel, "The Emerging Carlylean Hero in Bulwer's Novels of the 1830s," *Nineteenth-Century Fiction* 36, no. 3 (December 1981): 280.

77. Quoted in D. J. Trela, "Carlyle, Bulwer and the *New Monthly Magazine*," *Victorian Periodicals Review* 22, no. 4 (Winter 1989): 158, 159–160.

78. Thomas Carlyle, *Sartor Resartus*, ed. Kerry McSweeney and Peter Sabor (1833–34; Oxford: Oxford University Press, 2008), 211.

79. Latané, *William Maginn*, 326, 327.

80. His four predecessors were Sir Walter Scott, Caroline Norton, John Poole, and James Fenimore Cooper.

81. "Autobiography of Edward Lytton Bulwer, Esq.," *Fraser's Magazine for Town and Country* 3, no. 18 (July 1831): 714. Ann of Swansea was the penname of Ann Julia Hatton, author of *Cambrian Pictures* (1810) and *Secrets in Every Mansion* (1818).

82. "Autobiography of Edward Lytton Bulwer, Esq.," 714, 718.

83. Jorge Luis Borges, *Labyrinths: Selected Stories and Other Writings*, ed. Donald A. Yates and James E. Irby, rev. ed. (New York: New Directions, 1964), 43.

84. "Autobiography of Edward Lytton Bulwer, Esq.," 715.

85. Ibid. Cf. "Living Literary Characters, No. V. *Edward Lytton Bulwer*," *New Monthly Magazine and Literary Journal* 31, no. 125 (May 1831): 438. *Weeds and Wildflowers*, a collection of verse, was privately printed in 1825; *O'Neill; or, The Rebel* and *Falkland* both appeared in 1827.

86. "Autobiography of Edward Lytton Bulwer, Esq.," 716. Cf. "Living Literary Characters," 444.

87. "Autobiography of Edward Lytton Bulwer, Esq.," 716.

88. Ibid., 717. Cf. "Living Literary Characters," 443, 447.

89. *Wellesley* cites as its authority S. C. Hall, *Retrospect of a Long Life: From 1815 to 1883*, 2 vols. (London: Richard Bentley and Son, 1883).

90. "Elizabeth Brownrigge," parts 1–2, *Fraser's Magazine for Town and Country* 6, no. 31 (August 1832): 67–88; no. 32 (September 1832): 131–148. Subsequent references to this edition will be made parenthetically within the text.

91. Hollingsworth, *Newgate Novel*, 96.

92. Quoted in [E. R. Bulwer Lytton], *Life, Letters, and Literary Remains*, 1:127. Written in the 1850s and not published in his lifetime, Bulwer's memoirs halt at the age of twenty-two.

93. Thomas Babington Macaulay to Edward Bulwer, 24 June 1842, in [V. Bulwer Lytton], *Life of Edward Bulwer*, 2:92.

94. E. Bulwer, *Disowned*, 1:189, 1:194.

95. Ibid., 3:210.

96. Ibid., 2:4.

97. Ibid., 2:218–219.

98. This metaphor also appears in Laurence Sterne, *The Life and Opinions of Tristram Shandy, Gentleman*, ed. Graham Petrie (1759–67; London: Penguin Books, 1988), 51.

99. Earlier, Walter Scott anonymously reviewed one of his publications, *Tales of My Landlord* (*Quarterly Review* 16, no. 32 [January 1817]: 430–480). See [W. J. Fitzpatrick], *Who Wrote the Waverley Novels? Being an Investigation into Certain Mysterious Circumstances Attending Their Production and an Inquiry into the Literary Aid which Sir Walter Scott May Have Received from Other Persons* (London: Effingham Wilson; Edinburgh: John Menzies; Dublin: W. B. Kelly, 1856), 31.

100. [Edward Bulwer], "Modern Novelists and Recent Novels," *New Monthly Magazine and Literary Journal* 38, no. 150 (June 1833): 141.

101. Ibid., 142.

102. Ibid., 141.

103. Quoted in [E. R. Bulwer Lytton], *Life, Letters, and Literary Remains*, 2:284.

104. Ibid.

105. [E. R. Bulwer Lytton], *Life, Letters, and Literary Remains*, 2:283. The novelist published a parody of a living writer, Alfred Tennyson, in the pages of *The New Timon* (1846). "Let school-miss Alfred vent her chaste delight, / On 'darling little rooms so warm and bright'" (quoted in George O. Marshall, Jr., *Tennyson in Parody and Jest: An Essay and a Selection* [Lincoln: The Tennyson Society, 1975], 8).

106. E. Bulwer, "Preface to the Second Edition," in *Disowned*, 1:vi.

107. Ibid., 1:xxi

108. Ibid., 1:xxvii–xxviii.

109. Thompson Cooper, *Lord Lytton: A Biography* (London: George Routledge and Sons, 1873), 16–17; Edward Bulwer Lytton, quoted in [E. R. Bulwer Lytton], *Life, Letters, and Literary Remains*, 1:96.

110. Edward Bulwer Lytton, *A Word to the Public* (N.p., 1847), 36.

111. R. H. Horne, ed., *A New Spirit of the Age*, 2 vols. (London: Smith, Elder, and Co., 1844), 2:197.

112. Quoted in [E. R. Bulwer Lytton], *Life, Letters, and Literary Remains*, 2:192.

113. Ibid., 2:191.

114. Edward Bulwer to John Forster, 3 October 1838, in [V. Bulwer Lytton], *Life of Edward Bulwer*, 1:542.

115. E. Bulwer, *Ernest Maltravers*, 34.

116. Cooper, *Lord Lytton*, 132.

117. [Stephen], "Late Lord Lytton as a Novelist," 354.

118. Edward Bulwer to Elizabeth Bulwer Lytton, 17 June 1827, in [E. R. Bulwer Lytton], *Life, Letters, and Literary Remains*, 2:180.

119. Edward Bulwer, "The Knowledge of the World in Men and Books," in *The Student and Asmodeus at Large* (London: George Routledge and Sons, 1875), 186. This article originally appeared in the *New Monthly Magazine*, July 1831.

120. Quoted in [V. Bulwer Lytton], *Life of Edward Bulwer*, 2:398.

121. Edward Bulwer Lytton to Robert Lytton, 22 January 1862, in [V. Bulwer Lytton], *Life of Edward Bulwer*, 2:411.

122. Edward Bulwer Lytton to Robert Lytton, 7 October 1853, in ibid., 2:385–386.

123. Edward Bulwer Lytton to Robert Lytton, 1860, in ibid., 2:393.

124. E. Bulwer, *Disowned*, 1:283.

125. Quoted in [E. R. Bulwer Lytton], *Life, Letters, and Literary Remains*, 1:291.

126. Edward Bulwer, *England and the English* (1833; Chicago: University of Chicago Press, 1970), 297.

127. Ibid.

128. Demetrius, *Demetrius on Style*, 87; Bulwer, *England and the English*, 297.

129. Mitchell, *Bulwer Lytton*, 111.

130. Edward Bulwer, "On the Difference between Authors and the Impression Conveyed of Them by Their Works," in *Student*, 18.

131. Ibid., 15.

132. [E. R. Bulwer Lytton], *Life, Letters, and Literary Remains*, 2:6.

133. "Musings without Method," *Blackwood's Edinburgh Magazine* 173, no. 1051 (May 1903): 709.

134. John Sutherland, *Victorian Fiction: Writers, Publishers, Readers*, rev. ed. (Basingstoke: Palgrave Macmillan, 2006), 107.

135. Sadleir, *Bulwer and His Wife*, 305.

136. Review of *Paul Clifford*, *Athenaeum: Weekly Review of English and Foreign Literature, Fine Arts, and Works of Embellishment*, no. 133 (15 May 1830): 289.

137. [C. W. Russell], "The Novels of 1853," *Dublin Review* 34, no. 67 (March 1853): 179.

138. "Musings without Method," 713. A tale, *Zicci*, previously appeared in serial form, in the *Monthly Chronicle*.

139. [Roscoe], "Sir E. B. Lytton," 287.

140. "Epistles to the Literati. No. I," 525–526. Cf. E. Bulwer, *Ernest Maltravers*, 129: "Better hew wood and draw water than attach ourselves devotedly to an art in which we have not the capacity to excel."

141. Quoted in [V. Bulwer Lytton], *Life of Edward Bulwer*, 2:10.

142. Rosina Bulwer Lytton, *Lady Bulwer Lytton's Appeal to the Justice and Charity of the English Public* (London: Published for and by the Author, [1857]), 30n; Rosina Bulwer Lytton, *The Collected Letters of Rosina Bulwer Lytton*, ed. Marie Mulvey-Roberts with Steve Carpenter, 3 vols. (London: Pickering and Chatto, 2008), 2:170; quoted in Louisa Devey, *Life of Rosina, Lady Lytton, with Numerous Extracts from Her MS. Autobiography and Other Original Documents, Published in Vindication of Her Memory* (London: Swan Sonnenschein, Lowrey and Co., 1887), 273; Rosina Bulwer Lytton, *A Blighted Life* (1880; Bristol: Thoemmes Press, 1994), 35; quoted in Virginia Blain, "Rosina Bulwer Lytton and the Rage of the Unheard," *Huntington Library Quarterly* 53, no. 3 (Summer 1990): 231.

143. [Robertson], "Sir Lytton Bulwer," 41.

144. Marie Mulvey-Roberts, "Fame, Notoriety and Madness: Edward Bulwer-Lytton Paying the Price of Greatness," *Critical Survey* 13, no. 2 (2001): 133n37.

145. Quoted in Trodd, "Michael Angelo Titmarsh," 64.

146. Edward Bulwer, preface to *The Disowned* (1828; London: George Routledge and Sons, 1877), n.p.; Edward Bulwer, "Preface to the Present Edition," in *Eugene Aram* (1832; London: George Routledge and Sons, 1877), xxii.
147. Trodd, "Michael Angelo Titmarsh," 71.
148. E. Bulwer, *Ernest Maltravers*, 129.
149. Edward Bulwer, *Godolphin* (1833; London: Saunders and Otley, 1840), 103, 270.
150. Ibid., 242, 9, 301.
151. Quoted in Mitchell, *Bulwer Lytton*, 235.

Chapter 4 Thackeray versus Bulwer versus Bulwer: Parody and Appropriation

1. Quoted in Walter Hamilton, *Parodies of the Works of English and American Authors*, 6 vols. (1884–89; New York: Johnson Reprint Corporation, 1967), 2:103.
2. Christopher Stone, *Parody* (London: Martin Secker, [1914]), 50.
3. Arthur Quiller-Couch, "Foreword on the Gentle Art," in *Parodies and Imitations Old and New*, ed. J. A. Stanley Adam and Bernard C. White (London: Hutchinson and Co., 1912), xv.
4. Samuel Richardson to Lady Bradshaigh, [December 1749], in *Selected Letters of Samuel Richardson*, ed. John Carroll (Oxford: Clarendon Press, 1964), 133.
5. Dwight Macdonald, preface to *Parodies: An Anthology from Chaucer to Beerbohm – and After* (1960; London: Faber and Faber, 1964), xiii.
6. Rosemarie Bodenheimer, *Knowing Dickens* (2007; Ithaca, NY: Cornell University Press, 2010), 36.
7. Seamus Perry, "Sweet Counter-Song," *Times Literary Supplement*, 20 August 2010, 4.
8. Stone, *Parody*, 24.
9. Margaret A. Rose, *Parody: Ancient, Modern, and Post-modern* (1993; Cambridge: Cambridge University Press, 2000), 90.
10. Miriam M. H. Thrall, *Rebellious Fraser's: Nol Yorke's Magazine in the Days of Maginn, Thackeray, and Carlyle* (New York: Columbia University Press, 1934), 65.
11. "Mr. Thackeray's New Novel," *Times*, 22 December 1852, 8.
12. Quoted in Gordon N. Ray, "Dickens versus Thackeray: The Garrick Club Affair," *PMLA* 69, no. 4 (September 1954): 827.
13. Quoted in Gordon N. Ray, *Thackeray: The Uses of Adversity, 1811–1846* (New York: McGraw Hill Book Company, 1955), 377.
14. J. G. Riewald, "Parody as Criticism," *Neophilologus* 50, no. 1 (1 January 1966): 128, 127.

15. William Makepeace Thackeray to Edward FitzGerald, 13 September 1841, in *The Letters and Private Papers of William Makepeace Thackeray*, ed. Gordon N. Ray, 4 vols. (London: Oxford University Press, 1945–46), 2:39.

16. Gordon N. Ray, *The Buried Life: A Study of the Relation between Thackeray's Fiction and His Personal History* (London: Oxford University Press, 1952), 27; Ray, *Thackeray: The Uses of Adversity*, 241.

17. William Makepeace Thackeray to the Countess of Blessington, 1848, in Thackeray, *Letters and Private Papers*, 2:485.

18. Anthea Trodd, "Michael Angelo Titmarsh and the Knebworth Apollo," *Costerus: Essays in English and American Literature* 2 (1974): 62.

19. Proust says that after reading a book "we must do a deliberate pastiche" to get it out of our systems (quoted in Gérard Genette, *Palimpsests: Literature in the Second Degree*, trans. Channa Newman and Claude Doubinsky [Lincoln: University of Nebraska Press, 1997], 119).

20. Edward Bulwer, *Falkland*, in *The Coming Race; Falkland; Zicci; and Pausanias the Spartan* (London: George Routledge and Sons, 1878), 181.

21. Edward Bulwer, *Godolphin* (1833; London: Pickering and Chatto, 2005), 10. Subsequent references to this edition will be made parenthetically within the text.

22. William Makepeace Thackeray to Anne Carmichael-Smyth, 2–4 September 1829, in Thackeray, *Letters and Private Papers*, 1:98.

23. William Makepeace Thackeray, diary, 6 May 1832, in ibid., 1:198.

24. [William Makepeace Thackeray], review of *Ernest Maltravers*, *Times*, 30 September 1837, 5.

25. William Makepeace Thackeray, *Vanity Fair*, ed. John Sutherland (1847–48; Oxford: Oxford University Press, 2008), 1. The original title page announces that the work was "PUBLISHED AT THE PUNCH OFFICE."

26. Ibid., 878.

27. "Epistles to the Literati. No. I. To E. L. Bulwer," *Fraser's Magazine for Town and Country* 4, no. 23 (December 1831): 520.

28. William Makepeace Thackeray, *The Yellowplush Correspondence*, no. 2 (January 1838), in *Flore et Zéphyr; The Yellowplush Correspondence; The Tremendous Adventures of Major Gahagan* (New York: Garland Publishing, 1991), 10.

29. Thackeray, *Yellowplush Correspondence*, no. 7 (August 1838), in *Flore et Zéphyr*, 111.

30. Ibid., 116.

31. William Makepeace Thackeray to Anne Carmichael-Smyth, 1–2 December 1839, in Thackeray, *Letters and Private Papers*, 1:395.

32. Quoted in Thackeray, *Letters and Private Papers*, 1:408n7.

33. [William Makepeace Thackeray], "Epistles to the Literati. No. XIII. Ch-s Y-ll-wpl-sh, Esq., to Sir Edward Lytton Bulwer, Bart. John Thomas Smith, Esq. to C-s Y-h, Esq.," *Fraser's Magazine for Town and Country* 21, no. 121 (January 1840): 71, 73–74. Subsequent references to this edition will be made parenthetically within the text.

34. Edward Bulwer, preface to *The Sea-Captain; or, The Birthright*, 4th ed. (London: Saunders and Otley, 1839), vii.

35. Ray, *Thackeray: The Uses of Adversity*, 392.

36. Charles Dickens to William Makepeace Thackeray, 9 January 1848, in Thackeray, *Letters and Private Papers*, 2:336; William Makepeace Thackeray, *Punch's Prize Novelists*, in *The Snobs of England and Punch's Prize Novelists*, ed. Edgar F. Harden (Ann Arbor: University of Michigan Press, 2005), 1. Subsequent references to this edition will be made parenthetically within the text. *Punch's* was later republished, in altered form, as *Novels by Eminent Hands*.

37. William Makepeace Thackeray to Albany Fonblanque, 27 January 1847, in Thackeray, *Letters and Private Papers*, 2:270.

38. "Mr. Thackeray's New Novel," 8.

39. Edward Bulwer, *Eugene Aram*, 3 vols. (London: Henry Colburn and Richard Bentley, 1832), 3:171. Subsequent references to this edition will be made parenthetically within the text.

40. Printed as an appendix in Thackeray, *Vanity Fair*, 893n.

41. William Makepeace Thackeray to James Hannay, 29 June 1849, in Thackeray, *Letters and Private Papers*, 2:554.

42. William Makepeace Thackeray to Edward Bulwer Lytton, 21 June 1853, in ibid., 3:278. *The Caxtons* appeared in *Blackwood's Edinburgh Magazine*, April 1848–October 1849.

43. William Makepeace Thackeray to Sarah Baxter, 26 July–7 August 1853, in Thackeray, *Letters and Private Papers*, 3:298.

44. Ibid.

45. William Makepeace Thackeray to Anne Carmichael-Smyth, 7 January 1848, in Thackeray, *Letters and Private Papers*, 2:333.

46. Quoted in Virginia Blain, "Rosina Bulwer Lytton and the Rage of the Unheard," *Huntington Library Quarterly* 53, no. 3 (Summer 1990): 233. This chapter refers to the writer as Rosina, because it would be confusing to call her Bulwer or Bulwer Lytton.

47. David Lytton Cobbold, *A Blighted Marriage: The Life of Rosina Bulwer Lytton, Irish Beauty, Satirist and Tormented Victorian Wife, 1802–1882* (Knebworth, Herts: Knebworth House Education and Preservation Trust, 1999), 7.

48. Louisa Devey, *Life of Rosina, Lady Lytton, with Numerous Extracts from Her MS. Autobiography and Other Original Documents, Published in Vindication of Her Memory* (London: Swan Sonnenschein, Lowrey and Co., 1887), 255.

49. Ibid., 174–178.
50. Thackeray, *Letters and Private Papers*, 1:434n. "What the juice have Tom Thackeray & Lawson been about?" asked the novelist, in March 1840, after the shenanigans in Paris (ibid, 1:434).
51. Helen Small, *Love's Madness: Medicine, the Novel, and Female Insanity, 1800–1865* (1996; Oxford: Clarendon Press, 1998), 188.
52. Dickens, Thackeray, and Bulwer Lytton all consulted with Dr. John Connolly, in reference to their respective wives (Marie Mulvey-Roberts, "Fame, Notoriety and Madness: Edward Bulwer-Lytton Paying the Price of Greatness," *Critical Survey* 13, no. 2 [2001]: 123).
53. [Victor Alexander Bulwer Lytton], *The Life of Edward Bulwer First Lord Lytton*, 2 vols. (London: Macmillan and Co., 1913), 2:271–272.
54. Devey, *Life of Rosina*, 337–339.
55. Rosina Bulwer Lytton to Dr. Price, 26 September 1860, in ibid., 364.
56. [V. Bulwer Lytton], *Life of Edward Bulwer*, 2:267.
57. Marie Mulvey[-]Roberts, introduction to Rosina Bulwer Lytton, *A Blighted Life* (1880; Bristol: Thoemmes Press, 1994), xx.
58. Rosina Bulwer, preface to *The Budget of the Bubble Family*, 3 vols. (London: Edward Bull, 1840), 1:ix. Subsequent references to this edition will be made parenthetically within the text.
59. Edward Bulwer to Rosina Wheeler, [1827], in *Letters of the Late Edward Bulwer, Lord Lytton, to His Wife. With Extracts from Her MS. "Autobiography," and Other Documents, Published in Vindication of Her Memory*, ed. Louisa Devey (London: W. Swan Sonnenschein, 1884), 172–173.
60. Quoted in Devey, *Life of Rosina*, 29.
61. Devey, *Life of Rosina*, 30.
62. I[saac] D'Israeli, "Parodies," in *A Second Series of Curiosities of Literature: Consisting of Researches in Literary, Biographical, and Political History; of Critical and Philosophical Inquiries; and of Secret History*, 3 vols. (London: John Murray, 1823), 1:155.
63. Mulvey[-]Roberts, introduction to R. Bulwer Lytton, *Blighted Life*, xxi.
64. Edward Bull offered £300 for 1,500 copies of *Cheveley* (Rosina Bulwer Lytton, *The Collected Letters of Rosina Bulwer Lytton*, ed. Marie Mulvey-Roberts with Steve Carpenter, 3 vols. [London: Pickering and Chatto, 2008], 1:234) and £400 for the first 1,250 copies of *The Budget of the Bubble Family* (Devey, *Life of Rosina*, 198–199).
65. [V. Bulwer Lytton], *Life of Edward Bulwer*, 2:266, 2:264.
66. Rosina Bulwer to William Jerden, 29 April [1830], in R. Bulwer Lytton, *Collected Letters*, 1:42.
67. Rosina Bulwer to Richard Bentley, 10 January 1832, in ibid., 1:55.

68. Jane Preston, *That Odd Rich Old Woman: The Life and Troubled Times of Elizabeth Barbara Bulwer-Lytton of Knebworth House, 1773–1843* (Dorchester: Plush Publishing, 1998), 179.
69. Quoted in Devey, *Life of Rosina*, 75.
70. Quoted in ibid., 96.
71. Edward Bulwer to Rosina Bulwer, 22 January 1835, in [V. Bulwer Lytton], *Life of Edward Bulwer*, 1:298.
72. Leslie Mitchell, *Bulwer Lytton: The Rise and Fall of a Victorian Man of Letters* (London: Hambledon and London, 2003), 44; Mulvey[-]Roberts, introduction to R. Bulwer Lytton *Blighted Life*, xviii.
73. Rosina Bulwer Lytton to Edward Bulwer Lytton, 6 May 1851, in R. Bulwer Lytton, *Collected Letters*, 1:284.
74. Rosina Bulwer Lytton to Dr. Price, 12 April 1860, in Devey, *Life of Rosina*, 354.
75. Rosina Bulwer to Richard Bentley, 21 February 1839, in R. Bulwer Lytton, *Collected Letters*, 1:234.
76. Rosina Bulwer Lytton to William Shoberl, 20 January 1851, in Devey, *Life of Rosina*, 253.
77. Quoted in Devey, *Life of Rosina*, 261.
78. Rosina Bulwer Lytton to Dr. Price, 13 October 1860, in Devey, *Life of Rosina*, 365.
79. Quoted in Marie Mulvey-Roberts, introduction to Rosina Bulwer, *Cheveley; or, The Man of Honour* (1839; London: Pickering and Chatto, 2005), ix. Subsequent references to this edition will be made parenthetically within the text.
80. Rosina Bulwer to Richard Groom, 9 July 1838, in R. Bulwer Lytton, *Collected Letters*, 1:225.
81. Quoted in Devey, *Life of Rosina*, 207.
82. Preston, *Odd Rich Old Woman*, 207.
83. [V. Bulwer Lytton], *Life of Edward Bulwer*, 1:278.
84. Mulvey-Roberts, "Fame, Notoriety and Madness," 126.
85. Quoted in Blain, "Rosina Bulwer Lytton," 219.
86. Chris Baldick, *In Frankenstein's Shadow: Myth, Monstrosity, and Nineteenth-Century Writing* (Oxford: Clarendon Press, 1987), 10.
87. [Rosina Bulwer], "Bulwer's Dramatic Poetry," part 2, *Dublin University Magazine* 15, no. 88 (April 1840): 413.
88. [Rosina Bulwer], "Bulwer's Dramatic Poetry," part 1, *Dublin University Magazine* 15, no. 87 (March 1840): 272.
89. Ibid., 274. *Richelieu; or, The Conspiracy* first appeared in 1839.
90. [R. Bulwer], "Bulwer's Dramatic Poetry," part 2, 413.
91. Ibid., 414.

92. Quoted in Rosina Bulwer Lytton, *Lady Bulwer Lytton's Appeal to the Justice and Charity of the English Public* (London: Published for and by the Author, [1857]), 21.

93. For more on the afterlife of *Pompeii*, see William St. Clair and Annika Bautz, "Imperial Decadence: The Making of the Myths in Edward Bulwer-Lytton's *The Last Days of Pompeii*," *Victorian Literature and Culture* 40, no. 2 (September 2012): 359–396. The authors discuss "adaptations and spin-offs – theatre, songs, opera, pantomime, the circus, high and popular art, and book illustrations" (360).

94. Edward Bulwer, *The Last Days of Pompeii* (1834; London: George Routledge and Sons, 1875), 13; Rosina Bulwer, "Artaphernes the Platonist; or, The Supper at Sallust's," *Fraser's Magazine for Town and Country* 17, no. 100 (April 1838): 514. Her byline reads, "Mrs. Edward Lytton Bulwer."

95. R. Bulwer, "Artaphernes the Platonist," 516.

96. Ibid., 517.

97. Ibid.

98. Ibid., 513.

99. Cobbold, *Blighted Marriage*, 6.

100. For Colburn, see R. Bulwer Lytton, *Collected Letters*, 1:230.

101. Marie Mulvey-Roberts, "Writing for Revenge: The Battle of the Books of Edward and Rosina Bulwer Lytton," in *The Subverting Vision of Bulwer Lytton: Bicentenary Reflections*, ed. Allan Conrad Christensen (Newark: University of Delaware Press, 2004), 162.

102. Small, *Love's Madness*, 152; Mulvey-Roberts, introduction to R. Bulwer, *Cheveley*, xiii.

103. Review of *Cheveley*, *Athenaeum: Journal of English and Foreign Literature, Science, and the Fine Arts*, no. 596 (30 March 1839): 235.

104. Quoted in ibid.

105. Mulvey-Roberts, introduction to R. Bulwer, *Cheveley*, xxv.

106. Cf. Preston, *Odd Rich Old Woman*, 221.

107. Devey, *Life of Rosina*, 56.

108. Mulvey-Roberts, introduction to R. Bulwer, *Cheveley*, xxiii.

109. Recall that Becky learns "how to live well on nothing a year" (Thackeray, *Vanity Fair*, 452).

110. Henry Lytton Bulwer wrote *France, Social, Literary and Political* (1834), which in *Cheveley* becomes twisted into "An inquiry into the past, present and future State of the World in general, and Timbuctoo in particular" (92).

111. Preface to *Lady Cheveley; or, The Woman of Honour*, 2nd ed. (London: Edward Churton, 1839), xiv. Subsequent references to this edition will be made parenthetically within the text.

112. Devey suggests that Bulwer himself wrote it (*Life of Rosina*, 150); others hazard that it was his mother (William Alfred Frost, *Bulwer Lytton: An Exposure of the Errors of His Biographers* [London: Lynwood and Co., 1913], 87–88; Mulvey-Roberts, "Writing for Revenge," 166).
113. *Cheveley's Donkey; or, The Man in the Ass's Hide. A Romantic Fable* (London: James Pattie, 1839), 7.
114. Blain, "Rosina Bulwer Lytton," 232.
115. Indeed, "no Lytton hero would be called Smith" (Mitchell, *Bulwer Lytton*, 8).
116. "Elizabeth Brownrigge," part 1, *Fraser's Magazine for Town and Country* 6, no. 31 (August 1832): 75.
117. David Masson, in an 1858 lecture, referred to "a wholesome spirit of Realism." This would entail "a greater indifference to traditional ideas of beauty, and an increased willingness to accept, as worthy of study and representation, facts and objects accounted common, disagreeable, or even painful" (*British Novelists and Their Styles: Being a Critical Sketch of the History of British Prose Fiction* [1859; Folcroft, PA: The Folcroft Press, 1969], 257–259).
118. Lucille P. Shores, "Rosina Bulwer-Lytton: Strong-Minded Woman," *Massachusetts Studies in English* 6, nos. 3 and 4 (1978): 89; Mulvey-Roberts, "Writing for Revenge," 170.
119. Rosina Bulwer Lytton, *Memoirs of a Muscovite*, 3 vols. (London: T. C. Newby, 1844), 1:61–62. Popular in the eighteenth century, this form of elision is known as an *emvowel*; shading a name prevented "legal retribution" (Andrew Benjamin Bricker, "Libel and Satire: The Problem with Naming," *ELH* 81, no. 3 [Fall 2014]: 889).
120. R. Bulwer Lytton, *Memoirs of a Muscovite*, 2:159.
121. Ibid., 2:165. The same sum was initially granted to Rosina Bulwer.
122. Ibid., 2:170.
123. Rosina Bulwer Lytton, *Very Successful!*, 3 vols. (London: Whittaker and Co.; Taunton: Frederick R. Clarke, 1856), 2:61.
124. Ibid., 3:180.
125. Rosina Bulwer Lytton, *Miriam Sedley; or, The Tares and the Wheat. A Tale of Real Life*, 3 vols. (London: W. Shoberl, 1851), 1:2–3.
126. Mulvey[-]Roberts, introduction to R. Bulwer Lytton, *Blighted Life*, xxi.
127. Rosina Bulwer Lytton, *The Peer's Daughters*, 3 vols. (London: T. C. Newby, 1849), 1:151. Subsequent references to this edition will be made parenthetically within the text.
128. Rosina Bulwer Lytton, "Nemesis," quoted in Devey, *Life of Rosina*, 110–111.
129. Ibid., 130.
130. Ibid., 136.

Chapter 5 Being George Eliot: Imitation, Imposture, and Identity

1. John Holloway, *The Victorian Sage: Studies in Argument* (London: Macmillan and Co., 1953); Alexander Main's anthologies include *Wise, Witty, and Tender Sayings, in Prose and Verse, Selected from the Works of George Eliot* (Edinburgh: William Blackwood and Sons, 1872). Cf. Leah Price, *The Anthology and the Rise of the Novel: From Richardson to George Eliot* (2000; Cambridge: Cambridge University Press, 2003), chap. 3.

2. John M. Picker, "George Eliot and the Sequel Question," *New Literary History* 37, no. 2 (Spring 2006): 365.

3. John Rignall, ed., *Oxford Reader's Companion to George Eliot* (Oxford: Oxford University Press, 2000), 413. See also Margaret Reynolds, "After Eliot: Adapting *Adam Bede*," *English* 63, no. 242 (Autumn 2014): 201–202.

4. "Holborn Theatre," *Daily News*, 3 June 1884, 6.

5. Robert A. Colby, "An American Sequel to 'Daniel Deronda,'" *Nineteenth-Century Fiction* 12, no. 3 (December 1957): 231.

6. Picker, "Sequel Question," 366. Details on both appear below.

7. Price, *Anthology*, 135.

8. Gordon S. Haight, *George Eliot: A Biography* (New York: Oxford University Press, 1968), 25; Edith Simcox, "George Eliot," *Nineteenth Century* 9, no. 51 (May 1881): 779.

9. Kristin Brady, *George Eliot* (New York: St. Martin's Press, 1992), 47.

10. George Eliot to Charles Bray, 5 July 1859, in *The George Eliot Letters*, ed. Gordon S. Haight, 7 vols. (London: Oxford University Press; New Haven, CT: Yale University Press, 1954–56), 3:111. Haight edited volumes 8 and 9 and published them in 1978. Hereafter cited as *GE Letters*, followed by volume and page number.

11. George Eliot to James A. H. Murray, 5 December 1879, *GE Letters*, 9:279.

12. In this chapter I refer to the novelist as George Eliot; for the historical person, I use Mary Anne or Marian Evans.

13. Rosemary Ashton, *142 Strand: A Radical Address in Victorian London* (London: Chatto and Windus, 2006), 95.

14. George Eliot to Sara Sophia Hennell, 22 September 1856, *GE Letters*, 2:264.

15. George Eliot to John Blackwood, 1 December 1858, *GE Letters*, 2:505.

16. Henry Alley, *The Quest for Anonymity: The Novels of George Eliot* (Newark: University of Delaware Press, 1997), 15.

17. "Sayings and Doings," *Critic: Weekly Journal of Literature, Art, Science, and the Drama* 18, no. 459 (23 April 1859): 387.

18. Rosemarie Bodenheimer, *The Real Life of Mary Ann Evans: George Eliot, Her Letters and Fiction* (1994; Ithaca, NY: Cornell University Press, 1995), 125.

19. Haight, *George Eliot*, 135.

20. Alexander Welsh, *George Eliot and Blackmail* (Cambridge, MA: Harvard University Press, 1985), 113. Henry James illustrates such authorial self-division in his 1892 story "The Private Life" (*The Aspern Papers and Other Stories*, ed. Adrian Poole [1983; Oxford: Oxford University Press, 2009]).

21. Bodenheimer, *Real Life*, 144.

22. Ibid., 129.

23. Gillian Beer, *George Eliot* (Brighton: Harvester Press, 1986), 40.

24. Brady, *George Eliot*, 2.

25. Haight, *George Eliot*, 252, 251.

26. See, for example, David Carroll, ed., *George Eliot: The Critical Heritage* (London: Routledge and Kegan Paul, 1971), 67, 73.

27. Pam Hirsch, "Ligginitis, Three Georges, Perie-zadeh and Spitting Critics, or 'Will the Real Mr Eliot Please Stand Up?,'" *Critical Survey* 13, no. 2 (2001): 91; Rosemary Ashton, *George Eliot: A Life* (Harmondsworth: Allen Lane, The Penguin Press, 1996), 171.

28. Barbara Hardy, *The Novels of George Eliot: A Study in Form* (1959; London: University of London, The Athlone Press, 1963), 155.

29. George Eliot, *Scenes of Clerical Life*, ed. Thomas A. Noble (1857; Oxford: Clarendon Press, 1985), 32. Subsequent references to this edition will be made parenthetically within the text.

30. Elizabeth Gaskell to George Eliot, 3 June [1859]: "I have had the greatest compliment paid to me I ever had in my life. I have been suspected of having written 'Adam Bede'" (*GE Letters*, 3:74). For the others, see below.

31. George Eliot to Sara Sophia Hennell, 23 April [1862]: "I am NOT the author of the Chronicles of Carlingford" (*GE Letters*, 4:25); *Spectator*, 3 January 1874, quoted in Fionnuala Dillane, *Before George Eliot: Marian Evans and the Periodical Press* (Cambridge: Cambridge University Press, 2013), 1. *Chronicles of Carlingford: Salem Chapel* (its original title) appeared in *Blackwood's Edinburgh Magazine*, February 1862–January 1863. "Wit and wisdom," in the *Spectator* article, evokes Main's anthology *Wise, Witty, and Tender Sayings*.

32. Edwin P. Whipple, review of *Daniel Deronda*, *North American Review* 124, no. 254 (January 1877): 36.

33. Referring to *The Pirate*, Maggie says, "I made several endings; but they were all unhappy" (George Eliot, *The Mill on the Floss*, ed. Gordon S. Haight [1860; Oxford: Clarendon Press, 1980], 269).

34. Printed as an appendix in Haight, *George Eliot*, 554–560.

35. John Blackwood to George Henry Lewes, 28 April 1857, *GE Letters*, 2:322.

36. Edward Bulwer Lytton to John Blackwood, 14 April 1860, quoted in Carroll, *Critical Heritage*, 120.

37. Ashton, *George Eliot*, 231.

38. John Sutherland, *Victorian Fiction: Writers, Publishers, Readers*, rev. ed. (Basingstoke: Palgrave Macmillan, 2006), 117.

39. Edward Bulwer Lytton to John Blackwood, 29 October 1871, quoted in Sutherland, *Victorian Fiction*, 120.

40. [E. S. Dallas], review of *Adam Bede, Times*, 12 April 1859, 5.

41. Ibid.

42. Ibid.

43. George Eliot, *Adam Bede*, ed. Carol A. Martin (1859; Oxford: Clarendon Press, 2001), 145.

44. Bodenheimer, *Real Life*, 50; Beer, *George Eliot*, 78.

45. George Eliot, *Middlemarch*, ed. David Carroll (1871–72; Oxford: Clarendon Press, 1986), 138–139.

46. Welsh, *George Eliot and Blackmail*, 129.

47. Bodenheimer, *Real Life*, 131.

48. Susan de Sola Rodstein, "Sweetness and Dark: George Eliot's 'Brother Jacob,'" *Modern Language Quarterly* 52, no. 3 (September 1991): 311.

49. Ibid.

50. Review of *George Eliot's Life as Related in Her Letters and Journals, Saturday Review*, 7 February 1885, quoted in Carroll, *Critical Heritage*, 486.

51. R. N. Currey, "Joseph Liggins: A Slight Case of Literary Identity," *Times Literary Supplement*, 26 December 1958, 753.

52. Kathryn Hughes, *George Eliot: The Last Victorian* (London: Fourth Estate, 1998), 207.

53. Ruby V. Redinger, *George Eliot: The Emergent Self* (London: Bodley Head, 1975), 393.

54. "Notes of the Week," *Literary Gazette: A Weekly Journal of Literature, Science, Art, and General Information* 2, no. 51 (18 June 1859): 712.

55. Welsh, *George Eliot and Blackmail*, 128.

56. Kathryn Hughes, "'But Why Always Dorothea?' Marian Evans' Sisters, Cousins and Aunts," *George Eliot–George Henry Lewes Studies*, nos. 58–59 (September 2010): 48.

57. S. R. Hartnell to the Reverend G. E. Currie [*sic*], 26 January 1827, Archive, St. Catharine's College, Cambridge.

58. S. R. Hartnell to the Reverend Mr. Curie [*sic*], 9 October 1828, Archive, St. Catharine's College, Cambridge.

59. John Newman to the Tutor of St. Catherine's [*sic*] Hall, 2 August 1831, Archive, St. Catharine's College, Cambridge.

60. Haight, *George Eliot*, 211.

61. [John Gwyther] to Mrs. Lloyd, 23 February 1859, *GE Letters*, 3:21.

62. *Manx Sun*, 4 July 1857, quoted in in *GE Letters*, 2:337n7.

63. Hirsch, "Ligginitis," 79.

64. Bodenheimer, *Real Life*, 137; Brady, *George Eliot*, 48; Redinger, *George Eliot*, 333.
65. Hughes, "'But Why Always Dorothea?,'" 48.
66. Elizabeth Gaskell to Harriet Martineau, [29 October 1859], in *The Letters of Mrs Gaskell*, ed. J. A. V. Chapple and Arthur Pollard (Manchester: Manchester University Press, 1966), 583.
67. Hughes, "'But Why Always Dorothea?,'" 46.
68. Ibid., 44.
69. George Eliot to Mrs. Henry Houghton, 2 June 1857, *GE Letters*, 2:337.
70. *Manx Sun*, quoted in *GE Letters*, 2:337n7.
71. George Henry Lewes to John Blackwood, [19 July 1857], *GE Letters*, 2:366.
72. Haight, *George Eliot*, 245.
73. John Blackwood to George Henry Lewes, 23 May 1858, *GE Letters*, 2:457.
74. George Eliot to Sara Sophia Hennell, [11 April 1859], *GE Letters*, 3:46.
75. George Eliot to John Blackwood, 20 April 1859, *GE Letters*, 3:53.
76. To the Editor, *Times*, 15 April 1859, 10.
77. To the Editor, *Times*, 16 April 1859, 7.
78. Welsh, *George Eliot and Blackmail*, 129.
79. To the Editor, *Times*, 16 April 1859, 7.
80. [Sidney Godolphin Osborne], "The Great Unknown," *Times*, 3 June 1859, 10.
81. "The Authorship of *Adam Bede*," *Times*, 6 June 1859, 19.
82. Ibid.
83. "Our Weekly Gossip," *Athenaeum: Journal of English and Foreign Literature, Science, and the Fine Arts*, no. 1650 (11 June 1859): 780.
84. "Our Weekly Gossip," *Athenaeum: Journal of English and Foreign Literature, Science, and the Fine Arts*, no. 1651 (18 June 1859): 811.
85. All quotes from "Our Weekly Gossip," *Athenaeum: Journal of English and Foreign Literature, Science, and the Fine Arts*, no. 1653 (2 July 1859): 20.
86. *GE Letters*, 3:78n5.
87. "Notes of the Week," 712.
88. "Attleborough," *Nuneaton Observer and District Advertiser*, 23 November 1877, n.p.
89. Charles Dickens to George Henry Lewes, 6 August 1859, in *The Letters of Charles Dickens*, ed. Madeline House, Graham Storey, and Kathleen Tillotson, 12 vols. (Oxford: Clarendon Press, 1965–2002), 9:104. Hereafter cited as *CD Letters*.
90. George Eliot to John Blackwood, [28 June 1859], *GE Letters*, 3:102.
91. Bodenheimer, *Real Life*, 137.
92. *GE Letters*, 3:58n3.
93. "Attleborough," n.p.
94. C. H. Bracebridge to Charles Bray, n.d., *GE Letters*, 3:110n3.

95. Gaskell to Martineau, *Letters of Mrs Gaskell*, 585.
96. Hughes, "'But Why Always Dorothea?,'" 49; "Attleborough," n.p.
97. All quotes from "Notes of the Week," 711.
98. All quotes from "Attleborough", n.p. In this article, he sounds rather like an unpleasant version of Thomas Hardy's Jude the Obscure, who brandishes his learning for the benefit of fellow drinkers in a Christminster pub.
99. Currey, "Joseph Liggins," 753.
100. J. Liggins to the Rev. G. Corrie, 25 February 1827, Archive, St. Catharine's College, Cambridge.
101. *CD Letters*, 9:104n1.
102. Joseph Liggins, *A Refutation of the Calumnies Circulated by the Anti-Slavery Agency Committee, against the West India Planters* (London: Effingham Wilson, 1833), 35.
103. Ibid., 3, 4.
104. "Anti-Slavery Society Meeting," *Morning Chronicle*, 22 July 1833, n.p. The Collected Letters of Liggins of London include several to the editor of the *Morning Post* (8 August 1832, 5 March 1838, 23 November 1847) and an open letter to the Right Hon. Viscount Melbourne (*Morning Post*, 29 August 1832).
105. "Hinckley, Monday, June 9," *Leicester Chronicle; or, Commercial and Agricultural Advertiser*, 14 June 1834, n.p.
106. Obituary, *Leicester Chronicle; or Commercial and Agricultural Advertiser*, 3 February 1855, n.p.; Obituary, *Morning Post*, 26 June 1860, 7; "Latest Intelligence," *Hampshire Advertiser*, 8 December 1860, 2.
107. Eliot, *Adam Bede*, 8.
108. For more on Gwyther, see *GE Letters*, 3:83–86.
109. Hughes, "'But Why Always Dorothea?,'" 51.
110. Examples appear in Gordon S. Haight, *George Eliot's Originals and Contemporaries: Essays in Victorian Literary History and Biography*, ed. Hugh Witemeyer (Basingstoke: Macmillan, 1992).
111. Haight, *George Eliot*, 284.
112. George Eliot, "History of 'Adam Bede,'" in *GE Letters*, 2:503.
113. Hughes refers to "an interview with Samuel Evans given shortly before his death" ("'But Why Always Dorothea?,'" 55); the pamphlet cites "a short account penned by himself" (*Seth Bede, "the Methody:" His Life and Labours; Chiefly Written by Himself* [London: Tallant and Co., 1859], 7). Subsequent references to this edition will be made parenthetically within the text.
114. Price, *Anthology*, 105; Hardy, *Novels of George Eliot*, 12. Cf. Marian Evans on Charles Kingsley: "He has not that piercing insight which every now and then flashes to the depth of things" ([*Westward Ho!* and *Constance Herbert*],

in George Eliot, *Essays of George Eliot*, ed. Thomas Pinney [1963; New York: Columbia University Press, 1967], 127).

115. The date is handwritten on the copy in the Bodleian Library.

116. Adam Bede, *The Natural History of Puseyism: With a Short Account of the Sunday Opera at St. Paul's, Brighton* (Brighton: G. Smart, [1859]), 1.

117. Ibid., 3.

118. Ibid., 4.

119. Advertisement, *Times*, 11 November 1859, 11.

120. Advertisement, *Examiner*, 22 October 1859, 687.

121. Advertisement, *Times*, 29 October 1859, 13.

122. Advertisement, *Examiner*, 19 November 1859, 751.

123. Graham Handley, "Reclaimed," *George Eliot Fellowship Review*, no. 20 (1989): 38. I have not located a copy of *Adam Bede, Junior* in the catalogues of the British Library, the Bodleian, or other institutions.

124. George Henry Lewes to John Blackwood, [24 October 1859], *GE Letters*, 3:188–189.

125. John Blackwood to William Blackwood, 28 October 1859, *GE Letters*, 3:191n3.

126. Charles Dickens to George Henry Lewes, 20 November 1859, *CD Letters*, 9:168–169.

127. "Our Weekly Gossip," 11 June 1859, 780.

128. Picker, "Sequel Question," 367.

129. "A Venerable and a Non-Venerable Bede," *Punch; or, The London Charivari*, 3 December 1859, 224.

130. William Blackwood to John Blackwood, 20 June 1859, *GE Letters*, 3:89.

131. *GE Letters*, 3:89n3. I follow Haight in italicizing the title of this unpublished and possibly unwritten work.

132. Gérard Genette, *Palimpsests: Literature in the Second Degree*, trans. Channa Newman and Claude Doubinsky (Lincoln: University of Nebraska Press, 1997), 161.

133. The bibliography of Eliot, like that of Dickens, thus contains some unfinished, unpublished, lost, or mythical works, which I called pseudotexts. In Dickens's case they include *The Nickleby Papers* and *Lloyd's Everlasting Entertainments; or, Pickwickian Shadows*.

134. George Eliot to Charles Bray, 20 November [1859], *GE Letters*, 3:214.

135. George Eliot, *Silas Marner* (1861; Mahwah, NJ: Watermill Press, 1983), 191.

136. Eliot, *Middlemarch*, 819; George Eliot, *Daniel Deronda*, ed. Graham Handley (1876; Oxford: Clarendon Press, 1984), 656.

137. Haight, *George Eliot's Originals*, 14. Cf. Nancy Henry, *The Life of George Eliot: A Critical Biography* (Chichester, West Sussex: Wiley-Blackwell, 2012), 111.

138. Bodenheimer, *Real Life*, 146.
139. Welsh, *George Eliot and Blackmail*, 121.
140. Eliot, *Silas Marner*, 211.
141. Henry, *Life of George Eliot*, 6.
142. Ibid., 12.
143. Beer, *George Eliot*, 78. The third in Beer's list is "Poetry and Prose, from the Notebook of an Eccentric" (1846–47). These pieces appear in Eliot, *Essays*, 13–26.
144. Bodenheimer, *Real Life*, 135.
145. Ibid., 134.
146. George Henry Lewes to John Blackwood, [13 June 1859], *GE Letters*, 3:83: "It not being likely that L. would write on such a subject."
147. George Eliot, "The Lifted Veil," in *The Lifted Veil and Brother Jacob*, ed. Helen Small (Oxford: Oxford University Press, 2009), 15.
148. Beer, *George Eliot*, 80.
149. Eliot, "Lifted Veil," 4.
150. Rodstein, "Sweetness and Dark," 314. The name Faux suggests a fraud but also *fox* and *foe*.
151. George Eliot, "Brother Jacob," in *Lifted Veil and Brother Jacob*, 50.
152. Rodstein, "Sweetness and Dark," 310, 295.
153. Bodenheimer, *Real Life*, 150–151.
154. George Eliot to John Blackwood, 10 April 1859, *GE Letters*, 3:44.
155. Thomas Mallon, *Stolen Words: Forays into the Origins and Ravages of Plagiarism* (New York: Ticknor and Fields, 1989), 121.
156. Eliot, "Brother Jacob," 70.
157. Ibid., 74. Recall that Magwitch in *Great Expectations* passes for Pip's uncle.
158. Rodstein, "Sweetness and Dark," 299–300.
159. [Marian Evans], "Silly Novels by Lady Novelists," in Eliot, *Essays*, 317.
160. Rodstein, "Sweetness and Dark," 295.
161. Eliot, "Brother Jacob," 84.
162. Ibid., 87.
163. Henry, *Life of George Eliot*, 6.
164. Algernon Charles Swinburne, *A Note on Charlotte Brontë* (London: Chatto and Windus, 1877), 2.
165. Ibid., 3. Cf. F. R. Leavis: "It is tempting to retort that there is only one Brontë" (*The Great Tradition: A Study of the English Novel* [1948; Garden City, NY: Doubleday Anchor Books, 1954], 41).
166. Swinburne, *Note on Charlotte Brontë*, 31. *The Moorland Cottage*, a Christmas book in one volume, was published in December 1850.
167. Henry, *Life of George Eliot*, 2.
168. Haight, *George Eliot's Originals*, 31.

169. Henry, *Life of George Eliot*, 16.
170. Hirsch, "Ligginitis," 94.
171. Bodenheimer, *Real Life*, 240.
172. Simcox, "George Eliot," 799.
173. Robert Macfarlane, *Original Copy: Plagiarism and Originality in Nineteenth-Century Literature* (Oxford: Oxford University Press, 2007), 115.
174. George Eliot, *Impressions of Theophrastus Such* (Edinburgh: William Blackwood and Sons, 1879), 256. Subsequent references to this edition will be made parenthetically within the text.
175. Eliot, "Brother Jacob," 86. Cf. Rodstein, "Sweetness and Dark," 303.
176. *Punch* calls Newby and Co. a "Paternosteric firm" ("Venerable and a Non-Venerable Bede," 224).
177. Whipple, review of *Daniel Deronda*, 31.
178. Colby, "American Sequel," 231.
179. Henry James, *"Daniel Deronda*: A Conversation," *Atlantic Monthly*, December 1876, 686.
180. Ibid., 691.
181. Ibid., 690.
182. George Levine, "Isabel, Gwendolen, and Dorothea," *ELH* 30, no. 3 (September 1963): 244; Picker, "Sequel Question," 381.
183. Picker, "Sequel Question," 381.
184. Leavis, *Great Tradition*, 101.
185. Ibid., 102.
186. Claudia L. Johnson, "F. R. Leavis: The 'Great Tradition' of the English Novel and the Jewish Part," *Nineteenth-Century Literature* 56, no. 2 (September 2001): 210.
187. F. R. Leavis, "'Gwendolen Harleth,'" *London Review of Books*, 21 January–3 February 1982, 10.
188. Ibid.
189. Ibid., 11.
190. Picker, "Sequel Question," 362.
191. Johnson, "F. R. Leavis," 216.
192. "Contributors," *London Review of Books*, 21 January–3 February 1982, 2.
193. Picker, "Sequel Question," 387n46.
194. Colby, "American Sequel," 235.
195. Ibid., 234.
196. Picker, "Sequel Question," 374.
197. Ibid., 363.
198. Handley, "Reclaimed," 40.
199. Ibid., 39.
200. *New-York Times*, 30 March 1880, 4.

201. Anna Clay Beecher, *Gwendolen; or, Reclaimed. A Sequel to Daniel Deronda. By George Eliot* (Boston: William F. Gill and Co., 1878), 25. Subsequent references to this edition will be made parenthetically within the text.
202. Thackeray, *Vanity Fair*, 878.
203. Following the *Middlemarch* model, *Daniel Deronda* was published in eight installments, February–September 1876.
204. [Alfred Thompson], "Daniel Deronda. Book IX. – '*Tire and Side-on*,'" in *Punch's Pocket-Book for 1877, Containing a Calendar, Cash Account, Diary and Memoranda for Every Day of the Year, and a Variety of Useful Business Information* (London: Punch Office, 1877), 191.
205. Ibid., 190.
206. Ibid., 189.
207. Redinger, *George Eliot*, 334.
208. Quoted in Gillian Beer, "Knowing a Life: Edith Simcox – Sat est vixisse?," in *Knowing the Past: Victorian Literature and Culture*, ed. Suzy Anger (Ithaca, NY: Cornell University Press, 2001), 158.
209. Eliot, *Middlemarch*, 114.
210. Henry, *Life of George Eliot*, 237; Simcox, "George Eliot," 783.
211. Bodenheimer, *Real Life*, 241.
212. Ellen Bayuk Rosenman, "Mother Love: Edith Simcox, Maternity, and Lesbian Erotics," in *Other Mothers: Beyond the Maternal Ideal*, ed. Ellen Bayuk Rosenman and Claudia C. Klaver (Columbus: Ohio State University Press, 2008), 313.
213. [Edith Simcox], review of *Middlemarch*, *Academy: A Record of Literature, Learning, Science, and Art* 4, no. 63 (1 January 1873): 1.
214. Edith Simcox, *A Monument to the Memory of George Eliot: Edith J. Simcox's Autobiography of a Shirtmaker*, ed. Constance M. Fulmer and Margaret E. Barfield (New York: Garland Publishing, 1998), 20.
215. Rosemarie Bodenheimer, "Autobiography in Fragments: The Elusive Life of Edith Simcox," *Victorian Studies* 44, no. 3 (Spring 2002): 401.
216. Quoted in K. A. McKenzie, *Edith Simcox and George Eliot* (London: Oxford University Press, 1961), 88.
217. Rosenman, "Mother Love," 323.
218. Simcox, *Monument*, 122.
219. Ibid., 213.
220. Rosenman, "Mother Love," 325.
221. Gillian Beer, "A Troubled Friendship," *George Eliot Review*, no. 29 (1998): 26.
222. McKenzie, *Edith Simcox*, 58.
223. Bodenheimer, *Real Life*, 253.
224. Bodenheimer, "Autobiography in Fragments," 405.

225. Simcox, *Monument*, 7.

226. Ibid., 21.

227. Gordon S. Haight, introduction to McKenzie, *Edith Simcox*, xi.

228. Simcox, *Monument*, 185.

229. Rosenman, "Mother Love," 313.

230. Ibid., 331.

231. Edith Simcox, *Episodes in the Lives of Men, Women, and Lovers* (London: Trübner and Co., 1882), 100. Subsequent references to this edition will be made parenthetically within the text.

232. [Evans], "Silly Novels," in Eliot, *Essays*, 320.

Postscript, Posthumous Papers, Aftertexts

1. Elliot Engel, *Pickwick Papers: An Annotated Bibliography* (New York: Garland Publishing, 1990), 44.

2. H. Philip Bolton, *Dickens Dramatized* (London: Mansell, 1987), 75–76, 96.

3. Stephen Jarvis, *Death and Mr. Pickwick* (New York: Farrar, Straus and Giroux, 2015), 67. For more on the cultural afterlife of Dickens, see, for example, Juliet John, *Dickens and Mass Culture* (Oxford: Oxford University Press, 2010); Claire Wood, *Dickens and the Business of Death* (Cambridge: Cambridge University Press, 2015), conclusion.

4. Quoted in Anne Jamison, et al., *Fic: Why Fanfiction Is Taking Over the World* (Dallas: Smart Pop, 2013), 377.

5. Darren Wershler, "Conceptual Writing as Fanfiction," in ibid., 369. For the transmediation of Victorian authors, see, for instance, Jay Clayton, *Charles Dickens in Cyberspace: The Afterlife of the Nineteenth Century in Postmodern Culture* (New York: Oxford University Press, 2003).

6. David S. Roh, *Illegal Literature: Toward a Disruptive Creativity* (Minneapolis: University of Minnesota Press, 2015), 84.

7. Lawrence Lessig, *Remix: Making Art and Commerce Thrive in the Hybrid Economy* (2008; New York: Penguin Books, 2009), 28.

8. Roh, *Illegal Literature*, 127.

9. Quoted in Chris R. Vanden Bossche, "The Value of Literature: Representations of Print Culture in the Copyright Debate of 1837–1842," *Victorian Studies* 38, no. 1 (Autumn 1994): 45.

10. Cf. Lessig on technological advances (*Remix*, 101–102). For a phenomenon related to fanfiction, see Roh on *dojinshi*, in *Illegal Literature*, chap. 2.

11. Jamison, *Fic*, 4.

12. Henry Jenkins, *Textual Poachers: Television Fans and Participatory Culture*, rev. ed. (1992; New York: Routledge, 2013), 18.

13. Ibid., 23.

14. Lev Grossman, foreword to Jamison, *Fic*, xii.
15. Jamison, *Fic*, 17.
16. Ibid., 284.
17. Paul K. Saint-Amour, *The Copywrights: Intellectual Property and the Literary Imagination* (2003; Ithaca, NY: Cornell University Press, 2010), 4, 5. Cf. Laura J. Murray, "Plagiarism and Copyright Infringement: The Costs of Confusion," in *Originality, Imitation, and Plagiarism: Teaching Writing in the Digital Age*, ed. Caroline Eisner and Martha Vicinus (Ann Arbor: University of Michigan Press and the University of Michigan Library, 2008), 180: "this increasingly copyrightous world."
18. Dwight Macdonald, *Parodies: An Anthology from Chaucer to Beerbohm – and After* (1960; London: Faber and Faber, 1964), 157. Margaret A. Rose agrees that parody "ensures some continued form of existence for the parodied work" (*Parody: Ancient, Modern, and Post-modern* [1993; Cambridge: Cambridge University Press, 2000], 41).
19. Marjorie Garber, *Quotation Marks* (New York: Routledge, 2003), 78.
20. Sergei Eisenstein, "Dickens, Griffith, and the Film Today," in *Film Form: Essays in Film Theory* (1949; San Diego, CA: Harcourt Brace and Company, 1977).

Bibliography

The following sources are divided into chronological categories: I (Pre-1901), including later editions, and II (1901 to the Present).

For works by Charles Dickens, Edward Bulwer Lytton, Rosina Bulwer Lytton, and William Makepeace Thackeray that originally appeared anonymously or pseudonymously, the authors' names are not framed by square brackets.

I Pre-1901

À Beckett, Gilbert A. *Oliver Twist. A Burletta.* 1838. [Plays from the Lord Chamberlain's Office. British Museum Additional MS 42945.]

"An Act to Amend the Laws Relating to Dramatic Literary Property." *Athenaeum: Journal of English and Foreign Literature, Science, and the Fine Arts*, no. 295 (22 June 1833): 405.

Advertisement. *Athenaeum: Journal of English and Foreign Literature, Science, and the Fine Arts*, no. 439 (26 March 1836): 232.

Advertisement. *Bristol Mercury*, 7 July 1838, n.p.

Advertisement. *Examiner*, 22 October 1859, 687.

Advertisement. *Examiner*, 19 November 1859, 751.

Advertisement. *Morning Post*, 10 April 1839, 1.

Advertisement. *Northern Star, and Leeds General Advertiser*, 4 August 1838, 1.

Advertisement. *Times*, 15 December 1842, 2.

Advertisement. *Times*, 29 October, 1859, 13.

Advertisement. *Times*, 11 November 1859, 11.

Advertisement. *Times*, 19 November 1859, 13.

[Allen, Samuel Adams]. *My Own Home and Fireside: Being Illustrative of the Speculations of Martin Chuzzlewit and Co., among the "Wenom of the Walley of Eden."* By SYR. Philadelphia: John W. Moore; London: Wiley and Putnam, 1846.

Almar, George. *Oliver Twist. A Serio-Comic Burletta.* London: Sherwood, Gilbert, and Piper, [1840]. Leipsic: Herm. Hartung, 1842.

"Anti-Slavery Society Meeting." *Morning Chronicle*, 22 July 1833, n.p.

[Archer, Thomas]. *Richard of England; or, The Lion King.* London: F. Hextall, n.d.

Aristotle. *The "Art" of Rhetoric.* Trans. John Henry Freese. London: William Heinemann; New York: G. P. Putnam's Sons, 1926.

Poetics. Trans. Stephen Halliwell. In *Aristotle Poetics; Longinus on the Sublime; Demetrius on Style*. Loeb Classical Library. 1995. Cambridge, MA: Harvard University Press, 1999.

Athenaeum and Literary Chronicle, no.91 (22 July 1829): 450–451.

"Attleborough." *Nuneaton Observer and District Advertiser*, 23 November 1877, n.p.

"The Authorship of *Adam Bede*." *Times*, 6 June 1859, 19.

"Autobiography of Edward Lytton Bulwer, Esq." *Fraser's Magazine for Town and Country* 3, no. 18 (July 1831): 713–719.

Barnes, W[illiam]. "Plagiarism and Coincidence; or, Thought-Thievery and Thought-Likeness." *Macmillan's Magazine* 15, no. 85 (November 1866): 73–80.

Barnett, Charles Zachary. *A Christmas Carol; or, The Miser's Warning! A Drama*. London: John Duncombe, [1844].

 Oliver Twist; or, The Parish Boy's Progress. A Domestic Drama. London: J. Duncombe and Co., [1838?]

The Beauties of Pickwick. Collected and Arranged by Sam Weller. 1838. In *On the Origin of Sam Weller, and the Real Cause of the Success of the* Posthumous Papers of the Pickwick Club, *by a Lover of Charles Dickens's Works*. London: J. W. Jarvis and Son, 1883.

Bede, Adam. *The Natural History of Puseyism: With a Short Account of the Sunday Opera at St. Paul's, Brighton*. Brighton: G. Smart, [1859].

Beecher, Anna Clay. *Gwendolen; or, Reclaimed. A Sequel to Daniel Deronda. By George Eliot*. Boston: William F. Gill and Co., 1878.

Birrell, Augustine. *Seven Lectures on the Law and History of Copyright in Books*. London: Cassell and Company; New York: G. P. Putnam's Sons, 1899.

[Blackwood, John]. "The Death of Lord Lytton." *Blackwood's Edinburgh Magazine* 113, no. 688 (February 1873): 255–258.

Browning, Robert. *The Complete Works of Robert Browning*. Ed. Roma A. King, Jr., et al. 17 vols. Athens: Ohio University Press; Waco, TX: Baylor University, 1969–2011.

Buckstone, John Baldwin. *The Christening. A Farce*. London: William Strange, 1834.

The Bulwer Lytton Birthday Book. N.p.: George Routledge and Sons, [1884?]

Calverley, C. S. "An Examination Paper. 'The Posthumous Papers of the Pickwick Club.'" 1857. In *Fly Leaves*. Rev. ed. New York: Thomas Y. Crowell and Co., 1872.

Carlyle, Thomas. *On Heroes, Hero-Worship, and the Heroic in History. Six Lectures. Reported, with Emendations and Additions*. London: James Fraser, 1841.

 Sartor Resartus. 1833–34. Ed. Kerry McSweeney and Peter Sabor. Oxford: Oxford University Press, 2008.

Chamerovzow, L. A. *The Yule Log, for Everybody's Christmas Hearth; Showing Where It Grew; How It Was Cut and Brought Home; and How It Was Burnt*. London: T. C. Newby, 1847.

"Charles Dickens and His Works." *Fraser's Magazine for Town and Country* 21, no. 124 (April 1840): 381–400.

Cheveley's Donkey; or, The Man in the Ass's Hide. A Romantic Fable. London: James
Pattie, 1839.

The Christmas Log. A Tale of a Fireside That Had a Good Genius and a Bad One.
London: E. Lloyd, [1846].

[Cole, Alfred Whaley]. "The Martyrs of Chancery." *Household Words* 2, no. 37
(7 December 1850): 250–252.

The Comic Magazine [aka *The Penny Comic Magazine*]. London: W. Marshall, n.d.

Cooper, Frederic Fox. *Master Humphrey's Clock. A Domestic Drama.* London:
J. Duncombe and Co., [1840?]

Cooper, Thompson. *Lord Lytton: A Biography.* London: George Routledge and
Sons, 1873.

"Corn Law Repeal Humbug." *Northern Liberator*, 9 March 1839, n.p.

"Coroner's Inquest." *Times*, 22 April 1836, 7.

Coyne, Joseph Stirling. *Oliver Twist.* 1839. [Plays from the Lord Chamberlain's
Office. British Museum Additional MS 42950.]

Crowquill, Alfred [Alfred Forrester]. *The Pickwickians.* London: Ackermann and
Co., 1837.

   Seymour's Sketches, Illustrated in Prose and Verse. London: Published for the
Proprietor, by Joshua Thompson, 1838–39.

"The Cry of Plagiarism." *Spectator* 66, no. 3270 (28 February 1891): 305–306.

[Dallas, E. S.] Review of *Adam Bede. Times*, 12 April 1859, 5.

Defoe, Daniel. *An Essay on the Regulation of the Press.* London: n.p., 1704.

   "Miscellanea." *A Review of the State of the British Nation* 6, no. 129 (2 February
1710): 515–516.

Demetrius. *Demetrius on Style: The Greek Text of the Demetrius* De Elocutione
*Edited After the Paris Manuscript with Introduction, Translation, Facsimiles,
Etc.* Trans. W. Rhys Roberts. Cambridge: At the University Press, 1902.

[De Quincey, Thomas]. "Samuel Taylor Coleridge." By the English Opium-
Eater. *Tait's Edinburgh Magazine* 1, no. 8 (September 1834): 509–520.

[De Quincey, Thomas, trans.] *Walladmor: "Freely Translated into German from the
English of Sir Walter Scott." And Now Freely Translated from the German into
English.* 2 vols. London: Printed for Taylor and Hessey, 1825.

Devey, Louisa. *Life of Rosina, Lady Lytton, with Numerous Extracts from Her MS.
Autobiography and Other Original Documents, Published in Vindication of Her
Memory.* 2nd ed. London: Swan Sonnenschein, Lowrey and Co., 1887.

Dickens, Charles. *American Notes.* 1842. Ed. Patricia Ingham. London: Penguin
Books, 2004.

   Bleak House. 1852–53. Ed. Nicola Bradbury. London: Penguin Books, 2003.

   A Christmas Carol. In Prose. Being a Ghost Story of Christmas. London: Chapman
and Hall, 1843.

   David Copperfield. 1849–50. Ed. Nina Burgis. Oxford: Oxford University Press,
1997.

   Dombey and Son. 1844–46. Ed. Peter Fairclough. London: Penguin Books, 1985.

   Great Expectations. 1860–61. Ed. Edgar Rosenberg. New York: W. W. Norton
and Company, 1999.

The Letters of Charles Dickens. Ed. Madeline House, Graham Storey, and Kathleen Tillotson. 12 vols. Oxford: Clarendon Press, 1965–2002.

The Life and Adventures of Martin Chuzzlewit. Edited by Boz. London: Chapman and Hall, 1843–44.

The Life and Adventures of Nicholas Nickleby. Edited by "Boz." London: Chapman and Hall, 1838–39.

Master Humphrey's Clock. By "Boz." London: Chapman and Hall, 1840–41.

Nicholas Nickleby. 1838–39. Ed. Mark Ford. London: Penguin Books, 1999.

The Old Curiosity Shop. 1840–41. Ed. Elizabeth M. Brennan. Oxford: Oxford University Press, 1999.

The Old Curiosity Shop. In *Master Humphrey's Clock*. By "Boz." London: Chapman and Hall, 1840–41.

Oliver Twist; or, The Parish Boy's Progress. Parts 1–24. *Bentley's Miscellany*, nos. 2–28 (1 February 1837–1 April 1839).

"Passages in the Life of Mr. Watkins Tottle." Parts 1–2. *Monthly Magazine*, January 1835, 15–24; February 1835, 121–137.

The Posthumous Papers of the Pickwick Club. Edited by "Boz." London: Chapman and Hall, 1836–37.

The Posthumous Papers of the Pickwick Club. 1836–37. Ed. Robert L. Patten. London: Penguin Books, 1986.

Charles Dickens: The Public Readings. Ed. Philip Collins. Oxford: Clarendon Press, 1975.

Sketches by Boz and Other Early Papers, 1833–39. Ed. Michael Slater. Columbus: Ohio State University Press, 1994.

Sketches of Young Gentlemen and Young Couples. With Sketches of Young Ladies, by Edward Caswall. Oxford: Oxford University Press, 2012.

"Dickens v. Lee." *Jurist* (London) 8, no. 1 (1845): 183–186.

D'Israeli, I[saac]. *A Second Series of Curiosities of Literature: Consisting of Researches in Literary, Biographical, and Political History; of Critical and Philosophical Inquiries; and of Secret History*. 3 vols. London: John Murray, 1823.

"The Dominie's Legacy." *Fraser's Magazine for Town and Country* 1, no. 3 (April 1830): 318–335.

Droll Discussions and Queer Proceedings of the Magnum-Fundum Club. Accurately Reported by "Quiz." N.p., [1838].

Effingham Hazard, the Adventurer. London: Edward Ravenscroft; Foster and Hextall; John Foster, 1838–39.

Egan, Pierce. *The Finish to the Adventures of Tom, Jerry, and Logic, in Their Pursuits through Life in and out of London*. 1828. London: Reeves and Turner, 1887.

Eliot, George [née Mary Anne Evans]. *Adam Bede*. 1859. Ed. Carol A. Martin. Oxford: Clarendon Press, 2001.

Daniel Deronda. 1876. Ed. Graham Handley. Oxford: Clarendon Press, 1984.

Essays of George Eliot. Ed. Thomas Pinney. 1963. New York: Columbia University Press, 1967.

The George Eliot Letters. Ed. Gordon S. Haight. 7 vols. London: Oxford University Press; New Haven, CT: Yale University Press, 1954–56.

The George Eliot Letters. Ed. Gordon S. Haight. Vols. 8 and 9. New Haven, CT: Yale University Press, 1978.

Impressions of Theophrastus Such. Edinburgh: William Blackwood and Sons, 1879.

The Lifted Veil and Brother Jacob. Ed. Helen Small. Oxford: Oxford University Press, 2009.

Middlemarch. 1871–72. Ed. David Carroll. Oxford: Clarendon Press, 1986.

The Mill on the Floss. 1860. Ed. Gordon S. Haight. Oxford: Clarendon Press, 1980.

Scenes of Clerical Life. 1857. Ed. Thomas A. Noble. Oxford: Clarendon Press, 1985.

Silas Marner. 1861. Mahwah, NJ: Watermill Press, 1983.

"Elizabeth Brownrigge." Parts 1–2. *Fraser's Magazine for Town and Country* 6, no. 31 (August 1832): 67–88; no. 32 (September 1832): 131–148.

Emerson, Ralph Waldo. "Quotation and Originality." *In Ralph Waldo Emerson.* Ed. Richard Poirier. Oxford: Oxford University Press, 1990.

Enfield, William. *Observations on Literary Property.* London: Printed for Joseph Johnson, 1774.

"Epistles to the Literati. No. I. To E. L. Bulwer." *Fraser's Magazine for Town and Country* 4, no. 23 (December 1831): 520–526.

Fitzgerald, Percy. *Bozland: Dickens' Places and People.* London: Downey and Co., 1895.

The History of Pickwick: An Account of Its Characters, Localities, Allusions, and Illustrations. London: Chapman and Hall, 1891.

The Pickwickian Dictionary and Cyclopaedia. London: W. T. Spencer, [1900].

Pickwickian Manners and Customs. London: Roxburghe Press, [1898].

Pickwickian Studies. London: The New Century Press, 1899.

[Fitzpatrick, W. J.] *Who Wrote the Waverley Novels? Being an Investigation into Certain Mysterious Circumstances Attending Their Production and an Inquiry into the Literary Aid which Sir Walter Scott May Have Received from Other Persons.* London: Effingham Wilson; Edinburgh: John Menzies; Dublin: W. B. Kelly, 1856.

Forster, John. *The Life of Charles Dickens.* 3 vols. 1872–74. Cambridge: Cambridge University Press, 2011.

"From the London Gazette, Feb. 23." *Morning Post,* 24 February 1844, 7.

Gaskell, Elizabeth. *The Letters of Mrs Gaskell.* Ed. J. A. V. Chapple and Arthur Pollard. Manchester: Manchester University Press, 1966.

"A Good Tale Badly Told. By Mr. Edward Lytton Bulwer." *Fraser's Magazine for Town and Country* 5, no. 25 (February 1832): 107–113.

Gould, Edward S. "Review of the Writings of Bulwer." *Literary and Theological Review* 1, no. 3 (September 1834): 412–427.

Grant, James. *Sketches in London.* London: W. S. Orr and Co., 1838.

Grego, Joseph. *Pictorial Pickwickiana: Charles Dickens and His Illustrators.* 2 vols. London: Chapman and Hall, 1899.

Grub-Street Journal, no. 31 (6 August 1730): 1–4.

Hadden, J. Cuthbert. "Plagiarism and Coincidence." *Scottish Review* 27 (April 1896): 336–350.

Hall, Hammond. *Mr. Pickwick's Kent.* Rochester: W. and J. Mackay, 1899.

Hall, S. C. *Retrospect of a Long Life: From 1815 to 1883.* 2 vols. London: Richard Bentley and Son, 1883.

Hamilton, Walter. *Parodies of the Works of English and American Authors.* 6 vols. 1884–89. New York: Johnson Reprint Corporation, 1967.

Harte, Bret. *Condensed Novels and Other Papers.* New York: G. W. Carleton and Co., 1867.

[Hewitt, Henry]. "A Christmas Ghost Story." *Parley's Illuminated Library*, no. 16 (6 January 1844): 241–256.

"Hinckley, Monday, June 9." *Leicester Chronicle; or Commercial and Agricultural Advertiser*, 14 June 1834, n.p.

"Historical Romance. No. I. Sir Walter Scott and His Imitators." *Fraser's Magazine for Town and Country* 5, no. 25 (February 1832): 6–19.

[Hogg, James]. *The Poetic Mirror; or, The Living Bards of Britain.* London: Printed for Longman, Hurst, Rees, Orme, and Brown; and John Ballantyne, Edinburgh, 1816.

"Holborn Theatre." *Daily News*, 3 June 1884, 6.

Homer's Battle of the Frogs and Mice. With the Remarks of Zoilus. To Which Is Prefix'd, the Life of Said Zoilus. London: Printed for Bernard Lintot, 1707.

Horncastle, H. *The Infant Phenomenon; or, A Rehearsal Rehearsed* [aka *The Savage and the Maiden; or, Crummles and His Daughter* aka *The Crummleses; or, A Rehearsal Rehearsed*]. *A Dramatic Piece.* London: John Dicks, n.d.

Horne, R. H., ed. *A New Spirit of the Age.* 2 vols. London: Smith, Elder, and Co., 1844.

James, Henry. *The Aspern Papers and Other Stories.* Ed. Adrian Poole. 1983. Oxford: Oxford University Press, 2009.

   "*Daniel Deronda*: A Conversation." *Atlantic Monthly*, December 1876, 684–694.

[Jeffrey, Francis]. Review of *Rejected Addresses; or, The New Theatrum Poetarum. Edinburgh Review* 20, no. 40 (November 1812): 434–451.

"John Gilpin and Mazeppa." *Blackwood's Edinburgh Magazine* 5, no. 28 (July 1819): 434–439.

Johnson, Samuel. *The Yale Edition of the Works of Samuel Johnson.* Ed. E. L. McAdam, Jr., et al. 23 vols. New Haven, CT: Yale University Press, 1958–2012.

Keats, John. *The Letters of John Keats, 1814–1821.* Ed. Hyder Edward Rollins. 2 vols. Cambridge, MA: Harvard University Press, 1958.

Kent, Charles, ed. *The Wit and Wisdom of Edward Bulwer Lord Lytton with Impressive Humorous and Pathetic Passages from His Works.* London: George Routledge and Sons, 1883.

Kitton, Fred G. *Dickensiana: A Bibliography of the Literature Relating to Charles Dickens and His Writings.* London: George Redway, 1886.

   The Minor Writings of Charles Dickens: A Bibliography and Sketch. London: Elliot Stock, 1900.

Lacy, T. H. *The Pickwickians; or, The Peregrinations of Sam Weller. A Comic Drama, in Three Acts.* London: Samuel French, [1837].

Lady Cheveley; or, The Woman of Honour. A New Version of Cheveley, the Man of Honour. 2nd ed. London: Edward Churton, 1839.

Lang, A[ndrew]. "Literary Plagiarism." *Contemporary Review* 51 (June 1887): 831–840.

Langbaine, Gerard. *Momus Triumphans; or, The Plagiaries of the English Stage.* 1687. Los Angeles: University of California, 1971.

"Latest Intelligence." *Hampshire Advertiser*, 8 December 1860, 2.

Lewes, George Henry. *Ranthorpe.* 1847. Ed. Barbara Smalley. Athens: Ohio University Press, 1974.

The Life and Opinions of Bertram Montfichet, Esq; Written by Himself. 2 vols. London: Printed for C. G. Seyffert, [1761].

The Life and Opinions of Miss Sukey Shandy, of Bow-Street, Gentlewoman. In a Series of Letters to Her Dear Brother Tristram Shandy, Gent. London: Printed for R. Stevens, 1760.

Liggins, Joseph. *A Refutation of the Calumnies Circulated by the Anti-Slavery Agency Committee, against the West India Planters.* London: Effingham Wilson, 1833.

To Mr. John Crisp. *Morning Post*, 16 August 1832, n.p.

To the Editor. *Morning Post*, 8 August 1832, n.p.

To the Editor. *Morning Post*, 5 March 1838, n.p.

To the Editor. *Morning Post*, 23 November 1847, n.p.

To the Right Hon. Viscount Melbourne. *Morning Post*, 29 August 1832, n.p.

[Lister, T. H.] "Dickens's Tales." *Edinburgh Review* 68, no. 137 (October 1838): 75–97.

"Literary Impostures. – Alexandre Dumas." *North American Review* 78, no. 163 (April 1854): 305–345.

"Literary Recipes." *Punch; or, The London Charivari*, 7 August 1841, 39.

"Literature." *Morning Post*, 11 May 1836. In *Dickensian* 32, no. 239 (Summer 1936): 218.

"Living Literary Characters, No. V. *Edward Lytton Bulwer.*" *New Monthly Magazine and Literary Journal* 31, no. 125 (May 1831): 437–450.

Lloyd's Pickwickian Songster. London: E. Lloyd, [1837?].

[Locke, John]. *Two Treatises of Government: In the Former, the False Principles, and Foundation of Sir Robert Filmer, and His Followers, Are Detected and Overthrown. The Latter Is an Essay Concerning the True Original, Extent, and End of Civil Government.* London: Printed for Awnsham Churchill, 1690.

[Lockhart, John Gibson]. Review of *Zohrab the Hostage. Quarterly Review* 48, no. 96 (December 1832): 391–420.

"London Gazette." *Morning Chronicle*, 23 February 1839, n.p.

Lytton, Edward George Earle Lytton Bulwer [né Bulwer]. *The Caxtons: A Family Picture.* 1848–49. London: George Routledge and Sons, 1878.

Devereux. 1829. London: George Routledge and Sons, 1878.

The Disowned. 2nd ed. 3 vols. London: Henry Colburn, 1829.

The Disowned. 1828. London: George Routledge and Sons, 1877.

England and the English. 1833. Chicago: University of Chicago Press, 1970.

Ernest Maltravers. 1837. London: George Routledge and Sons, 1877.

Eugene Aram. 3 vols. London: Henry Colburn and Richard Bentley, 1832.

Eugene Aram. 1832. London: George Routledge and Sons, 1877.

Falkland. In *The Coming Race; Falkland; Zicci; and Pausanias the Spartan.* London: George Routledge and Sons, 1878.

Godolphin. 1833. London: Pickering and Chatto, 2005.

Godolphin. 1833. London: Saunders and Otley, 1840.

The Last Days of Pompeii. 1834. London: George Routledge and Sons, 1875.

Letters of the Late Edward Bulwer, Lord Lytton, to His Wife. With Extracts from Her MS. "Autobiography," and Other Documents, Published in Vindication of Her Memory. Ed. Louisa Devey. London: W. Swan Sonnenschein, 1884.

"Modern Novelists and Recent Novels." *New Monthly Magazine and Literary Journal* 38, no. 150 (June 1833): 135–142.

My Novel; or, Varieties in English Life. 1850–53. London: George Routledge and Sons, 1878.

Not So Bad as We Seem; or, Many Sides to a Character. A Comedy. London: Published for the Guild of Literature and Art, by Chapman and Hall, 1851.

"On Art in Fiction." Parts 1–2. *Monthly Chronicle* 1, no. 1 (March 1838): 42–51; no. 2 (April 1838): 138–149.

"On the Different Kinds of Prose Fiction, with Some Apology for the Fiction of the Author." In *The Works of Edward Lytton Bulwer, Esq.* 2 vols. Philadelphia: E. L. Carey and A. Hart, 1836.

Paul Clifford. 1830. London: George Routledge and Sons, 1877.

Pelham; or, Adventures of a Gentleman. 1828. London: George Routledge and Sons, 1877.

The Sea-Captain; or, The Birthright. A Drama. 4th ed. London: Saunders and Otley, 1839.

The Student and Asmodeus at Large. London: George Routledge and Sons, 1875.

A Word to the Public. N.p., 1847.

[Lytton, Edward Robert Bulwer]. *The Life, Letters, and Literary Remains of Edward Bulwer, Lord Lytton.* By his son. 2 vols. London: Kegan Paul, Trench and Co., 1883.

Lytton, Rosina Anne Doyle Bulwer [née Wheeler]. "Artaphernes the Platonist; or, The Supper at Sallust's." *Fraser's Magazine for Town and Country* 17, no. 100 (April 1838): 513–520.

Bianca Cappello. An Historical Romance. 3 vols. London: Edward Bull, 1843.

A Blighted Life. 1880. Bristol: Thoemmes Press, 1994.

The Budget of the Bubble Family. 3 vols. London: Edward Bull, 1840.

"Bulwer's Dramatic Poetry." Parts 1–2. *Dublin University Magazine* 15, no. 87 (March 1840): 267–284; no. 88 (April 1840): 412–423.

Cheveley; or, The Man of Honour. 1839. London: Pickering and Chatto, 2005.

The Collected Letters of Rosina Bulwer Lytton. Ed. Marie Mulvey-Roberts with Steve Carpenter. 3 vols. London: Pickering and Chatto, 2008.

Lady Bulwer Lytton's Appeal to the Justice and Charity of the English Public. London: Published for and by the Author, [1857].

Memoirs of a Muscovite. 3 vols. London: T. C. Newby, 1844.

Miriam Sedley; or, The Tares and the Wheat. A Tale of Real Life. 3 vols. London: W. Shoberl, 1851.

The Peer's Daughters. 3 vols. London: T. C. Newby, 1849.

Shells from the Sands of Time. London: Bickers and Son, 1876.

Very Successful! 3 vols. London: Whittaker and Co.; Taunton: Frederick R. Clarke, 1856.

[Madden, Richard Robert]. "Plagiarism and Accidental Imitation." *Dublin University Magazine* 73, no. 433 (January 1869): 107–120.

The Madras Miscellany. July 1839–March 1840. Madras: J. B. Pharoah, 1840.

Main, Alexander, ed. *Wise, Witty, and Tender Sayings in Prose and Verse: Selected from the Works of George Eliot.* Edinburgh: William Blackwood and Sons, 1872.

[Mallock, W. H.] *Every Man His Own Poet; or, The Inspired Singer's Recipe Book.* By a Newdigate Prizeman. Oxford: Thomas Shrimpton and Son, 1872.

"Maritime Romances, and Parliamentary Novels." *Fraser's Magazine for Town and Country* 4, no. 24 (January 1832): 661–671.

Martial. *Epigrams.* Trans. D. R. Shackleton Bailey. 3 vols. Loeb Classical Library. Cambridge, MA: Harvard University Press, 1993.

Masson, David. *British Novelists and Their Styles: Being a Critical Sketch of the History of British Prose Fiction.* 1859. Folcroft, PA: The Folcroft Press, 1969.

"Master Humphrey's Clock. From the Editor of the 'Town,' in His Easy Chair, to Master Humphrey, in His Chimney Corner." *Town,* 10 November 1841, 1852.

"Master Humphrey's Clock, Written by Himself." Parts 1–10. *Town,* 17 November 1841–26 January 1842.

"Master Humphrey's Turnip, a Chimney Corner Crotchet." By Poz. Parts 1–18. *Town,* 25 April–5 December 1840.

Matthews, James Brander. "The Ethics of Plagiarism." *In Pen and Ink: Papers on Subjects of More or Less Importance.* 1888. 3rd ed. New York: Charles Scribner's Sons, 1902.

[Meadows, Joseph K.] *Heads from Nicholas Nickleby. From Drawings by Miss La Creevy.* London: Robert Tyas, [1839].

Moncrieff, William Thomas. *Nickleby and Poor Smike; or, The Victim of the Yorkshire School.* 1839. [Plays from the Lord Chamberlain's Office. British Museum Additional MS 42951.]

Sam Weller; or, The Pickwickians. A Drama. London: Printed for the Author, 1837.

Morning Chronicle, 3 January 1850, 4.

"Mr. Bulwer's New Novel." *Spectator* 2, no. 56 (25 July 1829): 473–475.

"Mr. Edward Lytton Bulwer's Novels; and Remarks on Novel-Writing." *Fraser's Magazine for Town and Country* 1, no. 5 (June 1830): 511.

Mr. Pickwick's Collection of Songs. London: Smeeton, n.d.

"Mr. Pickwick's Hat-Box." Ed. Henry Ross. Parts 1–5. *New Monthly Belle Assemblée*, June, August–November 1840.

"Mr. Thackeray's New Novel." *Times*, 22 December 1852, 8.

Neale, C. M. *An Index to* Pickwick. London: Printed for the Author by J. Hitchcock, 1897.

New-York Times, 30 March 1880, 4.

Nicholson, Renton. *Dombey and Daughter: A Moral Fiction.* London: Thomas Faris, [1847].

"Notes of the Week." *Literary Gazette: A Weekly Journal of Literature, Science, Art, and General Information* 2, no. 51 (18 June 1859): 711–712.

"Notes on New Publications." *New Monthly Magazine and Humorist* 64, no. 253 (January 1842): 157–159.

"The Novels of the Season." *Fraser's Magazine for Town and Country* 3, no. 8 (February 1831): 95–113.

Obituary. *Leicester Chronicle; or, Commercial and Agricultural Advertiser*, 3 February 1855, n.p.

Obituary. *Morning Post*, 26 June 1860, 7.

[Oliphant, Margaret]. "Bulwer." *Blackwood's Edinburgh Magazine* 77, no. 472 (February 1855): 221–233.

Oliver Twiss, the Workhouse Boy. Edited by Poz. London: James Pattie, 1838.

Oliver Twist; or, The Parish Boy's Progress. A Drama. London: Thomas Hailes Lacy, n.d.

"An Omitted Pickwick Paper." Restored by Poz. In *The Token and Atlantic Souvenir.* Boston: William D. Ticknor, 1841.

On the Origin of Sam Weller, and the Real Cause of the Success of the Posthumous Papers of the Pickwick Club, by a Lover of Charles Dickens's Works. London: J. W. Jarvis and Son, 1883.

[Osborne, Sidney Godolphin]. "The Great Unknown." *Times*, 3 June 1859, 10.

"Our Civilization." *Saturday Review of Politics, Literature, Science, and Art* 35, no. 2 (28 June 1856): 195–196.

"Our Leader." *Thief*, no. 1 (21 April 1832): n.p.

"Our Weekly Gossip." *Athenaeum: Journal of English and Foreign Literature, Science, and the Fine Arts*, no. 1650 (11 June 1859): 780.

"Our Weekly Gossip." *Athenaeum: Journal of English and Foreign Literature, Science, and the Fine Arts*, no. 1651 (18 June 1859): 811.

"Our Weekly Gossip." *Athenaeum: Journal of English and Foreign Literature, Science, and the Fine Arts*, no. 1653 (2 July 1859): 20.

Palette, Peter. *Illustrations to Nicholas Nickleby.* London: Grattan and Gilbert,[1840].

Parley's Illuminated Library. Vol. 9. London: Cleave, [1843–44].

Parley's Penny Library; or, Treasury of Knowledge, Entertainment and Delight. Vol. 1. London: Cleave, [1841].

Parley's Penny Library; or, Treasury of Knowledge, Entertainment and Delight. Vol. 3. London: Cleave, [1842?]

Pemberton, Thomas Edgar. *Charles Dickens and the Stage: A Record of His Connection with the Drama as Playwright, Actor and Critic.* London: George Redway, 1888.

"Pickwick Abroad." *Cleave's Penny Gazette of Variety. Late the London Satirist* 1, no. 11 (23 December 1837): 1.

The Pickwick Comic Almanac for 1838. Containing Sam Weller's Diary of Fun and Pastime. London: W. Marshall, [1837].

Pickwick in India. Parts 1–7. *The Madras Miscellany.* July 1839–February 1840.

The Pickwick Treasury of Wit; or, Joe Miller's Jest Book. Dublin: James Duffy, 1840.

Posthumous Papers of the Cadgers' Club. London: E. Lloyd, [1837–38].

Posthumous Papers of the Wonderful Discovery Club, Formerly of Camden Town. Edited by Poz. London: William Mark Clark, 1838.

[Prest, Thomas Peckett]. *Barnaby Budge.* London: E. Lloyd, 1841.

The Life and Adventures of Oliver Twiss, the Workhouse Boy [aka *Life and History of Oliver Twiss*]. Edited by "Bos." London: E. Lloyd, [1837–39].

Mister Humfries' Clock [aka *Mister Humfrie's Clock*]. "Bos," Maker. London: E. Lloyd, 1840.

Nickelas Nickelbery. Edited by "Bos." London: E. Lloyl [*sic*], [1838–39].

The Penny Pickwick. Edited by "Bos." London: E. Lloyd, [1837–39]. Published in volume form as *The Post-Humourous Notes of the Pickwickian Club*, 1838–39.

Pickwick in America. Edited by "Bos." London: E. Lloyd, [1838–39]. Published in volume form as *Pickwick in America!*

Preface to *The Post-Humourous Notes of the Pickwickian Club.* Edited by "Bos." London: E. Lloyd, [1838–39].

The Sketch-Book by "Bos." London: E. Lloyd, [1837]. Also published as *The Sketch Book by "Bos," Containing a Great Number of Highly Interesting and Original Tales, Sketches, &c. &c.*

The Queerfish Chronicles, Forming a Correct Narrative of Divers Travels, Voyages, and Remarkable Adventures, That Have Come under the Notice of the Queerfish Society. Edited by Humphrey Trout. London: B. Steill, 1837.

"Recent English Romances." *Edinburgh Review* 65, no. 131 (April 1837): 180–204.

"Recent Novels." *Times*, 2 January 1859, 9.

"Recent Poetic Plagiarisms and Imitations." Parts 1–2. *London Magazine* (December 1823): 597–604; (March 1824): 277–285.

Rede, William Leman. *Peregrinations of Pickwick. A Drama.* London: W. Strange, 1837.

Refutation of an Audacious Forgery of the Dowager Lady Lytton's Name to a Book of the Publication of Which She Was Totally Ignorant. N.p., 1880.

Review of *The Caxtons. New Monthly Magazine and Humorist* 87, no. 347 (November 1849): 279–380.

Review of *Charles O'Malley, the Irish Dragoon. Monthly Review* 2, no. 3 (July 1840): 398–411.

Review of *Cheveley. Athenaeum: Journal of English and Foreign Literature, Science, and the Fine Arts*, no. 596 (30 March 1839): 235–236.

Review of *The Complete Works of Bret Harte. Athenaeum: Journal of English and Foreign Literature, Science, the Fine Arts, Music and the Drama*, no. 2786 (19 March 1881): 390–391.

Review of *Devereux*. *Athenaeum and Literary Chronicle*, no. 90 (15 July 1829): 433–434.

Review of *The Disowned*. *Monthly Magazine* 7, no. 37 (January 1829): 84–85.

Review of *Episodes in the Lives of Men, Women, and Lovers*. *Pall Mall Gazette: An Evening Newspaper and Review* 35, no. 5371 (17 May 1882): 4–5.

Review of *Eugene Aram*. *Athenaeum: Journal of English and Foreign Literature, Science, and the Fine Arts*, no. 219 (7 January 1832): 3–5.

Review of *Eugene Aram*. *Edinburgh Review* 55, no. 109 (April 1832): 208–219.

Review of *Eugene Aram*. *Monthly Magazine of Politics, Literature, and the Belles Lettres* 13, no. 74 (February 1832): 233–234.

Review of *A Flight to America; or, Ten Hours in New York*. *Times*, 8 November 1836, 5.

Review of *La Parodie chez les Grecs, chez les Romains, et chez les Modernes*. *Athenaeum: Journal of English and Foreign Literature, Science, the Fine Arts, Music and the Drama*, no. 2279 (1 July 1871): 12–13.

Review of *The Life and Adventures of Valentine Vox*. *Operative*, 5 May 1839, 11.

"Review of New Books." *London Literary Gazette; and Journal of Belles Lettres, Arts, Sciences, &c.*, no. 693 (1 May 1830): 281–284.

Review of *Paul Clifford*. *Athenaeum: Weekly Review of English and Foreign Literature, Fine Arts, and Works of Embellishment*, no. 133 (15 May 1830): 289–291.

Review of *Pelham; or, Adventures of a Gentleman*. *London Literary Gazette; and Journal of the Belles Lettres, Arts, Sciences, &c.*, no. 594 (7 June 1828): 357–358.

Review of *Pelham; or, Adventures of a Gentleman*. Parts 1–2. *Examiner*, no. 1076 (14 September 1828): 595–597; no. 1077 (21 September 1828): 613–614.

Review of *Pelham; or, Adventures of a Gentleman* ("Revised and improved"). *London Literary Gazette; and Journal of the Belles Lettres, Arts, Sciences, &c.*, no. 616 (8 November 1828): 710.

Review of *The Posthumous Papers of the Pickwick Club* and *Sketches by Boz*. *Quarterly Review* 59, no. 118 (October 1837): 484–518.

Review of *The Posthumous Papers of the Pickwick Club*. *Athenaeum: Journal of English and Foreign Literature, Science, and the Fine Arts*, no. 475 (3 December 1836): 841–843.

Reynolds, George W. M. "The Marriage of Mr. Pickwick." In *Master Timothy's Book-Case; or, The Magic-Lanthorn of the World*. 1842. London: William Emans, 1844. Previously published as "Pickwick Married," in *Teetotaller*, 23 January–19 June 1841.

"Noctes Pickwickianae." Parts 1–5. In *Dickensian* 13, no. 3 (March 1917): 69–71; no. 5 (May 1917): 126–128; no. 7 (July 1917): 187–189; no. 9 (September 1917): 244–245; no. 11 (November 1917): 301–302. Previously published in *Teetotaller*, 27 June–8 August 1840.

Pickwick Abroad; or, The Tour in France. 1837–39. London: Henry G. Bohn, 1864.

Richardson, Samuel. *Selected Letters of Samuel Richardson*. Ed. John Carroll. Oxford: Clarendon Press, 1964.

Rideal, Charles F. *Wellerisms from "Pickwick" & "Master Humphrey's Clock."* London: George Redway, 1886.

[Robertson, John]. "Sir Lytton Bulwer." *Westminster Review* 39, no. 1 (February 1843): 33–69.

Robinson, Charles J. Review of *Episodes in the Lives of Men, Women, and Lovers. Academy*, no. 521 (29 April 1882): 296–297.

[Roscoe, W. C.] "Sir E. B. Lytton, Novelist, Philosopher, and Poet." *National Review* 8, no. 16 (April 1859): 279–313.

[Russell, C. W.] "The Novels of 1853." *Dublin Review* 34, no. 67 (March 1853): 174–203.

Sam Weller; A Journal of Wit and Humour. Edited by Sam Slick. London: W. Strange, 1837.

Sam Weller's Budget of Recitations. London: J. Clements, 1838.

Sam Weller's Favorite Song Book. London: Smeeton, [1837].

Sam Weller's Pickwick Jest-Book. London: Berger; Pigot and Co.; W. M. Clark, 1837.

"Sayings and Doings." *Critic: Weekly Journal of Literature, Art, Science, and the Drama* 18, no. 459 (23 April 1859): 387.

[Scott, Walter]. *Ivanhoe; a Romance.* 3 vols. Edinburgh: Archibald Constable and Co.; London: Hurst, Robinson and Co., 1820.

Review of *Tales of My Landlord. Quarterly Review* 16, no. 32 (January 1817): 430–480.

Tales of My Landlord, Collected and Arranged by Jedidiah Cleishbotham, Schoolmaster and Parish-Clerk of Gandercleugh. 4 vols. Edinburgh: William Blackwood; London: John Murray, 1816.

Scenes from the Life of Nickleby Married. Edited by "Guess." London: John Williams, 1840.

[Senior, N. W.] "Sir E. Bulwer Lytton's Novels." *North British Review* 23, no. 46 (August 1855): 339–392.

Seth Bede, "the Methody:" His Life and Labours; Chiefly Written by Himself. London: Tallant and Co., 1859.

Seymour, Mrs. [Jane]. "An Account of the Origin of the 'Pickwick Papers.'" In *A Centenary Bibliography of the Pickwick Papers.* By W[illiam] Miller and E. H. Strange. London: Argonaut Press, 1936.

Seymour, Robert, Jr. "Seymour's Sketches." *Athenaeum: Journal of English and Foreign Literature, Science, and the Fine Arts*, no. 2004 (24 March 1866): 398–399.

Sibson, T. *Illustrations of Master Humphrey's Clock.* London: Robert Tyas, 1840.

Simcox, Edith. *Episodes in the Lives of Men, Women, and Lovers.* London: Trübner and Co., 1882.

"George Eliot." *Nineteenth Century* 9, no. 51 (May 1881): 778–801.

A Monument to the Memory of George Eliot: Edith J. Simcox's Autobiography of a Shirtmaker. Ed. Constance M. Fulmer and Margaret E. Barfield. New York: Garland Publishing, 1998.

Natural Law: An Essay in Ethics. London: Trübner and Co., 1877.

Primitive Civilizations; or, Outlines of the History of Ownership in Archaic Communities. 2 vols. London: Swan Sonnenschein and Co., 1894.

Review of *Middlemarch*. *Academy: A Record of Literature, Learning, Science, and Art* 4, no. 63 (1 January 1873): 1–4.

[Smith, James, and Horace Smith]. *Rejected Addresses; or, The New Theatrum Poetarum*. London: Printed for John Miller, 1812.

[Stephen, Leslie]. "The Late Lord Lytton as a Novelist." *Cornhill Magazine*, March 1873, 345–354.

Sterne, Laurence. *The Life and Opinions of Tristram Shandy, Gentleman. 1759–67*. Ed. Graham Petrie. London: Penguin Books, 1988.

Stirling, Edward. *A Christmas Carol; or, Past, Present and Future*. London: William Barth, [1844].

—— . *The Fortunes of Smike; or, A Sequel to Nicholas Nickleby: A Drama*. London: Sherwood, Gilbert, and Piper, [1840].

—— . *Nicholas Nickleby. A Farce*. London: Chapman and Hall, 1838.

—— . *The Old Curiosity Shop; or, One Hour from Humphrey's Clock. A Drama*. London: John Duncombe, [1844?]

—— . *Oliver Twist, a New Version* [aka *Oliver Twist; or, The Workhouse Boy*]. 1838. [Plays from the Lord Chamberlain's Office. British Museum Additional MS 42950 (first two acts only).]

—— . *The Pickwick Club; or, The Age We Live In! A Burletta Extravaganza!* Philadelphia: Frederick Turner, [1837].

[Swepstone, W. M.] *Christmas Shadows. A Tale of the Times*. London: T. C. Newby, [1850].

Swinburne, Algernon Charles. *A Note on Charlotte Brontë*. London: Chatto and Windus, 1877.

Thackeray, William Makepeace. "A Brother of the Press on the History of a Literary Man, Laman Blanchard, and the Chances of the Literary Profession." *Fraser's Magazine for Town and Country* 33, no. 195 (March 1846): 332–342.

—— . *Catherine: A Story*. By Ikey Solomons, Esq., Jr. 1839–40. Ann Arbor: University of Michigan Press, 1999.

—— . "Epistles to the Literati. No. XIII. Ch-s Y-ll-wpl-sh, Esq., to Sir Edward Lytton Bulwer, Bart. John Thomas Smith, Esq. to C-s Y-h, Esq." *Fraser's Magazine for Town and Country* 21, no. 121 (January 1840): 71–80.

—— . "Half-a-Crown's Worth of Cheap Knowledge." *Fraser's Magazine for Town and Country* 17, no. 99 (March 1838): 279–290.

—— . *The History of Pendennis. 1848–50*. Ed. John Sutherland. Oxford: Oxford University Press, 1999.

—— . *The Letters and Private Papers of William Makepeace Thackeray*. Ed. Gordon N. Ray. 4 vols. London: Oxford University Press, 1945–46.

—— . *The Newcomes. 1853–55*. Ed. David Pascoe. London: Penguin Books, 1996.

—— . "Proposals for a Continuation of *Ivanhoe*. In a Letter to Monsieur Alexandre Dumas, by Monsieur Michael Angelo Titmarsh." Parts 1–2. *Fraser's Magazine for Town and Country* 34, no. 200 (August 1846): 237–245; no. 201 (September 1846): 359–367.

Rebecca and Rowena: A Romance upon Romance. In *The Christmas Books of Mr M. A. Titmarsh*. London: Smith, Elder, and Co., 1879.

Review of *Alice; or, The Mysteries*. *Times*, 24 April 1838, 6.

Review of *Ernest Maltravers*. *Times*, 30 September 1837, 5.

Review of *The New Timon*. *Morning Chronicle*, 22 April 1846, 5.

The Snobs of England and Punch's Prize Novelists. Ed. Edgar F. Harden. Ann Arbor: University of Michigan Press, 2005.

Vanity Fair. 1847–48. Ed. John Sutherland. Oxford: Oxford University Press, 2008.

The Yellowplush Correspondence. In *Flore et Zéphyr; The Yellowplush Correspondence; The Tremendous Adventures of Major Gahagan*. Ed. Peter L. Shillingsburg. New York: Garland Publishing, 1991.

[Thackeray, William Makepeace, and William Maginn]. "Our Batch of Novels for Christmas, 1837." *Fraser's Magazine for Town and Country* 17, no. 97 (January 1838): 79–103.

[Thomas, J.] "Sam Weller's Adventures! A Song of the Pickwickians." *London Singer's Magazine and Reciter's Album*, no. 33 (1839).

[Thompson, Alfred]. "Daniel Deronda. Book IX. – 'Tire and Side-on.'" In *Punch's Pocket-Book for 1877, Containing a Calendar, Cash Account, Diary and Memoranda for Every Day of the Year, and a Variety of Useful Business Information*. London: Punch Office, 1877.

Three Portraits of Kate Nickleby, 'Tilda Price, and Madeline Bray. From Paintings by Frank Stone. Engraved by Edward Finden. London: Chapman and Hall, 1848.

To the Editor. *Times*, 15 April 1859, 10.

To the Editor. *Times*, 16 April 1859, 7.

Toulmin, Camilla [Camilla Dufour Crosland]. *Partners for Life: A Christmas Story*. London: Wm. S. Orr, and Co., 1847.

"A Touching Scene. (*From the Penny Pickwick*)." *Cleave's London Satirist, and Gazette of Variety* 1, no. 2 (21 October 1837): 1.

"A Venerable and a Non-Venerable Bede." *Punch; or, The London Charivari*, 3 December 1859, 224.

"Vice-Chancellor's Court. – This Day." *Standard*, 11 February 1839, 4.

"Vice-Chancellor's Court, Thursday, June 8." *Times*, 9 June 1837, 7.

"Vice-Chancellors' Court, Wednesday, May 2." *Times*, 3 May 1838, 6.

"Vice-Chancellors' Courts, Thursday, Jan. 11." *Times*, 12 January 1844, 6.

"Vice-Chancellors' Courts, Thursday, Jan. 18." *Times*, 19 January 1844, 7.

"Vice-Chancellors' Courts, Tuursday [*sic*], Jan. 25." *Times*, 26 January 1844, 7.

Wells, Stanley, ed. *Nineteenth-Century Shakespeare Burlesques*. 5 vols. London: Diploma Press, 1977–78.

Whipple, Edwin P. Review of *Daniel Deronda*. *North American Review* 124, no. 254 (January 1877): 31–52.

"William Ainsworth and Jack Sheppard." *Fraser's Magazine for Town and Country* 21, no. 122 (February 1840): 227–245.

[Wills, W. H., and Alfred Whaley Cole]. "The Martyrs of Chancery. Second Article." *Household Words* 2, no. 47 (15 February 1851): 493–496.

"Winkle's Journal (Omitted in *The Pickwick Papers*)." *Metropolitan Magazine* (October 1838): 158–176.

[Wise, J. R.] "Belles Lettres." *Westminster Review* 44, no. 1 (July 1873): 254–270.

[Young, Edward]. *Conjectures on Original Composition. In a Letter to the Author of Sir Charles Grandison.* London: Printed for A. Miller, 1759.

II 1901 to the Present

Abrams, M. H. "Burlesque." In *A Glossary of Literary Terms*. 6th ed. Fort Worth, TX: Harcourt Brace Jovanovich College Publishers, 1993.

Ackroyd, Peter. *Dickens*. 1990. New York: HarperPerennial, 1992.

Adam, J. A. Stanley, and Bernard C. White, eds. *Parodies and Imitations Old and New.* London: Hutchinson and Co., 1912.

Adamson, Sylvia. "Literary Language." In *The Cambridge History of the English Language,* Vol. 4: *1776–1997.* Ed. Suzanne Romaine. Cambridge: Cambridge University Press, 1998.

Addison, William. *In the Steps of Charles Dickens.* London: Rich and Cowan, 1955.

Allen, Graham. *Intertextuality.* 2nd ed. London: Routledge, 2011.

Alley, Henry. *The Quest for Anonymity: The Novels of George Eliot.* Newark: University of Delaware Press, 1997.

Altick, Richard D. *The English Common Reader: A Social History of the Mass Reading Public, 1800–1900.* 2nd ed. Columbus: Ohio State University Press, 1998.

Amos, William. *The Originals: Who's Really Who in Fiction.* London: Jonathan Cape, 1985.

Andrews, Malcolm. *Charles Dickens and His Performing Selves: Dickens and the Public Readings.* Oxford: Oxford University Press, 2006.

Ashton, Rosemary. *George Eliot: A Life.* Harmondsworth: Allen Lane, The Penguin Press, 1996.

   142 Strand: A Radical Address in Victorian London. London: Chatto and Windus, 2006.

Auden, W. H. *The Dyer's Hand and Other Essays.* New York: Random House, 1962.

Auerbach, Erich. *Mimesis: The Representation of Reality in Western Literature.* Trans. Willard R. Trask. 1946. Princeton, NJ: Princeton University Press, 2003.

Bakhtin, Mikhail M. *The Dialogic Imagination: Four Essays.* Trans. Caryl Emerson and Michael Holquist. 1981. Austin: University of Texas Press, 1990.

   Problems of Dostoevsky's Poetics. Trans. Caryl Emerson. 1984. Minneapolis: University of Minnesota Press, 2011.

   Rabelais and His World. Trans. Hélène Iswolsky. 1968. Bloomington: Indiana University Press, 1984.

Baldick, Chris. *In Frankenstein's Shadow: Myth, Monstrosity, and Nineteenth-Century Writing.* Oxford: Clarendon Press, 1987.

Barthes, Roland. "The Death of the Author." In *The Norton Anthology of Theory and Criticism*. Ed. Vincent B. Leitch, et al. New York: W. W. Norton and Company, 2001.

"From Work to Text." *In The Norton Anthology of Theory and Criticism*. Ed. Vincent B. Leitch, et al. New York: W. W. Norton and Co., 2001.

The Pleasure of the Text. Trans. Richard Miller. New York: Hill and Wang, 1975.

Bate, W. Jackson. *The Burden of the Past and the English Poet*. London: Chatto and Windus, 1971.

Baxandall, Michael. *Patterns of Intention: On the Historical Explanation of Pictures*. New Haven, CT: Yale University Press, 1985.

Beard, Joseph J. "Everything Old Is New Again: Dickens to Digital." *Loyola of Los Angeles Law Review* 38, no. 1 (Fall 2004): 19–69.

Beer, Gillian. *George Eliot*. Brighton: Harvester Press, 1986.

"Knowing a Life: Edith Simcox – Sat est vixisse?" In *Knowing the Past: Victorian Literature and Culture*. Ed. Suzy Anger. Ithaca, NY: Cornell University Press, 2001.

"A Troubled Friendship." *George Eliot Review*, no. 29 (1998): 24–29.

Beerbohm, Max. *A Christmas Garland*. London: William Heinemann, 1912.

Bell, E. G. *Introductions to the Prose Romances, Plays and Comedies of Edward Bulwer Lord Lytton*. Chicago: Walter M. Hill, 1914.

Benjamin, Walter. "The Work of Art in the Age of Mechanical Reproduction." In *Illuminations*. Trans. Harry Zohn. 1968. New York: Schocken Books, 1969.

Bennett, Andrew. *The Author*. London: Routledge, 2005.

Bergson, Henri. "Laughter." In *Comedy*. Ed. Wylie Sypher. 1956. Baltimore: Johns Hopkins University Press, 1980.

Besant, Walter. "The Examination." *Dickensian* 32, no. 237 (Winter 1935): 51–53.

Bevington, David M. "Seasonal Relevance in *The Pickwick Papers*." *Nineteenth-Century Fiction* 16, no. 3 (December 1961): 219–230.

Bevis, Matthew. *The Art of Eloquence: Bryon, Dickens, Tennyson, Joyce*. Oxford: Oxford University Press, 2007.

Blain, Virginia. "Rosina Bulwer Lytton and the Rage of the Unheard." *Huntington Library Quarterly* 53, no. 3 (Summer 1990): 210–236.

Blake, Robert. "Bulwer-Lytton." *Cornhill Magazine*, Autumn 1973, 67–76.

Bloom, Harold. *The Anxiety of Influence: A Theory of Poetry*. 1973. London: Oxford University Press, 1975.

A Map of Misreading. 1975. Oxford: Oxford University Press, 1980.

Bloom, Harold, et al. "Plagiarism – A Symposium." *Times Literary Supplement*, 9 April 1982, 413–415.

Bodenheimer, Rosemarie. "Autobiography in Fragments: The Elusive Life of Edith Simcox." *Victorian Studies* 44, no. 3 (Spring 2002): 399–422.

Knowing Dickens. 2007. Ithaca, NY: Cornell University Press, 2010.

The Real Life of Mary Ann Evans: George Eliot, Her Letters and Fiction. 1994. Ithaca, NY: Cornell University Press, 1995.

Bolton, H. Philip. *Dickens Dramatized*. London: Mansell, 1987.

Scott Dramatized. London: Mansell, 1992.

Borges, Jorge Luis. *Labyrinths: Selected Stories and Other Writings*. Ed. Donald A. Yates and James E. Irby. 1962. Rev. ed. New York: New Directions, 1964.

Bowen, John. *Other Dickens: Pickwick to Chuzzlewit*. 2000. Oxford: Oxford University Press, 2003.

Bracher, Peter. "Thwarting the Pirates: Timing the Publication of *American Notes*." *Dickens Studies Newsletter* 7, no. 2 (June 1976): 33–34.

Brady, Kristin. *George Eliot*. New York: St. Martin's Press, 1992.

Brett, Simon, ed. *The Faber Book of Parodies*. London: Faber and Faber, 1984.

Brewer, David A. *The Afterlife of Character, 1726–1825*. Philadelphia: University of Pennsylvania Press, 2005.

Bricker, Andrew Benjamin. "Libel and Satire: The Problem with Naming." *ELH* 81, no. 3 (Fall 2014): 889–921.

Broadbent, A., ed. *A Lytton Treasury*. Manchester: Albert Broadbent, 1908.

Bromwich, David. "Parody, Pastiche, and Allusion." In *Lyric Poetry: Beyond New Criticism*. Ed. Chaviva Hosek and Patricia Parker. Ithaca, NY: Cornell University Press, 1985.

Butt, John, and Kathleen Tillotson. *Dickens at Work*. London: Methuen, 1957.

Byatt, A. S. *Possession: A Romance*. New York: Random House, 1990.

Cabajsky, Andrea. "Plagiarizing Sir Walter Scott: The Afterlife of *Kenilworth* in Victorian Quebec." *Novel: A Forum on Fiction* 44, no. 3 (Fall 2011): 354–381.

Calè, Luisa. "Dickens Extra-Illustrated: Heads and Scenes in Monthly Parts (The Case of *Nicholas Nickleby*)." *Yearbook of English Studies* 40, nos. 1/2 (2010): 8–32.

Cardwell, Sarah. *Adaptation Revisited: Television and the Classic Novel*. Manchester: Manchester University Press, 2002.

Carey, John. *The Violent Effigy: A Study of Dickens' Imagination*. 2nd ed. London: Faber and Faber, 1991.

Carlton, William J. "A *Pickwick* Lawsuit in 1837." *Dickensian* 52, no. 317 (December 1955): 33–38.

Carroll, David, ed. *George Eliot: The Critical Heritage*. London: Routledge and Kegan Paul, 1971.

Castillo, Larisa T. "Natural Authority in Charles Dickens's *Martin Chuzzlewit* and the Copyright Act of 1842." *Nineteenth-Century Literature* 62, no. 4 (March 2008): 435–464.

Castle, Terry. *Masquerade and Civilization: The Carnivalesque in Eighteenth-Century English Culture and Fiction*. Stanford, CA: Stanford University Press, 1986.

"Charles Dickens in Chancery." *Dickensian* 10, no. 8 (August 1914): 216–217.

Chartier, Roger. *The Order of Books: Readers, Authors, and Libraries in Europe between the Fourteenth and Eighteenth Centuries*. Trans. Lydia G. Cochrane. Stanford, CA: Stanford University Press, 1994.

Chesterton, G. K. *Charles Dickens*. 1906. London: Methuen and Co., 1960.

Criticisms and Appreciations of the Works of Charles Dickens. 1911. London: J. M. Dent and Sons, 1933.

Childers, Joseph W. "Victorian Theories of the Novel." In *A Companion to the Victorian Novel.* Ed. Patrick Brantlinger and William B. Thesing. Oxford: Blackwell Publishing, 2002.

Chittick, Kathryn. *The Critical Reception of Charles Dickens, 1833–1841.* New York: Garland Publishing, 1989.

Dickens and the 1830s. 1990. Cambridge: Cambridge University Press, 2009.

Christensen, Allan Conrad. *Edward Bulwer-Lytton: The Fiction of New Regions.* Athens: University of Georgia Press, 1976.

Churchill, R. C., ed. *A Bibliography of Dickensian Criticism, 1836–1975.* New York: Garland Publishing, 1975.

Clark, Peter. *British Clubs and Societies, 1580–1800: The Origins of an Associational World.* Oxford: Oxford University Press, 2000.

Clayton, Jay. *Charles Dickens in Cyberspace: The Afterlife of the Nineteenth Century in Postmodern Culture.* New York: Oxford University Press, 2003.

Clendening, Logan. *A Handbook to Pickwick Papers.* New York: Alfred A. Knopf, 1936.

Clinton-Baddeley, V. C. "Benevolent Teachers of Youth." *Cornhill Magazine,* Autumn 1957, 360–382.

Cobbold, David Lytton. *A Blighted Marriage: The Life of Rosina Bulwer Lytton, Irish Beauty, Satirist and Tormented Victorian Wife, 1802–1882.* Knebworth, Herts: Knebworth House Education and Preservation Trust, 1999.

Cohen, Jane R. *Charles Dickens and His Original Illustrators.* Columbus: Ohio State University Press, 1980.

Cohen, Marc D. "'By the Express Permission of the Author': Intellectual Property and the Authorized Adaptations of Charles Dickens." Doctoral thesis, University of North Carolina at Chapel Hill, 2011.

"How Dickens Co-opted the British Theatrical Adaptation Industry in 1844: Part I." *Dickensian* 108, no. 487 (Summer 2012): 126–140.

Cohen, Monica F. "Making Piracy Pay: Fagin and Contested Authorship in Victorian Print Culture." *Dickens Studies Annual: Essays on Victorian Fiction* 44 (2013): 43–54.

Pirating Fictions: Ownership and Creativity in Nineteenth-Century Popular Culture. Charlottesville: University of Virginia Press, 2017.

Colby, Robert A. "An American Sequel to 'Daniel Deronda.'" *Nineteenth-Century Fiction* 12, no. 3 (December 1957): 231–235.

Collins, Philip, ed. *Dickens: The Critical Heritage.* London: Routledge and Kegan Paul, 1971.

Contributors. *London Review of Books,* 21 January–3 February 1982, 2.

Cross, Nigel. *The Common Writer: Life in Nineteenth-Century Grub Street.* 1985. Cambridge: Cambridge University Press, 2010.

Cruse, Amy. *The Victorians and Their Books.* London: George Allen and Unwin, 1935.

Currey, R. N. "Joseph Liggins: A Slight Case of Literary Identity." *Times Literary Supplement,* 26 December 1958, 753.

Darnton, Robert. "What Is the History of Books?" *In The Kiss of Lamourette: Reflections in Cultural History*. New York: W. W. Norton and Company, 1990.

Davis, Paul. *The Lives and Times of Ebenezer Scrooge*. New Haven, CT: Yale University Press, 1990.

Deane, Bradley. *The Making of the Victorian Novelist: Anxieties of Authorship in the Mass Market*. New York: Routledge, 2003.

De Certeau, Michel. *The Practice of Everyday Life*. Trans. Steven Rendall. 1984. Berkeley: University of California Press, 1988.

Dentith, Simon. *Parody*. 2000. London: Routledge, 2005.

DeVries, Duane. *Dickens's Apprentice Years: The Making of a Novelist*. Hassocks, Sussex: Harvester Press; New York: Barnes and Noble Books, 1976.

Dexter, Walter, and J. W. T. Ley. *The Origin of Pickwick: New Facts Now First Published in the Year of the Centenary*. London: Chapman and Hall, 1936.

"Dickens in Chancery." *Times Literary Supplement*, 2 July 1914, 319.

"Dickens's Imitators." *Times Literary Supplement*, 13 April 1922, 248.

Dillane, Fionnuala. *Before George Eliot: Marian Evans and the Periodical Press*. Cambridge: Cambridge University Press, 2013.

Douglas-Fairhurst, Robert. *Becoming Dickens: The Invention of a Novelist*. Cambridge, MA: Belknap Press of Harvard University Press, 2011.
    Victorian Afterlives: The Shaping Influence of Nineteenth-Century Literature. 2002. Oxford: Oxford University Press, 2004.

Dunn, Richard J. *David Copperfield: An Annotated Bibliography*. New York: Garland Publishing, 1981.

Easson, Angus. "*The Old Curiosity Shop*: From Manuscript to Print." *Dickens Studies Annual* 1 (1970): 93–128.

Eigner, Edwin M. *The Metaphysical Novel in England and America: Dickens, Bulwer, Melville, and Hawthorne*. Berkeley: University of California Press, 1978.

Eigner, Edwin M., and George J. Worth, eds. *Victorian Criticism of the Novel*. Cambridge: Cambridge University Press, 1985.

Eisenstein, Sergei. "Dickens, Griffith, and the Film Today." In *Film Form: Essays in Film Theory*. 1949. San Diego, CA: Harcourt Brace and Company, 1977.

Eisner, Caroline, and Martha Vicinus, eds. *Originality, Imitation, and Plagiarism: Teaching Writing in the Digital Age*. Ann Arbor: University of Michigan Press and the University of Michigan Library, 2008.

Eliot, T. S. "Tradition and the Individual Talent." In *Selected Essays, 1917–1932*. New York: Harcourt, Brace and Company, 1932.

Ellis, S. M. *William Harrison Ainsworth and His Friends*. 2 vols. London: John Lane, the Bodley Head; New York: John Lane Company, 1911.

Engel, Elliot. *Pickwick Papers: An Annotated Bibliography*. New York: Garland Publishing, 1990.

Engel, Elliot D., and Margaret F. King. "*Pickwick*'s Progress: The Critical Reception of *The Pickwick Papers* from 1836 to 1986." *Dickens Quarterly* 3, no. 1 (March 1986): 56–66.

Escott, T. H. S. *Edward Bulwer First Baron Lytton of Knebworth: A Social, Personal, and Political Monograph*. London: George Routledge and Sons, 1910.

Fadiman, Clifton. "Pickwick Lives Forever." *Atlantic Monthly*, December 1949, 23–29.

Feather, John. "The Book Trade in Politics: The Making of the Copyright Act of 1710." *Publishing History: The Social, Economic and Literary History of Book, Newspaper and Magazine Publishing* 8 (1980): 19–44.

   Publishing, Piracy and Politics: An Historical Study of Copyright in Britain. London: Mansell, 1994.

Feltes, N. N. *Modes of Production of Victorian Novels*. Chicago: University of Chicago Press, 1986.

Fitzgerald, Percy. *Memories of Charles Dickens*. Bristol: J. W. Arrowsmith; London: Simpkin, Marshall, Hamilton, Kent and Co., 1913.

   Pickwick Riddles and Perplexities. London: Gay and Hancock, 1912.

Fitzgerald, Percy, ed. *Bardell v. Pickwick: The Trial for Breach of Promise of Marriage Held at the Guildhall Sittings, on April 1, 1828, before Mr. Justice Stareleigh and a Special Jury of the City of London*. London: Elliot Stock, 1902.

   Pickwickian Wit and Humour. London: Gay and Bird, 1903.

Flower, Sibylla Jane. *Bulwer-Lytton: An Illustrated Life of the First Baron Lytton, 1803–1873*. Aylesbury, Bucks: Shire Publications, 1973.

Ford, George H. *Dickens and His Readers: Aspects of Novel-Criticism since 1836*. 1955. New York: W. W. Norton and Company, 1965.

Franklyn, Julian. *The Cockney: A Survey of London Life and Language*. London: Andre Deutsch Limited, 1953.

Freud, Sigmund. *The Uncanny*. Trans. David McLintock. 1919. London: Penguin Books, 2003.

Frost, William Alfred. *Bulwer Lytton: An Exposure of the Errors of His Biographers*. London: Lynwood and Co., 1913.

Fruman, Norman. *Coleridge, the Damaged Archangel*. New York: George Braziller, 1971.

Garber, Marjorie. *Quotation Marks*. New York: Routledge, 2003.

Garcha, Amanpal. *From Sketch to Novel: The Development of Victorian Fiction*. Cambridge: Cambridge University Press, 2009.

Gardiner, John. "The Dickensian and Us." *History Workshop Journal*, no. 51 (Spring 2001): 226–237.

Genette, Gérard. *Palimpsests: Literature in the Second Degree*. Trans. Channa Newman and Claude Doubinsky. Lincoln: University of Nebraska Press, 1997.

   Paratexts: Thresholds of Interpretation. Trans. Jane E. Lewin. 1997. Cambridge: Cambridge University Press, 2001.

Gettmann, Royal A. *A Victorian Publisher: A Study of the Bentley Papers*. Cambridge: Cambridge University Press, 1960.

Gill, Stephen C. "'Pickwick Papers' and the 'Chroniclers by the Line': A Note on Style." *Modern Language Review* 63, no. 1 (January 1968): 33–36.

Gissing, George. *The Immortal Dickens*. London: Cecil Palmer, 1925.

Glancy, Ruth F. *Dickens's Christmas Books, Christmas Stories, and Other Short Fiction: An Annotated Bibliography*. New York: Garland Publishing, 1985.

Glavin, John. *After Dickens: Reading, Adaptation and Performance*. Cambridge: Cambridge University Press, 1999.

Glavin, John, ed. *Dickens Adapted*. Farnham, Surrey: Ashgate, 2012.

Goodman, Nelson. *Languages of Art: An Approach to a Theory of Symbols*. London: Oxford University Press, 1969.

Grafton, Anthony. *Forgers and Critics: Creativity and Duplicity in Western Scholarship*. London: Juliet Gardiner Books, Collins and Brown, 1990.

Graham, Kenneth. *English Criticism of the Novel, 1865–1900*. Oxford: Oxford University Press, 1965.

Griest, Guinevere L. *Mudie's Circulating Library and the Victorian Novel*. Bloomington: Indiana University Press, 1970.

Groom, Nick. *The Forger's Shadow: How Forgery Changed the Course of Literature*. London: Picador, 2002.

Gross, John, ed. *The Oxford Book of Parodies*. Oxford: Oxford University Press, 2010.

Grossman, Jonathan H. *Charles Dickens's Networks: Public Transport and the Novel*. Oxford: Oxford University Press, 2012.

Guida, Fred. *A Christmas Carol and Its Adaptations: A Critical Examination of Dickens's Story and Its Productions on Screen and Television*. Jefferson, NC: McFarland and Company, 2000.

Hack, Daniel. *The Material Interests of the Victorian Novel*. Charlottesville: University of Virginia Press, 2005.

Reaping Something New: African American Transformations of Victorian Literature. Princeton, NJ: Princeton University Press, 2017.

Haight, Gordon S. *George Eliot: A Biography*. New York: Oxford University Press, 1968.

George Eliot and John Chapman: With Chapman's Diaries. 2nd ed. N.p.: Archon Books, 1969.

George Eliot's Originals and Contemporaries: Essays in Victorian Literary History and Biography. Ed. Hugh Witemeyer. Basingstoke: Macmillan, 1992.

Han, Carrie Sickmann. "Pickwick's Other Papers: Continually Reading Dickens." *Victorian Literature and Culture* 44, no. 1 (March 2016): 19–41.

Hancher, Michael. "Dickens's First Effusion." *Dickens Quarterly* 31, no. 4 (December 2014): 285–297.

"Grafting *A Christmas Carol*." *SEL Studies in English Literature 1500–1900* 48, no. 4 (Autumn 2008): 813–827.

Handley, Graham. "Reclaimed." *George Eliot Fellowship Review*, no. 20 (1989): 38–40.

Hanna, Robert C. *Dickens's Nonfictional, Theatrical, and Poetical Writings: An Annotated Bibliography, 1820–2000*. New York: AMS Press, 2007.

Hardy, Barbara. *The Novels of George Eliot: A Study in Form*. 1959. London: University of London, Athlone Press, 1963.

Harvey, J. R. *Victorian Novelists and Their Illustrators*. London: Sidgwick and Jackson, 1970.

Hearn, Michael Patrick. *The Annotated Christmas Carol*. New York: Clarkson N. Potter, 1976.

Henry, Nancy. *The Life of George Eliot: A Critical Biography*. Chichester, West Sussex: Wiley-Blackwell, 2012.

Hill, T. W. "A Pickwick Examination." *Dickensian* 32, no. 240 (Autumn 1936): 240.

Hirsch, Pam. "'Ligginitis, Three Georges, Perie-zadeh and Spitting Critics, or 'Will the Real Mr Eliot Please Stand Up?'" *Critical Survey* 13, no. 2 (2001): 78–97.

Hoggart, P. R. "The Father of the Cheap Press." *Dickensian* 80, no. 402 (Spring 1984): 33–38.

Holdsworth, William S. *Charles Dickens as Legal Historian*. New Haven, CT: Yale University Press, 1928.

Hollingsworth, Keith. *The Newgate Novel, 1830–1847: Bulwer, Ainsworth, Dickens and Thackeray*. Detroit: Wayne State University Press, 1963.

Holloway, John. *The Victorian Sage: Studies in Argument*. London: Macmillan and Co., 1953.

House, Humphry. *The Dickens World*. London: Oxford University Press, 1941.

Householder, Fred W., Jr. "ΠΑΡΩΙΔΙΑ." *Classical Philology* 39, no. 1 (January 1944): 1–9.

Hughes, Kathryn. "'But Why Always Dorothea?' Marian Evans' Sisters, Cousins and Aunts." *George Eliot–George Henry Lewes Studies*, nos. 58/59 (September 2010): 43–60.

George Eliot: The Last Victorian. London: Fourth Estate, 1998.

Hutcheon, Linda. *A Theory of Parody: The Teachings of Twentieth-Century Art Forms*. 1985. Urbana: University of Illinois Press, 2000.

Hutcheon, Linda, with Siobhan O'Flynn. *A Theory of Adaptation*. 2nd ed. London: Routledge, 2013.

James, Louis. *Fiction for the Working Man, 1830–1850: A Study of the Literature Produced for the Working Classes in Early Victorian Urban England*. London: Oxford University Press, 1963.

"Pickwick in America!" Dickens Studies Annual 1 (1970): 65–80.

"The View from Brick Lane: Contrasting Perspectives in Working-Class and Middle-Class Fiction in the Early Victorian Period." *Yearbook of English Studies* 11 (1981): 87–101.

Jameson, Fredric. "Postmodernism and Consumer Culture." In *Postmodern Culture*. Ed. Hal Foster. 1983. London: Pluto Press, 1985. Previously published as *The Anti-Aesthetic*.

Jamison, Anne, et al. *Fic: Why Fanfiction Is Taking Over the World*. Dallas: Smart Pop, 2013.

Jaques, E. T. *Charles Dickens in Chancery: Being an Account of His Proceedings in Respect of the "Christmas Carol" with Some Gossip in Relation to the Old Law Courts at Westminster*. London: Longman, Green and Co., 1914.

Jarvis, Stephen. *Death and Mr. Pickwick*. New York: Farrar, Straus and Giroux, 2015.

Jauss, Hans Robert. *Toward an Aesthetic of Reception*. Trans. Timothy Bahti. Brighton: Harvester Press, 1982.

Jenkins, Henry. *Textual Poachers: Television Fans and Participatory Culture*. 1992. Rev. ed. New York: Routledge, 2013.

Jerrold, Walter, and R. M. Leonard, eds. *A Century of Parody and Imitation*. London: Oxford University Press, 1913.

John, Juliet. *Dickens and Mass Culture*. Oxford: Oxford University Press, 2010.

Johns, Adrian. *Piracy: The Intellectual Property Wars from Gutenberg to Gates*. Chicago: University of Chicago Press, 2009.

Johnson, Claudia L. "F. R. Leavis: The 'Great Tradition' of the English Novel and the Jewish Part." *Nineteenth-Century Literature* 56, no. 2 (September 2001): 198–227.

Johnson, Edgar. *Charles Dickens: His Tragedy and Triumph*. 2 vols. New York: Simon and Schuster, 1952.

Jones, Mark, ed. *Fake? The Art of Deception*. Berkeley: University of California Press, 1990.

Jordan, John O. "The Purloined Handkerchief." *Dickens Studies Annual: Essays on Victorian Fiction* 18 (1989): 1–17.

Jordan, John O., ed. *The Cambridge Companion to Charles Dickens*. Cambridge: Cambridge University Press, 2001.

Jump, John D. *Burlesque*. London: Methuen and Co., 1972.

Keats, Jonathon. *Forged: Why Fakes Are the Great Art of Our Age*. Oxford: Oxford University Press, 2013.

Keitt, Diane. "Charles Dickens and Robert Seymour: The Battle of Wills." *Dickensian* 82, no. 408 (Spring 1986): 2–11.

Kerr, Matthew P. M. "With Many Voices: The Sea in Victorian Fiction." Doctoral thesis, University of Oxford, 2012.

Keymer, Thomas. *Sterne, the Moderns, and the Novel*. Oxford: Oxford University Press, 2002.

Keymer, Thomas, and Peter Sabor. Pamela *in the Marketplace: Literary Controversy and Print Culture in Eighteenth-Century Britain and Ireland*. Cambridge: Cambridge University Press, 2005.

Kincaid, James R. *Dickens and the Rhetoric of Laughter*. Oxford: Oxford University Press, 1971.

King, Margaret F., and Elliot Engel. "The Emerging Carlylean Hero in Bulwer's Novels of the 1830s." *Nineteenth-Century Fiction* 36, no. 3 (December 1981): 277–295.

Kitchin, George. *A Survey of Burlesque and Parody in English*. Edinburgh: Oliver and Boyd, 1931.

Lamarque, Peter. *Work and Object: Explorations in the Metaphysics of Art*. Oxford: Oxford University Press, 2010.

Lambert, Samuel W. *When Mr. Pickwick Went Fishing*. New York: The Brick Row Book Shop, 1924.

Lanham, Richard A. *A Handlist of Rhetorical Terms*. 2nd ed. Berkeley: University of California Press, 1991.

Latané, David E. *William Maginn and the British Press: A Critical Biography*. Farnham, Surrey: Ashgate, 2013.

Leader, Zachary. *Revision and Romantic Authorship*. Oxford: Clarendon Press, 1996.

Leavis, F. R. *The Great Tradition: A Study of the English Novel*. 1948. Garden City, NY: Doubleday Anchor Books, 1954.

"'Gwendolen Harleth.'" *London Review of Books*, 21 January–3 February 1982, 10–12.

Lessig, Lawrence. *Remix: Making Art and Commerce Thrive in the Hybrid Economy*. 2008. New York: Penguin Books, 2009.

Levine, George. "Isabel, Gwendolen, and Dorothea." *ELH* 30, no. 3 (September 1963): 244–257.

Levine, George, ed. *The Cambridge Companion to George Eliot*. Cambridge: Cambridge University Press, 2001.

Litvack, Charles L. *Charles Dickens's Dombey and Son: An Annotated Bibliography*. New York: AMS Press, 1999.

Loewenstein, Joseph. *The Author's Due: Printing and the Prehistory of Copyright*. Chicago: University of Chicago Press, 2002.

Long, William F. "'Boz': Reinforcement of the Received Wisdom." *Dickens Quarterly* 31, no. 2 (June 2014): 165–166.

Lougy, Robert E. *Martin Chuzzlewit: An Annotated Bibliography*. New York: Garland Publishing, 1990.

Lüthi, Max. *The European Folktale: Form and Nature*. Trans. John D. Niles. 1947. Philadelphia: Institute for the Study of Human Issues, 1982.

[Lytton, Victor Alexander Bulwer]. *The Life of Edward Bulwer First Lord Lytton*. By his grandson. 2 vols. London: Macmillan and Co., 1913.

Macdonald, Dwight, ed. *Parodies: An Anthology from Chaucer to Beerbohm – and After*. 1960. London: Faber and Faber, 1964.

Macfarlane, Robert. *Original Copy: Plagiarism and Originality in Nineteenth-Century Literature*. Oxford: Oxford University Press, 2007.

Mallon, Thomas. *Stolen Words: Forays into the Origins and Ravages of Plagiarism*. New York: Ticknor and Fields, 1989.

Marcus, Steven. *Dickens from Pickwick to Dombey*. 1965. New York: Simon and Schuster, 1968.

"Language into Structure: Pickwick Revisited." *Daedalus* 101, no. 1 (Winter 1972): 183–202.

Marshall, George O., Jr. *Tennyson in Parody and Jest: An Essay and a Selection*. Lincoln: The Tennyson Society, 1975.

Matz, B. W. *The Inns and Taverns of "Pickwick": With Some Observances on Their Other Associations*. London: Cecil Palmer, 1921.

Matz, B. W., and J. W. T. Ley. *The Pickwick Exhibition: Catalogue of Exhibits*. London: The Dickens Fellowship, 1907.

Mazzeno, Laurence M. *The Dickens Industry: Critical Perspectives, 1836–2005*. 2008. Rochester, NY: Camden House, 2011.

Mazzeo, Tilar J. *Plagiarism and Literary Property in the Romantic Period*. Philadelphia: University of Pennsylvania Press, 2007.

McDonagh, Josephine. "Writings on the Mind: Thomas De Quincey and the Importance of the Palimpsest in Nineteenth Century Thought." *Prose Studies: History, Theory, Criticism* 10, no. 2 (1987): 207–224.

McFarland, Thomas. *Originality and Imagination*. Baltimore: Johns Hopkins University Press, 1985.

McGann, Jerome J. *The Beauty of Inflections: Literary Investigations in Historical Method and Theory*. Oxford: Clarendon Press, 1985.

  A Critique of Modern Textual Criticism. Chicago: University of Chicago Press, 1983.

  The Textual Condition. Princeton, NJ: Princeton University Press, 1991.

McGill, Meredith L. *American Literature and the Culture of Reprinting, 1834–1853*. Philadelphia: University of Pennsylvania Press, 2003.

McGowan, Mary Teresa. "Pickwick and the Pirates: A Study of Some Early Imitations, Dramatisations and Plagiarisms of *Pickwick Papers*." Doctoral thesis, University of London, 1975.

McKenzie, D. F. *Bibliography and the Sociology of Texts*. London: The British Library, 1986.

  Making Meaning: "Printers of the Mind" and Other Essays. Ed. Peter D. McDonald and Michael F. Suarez. Amherst: University of Massachusetts Press, 2002.

McKenzie, K. A. *Edith Simcox and George Eliot*. London: Oxford University Press, 1961.

McKeon, Richard. "Literary Criticism and the Concept of Imitation in Antiquity." In *Critics and Criticism: Ancient and Modern*. Ed. R. S. Crane. Chicago: University of Chicago Press, 1952.

Mead, Rebecca. *My Life in Middlemarch*. New York: Crown Publishers, 2014.

Mee, Jon. *The Cambridge Introduction to Charles Dickens*. Cambridge: Cambridge University Press, 2010.

Melville, Lewis. "The Centenary of Bulwer-Lytton: May 25th, 1903." *Bookman* 24, no. 140 (May 1903): 49–52.

Miller, D. A. *Narrative and Its Discontents: Problems of Closure in the Traditional Novel*. Princeton, NJ: Princeton University Press, 1981.

Miller, J. Hillis. *Charles Dickens: The World of His Novels*. Cambridge, MA: Harvard University Press, 1958.

Miller, William, ed. *Catalogue of a Pickwick Exhibition*. London: The Dickens Fellowship, 1936.

  The Dickens Student and Collector: A List of Writings Relating to Charles Dickens and His Works, 1836–1945. London: Chapman and Hall, 1946.

  "G. W. M. Reynolds and Pickwick." *Dickensian* 13, no. 1 (January 1917): 8–12.

  "Imitations of Pickwick." *Dickensian* 32, no. 237 (Winter 1935): 4–5.

Miller, W[illiam], and E. H. Strange. *A Centenary Bibliography of the Pickwick Papers*. London: Argonaut Press, 1936.

Mitchell, Leslie. *Bulwer Lytton: The Rise and Fall of a Victorian Man of Letters*. London: Hambledon and London, 2003.

Moretti, Franco. *Distant Reading*. London: Verso, 2013.

Morley, Malcolm. "Curtain Up on *A Christmas Carol*." *Dickensian* 47, no. 299 (June 1951): 159–164.

"Early Dramas of *Oliver Twist*." *Dickensian* 43, no. 282 (1 March 1947): 74–79.

"*Martin Chuzzlewit* in the Theatre." *Dickensian* 47, no. 298 (March 1951): 98–102.

"Nicholas Nickleby on the Boards." *Dickensian* 43, no. 283 (1 June 1947): 137–141.

"Pickwick Makes His Stage Début." *Dickensian* 42, no. 280 (Autumn 1946): 204–206.

"Plays in *Master Humphrey's Clock*." *Dickensian* 43, no. 284 (1 September 1947): 202–205.

Mulvey-Roberts, Marie. "Fame, Notoriety and Madness: Edward Bulwer-Lytton Paying the Price of Greatness." *Critical Survey* 13, no. 2 (2001): 115–134.

"Pleasures Engendered by Gender: Homosociality and the Club." *In Pleasure in the Eighteenth Century*. Ed. Roy Porter and Marie Mulvey[-]Roberts. Basingstoke: Macmillan, 1996.

"Writing for Revenge: The Battle of the Books of Edward and Rosina Bulwer Lytton." In *The Subverting Vision of Bulwer Lytton: Bicentenary Reflections*. Ed. Allan Conrad Christensen. Newark: University of Delaware Press, 2004.

Murray, Simone. *The Adaptation Industry: The Cultural Economy of Contemporary Literary Adaptation*. New York: Routledge, 2012.

"Musings without Method." *Blackwood's Edinburgh Magazine* 173, no. 1051 (May 1903): 707–719.

New, Melvyn, ed. *Critical Essays on Laurence Sterne*. New York: G. K. Hall and Co., 1998.

Novak, Maximillian E., and Carl Fisher, eds. *Approaches to Teaching Defoe's* Robinson Crusoe. New York: Modern Language Association of America, 2005.

Olmsted, John Charles. *A Victorian Art of Fiction: Essays on the Novel in British Periodicals, 1830–1850*. New York: Garland Publishers, 1979.

Orwell, George. "Charles Dickens." In *A Collection of Essays*. 1946. San Diego, CA: Harcourt, 1981.

Pakenham, Pansy. "The Way to Dingley Dell." *Dickensian* 52, no. 320 (September 1956): 163.

Parker, David. "The *Pickwick* Prefaces." *Dickens Studies Annual: Essays on Victorian Fiction* 43 (2012): 67–79.

Paroissien, David. *Oliver Twist: An Annotated Bibliography*. New York: Garland Publishing, 1986.

"'What's in a name?' Some Speculations about Fagin." *Dickensian* 80, no. 402 (Spring 1984): 41–45.

Patten, Robert L. "The Art of *Pickwick's* Interpolated Tales." *ELH* 34, no. 3 (September 1967): 349–366.

Charles Dickens and "Boz": The Birth of the Industrial-Age Author. Cambridge: Cambridge University Press, 2012.

Charles Dickens and His Publishers. Oxford: Oxford University Press, 1978.

"*Pickwick Papers* and the Development of Serial Fiction." *Rice University Studies* 61, no. 1 (Winter 1975): 51–74.

"The Unpropitious Muse: *Pickwick*'s 'Interpolated' Tales." *Dickens Studies Newsletter*, no. 1 (March 1970): 7–10.

Paull, H. M. *Literary Ethics: A Study in the Growth of the Literary Conscience.* London: Thornton Butterworth, 1928.

Perry, Seamus. "Sweet Counter-Song." *Times Literary Supplement*, 20 August 2010, 3–4.

Peters, Catherine. *Thackeray: A Writer's Life.* 1987. Rev. ed. Stroud: Sutton Publishing, 1999. Previously published as *Thackeray's Universe: Shifting Worlds of Imagination and Reality.*

Pettitt, Clare. *Patent Inventions: Intellectual Property and the Victorian Novel.* Oxford: Oxford University Press, 2004.

Picker, John M. "George Eliot and the Sequel Question." *New Literary History* 37, no. 2 (Spring 2006): 361–388.

Pierce, Dorothy. "Special Bibliography: The Stage Versions of Dickens's Novels." Parts 1–2. *Bulletin of Bibliography* 16, no. 1 (September–December 1936): 10; no. 2 (January–April 1937): 30–31.

Poirier, Richard. "The Politics of Self-Parody." *Partisan Review* 35, no. 3 (Summer 1968): 339–353.

Poole, Adrian. *Shakespeare and the Victorians.* London: Arden Shakespeare, 2004.

Posner, Richard A. *Law and Literature.* 1988. Rev. ed. Cambridge, MA: Harvard University Press, 2002.

Preston, Jane. *That Odd Rich Old Woman: The Life and Troubled Times of Elizabeth Barbara Bulwer-Lytton of Knebworth House, 1773–1843.* Dorchester: Plush Publishing, 1998.

Price, Leah. *The Anthology and the Rise of the Novel: From Richardson to George Eliot.* 2000. Cambridge: Cambridge University Press, 2003.

How to Do Things with Books in Victorian Britain. Princeton, NJ: Princeton University Press, 2012.

Priestman, Judith. "The Age of Parody: Literary Parody and Some Nineteenth-Century Perspectives." Doctoral thesis, University of Kent at Canterbury, 1980.

Proust, Marcel. *Against Sainte-Beuve and Other Essays.* Trans. John Sturrock. London: Penguin Books, 1988.

Pugh, Edwin. *The Charles Dickens Originals.* 1912. New York: AMS Press, 1975.

Rabinowitz, Peter J. "What's Hecuba to Us?" *In The Reader in the Text: Essays on Audience and Interpretation.* Ed. Susan R. Suleiman and Inge Crosman. Princeton, NJ: Princeton University Press, 1980.

Randall, Marilyn. *Pragmatic Plagiarism: Authorship, Profit, and Power.* Toronto: University of Toronto Press, 2001.

Ransom, Harry. *The First Copyright Statute: An Essay on An Act for the Encouragement of Learning, 1710.* Austin: University of Texas Press, 1956.

Ray, Gordon N. *The Buried Life: A Study of the Relation between Thackeray's Fiction and His Personal History.* Published for the Royal Society of Literature by George Cumberlege. London: Oxford University Press, 1952.

"Dickens versus Thackeray: The Garrick Club Affair." *PMLA* 69, no. 4 (September 1954): 815–832.

Thackeray: The Age of Wisdom, 1847–1863. New York: McGraw Hill Book Company, 1958.

Thackeray: The Uses of Adversity, 1811–1846. New York: McGraw Hill Book Company, 1955.

Read, Newbury Frost. "Facts and Figures from 'Pickwick.'" *Dickensian* 32, no. 238 (Spring 1936): 132.

Redinger, Ruby V. *George Eliot: The Emergent Self.* London: Bodley Head, 1975.

Reinhold, Heinz. "'The Stroller's Tale' in *Pickwick.*" Trans. Margaret Jury. *Dickensian* 64, no. 356 (September 1968): 141–151.

Rem, Tore. "Dickens and Parody." Doctoral thesis, University of Oxford, 1998.

Reynolds, Margaret. "After Eliot: Adapting *Adam Bede.*" *English* 63, no. 242 (Autumn 2014): 198–223.

Rice, Scott, ed. *It Was a Dark and Stormy Night: The Best (?) from the Bulwer-Lytton Contest.* New York: Penguin Books, 1984.

Son of "It Was a Dark and Stormy Night": More of the Best (?) from the Bulwer-Lytton Contest. New York: Penguin Books, 1986.

Richardson, Ruth. "'BOZ': Another Explanation." *Dickens Quarterly* 30, no. 1 (March 2013): 64–65.

Ricks, Christopher. *Allusion to the Poets.* 2002. Oxford: Oxford University Press, 2007.

Riewald, J. G. "Parody as Criticism." *Neophilologus* 50, no. 1 (1 January 1966): 125–148.

Rignall, John, ed. *Oxford Reader's Companion to George Eliot.* Oxford: Oxford University Press, 2000.

Rigney, Ann. *The Afterlives of Walter Scott: Memory on the Move.* Oxford: Oxford University Press, 2012.

Rodstein, Susan de Sola. "Sweetness and Dark: George Eliot's 'Brother Jacob.'" *Modern Language Quarterly* 52, no. 3 (September 1991): 295–317.

Rogers, Philip. "Mr. Pickwick's Innocence." *Nineteenth-Century Fiction* 27, no. 1 (June 1962): 21–37.

Roh, David S. *Illegal Literature: Toward a Disruptive Creativity.* Minneapolis: University of Minnesota Press, 2015.

Rose, Margaret A. *Parody: Ancient, Modern, and Post-modern.* 1993. Cambridge: Cambridge University Press, 2000.

Rose, Mark. *Authors and Owners: The Invention of Copyright.* Cambridge, MA: Harvard University Press, 1993.

Rosenman, Ellen Bayuk. "Mother Love: Edith Simcox, Maternity, and Lesbian Erotics." In *Other Mothers: Beyond the Maternal Ideal.* Ed. Ellen Bayuk Rosenman and Claudia C. Klaver. Columbus: Ohio State University Press, 2008.

Ross, Trevor. "The Fate of Style in an Age of Literary Property." *ELH* 80, no. 3 (Fall 2013): 747–782.

Rust, S. J. "At the Dickens House: Legal Documents Relating to the Piracy of *A Christmas Carol.*" *Dickensian* 34, no. 245 (Winter 1937–38): 41–44.

Ruthven, K. K. *Faking Literature*. 2001. Cambridge: Cambridge University Press, 2010.

Sadleir, Michael. *Bulwer and His Wife: A Panorama, 1803–1836*. 1931. New ed. London: Constable and Co., 1933. Previously published as *Edward and Rosina, 1803–1836*.

Sadrin, Anny. "Fragmentation in *The Pickwick Papers*." *Dickens Studies Annual: Essays on Victorian Fiction* 22 (1993): 21–34.

Saint-Amour, Paul K. *The Copywrights: Intellectual Property and the Literary Imagination*. 2003. Ithaca, NY: Cornell University Press, 2010.

Saintsbury, George. "Dickens." In *The Cambridge History of English Literature*, Vol. 13: *The Nineteenth Century 2*. Ed. A. W. Ward and A. R. Walker. New York: G. P. Putnam's Sons, 1917.

Saint Victor, Carol de. "*Master Humphrey's Clock*: Dickens' 'Lost' Book." *Texas Studies in Literature and Language* 10, no. 4 (Winter 1969): 569–584.

Sallis, Eva. *Sheherazade through the Looking Glass: The Metamorphosis of the Thousand and One Nights*. Richmond, Surrey: Curzon, 1999.

Salmon, Richard. *The Formation of the Victorian Literary Profession*. Cambridge: Cambridge University Press, 2013.

Sanders, Julie. *Adaptation and Appropriation*. London: Routledge, 2006.

Schlicke, Paul. *Dickens and Popular Entertainment*. London: Allen and Unwin, 1985.
   "Dickens and the Pirates: The Case of *The Odd Fellow*." *Dickensian* 100, no. 464 (Winter 2004): 224–225.
   "Dickens in the Circus." *Theatre Notebook: A Journal of the History and Technique of the British Theatre* 47, no. 1 (1993): 3–19.

Schlicke, Priscilla, and Paul Schlicke. *The Old Curiosity Shop: An Annotated Bibliography*. New York: Garland Publishing, 1988.

Schreiner, T. W. "Warren's Blacking." *Dickensian* 32, no. 237 (Winter 1935): 73.

Schwartz, Hillel. *The Culture of the Copy: Striking Likenesses, Unreasonable Facsimiles*. New York: Zone Books, 1996.

Seville, Catherine. "Edward Bulwer Lytton Dreams of Copyright: 'It Might Make Me a Rich Man.'" In *Victorian Literature and Finance*. Ed. Francis O'Gorman. Oxford: Oxford University Press, 2007.

Shattock, Joanne, ed. *The Cambridge Bibliography of English Literature*, Vol. 4: *1800–1900*. Cambridge: Cambridge University Press, 1999.

Shaw, Peter. "Plagiary." *American Scholar* 51, no. 3 (Summer 1982): 325–337.

Shores, Lucille P. "Rosina Bulwer-Lytton: Strong-Minded Woman." *Massachusetts Studies in English* 6, nos. 3 and 4 (1978): 83–92.

Simonds, C. H. "Peter Parley and Dickens." *Dickensian* 19, no. 3 (July 1923): 129–132.

Slater, Michael. *The Composition and Monthly Publication of Nicholas Nickleby*. Menston, Yorkshire: Scolar Press, 1973.

Small, Helen. *Love's Madness: Medicine, the Novel, and Female Insanity, 1800–1865*. 1996. Oxford: Clarendon Press, 1998.

Stang, Richard. *The Theory of the Novel in England, 1850–1870*. London: Routledge and Kegan Paul, 1959.

St. Clair, William, and Annika Bautz. "Imperial Decadence: The Making of the Myths in Edward Bulwer-Lytton's *The Last Days of Pompeii.*" *Victorian Literature and Culture* 40, no. 2 (September 2012): 359–396.

Stephen, Leslie. *George Eliot.* New York: Macmillan Company, 1902.

Stewart, Garrett. *Dickens and the Trials of the Imagination.* Cambridge, MA: Harvard University Press, 1974.

Stillinger, Jack. *Multiple Authorship and the Myth of Solitary Genius.* New York: Oxford University Press, 1991.

Stone, Christopher. *Parody.* London: Martin Secker, [1914].

Stone, Harry. *The Night Side of Dickens: Cannibalism, Passion, Necessity.* Columbus: Ohio State University Press, 1994.

Stoneman, Patsy. *Brontë Transformations: The Cultural Dissemination of Jane Eyre and Wuthering Heights.* London: Prentice Hall/Harvester Wheatsheaf, 1996.

Sutherland, John. *The Stanford Companion to Victorian Fiction.* Stanford, CA: Stanford University Press, 1989. Previously published as *The Longman Companion to Victorian Fiction.*

———. *Victorian Fiction: Writers, Publishers, Readers.* 1995. Rev. ed. Basingstoke: Palgrave Macmillan, 2006.

———. *Victorian Novelists and Publishers.* 1976. Chicago: University of Chicago Press, 1978.

Symons, Arthur, ed. *A Book of Parodies.* London: Blackie and Son, 1908.

Tanselle, G. Thomas. *A Rationale of Textual Criticism.* 1989. Philadelphia: University of Pennsylvania Press, 1992.

Terry, Richard. *The Plagiarism Allegation in English Literature from Butler to Sterne.* Basingstoke: Palgrave Macmillan, 2010.

Thomas, L. H. C. "'Walladmor': A Pseudo-Translation of Sir Walter Scott." *Modern Language Review* 46, no. 2 (January 1951): 218–231.

Thompson, Kenneth Carlyle. "Boz and the Hacks: Literature and Social Exchange in Early Victorian England." Doctoral thesis, University of Virginia, 1993.

Thrall, Miriam M. H. *Rebellious Fraser's: Nol Yorke's Magazine in the Days of Maginn, Thackeray, and Carlyle.* New York: Columbia University Press, 1934.

Tillotson, Kathleen. Introduction to *Oliver Twist*, by Charles Dickens. Oxford: Clarendon Press, 1966.

Tobias, J. J. "Ikey Solomons – A Real-Life Fagin." *Dickensian* 65, no. 359 (September 1969): 171–175.

Trela, D. J. "Carlyle, Bulwer and the *New Monthly Magazine.*" *Victorian Periodicals Review* 22, no. 4 (Winter 1989): 157–162.

Trodd, Anthea. "Michael Angelo Titmarsh and the Knebworth Apollo." *Costerus: Essays in English and American Literature* 2 (1974): 59–81.

Tyler, Daniel, ed. *Dickens's Style.* Cambridge: Cambridge University Press, 2013.

Vaidhyanathan, Siva. *Copyrights and Copywrongs: The Rise of Intellectual Property and How It Threatens Creativity.* New York: New York University Press, 2001.

Vanden Bossche, Chris R. "The Value of Literature: Representations of Print Culture in the Copyright Debate of 1837–1842." *Victorian Studies* 38, no. 1 (Autumn 1994): 41–68.

Vann, J. Don. "*Pickwick* in the London Newspapers." *Dickensian* 70, no. 372 (January 1974): 49–52.

Victorian Novels in Serial. New York: Modern Language Association of America, 1985.

Ward, H. Snowden, and Catharine W. B. Ward. *The Real Dickens Land.* London: Chapman and Hall, 1904.

Watts, Harold H. "Lytton's Theories of Prose Fiction." *PMLA* 50, no. 1 (March 1935): 274–289.

Weinsheimer, Joel. "Conjectures on Unoriginal Composition." *Eighteenth Century* 22, no. 1 (Winter 1981): 58–73.

Welcher, J. K. "Gulliver in the Market-place." *Studies on Voltaire and the Eighteenth Century,* no. 217 (1983): 129–139.

Wells, Carolyn, ed. *A Parody Anthology.* New York: Charles Scribner's Sons, 1904.

Welsh, Alexander. *From Copyright to Copperfield: The Identity of Dickens.* Cambridge, MA: Harvard University Press, 1987.

George Eliot and Blackmail. Cambridge, MA: Harvard University Press, 1985.

Wheeler, Burton, M. "The Text and Plan of *Oliver Twist.*" *Dickens Studies Annual: Essays on Victorian Fiction* 12 (1983): 41–61.

Williams, Carolyn. *Gilbert and Sullivan: Gender, Genre, Parody.* 2011. New York: Columbia University Press, 2012.

Wilson, Edmund. "Dickens: The Two Scrooges." In *The Wound and the Bow: Seven Studies in Literature.* 1941. Athens: Ohio University Press, 1997.

Wollheim, Richard. "Style in Painting." In *The Question of Style in Philosophy and the Arts.* Ed. Caroline van Eck, James McAllister, and Renée van de Vall. Cambridge: Cambridge University Press, 1995.

Wood, Claire. *Dickens and the Business of Death.* Cambridge: Cambridge University Press, 2015.

Woodmansee, Martha. *The Author, Art, and the Market: Rereading the History of Aesthetics.* New York: Columbia University Press, 1994.

Woodmansee, Martha, and Peter Jaszi, eds. *The Construction of Authorship: Textual Appropriation in Law and Literature.* Durham, NC: Duke University Press, 1994.

Worton, Michael, and Judith Still, eds. *Intertextuality: Theories and Practice.* Manchester: Manchester University Press, 1990.

Index

Ackroyd, Peter, 26, 51
Adam Bede
    authorship of, 139
    and Joseph Liggins, 150
    and memory, 154
    and *The Poysers at the Seaside*, 158
    publication of, 142, 147
    review of, 143
    sales of, 159
    successors to, 157, 166
Adam Bede, Junior, 157–159
adaptation, 14
Adventures of Marmaduke Midge, the Pickwickian Legatee, The, 180
aftertext
    and copyright, 183
    dangers of, 135
    definition of, 18
    and Dickens, 90
    and Dickensian, 74
    and doubling, 29
    as literary criticism, 28, 42
    and literary history, 19–22, 92, 179, 184
    and Bulwer Lytton, 113
    multiplications of, 130
    and new media, 185
    and straying, 60, 63
    unrealized, 159, 167
Ainsworth, William Harrison, 13, 21
Alice, 99
Alley, Henry, 139
All the Year Round, 92, 157, 177
American Notes, 88
Amis, Martin, 5
Anders, Henry Smith, 147
anonymity, 139
Arabian Nights, The. See *One Thousand and One Nights*
Aristotle, 3, 16, 94
Arnold, Matthew, 16
"Artaphernes the Platonist," 126–127

Ashton, Rosemary, 139, 140
Auden, W. H., 45
Austen, Jane, 18
"Autobiography of a Shirtmaker," 174
"Autobiography of Edward Lytton Bulwer, Esq.," 103–104

Bakhtin, Mikhail, 48, 54
Baldick, Chris, 125
Barnaby Rudge, 23, 78
Barthes, Roland, 19
Bate, Walter Jackson, 1
Beecher, Anna Clay, 168
Beer, Gillian, 140, 143, 161, 175
Beerbohm, Max, 18
Bentley, Richard, 101
Bergson, Henri, 100
Bevington, David M., 33, 44
Birrell, Augustine, 10, 85
Blackwood, John, 142, 147
Blackwood, William, 158
Blackwood, William, and Sons, 142
Blackwood's Edinburgh Magazine, 139, 146, 151, 161
Blanchard, Edward Leman, 85, 86
Bleak House, 87
Bloom, Harold, 6
Bodenheimer, Rosemarie
    on Dickens, 38, 55, 85
    on Eliot, 139, 143, 144, 149, 150, 160, 162, 173, 175
    on parody, 114
Bolton, H. Philip, 12
Borges, Jorge Luis, 103
Bos. See Prest, Thomas Peckett
Bowen, John, 25, 26, 60, 73
Boz. See Dickens, Charles
Bracebridge, Charles Holte, 151, 154, 160, 166
Bradbury and Evans, 118
Brady, Kristin, 138
Brewer, David A., 10, 13

275

CAMBRIDGE STUDIES IN NINETEENTH-CENTURY
LITERATURE AND CULTURE

GENERAL EDITOR: Gillian Beer, University of Cambridge

Titles published

CPSIA information can be obtained
at www.ICGtesting.com
Printed in the USA
LVHW080258060620
657512LV00009B/247